PLANET OF THE HAIRLESS BEACH APES

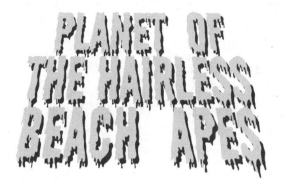

Other Books by Jim Toomey

Sherman's Lagoon: Ate That, What's Next?

Poodle: The Other White Meat

An Illustrated Guide to Shark Etiquette

Another Day in Paradise

Greetings from Sherman's Lagoon

Surf's Up!

The Shark Diaries

Catch of the Day

A Day at the Beach

Surfer Safari

Treasuries

***Sherman's Lagoon 1991 to 2001:
Greatest Hits and Near Misses***

In Shark Years I'm Dead: Sherman's Lagoon Turns Fifteen

PLANET OF THE HAIRLESS BEACH APES

THE ELEVENTH *Sherman's Lagoon* COLLECTION
BY JIM TOOMEY

Andrews McMeel
Publishing, LLC
Kansas City

Sherman's Lagoon is distributed internationally by King Features Syndicate, Inc. For information, write King Features Syndicate, Inc., 888 Seventh Avenue, New York, New York 10019.

 For information, write Andrews McMeel Publishing, LLC, an Andrews McMeel Universal company, 4520 Main Street, Kansas City, Missouri 64111.

06 07 08 09 10 BBG 10 9 8 7 6 5 4 3 2 1

ISBN-13: 978-0-7407-6056-3
ISBN-10: 0-7407-6056-4

Library of Congress Control Number: 2006925239

www.andrewsmcmeel.com

Special thanks to Daryl Van Humbeck for suggesting the title to this book.

Sherman's Lagoon may be viewed on the Internet at
www.shermanslagoon.com.

──── **ATTENTION: SCHOOLS AND BUSINESSES** ────

Andrews McMeel books are available at quantity discounts with bulk purchase for educational, business, or sales promotional use. For information, please write to: Special Sales Department, Andrews McMeel Publishing, LLC, 4520 Main Street, Kansas City, Missouri 64111.

Mother Mother Ocean
After all the years I've found
My occupational hazard being my occupation's just not around

—Jimmy Buffett

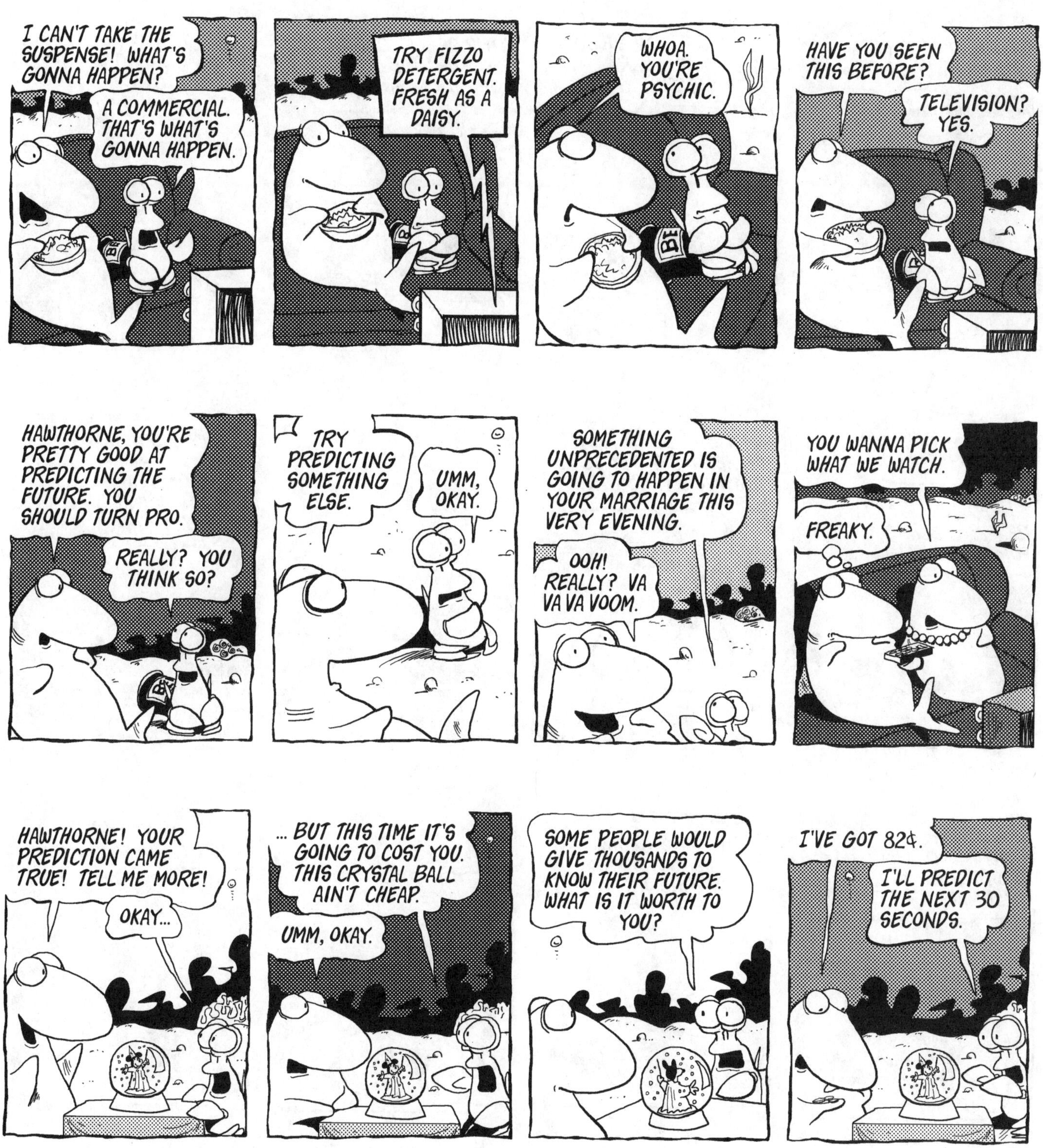

I CAN'T TAKE THE SUSPENSE! WHAT'S GONNA HAPPEN?
A COMMERCIAL. THAT'S WHAT'S GONNA HAPPEN.
TRY FIZZO DETERGENT. FRESH AS A DAISY.
WHOA. YOU'RE PSYCHIC.
HAVE YOU SEEN THIS BEFORE?
TELEVISION? YES.
HAWTHORNE, YOU'RE PRETTY GOOD AT PREDICTING THE FUTURE. YOU SHOULD TURN PRO.
REALLY? YOU THINK SO?
TRY PREDICTING SOMETHING ELSE.
UMM, OKAY.
SOMETHING UNPRECEDENTED IS GOING TO HAPPEN IN YOUR MARRIAGE THIS VERY EVENING.
OOH! REALLY? VA VA VA VOOM.
YOU WANNA PICK WHAT WE WATCH.
FREAKY.
HAWTHORNE! YOUR PREDICTION CAME TRUE! TELL ME MORE!
OKAY...
... BUT THIS TIME IT'S GOING TO COST YOU. THIS CRYSTAL BALL AIN'T CHEAP.
UMM, OKAY.
SOME PEOPLE WOULD GIVE THOUSANDS TO KNOW THEIR FUTURE. WHAT IS IT WORTH TO YOU?
I'VE GOT 82¢.
I'LL PREDICT THE NEXT 30 SECONDS.

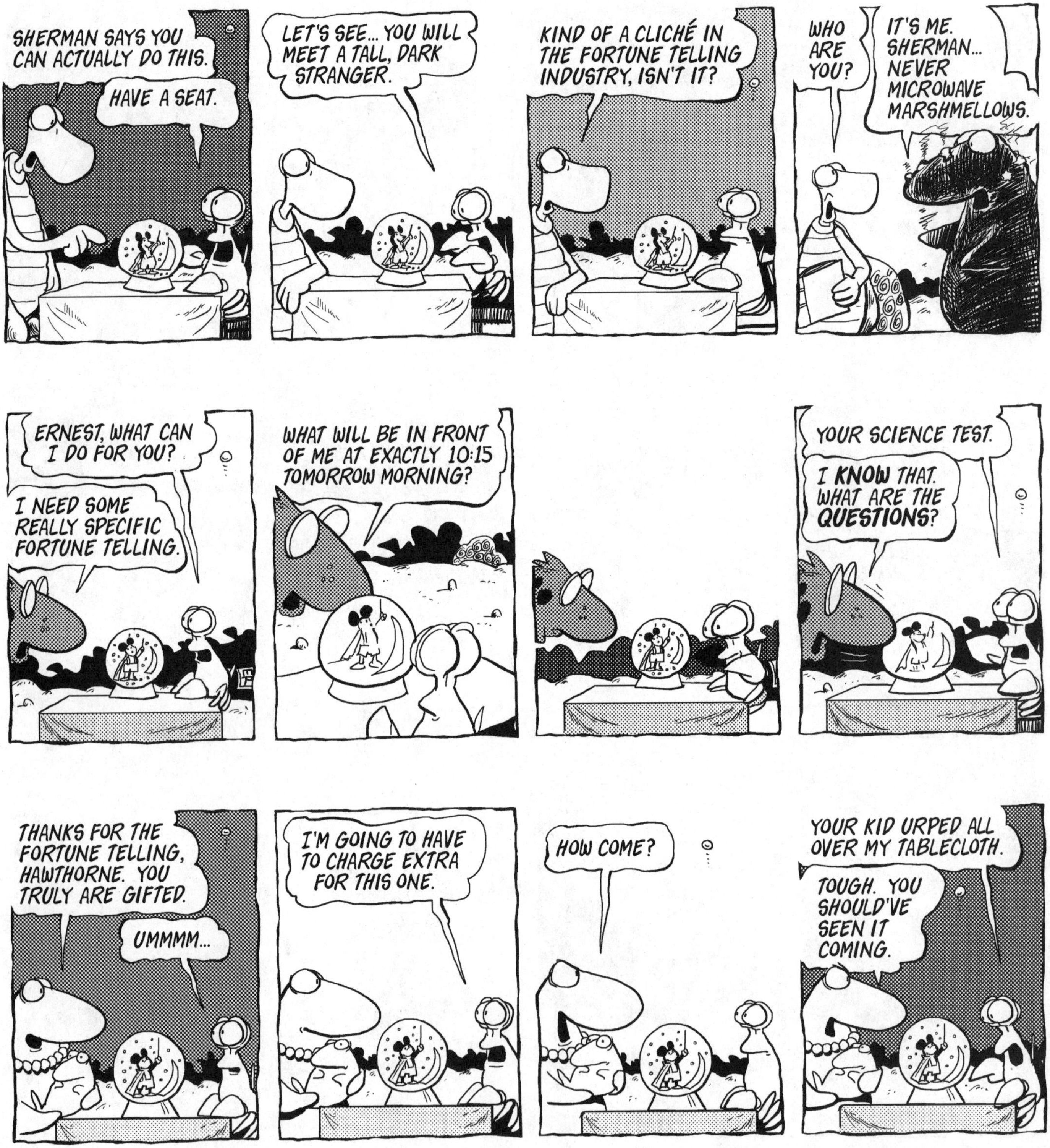
SHERMAN SAYS YOU CAN ACTUALLY DO THIS.
HAVE A SEAT.
LET'S SEE... YOU WILL MEET A TALL, DARK STRANGER.
KIND OF A CLICHÉ IN THE FORTUNE TELLING INDUSTRY, ISN'T IT?
WHO ARE YOU?
IT'S ME. SHERMAN... NEVER MICROWAVE MARSHMELLOWS.
ERNEST, WHAT CAN I DO FOR YOU?
I NEED SOME REALLY SPECIFIC FORTUNE TELLING.
WHAT WILL BE IN FRONT OF ME AT EXACTLY 10:15 TOMORROW MORNING?
YOUR SCIENCE TEST.
I KNOW THAT. WHAT ARE THE QUESTIONS?
THANKS FOR THE FORTUNE TELLING, HAWTHORNE. YOU TRULY ARE GIFTED.
UMMMM...
I'M GOING TO HAVE TO CHARGE EXTRA FOR THIS ONE.
HOW COME?
YOUR KID URPED ALL OVER MY TABLECLOTH.
TOUGH. YOU SHOULD'VE SEEN IT COMING.

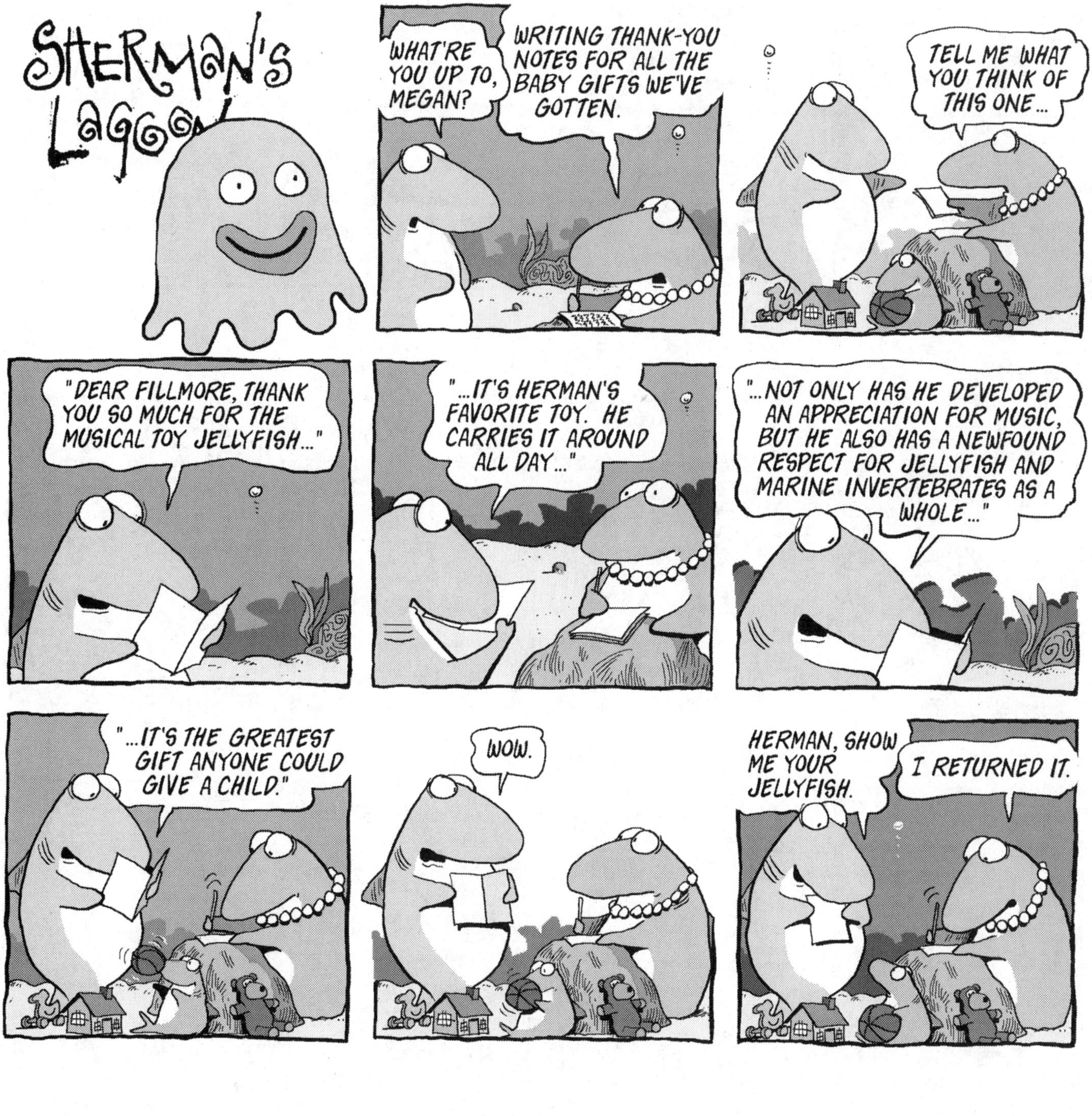
SHERMAN'S LAGOON
WHAT'RE YOU UP TO, MEGAN?
WRITING THANK-YOU NOTES FOR ALL THE BABY GIFTS WE'VE GOTTEN.
TELL ME WHAT YOU THINK OF THIS ONE...
"DEAR FILLMORE, THANK YOU SO MUCH FOR THE MUSICAL TOY JELLYFISH..."
"...IT'S HERMAN'S FAVORITE TOY. HE CARRIES IT AROUND ALL DAY..."
"...NOT ONLY HAS HE DEVELOPED AN APPRECIATION FOR MUSIC, BUT HE ALSO HAS A NEWFOUND RESPECT FOR JELLYFISH AND MARINE INVERTEBRATES AS A WHOLE..."
"...IT'S THE GREATEST GIFT ANYONE COULD GIVE A CHILD."
WOW.
HERMAN, SHOW ME YOUR JELLYFISH.
I RETURNED IT.

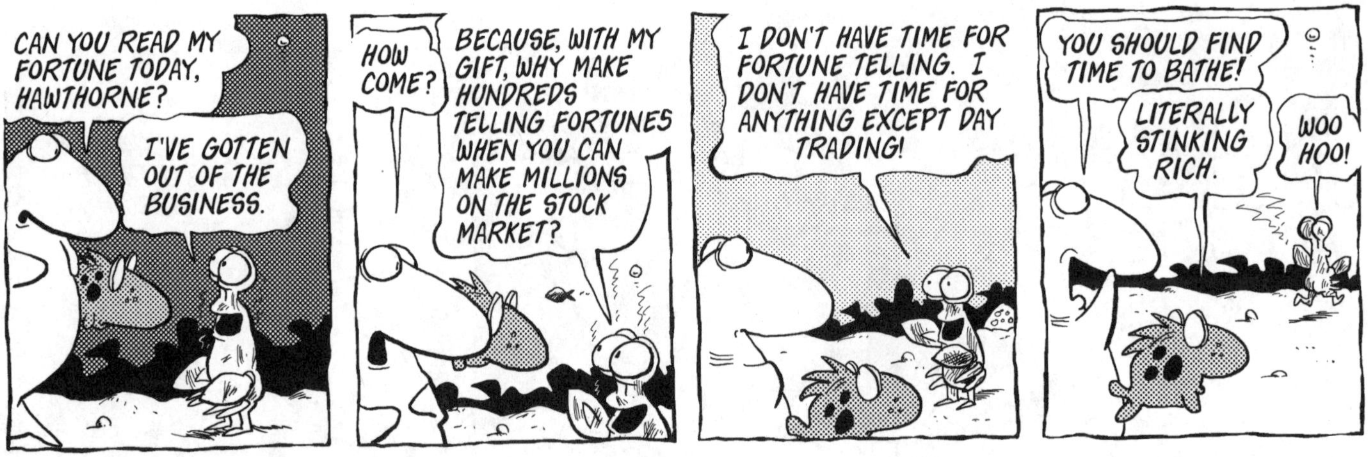
CAN YOU READ MY FORTUNE TODAY, HAWTHORNE?
I'VE GOTTEN OUT OF THE BUSINESS.
HOW COME?
BECAUSE, WITH MY GIFT, WHY MAKE HUNDREDS TELLING FORTUNES WHEN YOU CAN MAKE MILLIONS ON THE STOCK MARKET?
I DON'T HAVE TIME FOR FORTUNE TELLING. I DON'T HAVE TIME FOR ANYTHING EXCEPT DAY TRADING!
YOU SHOULD FIND TIME TO BATHE!
LITERALLY STINKING RICH.
WOO HOO!

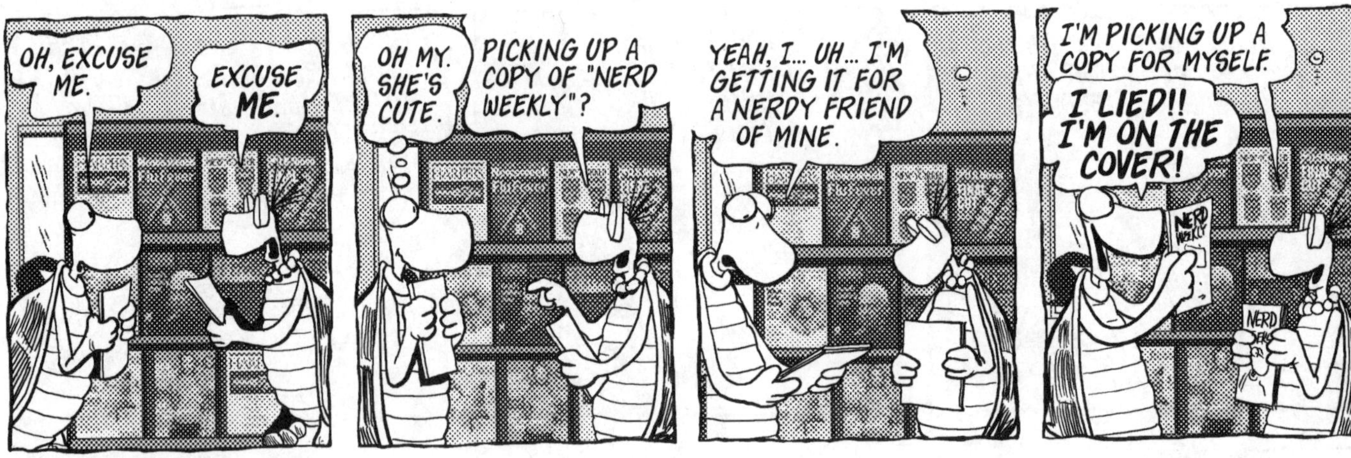
OH, EXCUSE ME.
EXCUSE **ME**.
OH MY. SHE'S CUTE.
PICKING UP A COPY OF "NERD WEEKLY"?
YEAH, I... UH... I'M GETTING IT FOR A NERDY FRIEND OF MINE.
I'M PICKING UP A COPY FOR MYSELF.
I LIED!! I'M ON THE COVER!
NERD WEEKLY

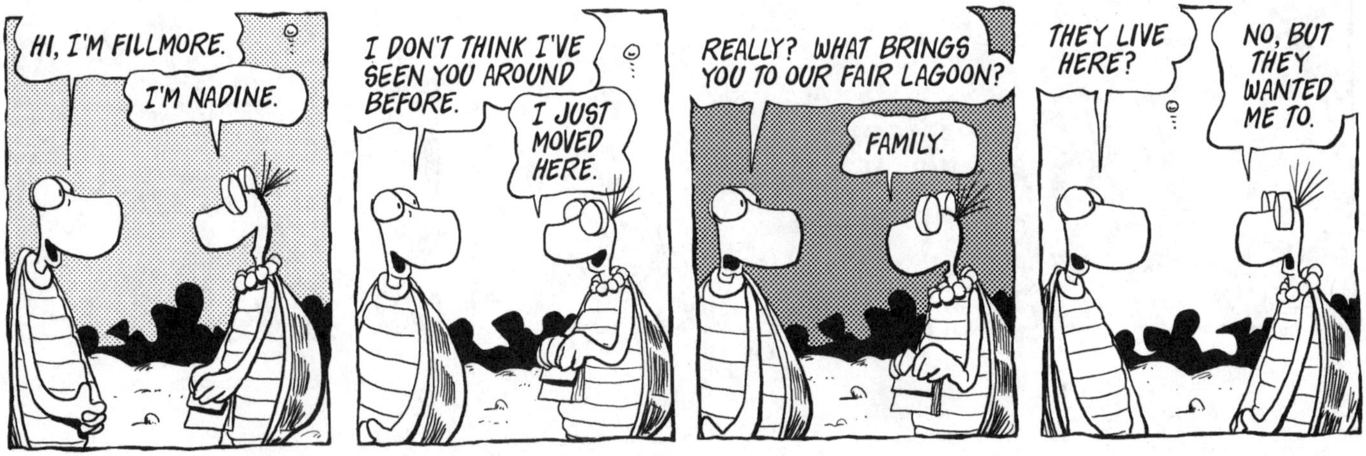
HI, I'M FILLMORE.
I'M NADINE.
I DON'T THINK I'VE SEEN YOU AROUND BEFORE.
I JUST MOVED HERE.
REALLY? WHAT BRINGS YOU TO OUR FAIR LAGOON?
FAMILY.
THEY LIVE HERE?
NO, BUT THEY WANTED ME TO.

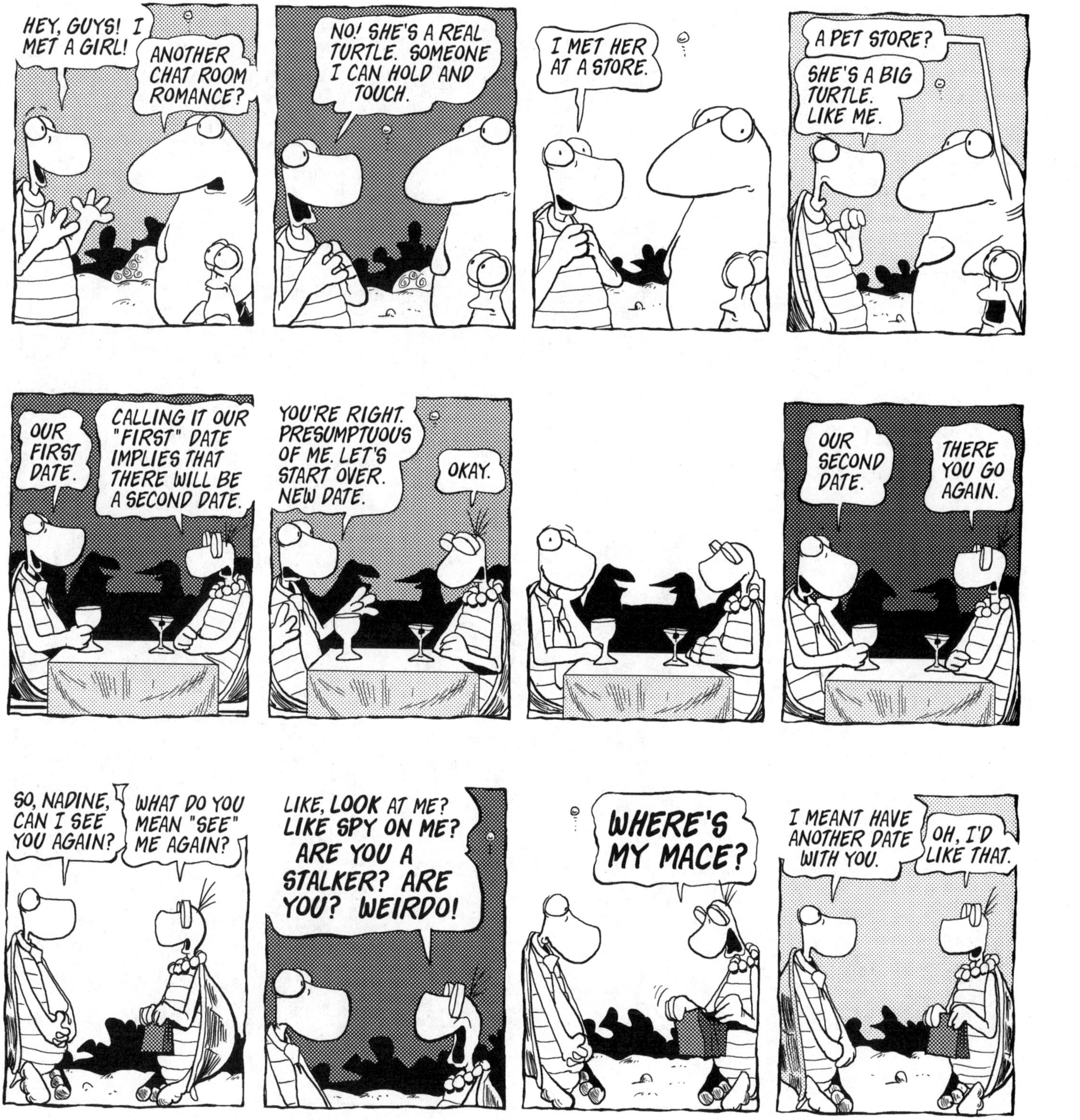
HEY, GUYS! I MET A GIRL!
ANOTHER CHAT ROOM ROMANCE?
NO! SHE'S A REAL TURTLE. SOMEONE I CAN HOLD AND TOUCH.
I MET HER AT A STORE.
A PET STORE?
SHE'S A BIG TURTLE. LIKE ME.
OUR FIRST DATE.
CALLING IT OUR "FIRST" DATE IMPLIES THAT THERE WILL BE A SECOND DATE.
YOU'RE RIGHT. PRESUMPTUOUS OF ME. LET'S START OVER. NEW DATE.
OKAY.
OUR SECOND DATE.
THERE YOU GO AGAIN.
SO, NADINE, CAN I SEE YOU AGAIN?
WHAT DO YOU MEAN "SEE" ME AGAIN?
LIKE, LOOK AT ME? LIKE SPY ON ME? ARE YOU A STALKER? ARE YOU? WEIRDO!
WHERE'S MY MACE?
I MEANT HAVE ANOTHER DATE WITH YOU.
OH, I'D LIKE THAT.

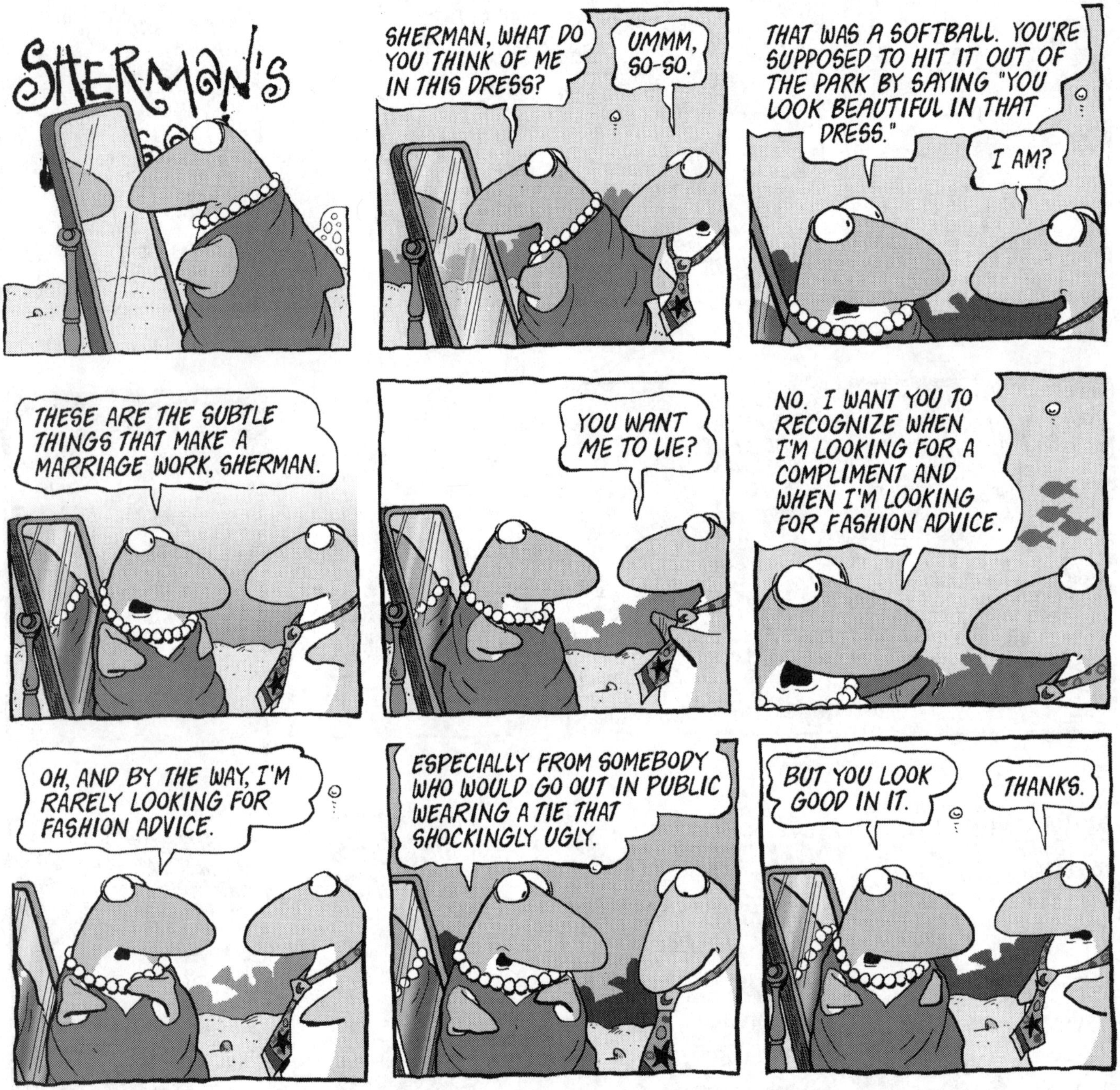
SHERMAN'S
SHERMAN, WHAT DO YOU THINK OF ME IN THIS DRESS?
UMMM, SO-SO.
THAT WAS A SOFTBALL. YOU'RE SUPPOSED TO HIT IT OUT OF THE PARK BY SAYING "YOU LOOK BEAUTIFUL IN THAT DRESS."
I AM?
THESE ARE THE SUBTLE THINGS THAT MAKE A MARRIAGE WORK, SHERMAN.
YOU WANT ME TO LIE?
NO. I WANT YOU TO RECOGNIZE WHEN I'M LOOKING FOR A COMPLIMENT AND WHEN I'M LOOKING FOR FASHION ADVICE.
OH, AND BY THE WAY, I'M RARELY LOOKING FOR FASHION ADVICE.
ESPECIALLY FROM SOMEBODY WHO WOULD GO OUT IN PUBLIC WEARING A TIE THAT SHOCKINGLY UGLY.
BUT YOU LOOK GOOD IN IT.
THANKS.

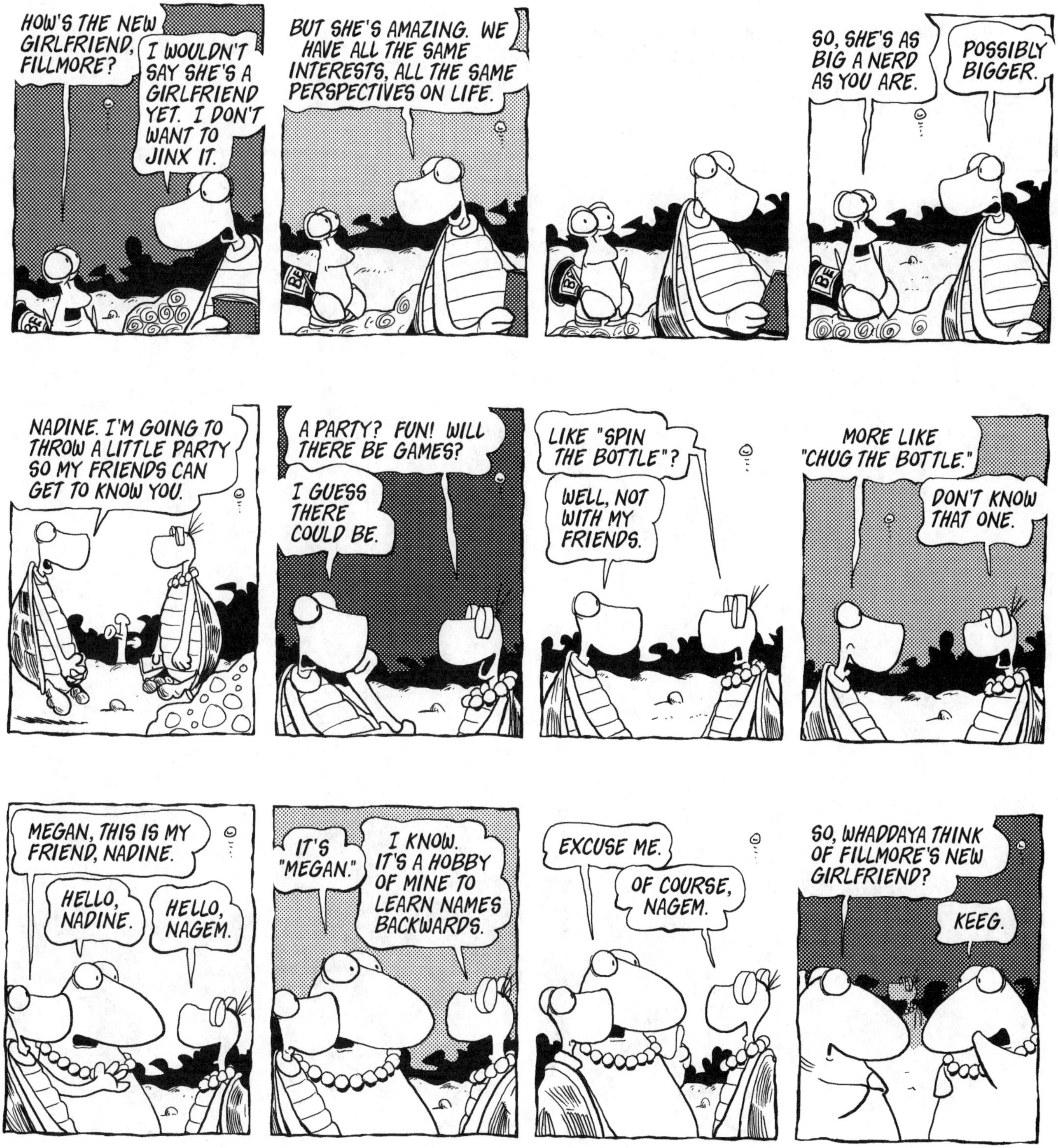
HOW'S THE NEW GIRLFRIEND, FILLMORE?
I WOULDN'T SAY SHE'S A GIRLFRIEND YET. I DON'T WANT TO JINX IT.
BUT SHE'S AMAZING. WE HAVE ALL THE SAME INTERESTS, ALL THE SAME PERSPECTIVES ON LIFE.
BE
SO, SHE'S AS BIG A NERD AS YOU ARE.
POSSIBLY BIGGER.
NADINE. I'M GOING TO THROW A LITTLE PARTY SO MY FRIENDS CAN GET TO KNOW YOU.
A PARTY? FUN! WILL THERE BE GAMES?
I GUESS THERE COULD BE.
LIKE "SPIN THE BOTTLE"?
WELL, NOT WITH MY FRIENDS.
MORE LIKE "CHUG THE BOTTLE."
DON'T KNOW THAT ONE.
MEGAN, THIS IS MY FRIEND, NADINE.
HELLO, NADINE.
HELLO, NAGEM.
IT'S "MEGAN."
I KNOW. IT'S A HOBBY OF MINE TO LEARN NAMES BACKWARDS.
EXCUSE ME.
OF COURSE, NAGEM.
SO, WHADDAYA THINK OF FILLMORE'S NEW GIRLFRIEND?
KEEG.

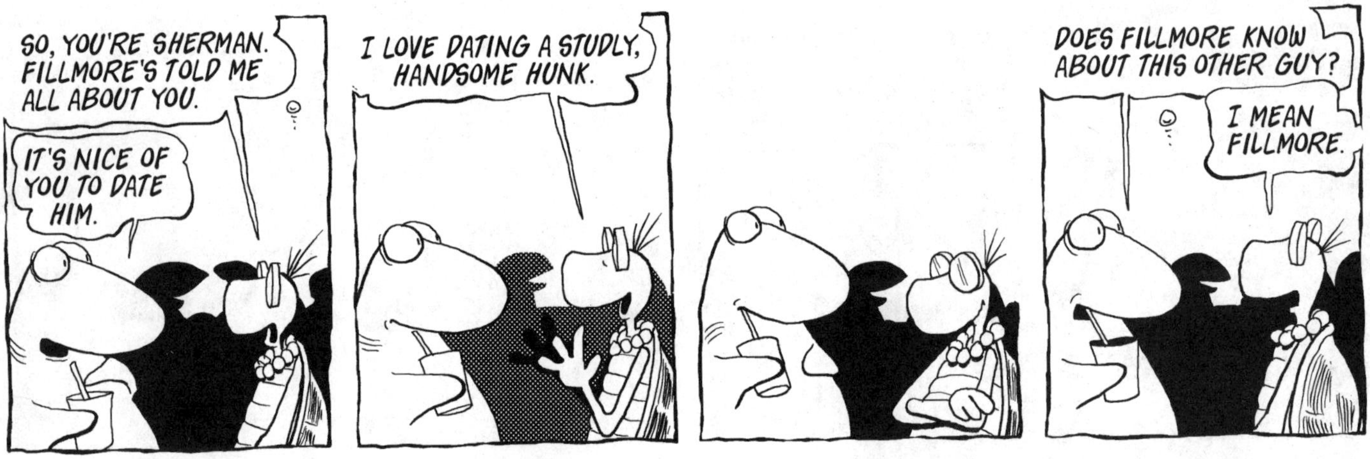
SO, YOU'RE SHERMAN. FILLMORE'S TOLD ME ALL ABOUT YOU.
IT'S NICE OF YOU TO DATE HIM.
I LOVE DATING A STUDLY, HANDSOME HUNK.
DOES FILLMORE KNOW ABOUT THIS OTHER GUY?
I MEAN FILLMORE.

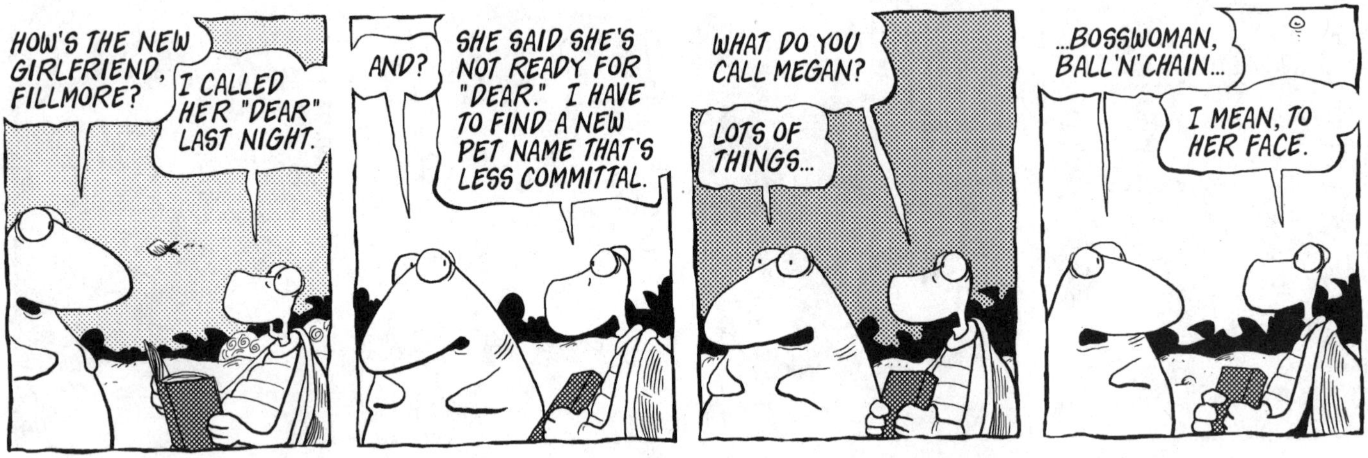
HOW'S THE NEW GIRLFRIEND, FILLMORE?
I CALLED HER "DEAR" LAST NIGHT.
AND?
SHE SAID SHE'S NOT READY FOR "DEAR." I HAVE TO FIND A NEW PET NAME THAT'S LESS COMMITTAL.
WHAT DO YOU CALL MEGAN?
LOTS OF THINGS...
...BOSSWOMAN, BALL'N'CHAIN...
I MEAN, TO HER FACE.

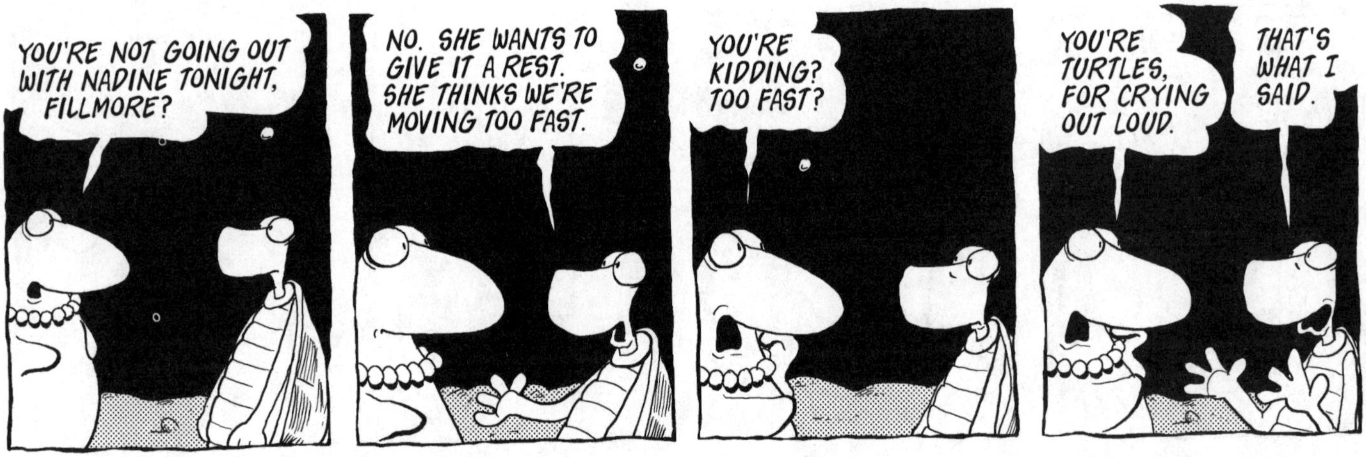
YOU'RE NOT GOING OUT WITH NADINE TONIGHT, FILLMORE?
NO. SHE WANTS TO GIVE IT A REST. SHE THINKS WE'RE MOVING TOO FAST.
YOU'RE KIDDING? TOO FAST?
YOU'RE TURTLES, FOR CRYING OUT LOUD.
THAT'S WHAT I SAID.

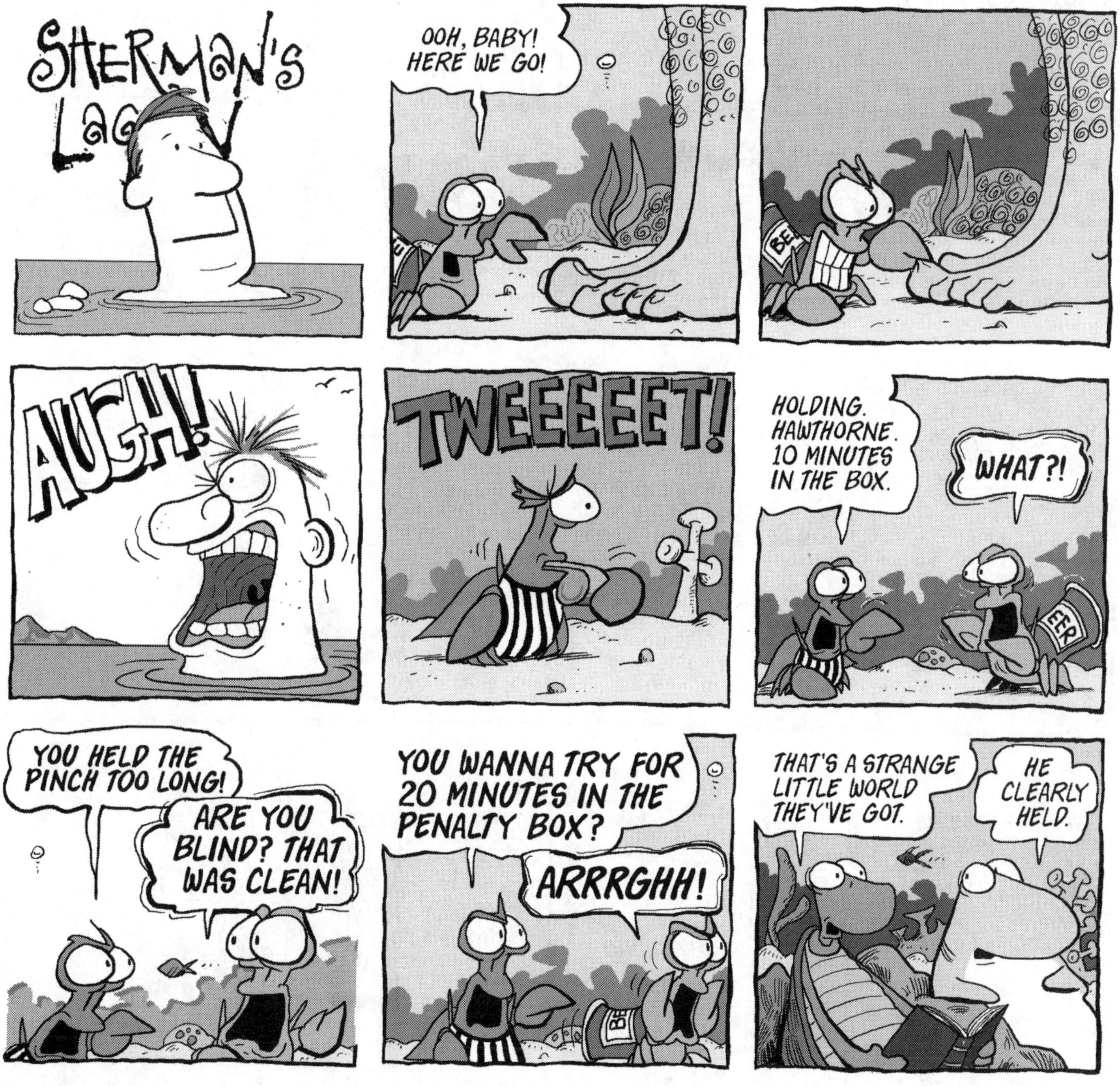
SHERMAN'S LAGOON
OOH, BABY! HERE WE GO!
AUGH!
TWEEEEET!
HOLDING. HAWTHORNE. 10 MINUTES IN THE BOX.
WHAT?!
YOU HELD THE PINCH TOO LONG!
ARE YOU BLIND? THAT WAS CLEAN!
YOU WANNA TRY FOR 20 MINUTES IN THE PENALTY BOX?
ARRRGHH!
THAT'S A STRANGE LITTLE WORLD THEY'VE GOT.
HE CLEARLY HELD.

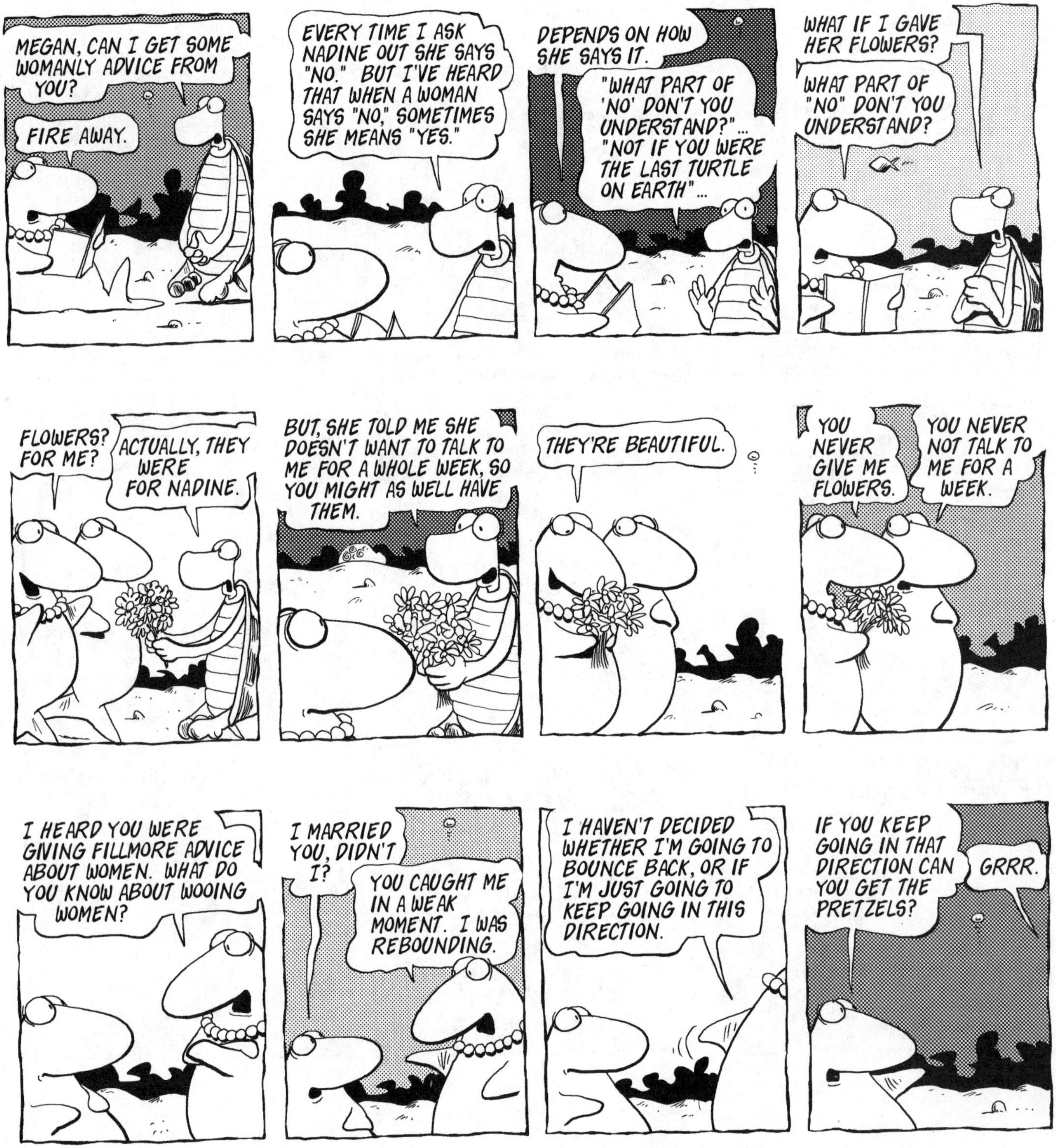
MEGAN, CAN I GET SOME WOMANLY ADVICE FROM YOU?
FIRE AWAY.
EVERY TIME I ASK NADINE OUT SHE SAYS "NO." BUT I'VE HEARD THAT WHEN A WOMAN SAYS "NO," SOMETIMES SHE MEANS "YES."
DEPENDS ON HOW SHE SAYS IT.
"WHAT PART OF 'NO' DON'T YOU UNDERSTAND?"... "NOT IF YOU WERE THE LAST TURTLE ON EARTH"...
WHAT IF I GAVE HER FLOWERS?
WHAT PART OF "NO" DON'T YOU UNDERSTAND?
FLOWERS? FOR ME?
ACTUALLY, THEY WERE FOR NADINE.
BUT, SHE TOLD ME SHE DOESN'T WANT TO TALK TO ME FOR A WHOLE WEEK, SO YOU MIGHT AS WELL HAVE THEM.
THEY'RE BEAUTIFUL.
YOU NEVER GIVE ME FLOWERS.
YOU NEVER NOT TALK TO ME FOR A WEEK.
I HEARD YOU WERE GIVING FILLMORE ADVICE ABOUT WOMEN. WHAT DO YOU KNOW ABOUT WOOING WOMEN?
I MARRIED YOU, DIDN'T I?
YOU CAUGHT ME IN A WEAK MOMENT. I WAS REBOUNDING.
I HAVEN'T DECIDED WHETHER I'M GOING TO BOUNCE BACK, OR IF I'M JUST GOING TO KEEP GOING IN THIS DIRECTION.
IF YOU KEEP GOING IN THAT DIRECTION CAN YOU GET THE PRETZELS?
GRRR.

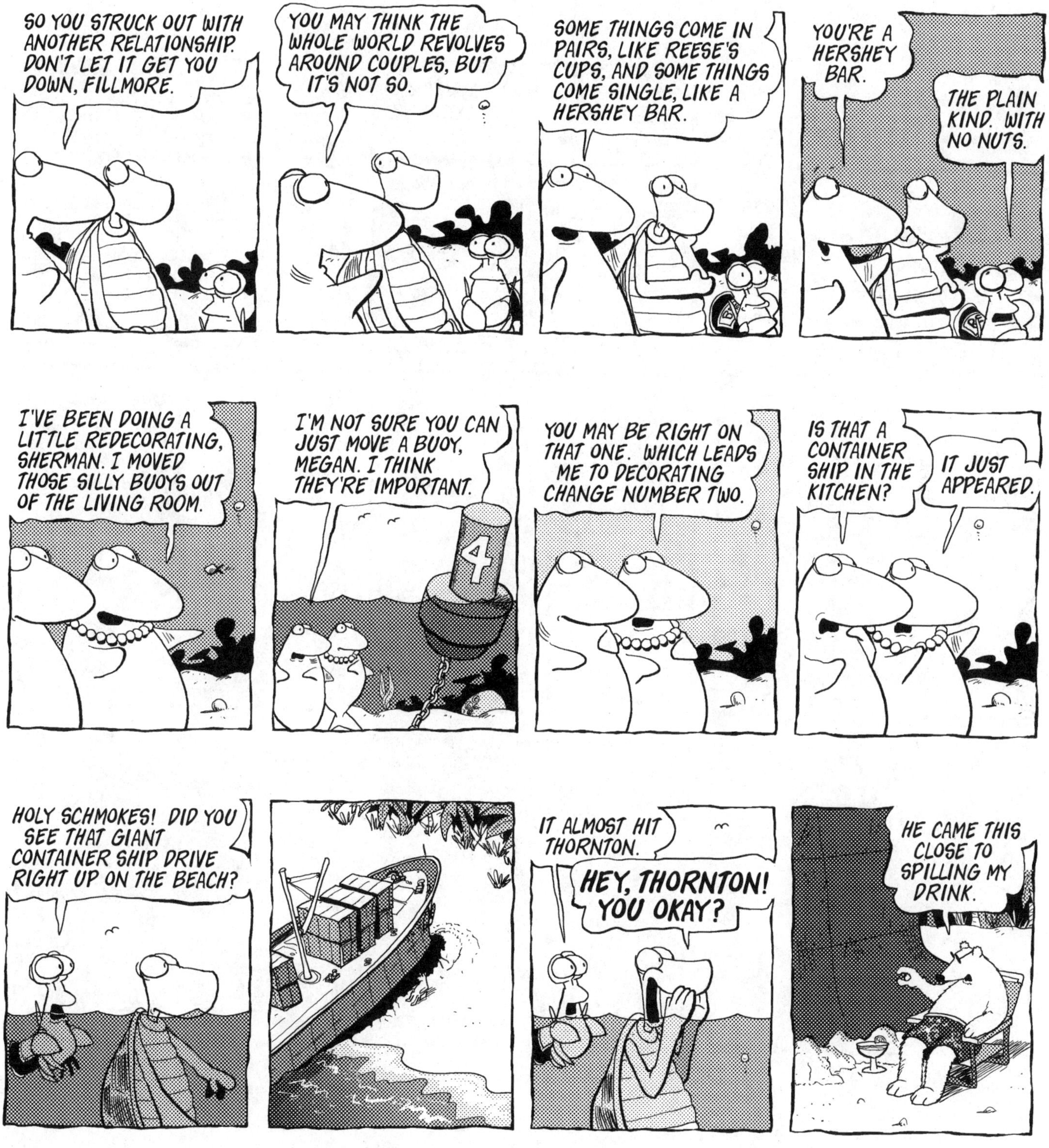
SO YOU STRUCK OUT WITH ANOTHER RELATIONSHIP. DON'T LET IT GET YOU DOWN, FILLMORE.
YOU MAY THINK THE WHOLE WORLD REVOLVES AROUND COUPLES, BUT IT'S NOT SO.
SOME THINGS COME IN PAIRS, LIKE REESE'S CUPS, AND SOME THINGS COME SINGLE, LIKE A HERSHEY BAR.
YOU'RE A HERSHEY BAR.
THE PLAIN KIND. WITH NO NUTS.
I'VE BEEN DOING A LITTLE REDECORATING, SHERMAN. I MOVED THOSE SILLY BUOYS OUT OF THE LIVING ROOM.
I'M NOT SURE YOU CAN JUST MOVE A BUOY, MEGAN. I THINK THEY'RE IMPORTANT.
4
YOU MAY BE RIGHT ON THAT ONE. WHICH LEADS ME TO DECORATING CHANGE NUMBER TWO.
IS THAT A CONTAINER SHIP IN THE KITCHEN?
IT JUST APPEARED.
HOLY SCHMOKES! DID YOU SEE THAT GIANT CONTAINER SHIP DRIVE RIGHT UP ON THE BEACH?
IT ALMOST HIT THORNTON.
HEY, THORNTON! YOU OKAY?
HE CAME THIS CLOSE TO SPILLING MY DRINK.

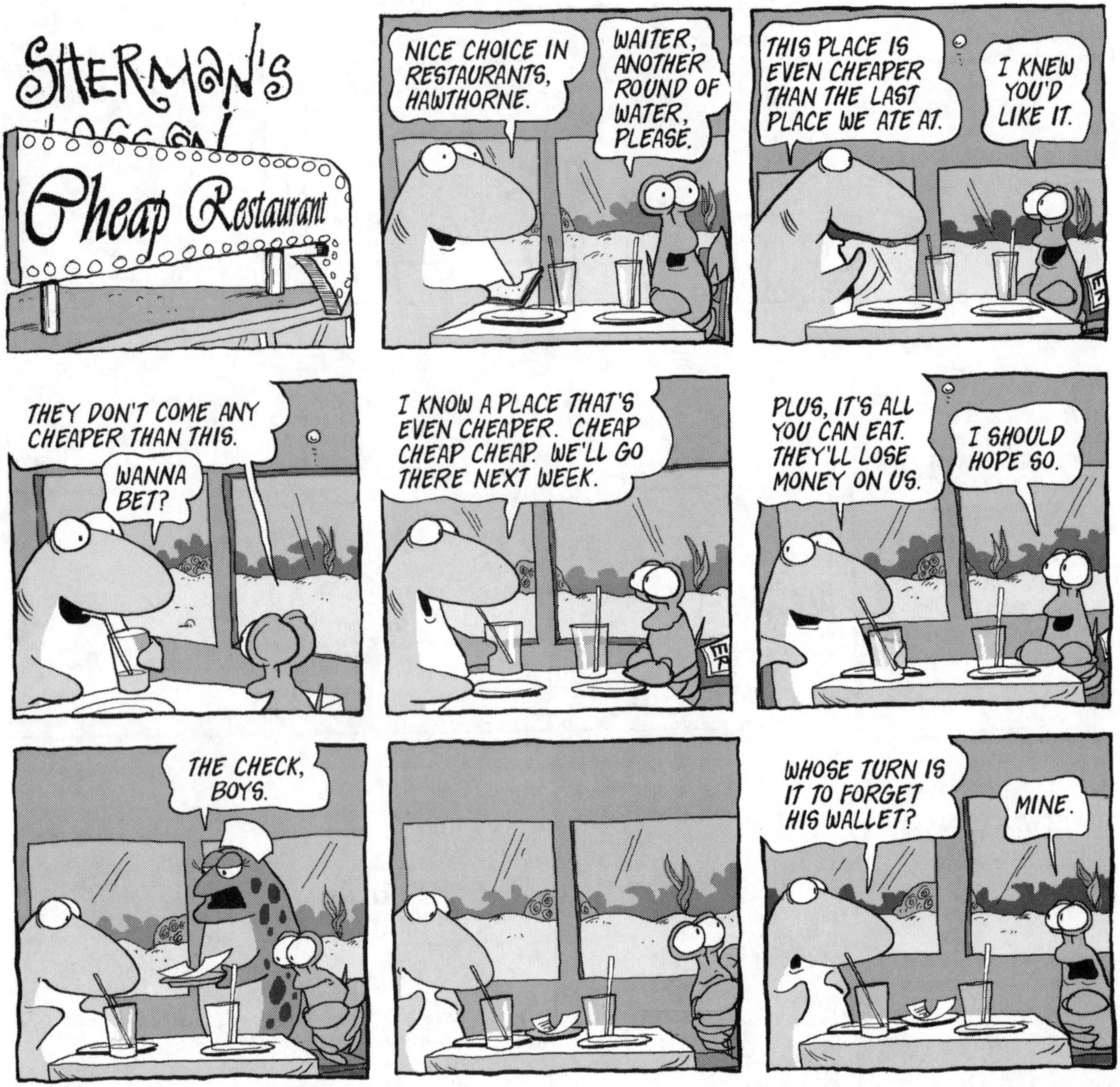
SHERMAN'S
Cheap Restaurant
NICE CHOICE IN RESTAURANTS, HAWTHORNE.
WAITER, ANOTHER ROUND OF WATER, PLEASE.
THIS PLACE IS EVEN CHEAPER THAN THE LAST PLACE WE ATE AT.
I KNEW YOU'D LIKE IT.
THEY DON'T COME ANY CHEAPER THAN THIS.
WANNA BET?
I KNOW A PLACE THAT'S EVEN CHEAPER. CHEAP CHEAP CHEAP. WE'LL GO THERE NEXT WEEK.
PLUS, IT'S ALL YOU CAN EAT. THEY'LL LOSE MONEY ON US.
I SHOULD HOPE SO.
THE CHECK, BOYS.
WHOSE TURN IS IT TO FORGET HIS WALLET?
MINE.

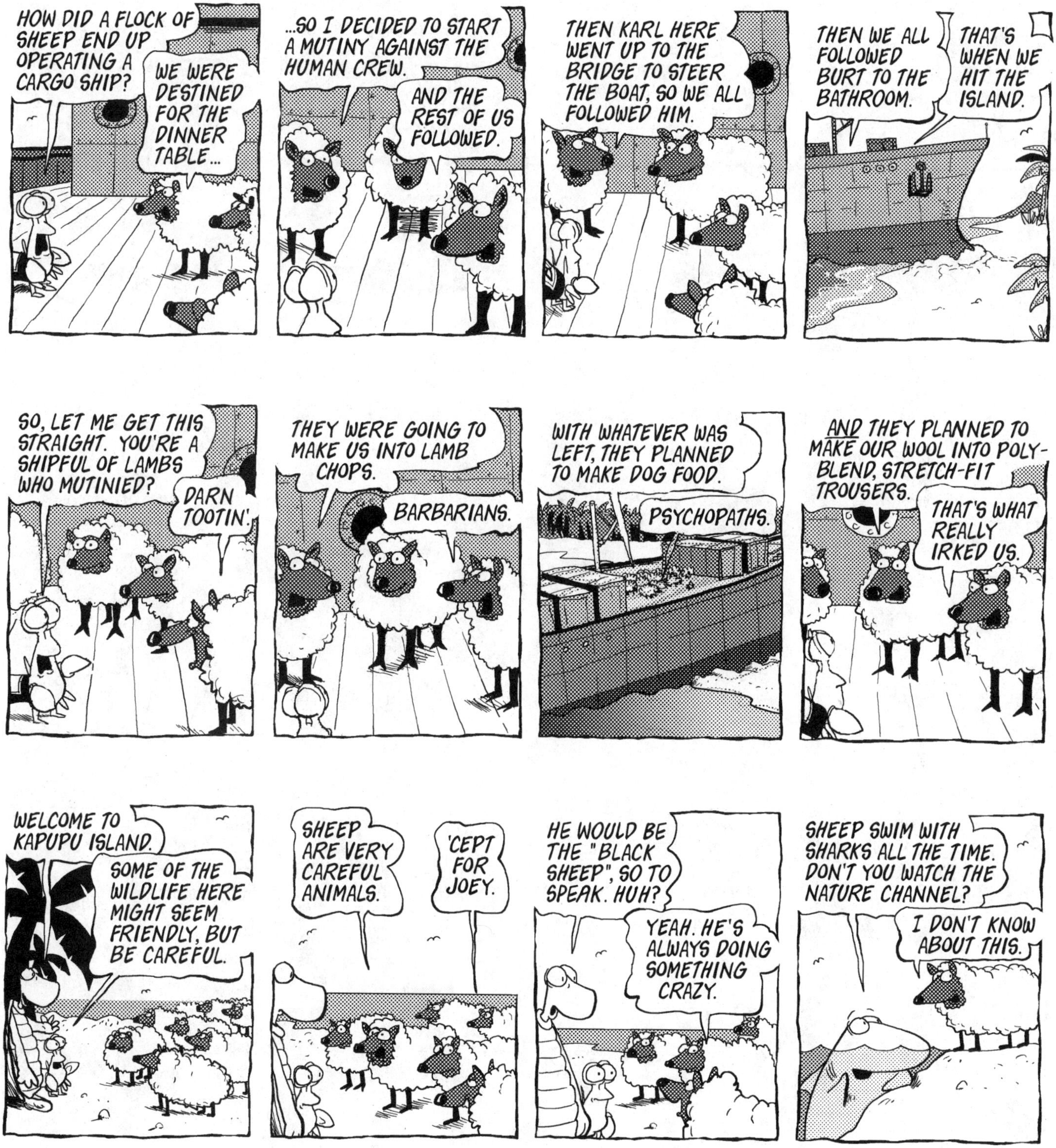
HOW DID A FLOCK OF SHEEP END UP OPERATING A CARGO SHIP?
WE WERE DESTINED FOR THE DINNER TABLE...
...SO I DECIDED TO START A MUTINY AGAINST THE HUMAN CREW.
AND THE REST OF US FOLLOWED.
THEN KARL HERE WENT UP TO THE BRIDGE TO STEER THE BOAT, SO WE ALL FOLLOWED HIM.
THEN WE ALL FOLLOWED BURT TO THE BATHROOM.
THAT'S WHEN WE HIT THE ISLAND.
SO, LET ME GET THIS STRAIGHT. YOU'RE A SHIPFUL OF LAMBS WHO MUTINIED?
DARN TOOTIN'.
THEY WERE GOING TO MAKE US INTO LAMB CHOPS.
BARBARIANS.
WITH WHATEVER WAS LEFT, THEY PLANNED TO MAKE DOG FOOD.
PSYCHOPATHS.
AND THEY PLANNED TO MAKE OUR WOOL INTO POLY-BLEND, STRETCH-FIT TROUSERS.
THAT'S WHAT REALLY IRKED US.
WELCOME TO KAPUPU ISLAND.
SOME OF THE WILDLIFE HERE MIGHT SEEM FRIENDLY, BUT BE CAREFUL.
SHEEP ARE VERY CAREFUL ANIMALS.
'CEPT FOR JOEY.
HE WOULD BE THE "BLACK SHEEP", SO TO SPEAK. HUH?
YEAH. HE'S ALWAYS DOING SOMETHING CRAZY.
SHEEP SWIM WITH SHARKS ALL THE TIME. DON'T YOU WATCH THE NATURE CHANNEL?
I DON'T KNOW ABOUT THIS.

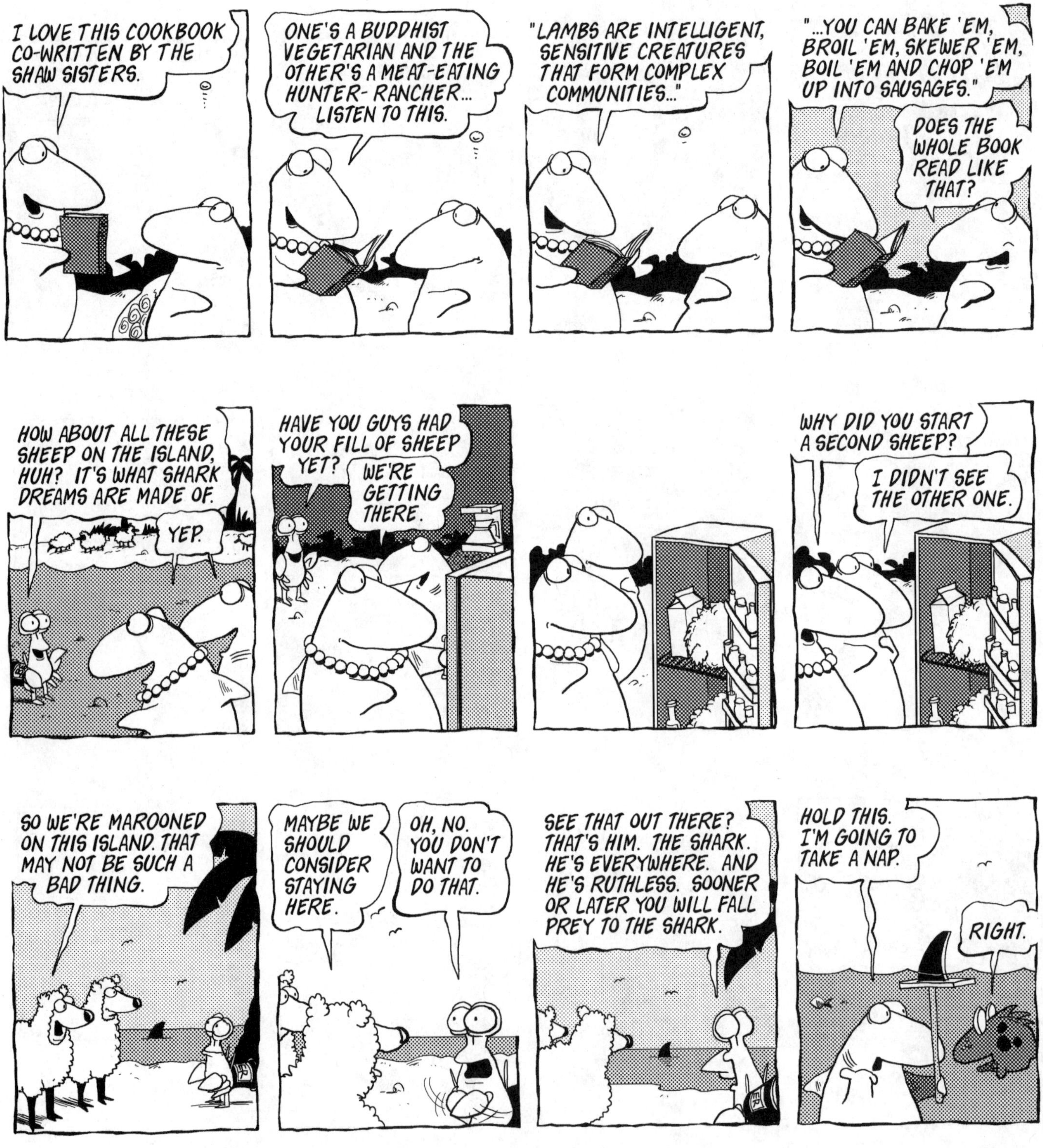
I LOVE THIS COOKBOOK CO-WRITTEN BY THE SHAW SISTERS.
ONE'S A BUDDHIST VEGETARIAN AND THE OTHER'S A MEAT-EATING HUNTER- RANCHER... LISTEN TO THIS.
"LAMBS ARE INTELLIGENT, SENSITIVE CREATURES THAT FORM COMPLEX COMMUNITIES..."
"...YOU CAN BAKE 'EM, BROIL 'EM, SKEWER 'EM, BOIL 'EM AND CHOP 'EM UP INTO SAUSAGES."
DOES THE WHOLE BOOK READ LIKE THAT?
HOW ABOUT ALL THESE SHEEP ON THE ISLAND, HUH? IT'S WHAT SHARK DREAMS ARE MADE OF.
YEP.
HAVE YOU GUYS HAD YOUR FILL OF SHEEP YET?
WE'RE GETTING THERE.
WHY DID YOU START A SECOND SHEEP?
I DIDN'T SEE THE OTHER ONE.
SO WE'RE MAROONED ON THIS ISLAND. THAT MAY NOT BE SUCH A BAD THING.
MAYBE WE SHOULD CONSIDER STAYING HERE.
OH, NO. YOU DON'T WANT TO DO THAT.
SEE THAT OUT THERE? THAT'S HIM. THE SHARK. HE'S EVERYWHERE. AND HE'S RUTHLESS. SOONER OR LATER YOU WILL FALL PREY TO THE SHARK.
HOLD THIS. I'M GOING TO TAKE A NAP.
RIGHT.

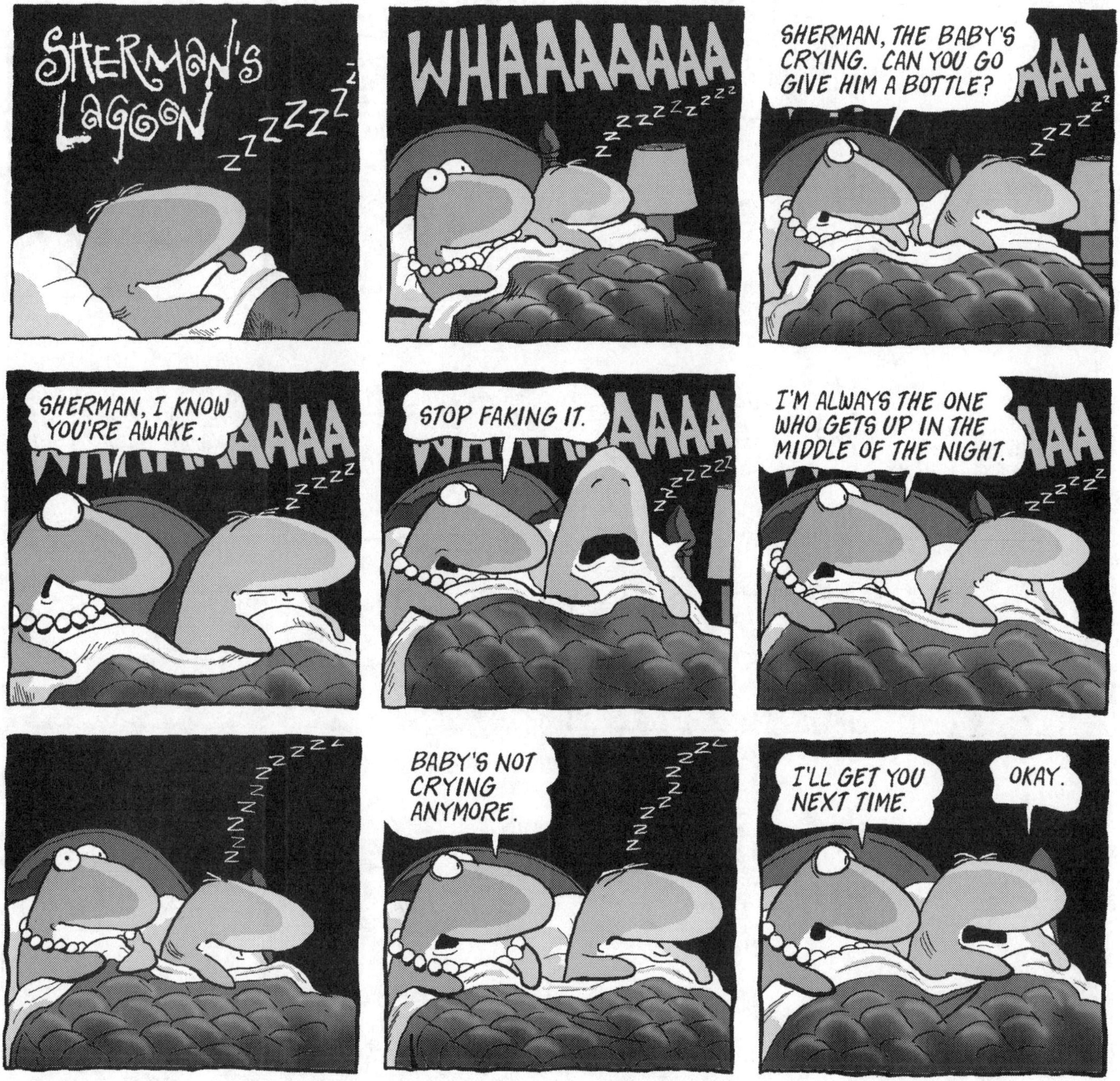
SHERMAN'S LAGOON
ZZZZZZZ
WHAAAAAAA
ZZZZZZZZZ
SHERMAN, THE BABY'S CRYING. CAN YOU GO GIVE HIM A BOTTLE?
SHERMAN, I KNOW YOU'RE AWAKE.
STOP FAKING IT.
I'M ALWAYS THE ONE WHO GETS UP IN THE MIDDLE OF THE NIGHT.
BABY'S NOT CRYING ANYMORE.
I'LL GET YOU NEXT TIME.
OKAY.

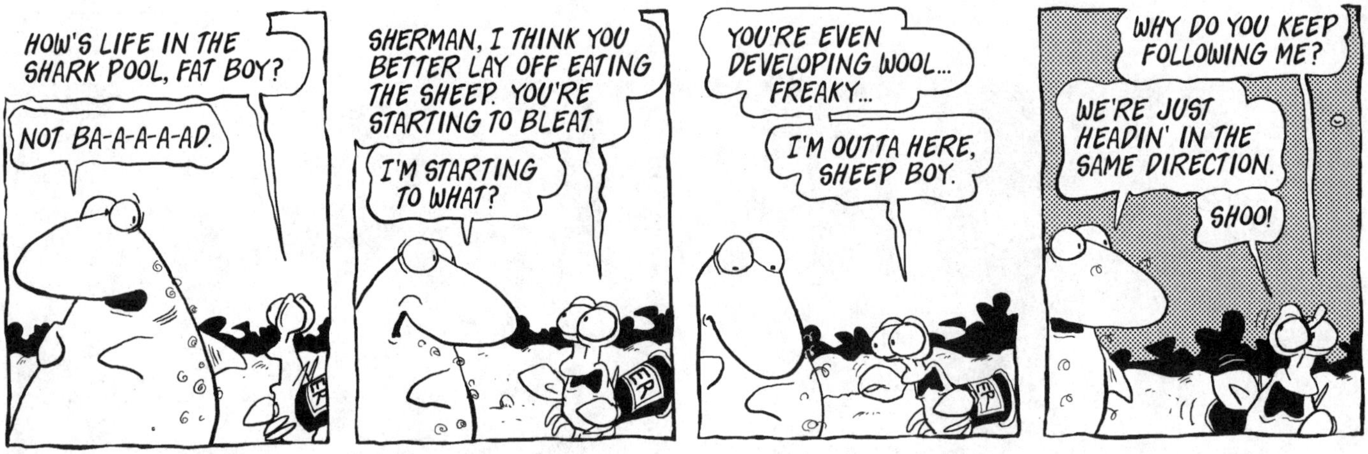
HOW'S LIFE IN THE SHARK POOL, FAT BOY?
NOT BA-A-A-A-AD.
SHERMAN, I THINK YOU BETTER LAY OFF EATING THE SHEEP. YOU'RE STARTING TO BLEAT.
I'M STARTING TO WHAT?
YOU'RE EVEN DEVELOPING WOOL... FREAKY...
I'M OUTTA HERE, SHEEP BOY.
WHY DO YOU KEEP FOLLOWING ME?
WE'RE JUST HEADIN' IN THE SAME DIRECTION.
SHOO!

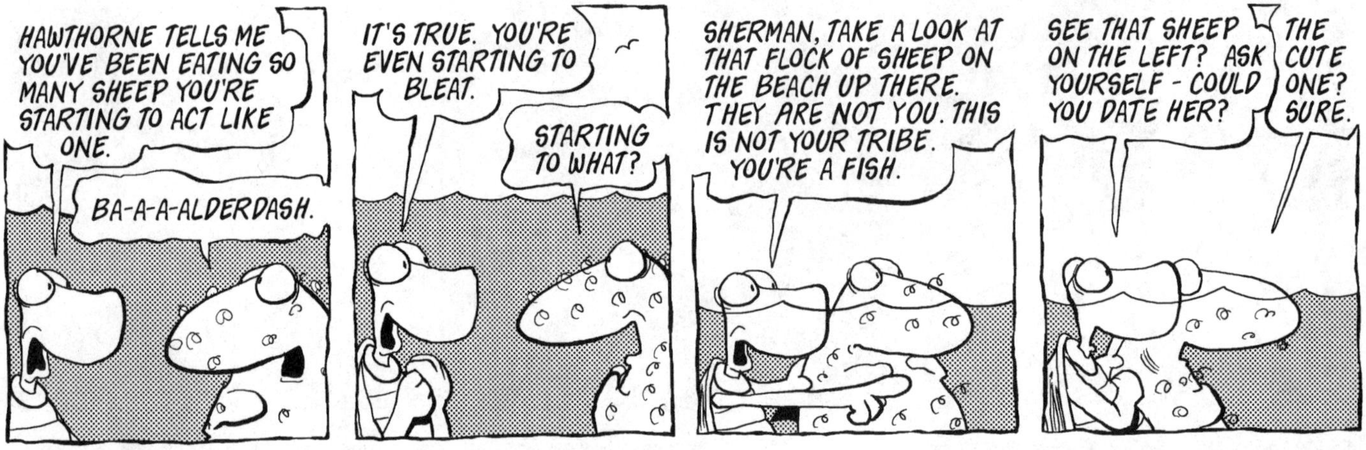
HAWTHORNE TELLS ME YOU'VE BEEN EATING SO MANY SHEEP YOU'RE STARTING TO ACT LIKE ONE.
BA-A-A-ALDERDASH.
IT'S TRUE. YOU'RE EVEN STARTING TO BLEAT.
STARTING TO WHAT?
SHERMAN, TAKE A LOOK AT THAT FLOCK OF SHEEP ON THE BEACH UP THERE. THEY ARE NOT YOU. THIS IS NOT YOUR TRIBE. YOU'RE A FISH.
SEE THAT SHEEP ON THE LEFT? ASK YOURSELF - COULD YOU DATE HER?
THE CUTE ONE? SURE.

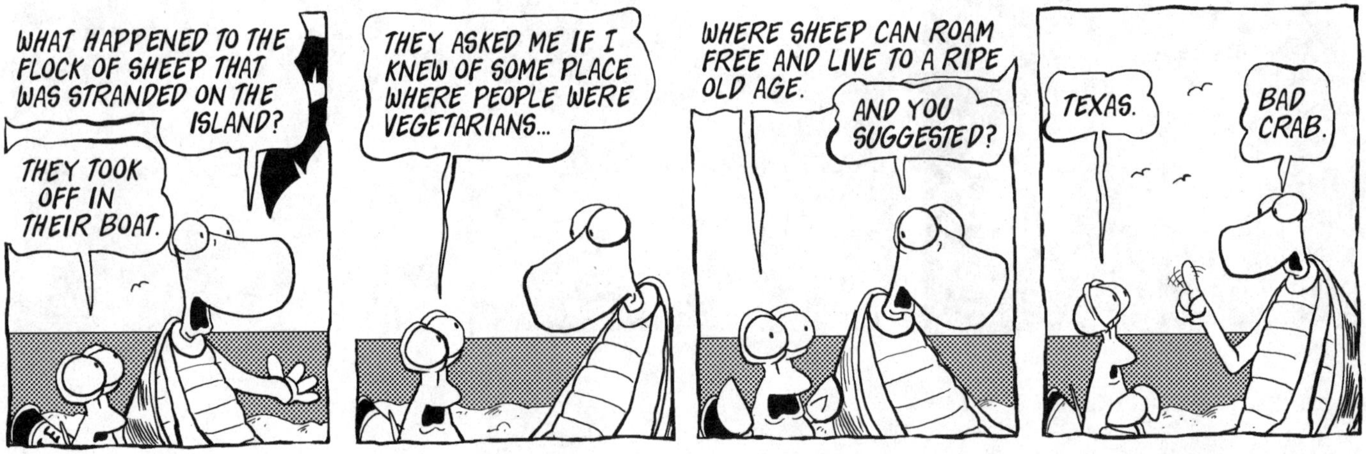
WHAT HAPPENED TO THE FLOCK OF SHEEP THAT WAS STRANDED ON THE ISLAND?
THEY TOOK OFF IN THEIR BOAT.
THEY ASKED ME IF I KNEW OF SOME PLACE WHERE PEOPLE WERE VEGETARIANS...
WHERE SHEEP CAN ROAM FREE AND LIVE TO A RIPE OLD AGE.
AND YOU SUGGESTED?
TEXAS.
BAD CRAB.

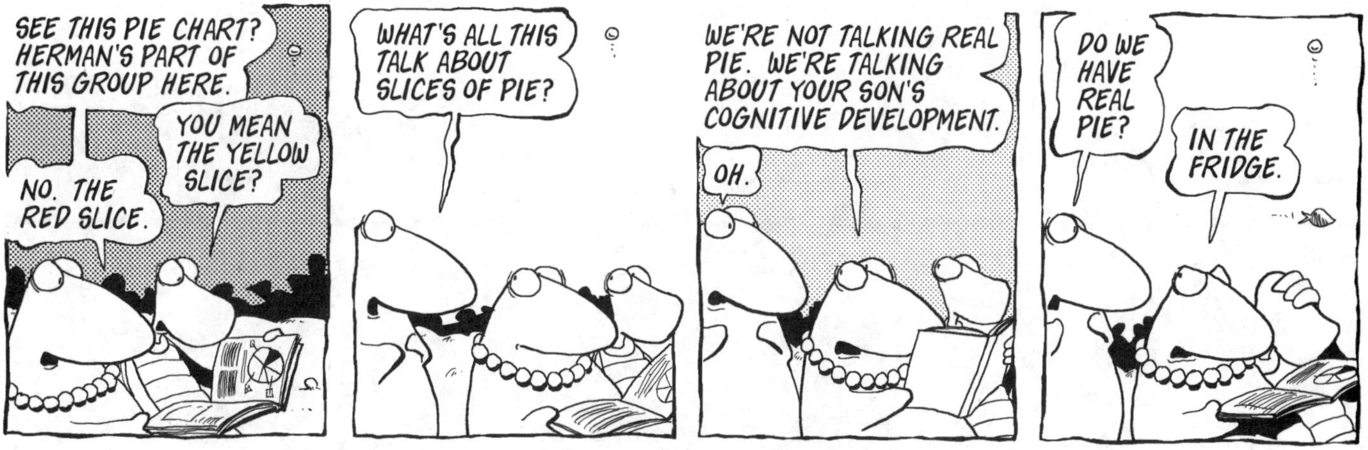
SEE THIS PIE CHART? HERMAN'S PART OF THIS GROUP HERE.
YOU MEAN THE YELLOW SLICE?
NO. THE RED SLICE.
WHAT'S ALL THIS TALK ABOUT SLICES OF PIE?
WE'RE NOT TALKING REAL PIE. WE'RE TALKING ABOUT YOUR SON'S COGNITIVE DEVELOPMENT.
OH.
DO WE HAVE REAL PIE?
IN THE FRIDGE.

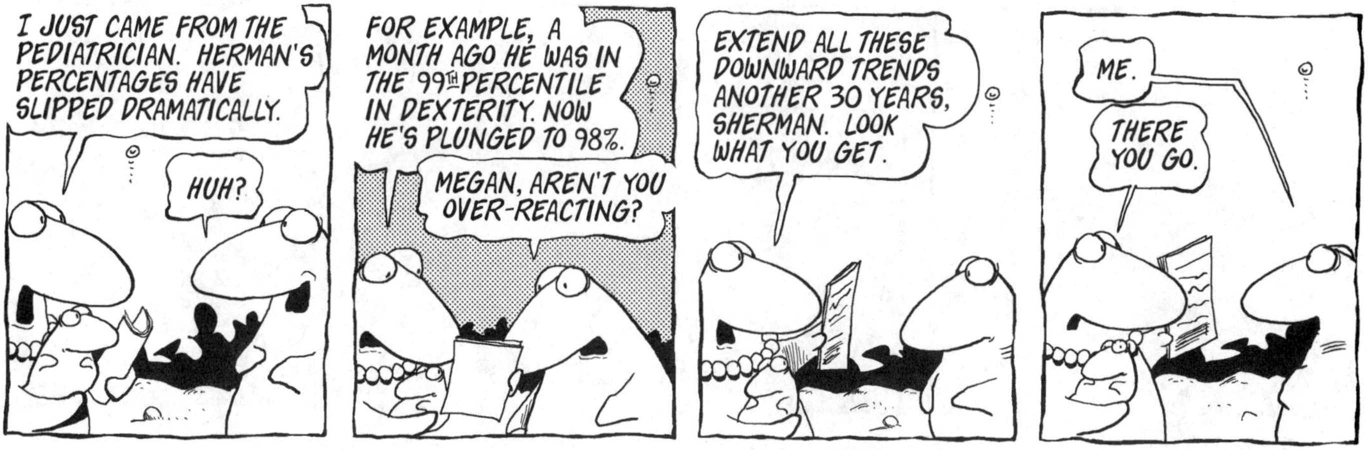
I JUST CAME FROM THE PEDIATRICIAN. HERMAN'S PERCENTAGES HAVE SLIPPED DRAMATICALLY.
HUH?
FOR EXAMPLE, A MONTH AGO HE WAS IN THE 99TH PERCENTILE IN DEXTERITY. NOW HE'S PLUNGED TO 98%.
MEGAN, AREN'T YOU OVER-REACTING?
EXTEND ALL THESE DOWNWARD TRENDS ANOTHER 30 YEARS, SHERMAN. LOOK WHAT YOU GET.
ME.
THERE YOU GO.

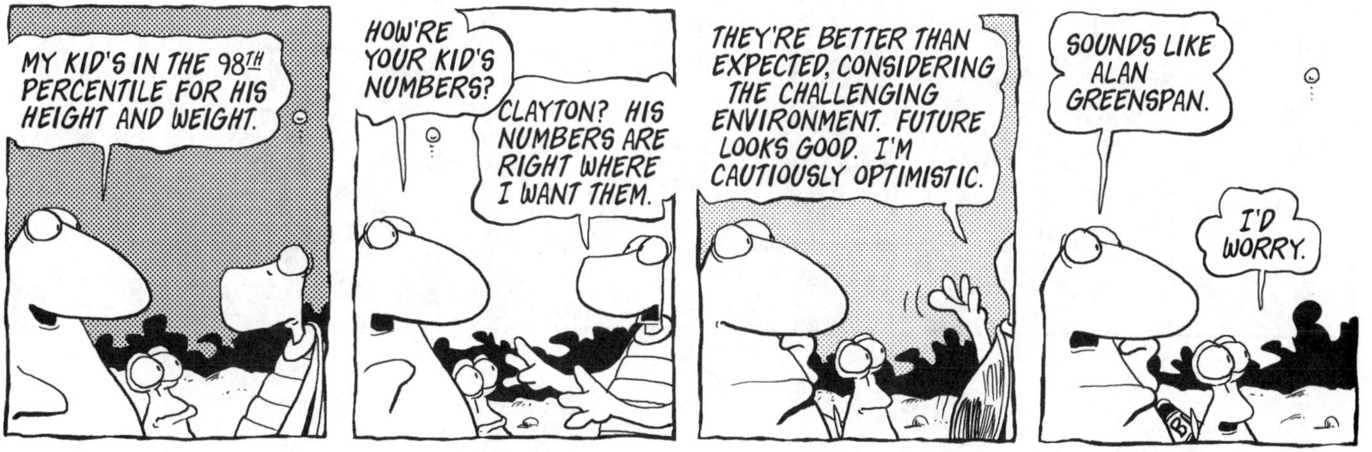
MY KID'S IN THE 98TH PERCENTILE FOR HIS HEIGHT AND WEIGHT.
HOW'RE YOUR KID'S NUMBERS?
CLAYTON? HIS NUMBERS ARE RIGHT WHERE I WANT THEM.
THEY'RE BETTER THAN EXPECTED, CONSIDERING THE CHALLENGING ENVIRONMENT. FUTURE LOOKS GOOD. I'M CAUTIOUSLY OPTIMISTIC.
SOUNDS LIKE ALAN GREENSPAN.
I'D WORRY.

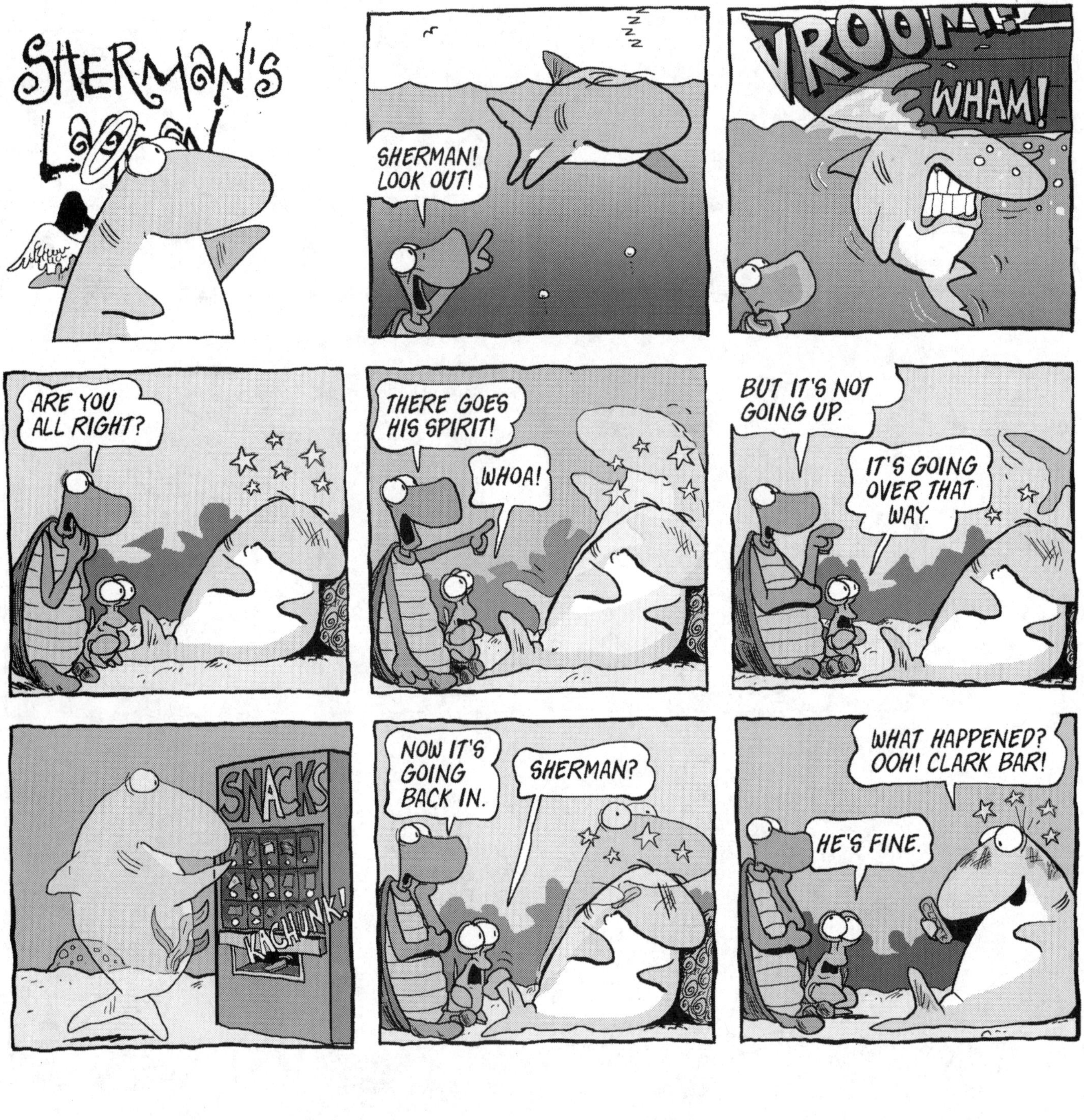
SHERMAN'S LAGOON
SHERMAN! LOOK OUT!
WHAM!
ARE YOU ALL RIGHT?
THERE GOES HIS SPIRIT!
WHOA!
BUT IT'S NOT GOING UP.
IT'S GOING OVER THAT WAY.
SNACKS
KACHUNK!
NOW IT'S GOING BACK IN.
SHERMAN?
WHAT HAPPENED? OOH! CLARK BAR!
HE'S FINE.

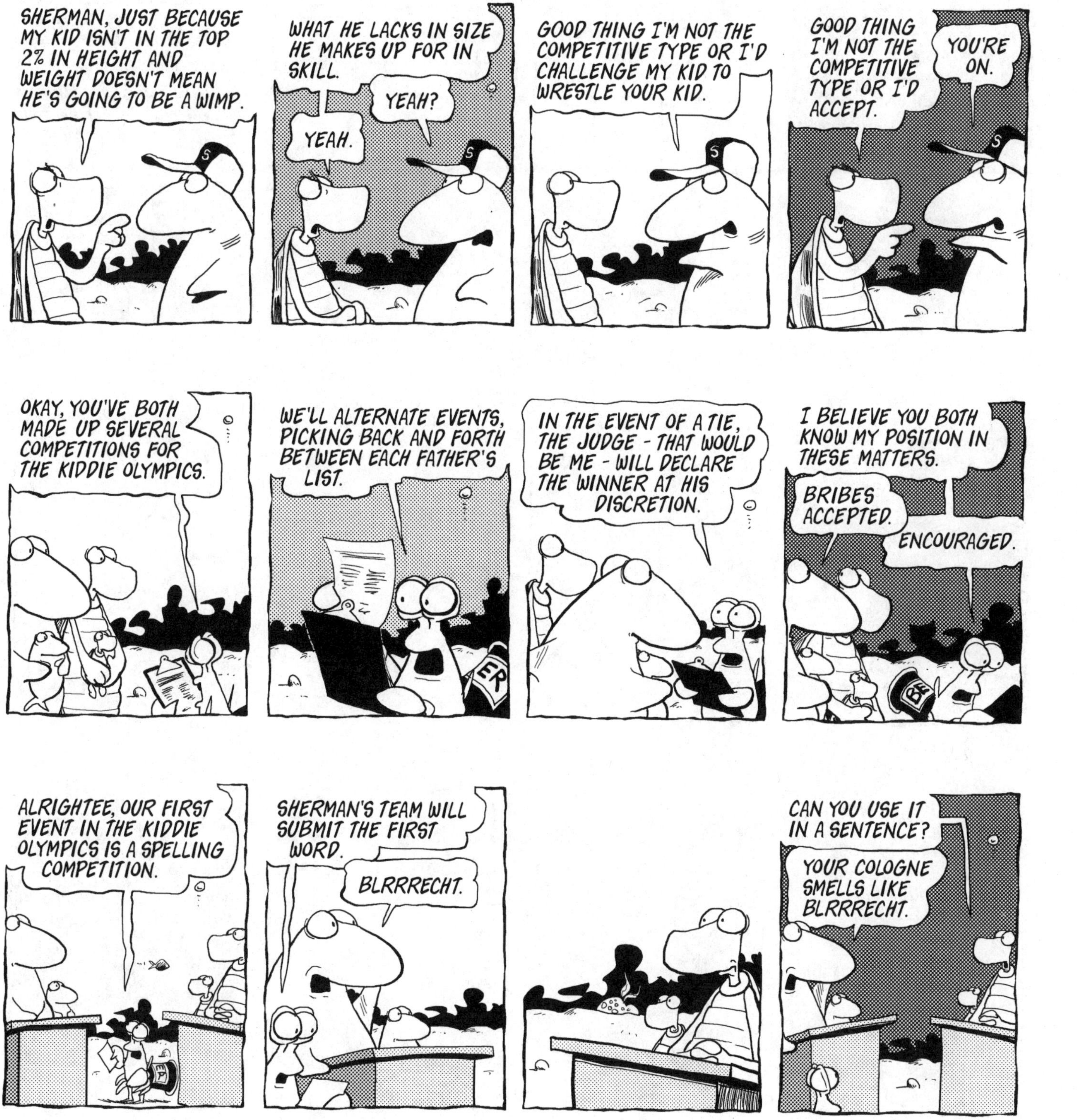
SHERMAN, JUST BECAUSE MY KID ISN'T IN THE TOP 2% IN HEIGHT AND WEIGHT DOESN'T MEAN HE'S GOING TO BE A WIMP.
WHAT HE LACKS IN SIZE HE MAKES UP FOR IN SKILL.
YEAH?
YEAH.
GOOD THING I'M NOT THE COMPETITIVE TYPE OR I'D CHALLENGE MY KID TO WRESTLE YOUR KID.
GOOD THING I'M NOT THE COMPETITIVE TYPE OR I'D ACCEPT.
YOU'RE ON.
S
OKAY, YOU'VE BOTH MADE UP SEVERAL COMPETITIONS FOR THE KIDDIE OLYMPICS.
WE'LL ALTERNATE EVENTS, PICKING BACK AND FORTH BETWEEN EACH FATHER'S LIST.
ER
IN THE EVENT OF A TIE, THE JUDGE - THAT WOULD BE ME - WILL DECLARE THE WINNER AT HIS DISCRETION.
I BELIEVE YOU BOTH KNOW MY POSITION IN THESE MATTERS.
BRIBES ACCEPTED.
ENCOURAGED.
ALRIGHTEE, OUR FIRST EVENT IN THE KIDDIE OLYMPICS IS A SPELLING COMPETITION.
SHERMAN'S TEAM WILL SUBMIT THE FIRST WORD.
BLRRRECHT.
CAN YOU USE IT IN A SENTENCE?
YOUR COLOGNE SMELLS LIKE BLRRRECHT.

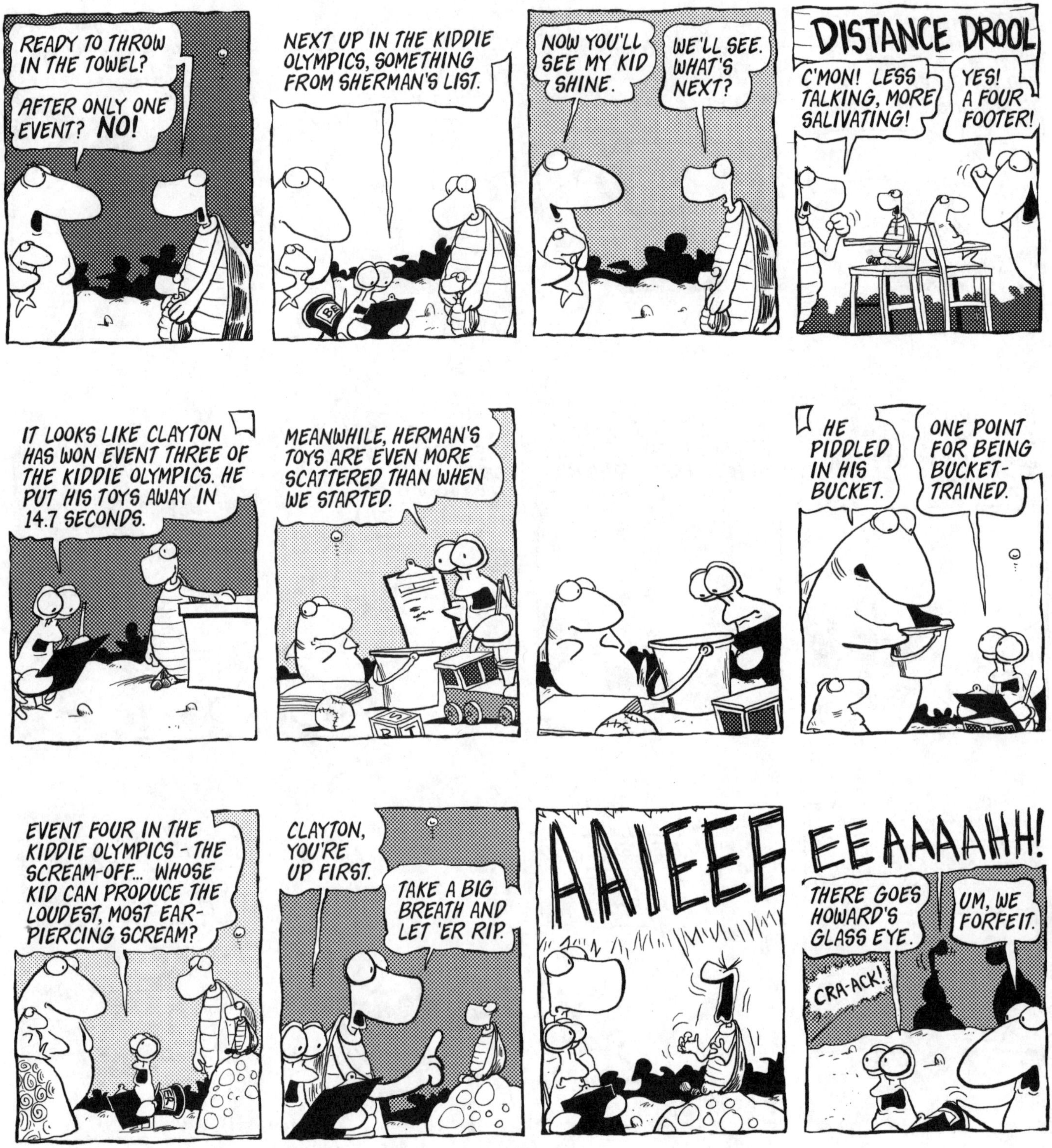
READY TO THROW IN THE TOWEL?
AFTER ONLY ONE EVENT? NO!
NEXT UP IN THE KIDDIE OLYMPICS, SOMETHING FROM SHERMAN'S LIST.
NOW YOU'LL SEE MY KID SHINE.
WE'LL SEE. WHAT'S NEXT?
DISTANCE DROOL
C'MON! LESS TALKING, MORE SALIVATING!
YES! A FOUR FOOTER!
IT LOOKS LIKE CLAYTON HAS WON EVENT THREE OF THE KIDDIE OLYMPICS. HE PUT HIS TOYS AWAY IN 14.7 SECONDS.
MEANWHILE, HERMAN'S TOYS ARE EVEN MORE SCATTERED THAN WHEN WE STARTED.
HE PIDDLED IN HIS BUCKET.
ONE POINT FOR BEING BUCKET-TRAINED.
EVENT FOUR IN THE KIDDIE OLYMPICS - THE SCREAM-OFF... WHOSE KID CAN PRODUCE THE LOUDEST, MOST EAR-PIERCING SCREAM?
CLAYTON, YOU'RE UP FIRST.
TAKE A BIG BREATH AND LET 'ER RIP.
AAIEEE
EEAAAAHH!
THERE GOES HOWARD'S GLASS EYE.
UM, WE FORFEIT.
CRA-ACK!

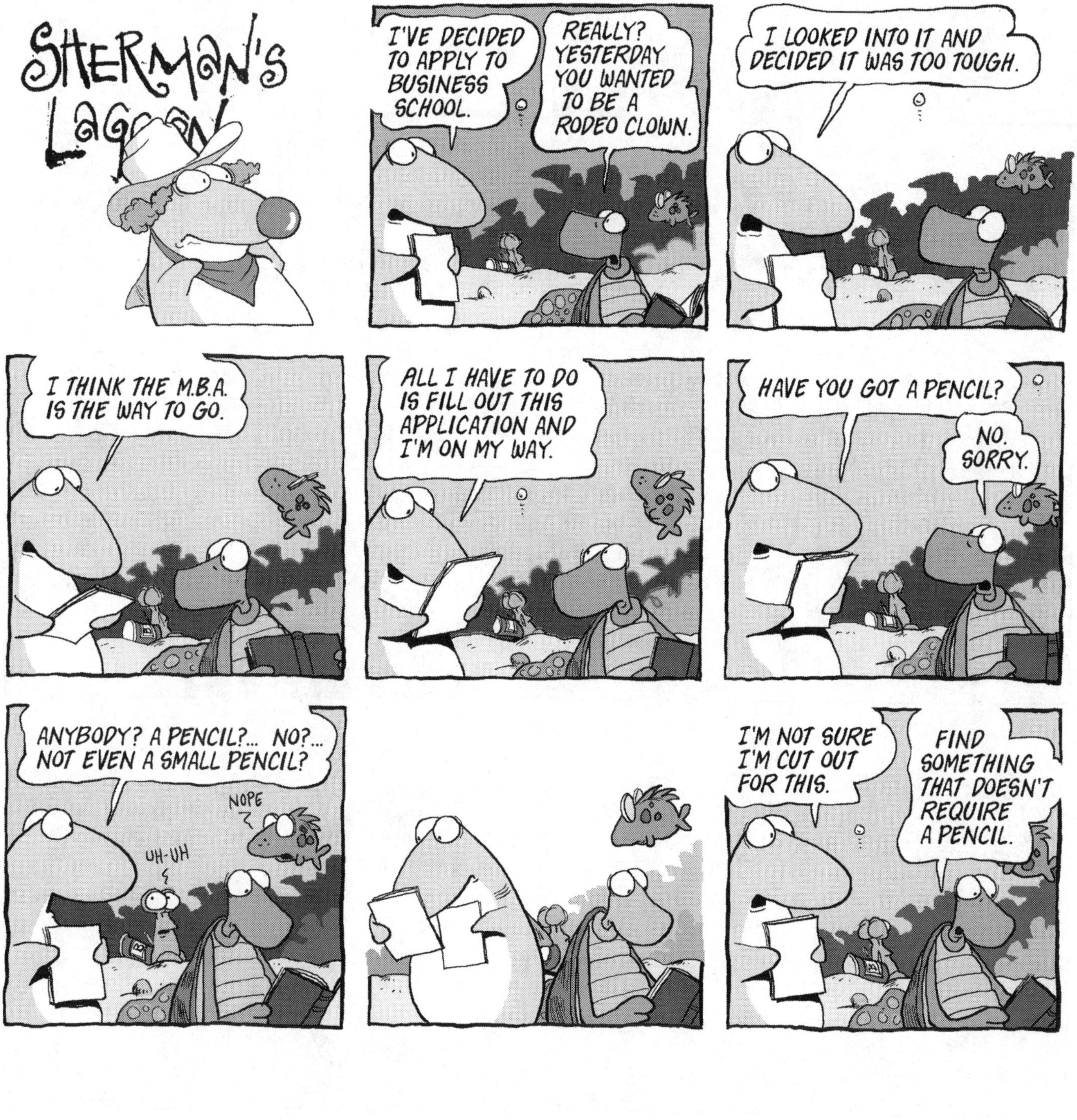

SHERMAN'S LAGOON
I'VE DECIDED TO APPLY TO BUSINESS SCHOOL.
REALLY? YESTERDAY YOU WANTED TO BE A RODEO CLOWN.
I LOOKED INTO IT AND DECIDED IT WAS TOO TOUGH.
I THINK THE M.B.A. IS THE WAY TO GO.
ALL I HAVE TO DO IS FILL OUT THIS APPLICATION AND I'M ON MY WAY.
HAVE YOU GOT A PENCIL?
NO. SORRY.
ANYBODY? A PENCIL?... NO?... NOT EVEN A SMALL PENCIL?
UH-UH
NOPE
I'M NOT SURE I'M CUT OUT FOR THIS.
FIND SOMETHING THAT DOESN'T REQUIRE A PENCIL.

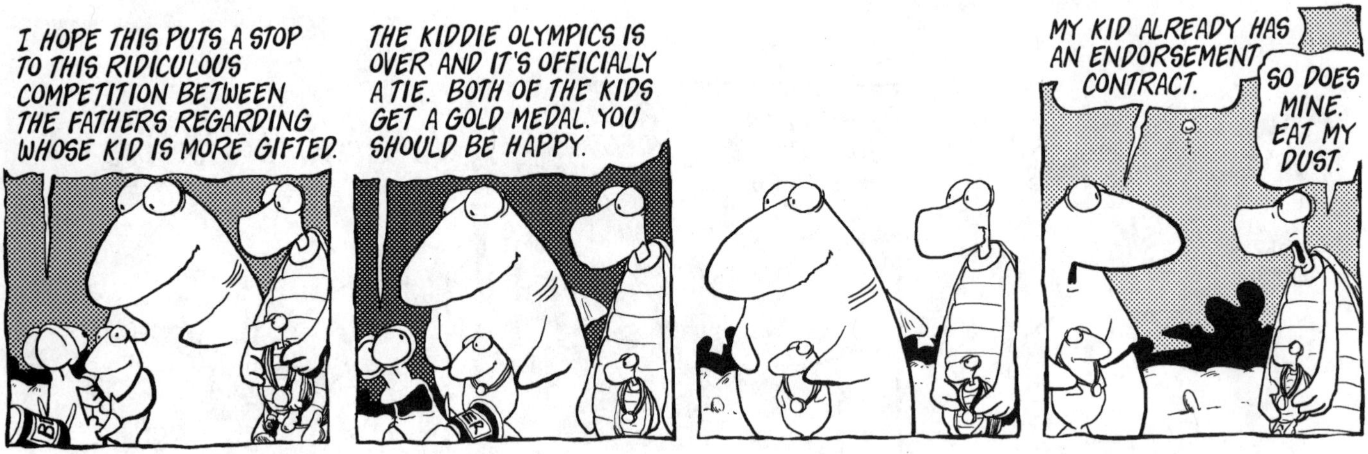
I HOPE THIS PUTS A STOP TO THIS RIDICULOUS COMPETITION BETWEEN THE FATHERS REGARDING WHOSE KID IS MORE GIFTED.
THE KIDDIE OLYMPICS IS OVER AND IT'S OFFICIALLY A TIE. BOTH OF THE KIDS GET A GOLD MEDAL. YOU SHOULD BE HAPPY.
MY KID ALREADY HAS AN ENDORSEMENT CONTRACT.
SO DOES MINE. EAT MY DUST.

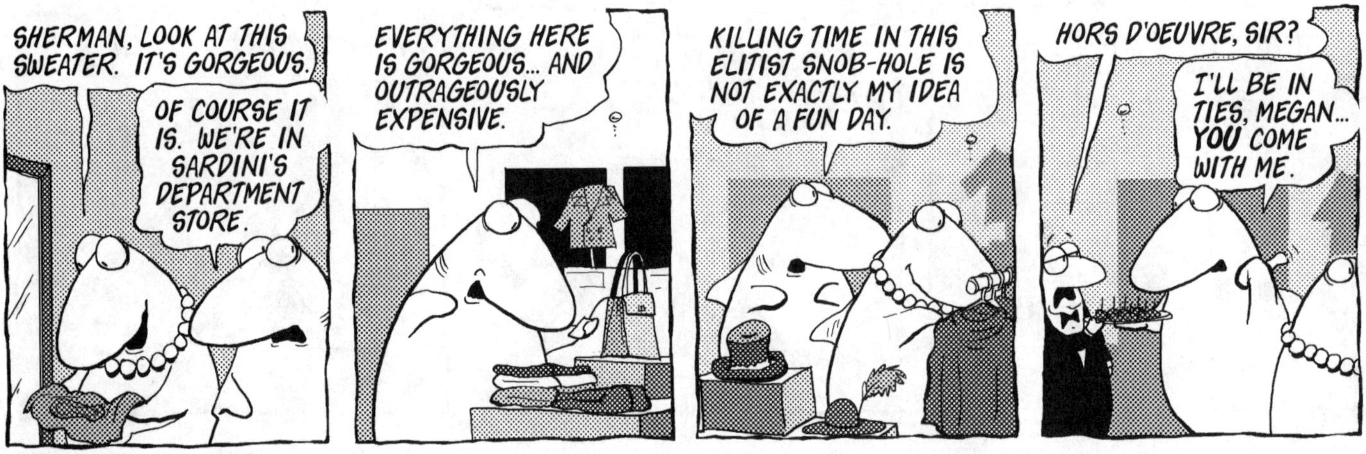
SHERMAN, LOOK AT THIS SWEATER. IT'S GORGEOUS.
OF COURSE IT IS. WE'RE IN SARDINI'S DEPARTMENT STORE.
EVERYTHING HERE IS GORGEOUS... AND OUTRAGEOUSLY EXPENSIVE.
KILLING TIME IN THIS ELITIST SNOB-HOLE IS NOT EXACTLY MY IDEA OF A FUN DAY.
HORS D'OEUVRE, SIR?
I'LL BE IN TIES, MEGAN... **YOU** COME WITH ME.

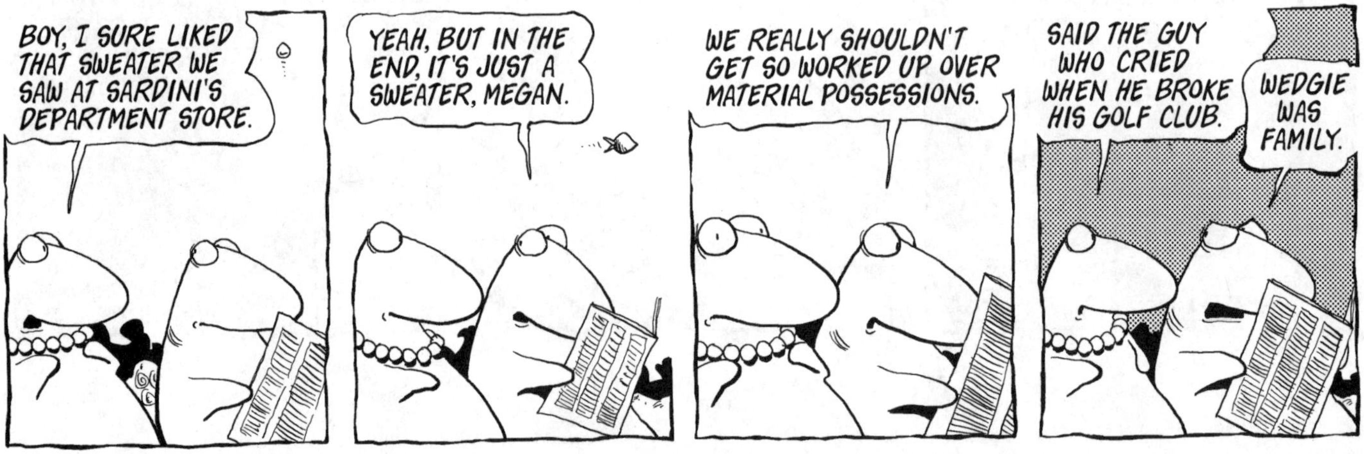
BOY, I SURE LIKED THAT SWEATER WE SAW AT SARDINI'S DEPARTMENT STORE.
YEAH, BUT IN THE END, IT'S JUST A SWEATER, MEGAN.
WE REALLY SHOULDN'T GET SO WORKED UP OVER MATERIAL POSSESSIONS.
SAID THE GUY WHO CRIED WHEN HE BROKE HIS GOLF CLUB.
WEDGIE WAS FAMILY.

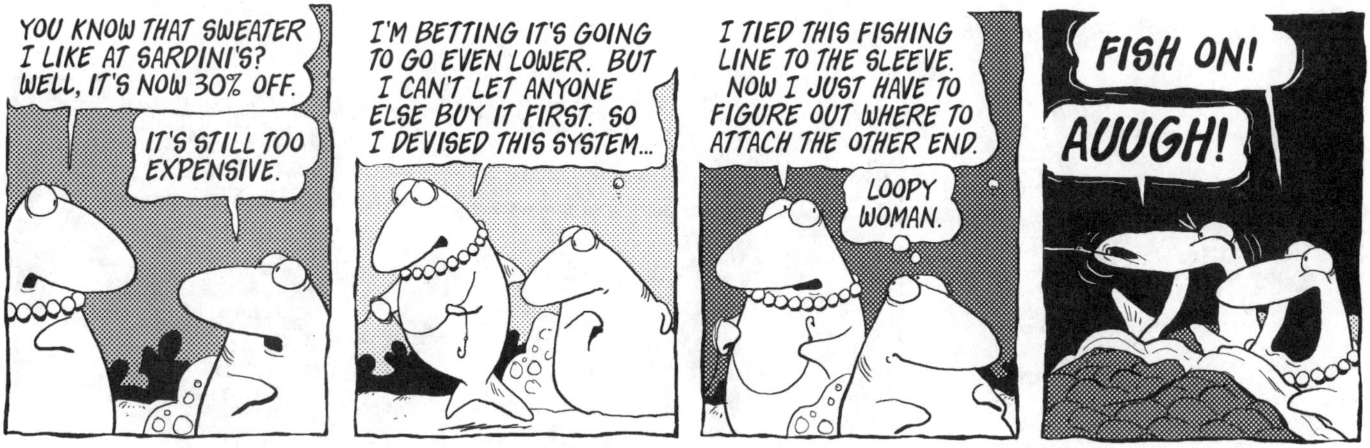
YOU KNOW THAT SWEATER I LIKE AT SARDINI'S? WELL, IT'S NOW 30% OFF.
IT'S STILL TOO EXPENSIVE.
I'M BETTING IT'S GOING TO GO EVEN LOWER. BUT I CAN'T LET ANYONE ELSE BUY IT FIRST. SO I DEVISED THIS SYSTEM...
I TIED THIS FISHING LINE TO THE SLEEVE. NOW I JUST HAVE TO FIGURE OUT WHERE TO ATTACH THE OTHER END.
LOOPY WOMAN.
FISH ON!
AUUGH!

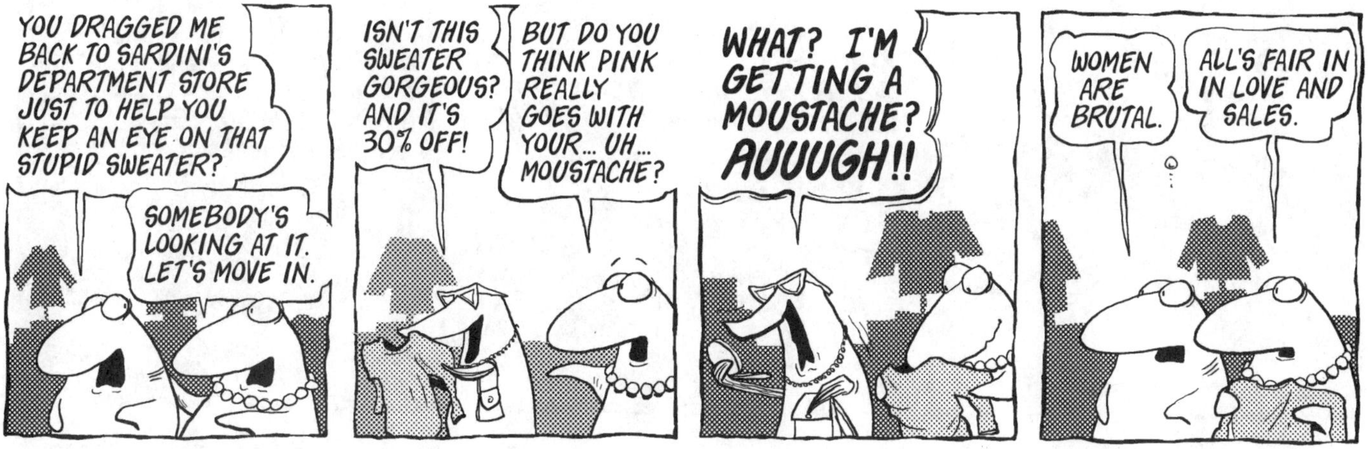
YOU DRAGGED ME BACK TO SARDINI'S DEPARTMENT STORE JUST TO HELP YOU KEEP AN EYE ON THAT STUPID SWEATER?
SOMEBODY'S LOOKING AT IT. LET'S MOVE IN.
ISN'T THIS SWEATER GORGEOUS? AND IT'S 30% OFF!
BUT DO YOU THINK PINK REALLY GOES WITH YOUR... UH... MOUSTACHE?
WHAT? I'M GETTING A MOUSTACHE? AUUUGH!!
WOMEN ARE BRUTAL.
ALL'S FAIR IN IN LOVE AND SALES.

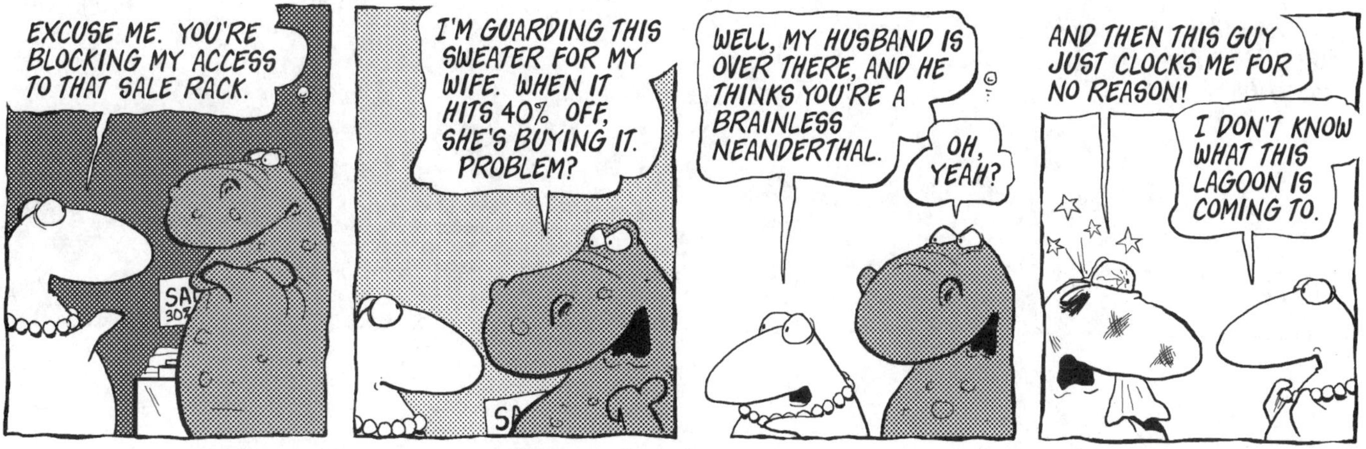
EXCUSE ME. YOU'RE BLOCKING MY ACCESS TO THAT SALE RACK.
I'M GUARDING THIS SWEATER FOR MY WIFE. WHEN IT HITS 40% OFF, SHE'S BUYING IT. PROBLEM?
WELL, MY HUSBAND IS OVER THERE, AND HE THINKS YOU'RE A BRAINLESS NEANDERTHAL.
OH, YEAH?
AND THEN THIS GUY JUST CLOCKS ME FOR NO REASON!
I DON'T KNOW WHAT THIS LAGOON IS COMING TO.

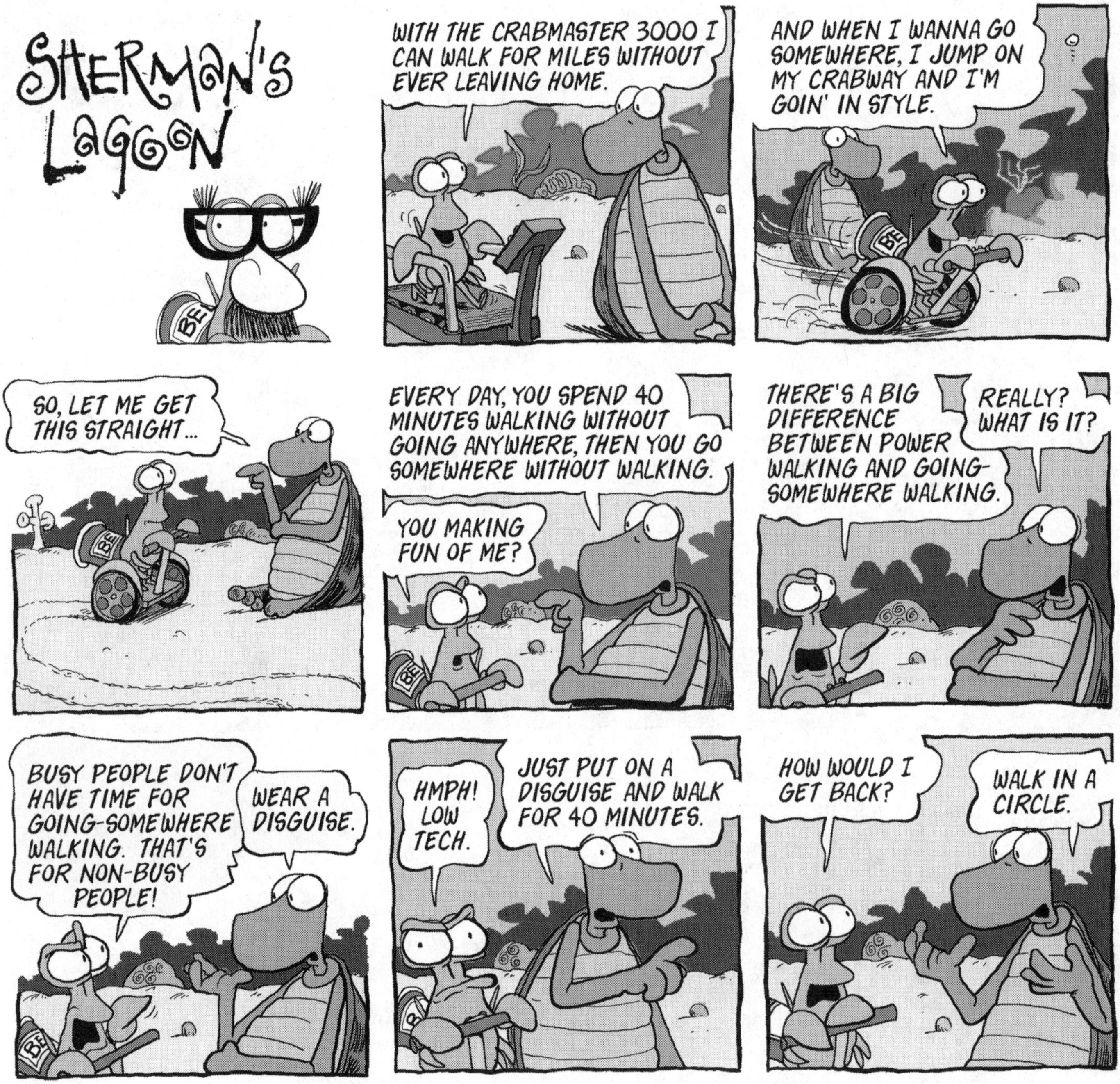
SHERMAN'S LAGOON
WITH THE CRABMASTER 3000 I CAN WALK FOR MILES WITHOUT EVER LEAVING HOME.
AND WHEN I WANNA GO SOMEWHERE, I JUMP ON MY CRABWAY AND I'M GOIN' IN STYLE.
BE
SO, LET ME GET THIS STRAIGHT...
EVERY DAY, YOU SPEND 40 MINUTES WALKING WITHOUT GOING ANYWHERE, THEN YOU GO SOMEWHERE WITHOUT WALKING.
YOU MAKING FUN OF ME?
THERE'S A BIG DIFFERENCE BETWEEN POWER WALKING AND GOING-SOMEWHERE WALKING.
REALLY? WHAT IS IT?
BUSY PEOPLE DON'T HAVE TIME FOR GOING-SOMEWHERE WALKING. THAT'S FOR NON-BUSY PEOPLE!
WEAR A DISGUISE.
HMPH! LOW TECH.
JUST PUT ON A DISGUISE AND WALK FOR 40 MINUTES.
HOW WOULD I GET BACK?
WALK IN A CIRCLE.

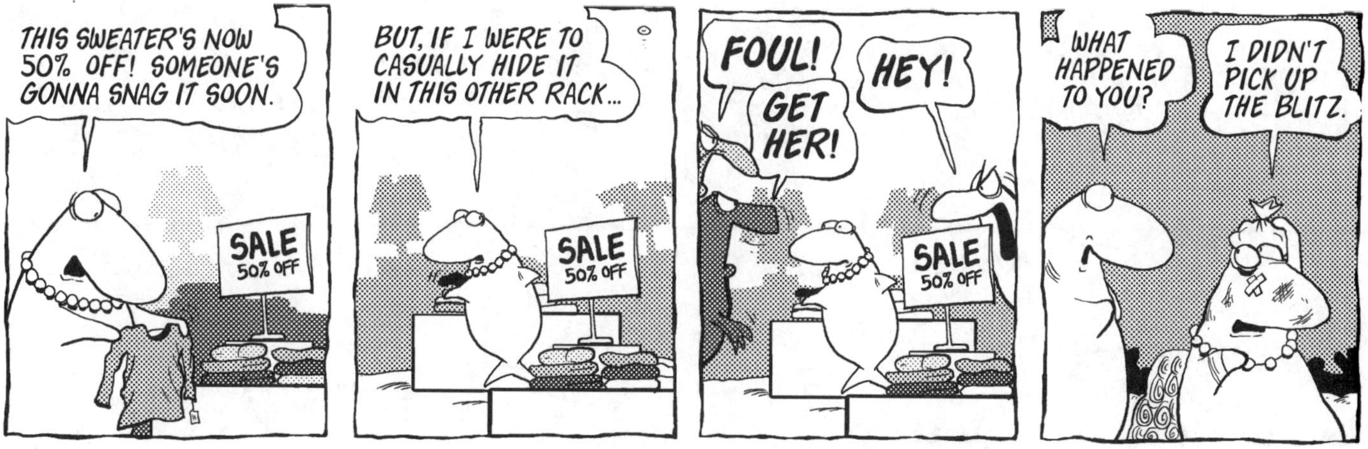
THIS SWEATER'S NOW 50% OFF! SOMEONE'S GONNA SNAG IT SOON.
SALE 50% OFF
BUT, IF I WERE TO CASUALLY HIDE IT IN THIS OTHER RACK...
SALE 50% OFF
FOUL!
GET HER!
HEY!
SALE 50% OFF
WHAT HAPPENED TO YOU?
I DIDN'T PICK UP THE BLITZ.

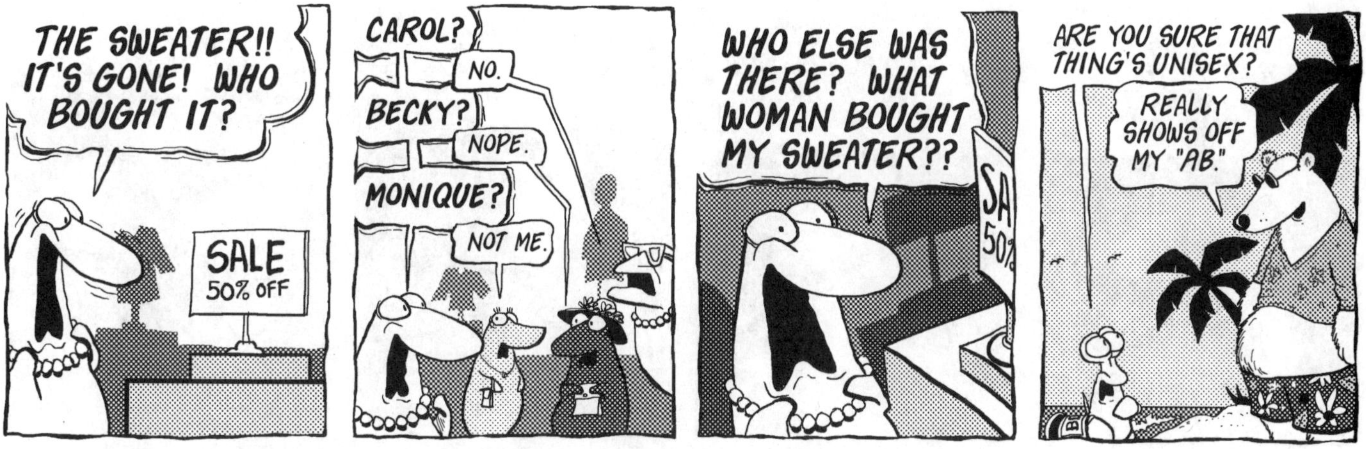
THE SWEATER!! IT'S GONE! WHO BOUGHT IT?
SALE 50% OFF
CAROL?
NO.
BECKY?
NOPE.
MONIQUE?
NOT ME.
WHO ELSE WAS THERE? WHAT WOMAN BOUGHT MY SWEATER??
ARE YOU SURE THAT THING'S UNISEX?
REALLY SHOWS OFF MY "AB."

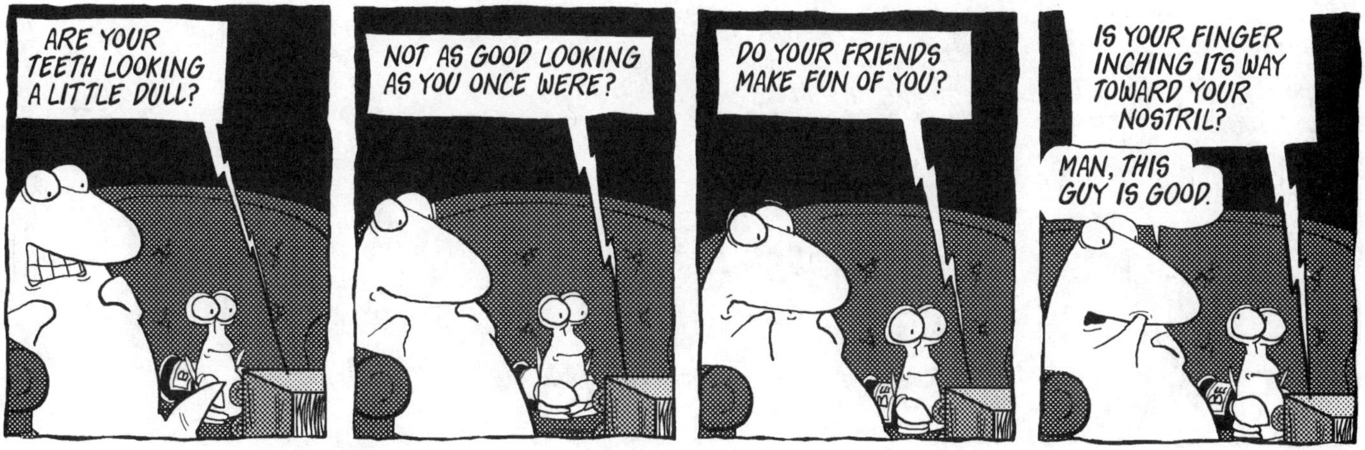
ARE YOUR TEETH LOOKING A LITTLE DULL?
NOT AS GOOD LOOKING AS YOU ONCE WERE?
DO YOUR FRIENDS MAKE FUN OF YOU?
IS YOUR FINGER INCHING ITS WAY TOWARD YOUR NOSTRIL?
MAN, THIS GUY IS GOOD.

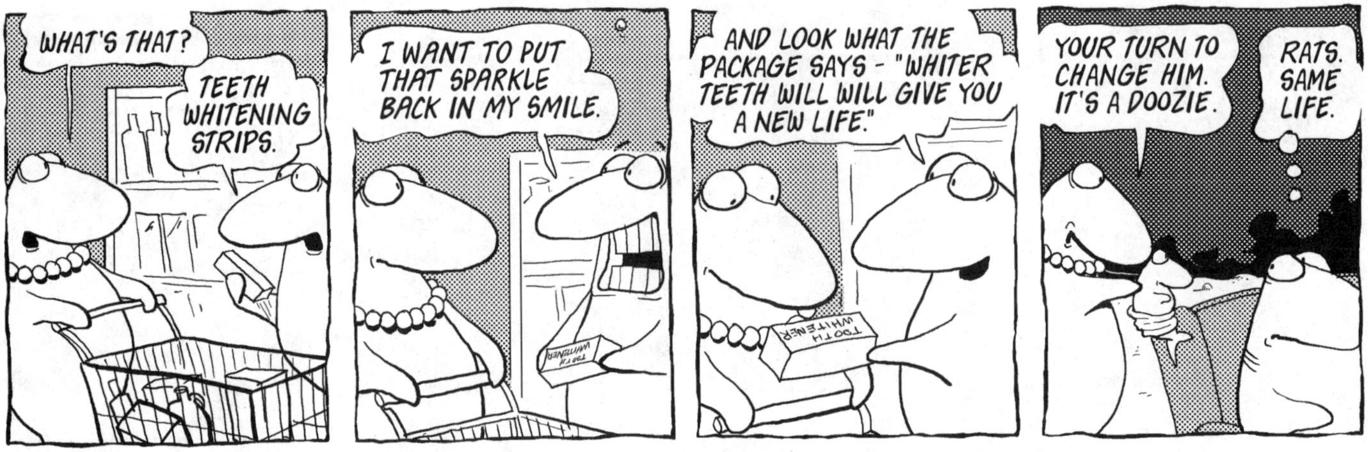
WHAT'S THAT?
TEETH WHITENING STRIPS.
I WANT TO PUT THAT SPARKLE BACK IN MY SMILE.
AND LOOK WHAT THE PACKAGE SAYS - "WHITER TEETH WILL WILL GIVE YOU A NEW LIFE."
YOUR TURN TO CHANGE HIM. IT'S A DOOZIE.
RATS. SAME LIFE.

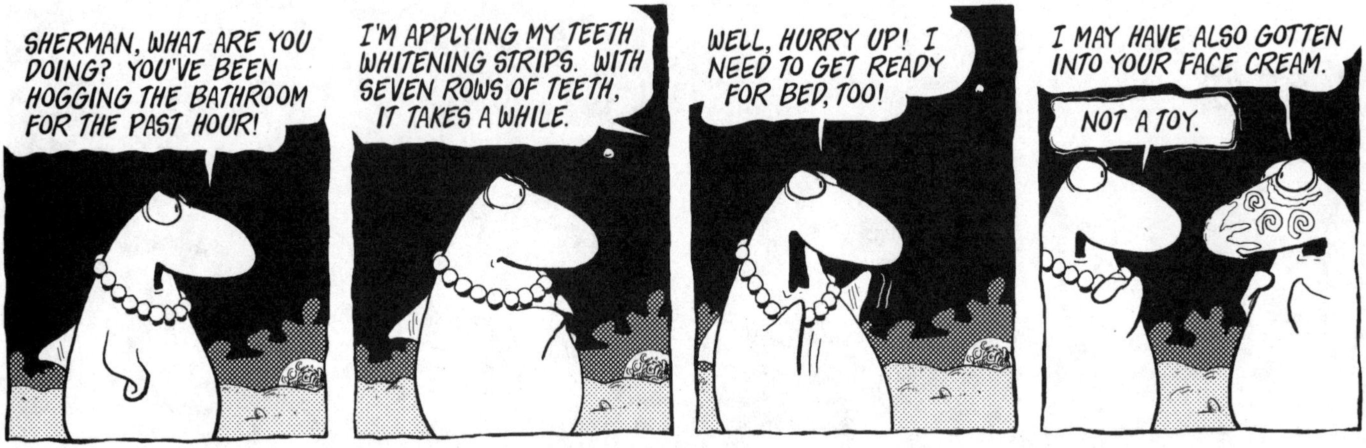
SHERMAN, WHAT ARE YOU DOING? YOU'VE BEEN HOGGING THE BATHROOM FOR THE PAST HOUR!
I'M APPLYING MY TEETH WHITENING STRIPS. WITH SEVEN ROWS OF TEETH, IT TAKES A WHILE.
WELL, HURRY UP! I NEED TO GET READY FOR BED, TOO!
I MAY HAVE ALSO GOTTEN INTO YOUR FACE CREAM.
NOT A TOY.

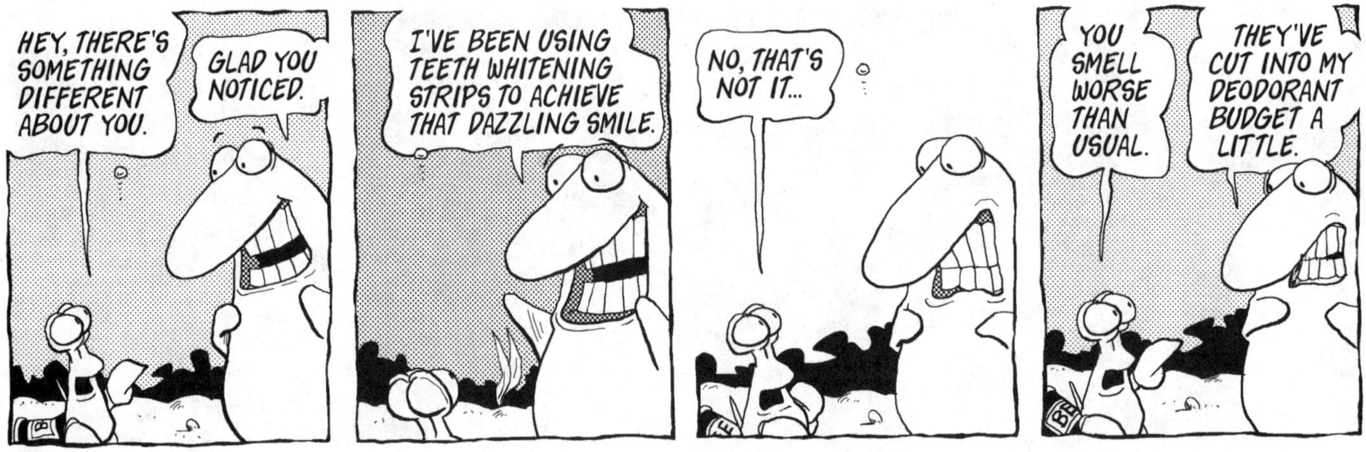
HEY, THERE'S SOMETHING DIFFERENT ABOUT YOU.
GLAD YOU NOTICED.
I'VE BEEN USING TEETH WHITENING STRIPS TO ACHIEVE THAT DAZZLING SMILE.
NO, THAT'S NOT IT...
YOU SMELL WORSE THAN USUAL.
THEY'VE CUT INTO MY DEODORANT BUDGET A LITTLE.

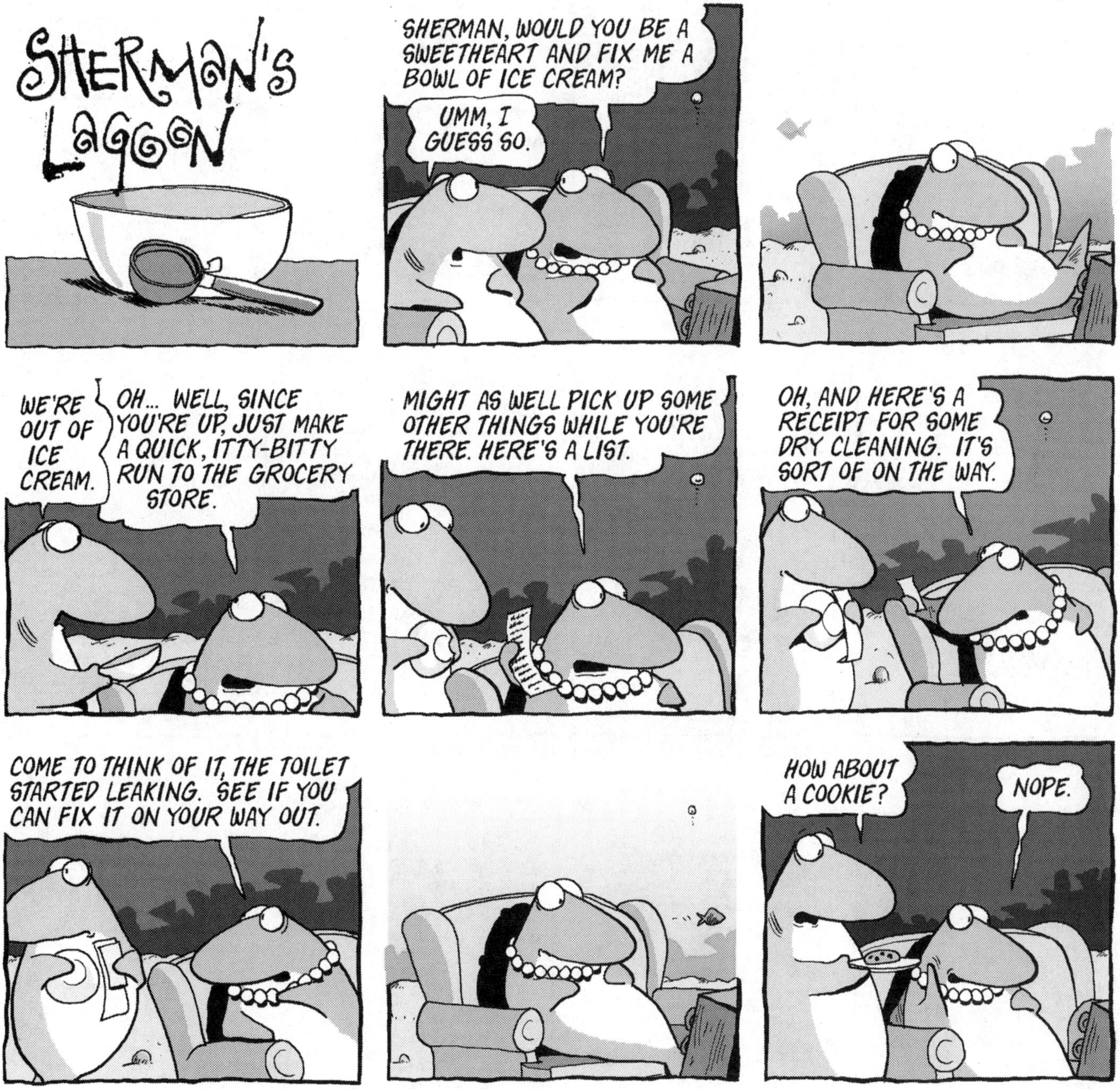
SHERMAN'S LAGOON
SHERMAN, WOULD YOU BE A SWEETHEART AND FIX ME A BOWL OF ICE CREAM?
UMM, I GUESS SO.
WE'RE OUT OF ICE CREAM.
OH... WELL, SINCE YOU'RE UP, JUST MAKE A QUICK, ITTY-BITTY RUN TO THE GROCERY STORE.
MIGHT AS WELL PICK UP SOME OTHER THINGS WHILE YOU'RE THERE. HERE'S A LIST.
OH, AND HERE'S A RECEIPT FOR SOME DRY CLEANING. IT'S SORT OF ON THE WAY.
COME TO THINK OF IT, THE TOILET STARTED LEAKING. SEE IF YOU CAN FIX IT ON YOUR WAY OUT.
HOW ABOUT A COOKIE?
NOPE.

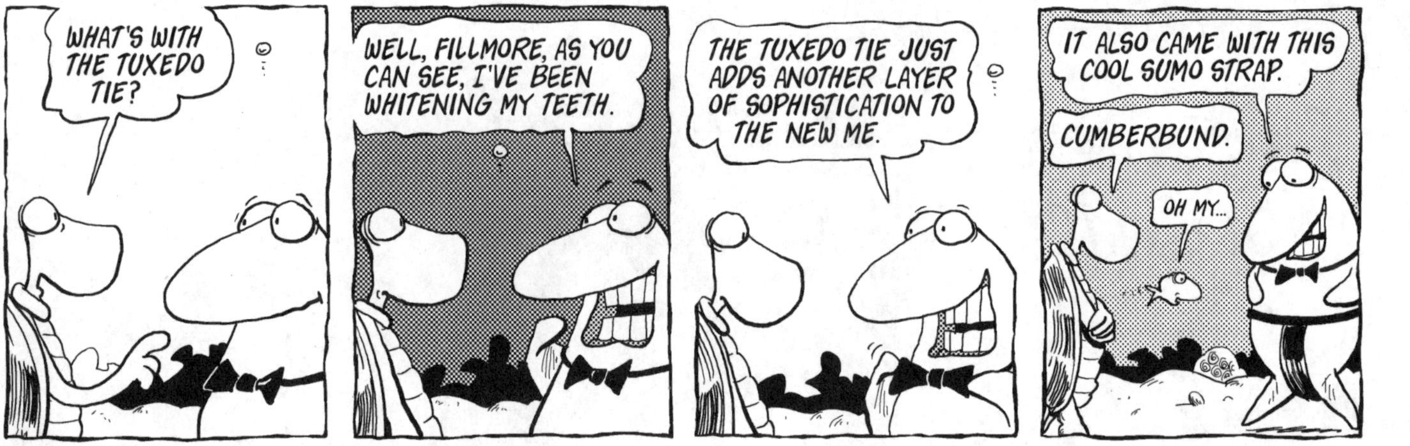
WHAT'S WITH THE TUXEDO TIE?
WELL, FILLMORE, AS YOU CAN SEE, I'VE BEEN WHITENING MY TEETH.
THE TUXEDO TIE JUST ADDS ANOTHER LAYER OF SOPHISTICATION TO THE NEW ME.
IT ALSO CAME WITH THIS COOL SUMO STRAP.
CUMBERBUND.
OH MY...

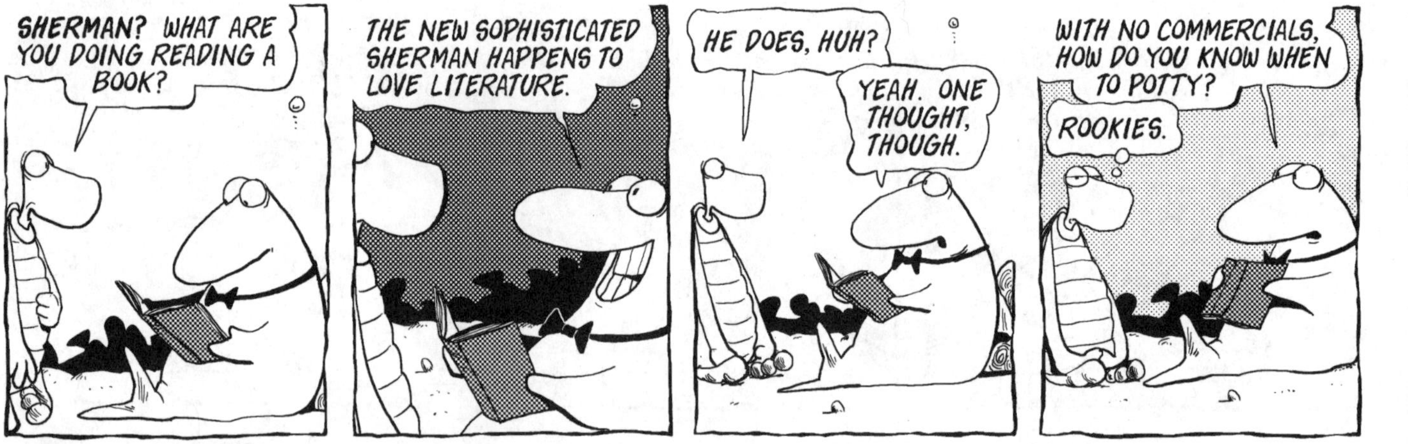
SHERMAN? WHAT ARE YOU DOING READING A BOOK?
THE NEW SOPHISTICATED SHERMAN HAPPENS TO LOVE LITERATURE.
HE DOES, HUH?
YEAH. ONE THOUGHT, THOUGH.
WITH NO COMMERCIALS, HOW DO YOU KNOW WHEN TO POTTY?
ROOKIES.

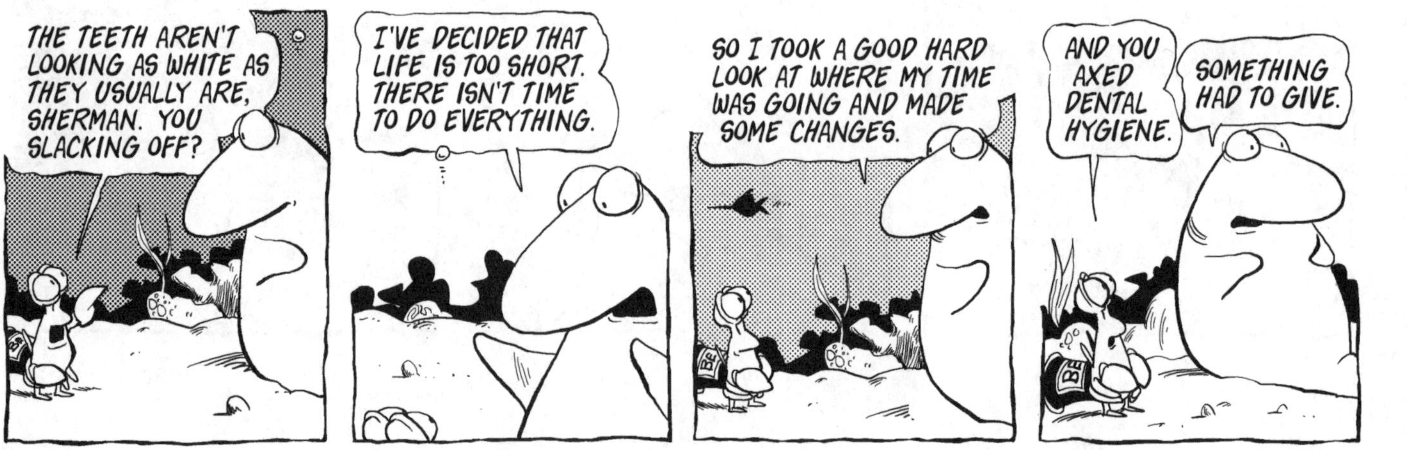
THE TEETH AREN'T LOOKING AS WHITE AS THEY USUALLY ARE, SHERMAN. YOU SLACKING OFF?
I'VE DECIDED THAT LIFE IS TOO SHORT. THERE ISN'T TIME TO DO EVERYTHING.
SO I TOOK A GOOD HARD LOOK AT WHERE MY TIME WAS GOING AND MADE SOME CHANGES.
AND YOU AXED DENTAL HYGIENE.
SOMETHING HAD TO GIVE.

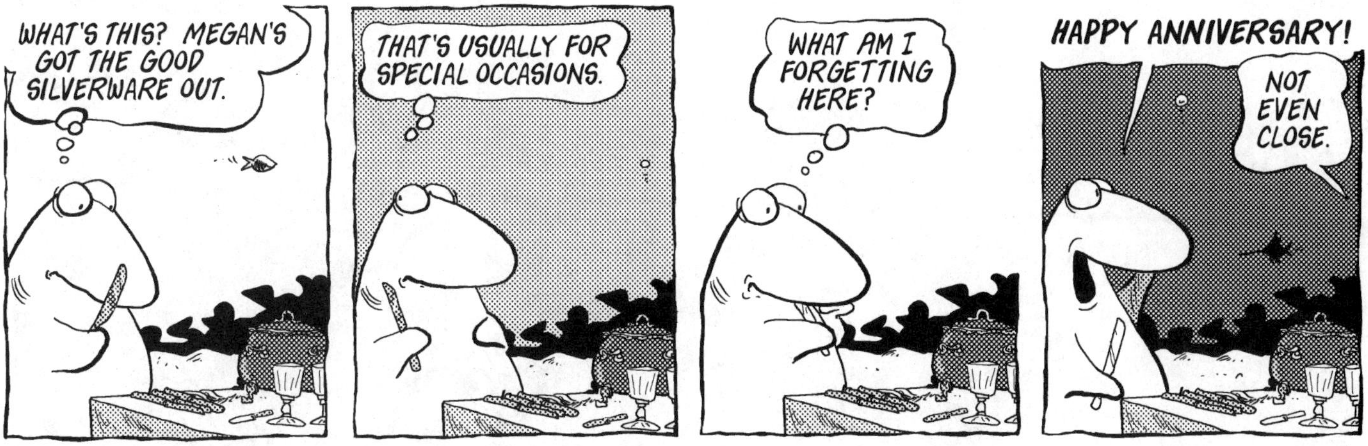

WHAT'S THIS? MEGAN'S GOT THE GOOD SILVERWARE OUT.
THAT'S USUALLY FOR SPECIAL OCCASIONS.
WHAT AM I FORGETTING HERE?
HAPPY ANNIVERSARY!
NOT EVEN CLOSE.

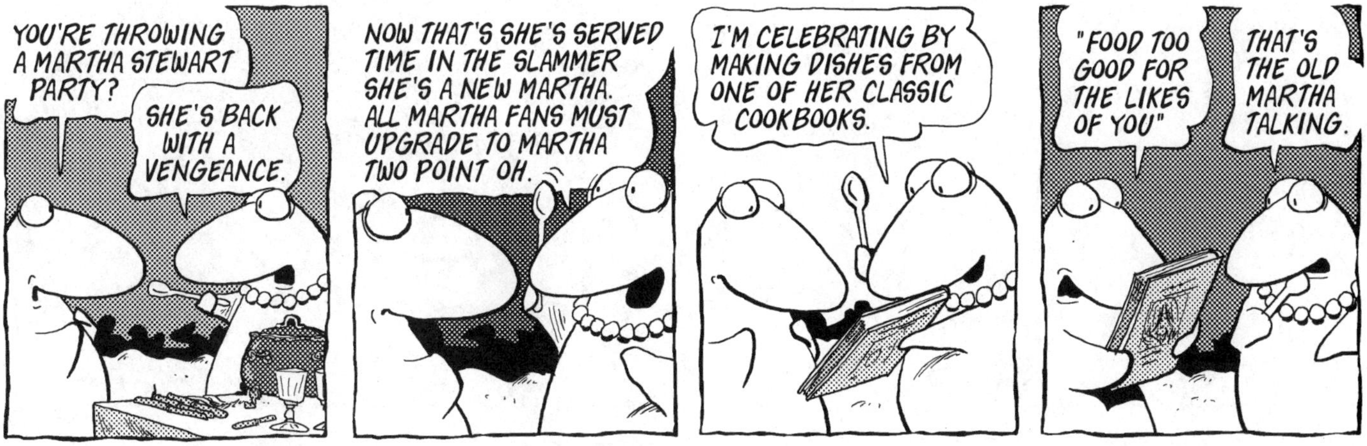

YOU'RE THROWING A MARTHA STEWART PARTY?
SHE'S BACK WITH A VENGEANCE.
NOW THAT'S SHE'S SERVED TIME IN THE SLAMMER SHE'S A NEW MARTHA. ALL MARTHA FANS MUST UPGRADE TO MARTHA TWO POINT OH.
I'M CELEBRATING BY MAKING DISHES FROM ONE OF HER CLASSIC COOKBOOKS.
"FOOD TOO GOOD FOR THE LIKES OF YOU"
THAT'S THE OLD MARTHA TALKING.

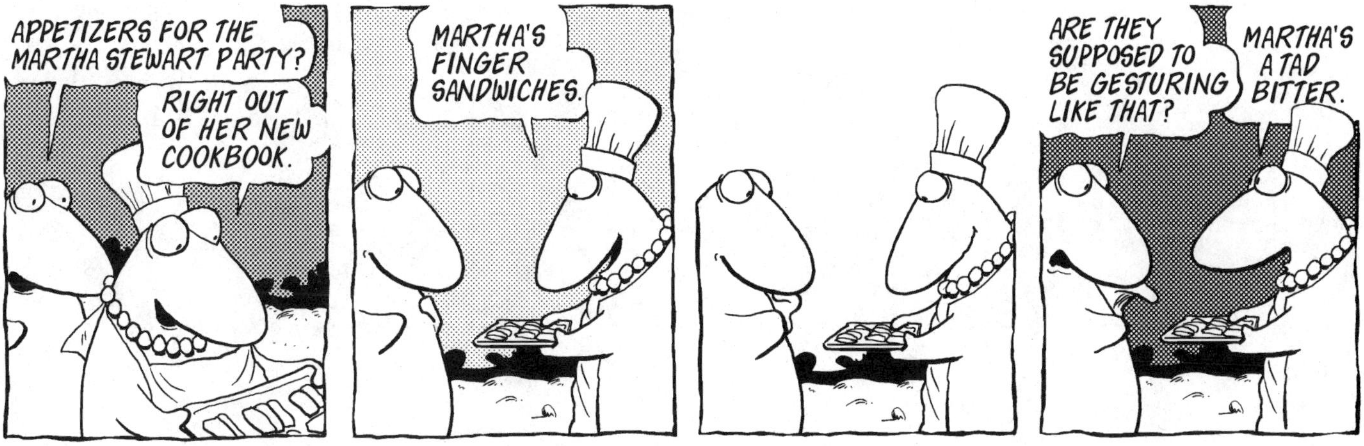

APPETIZERS FOR THE MARTHA STEWART PARTY?
RIGHT OUT OF HER NEW COOKBOOK.
MARTHA'S FINGER SANDWICHES.
ARE THEY SUPPOSED TO BE GESTURING LIKE THAT?
MARTHA'S A TAD BITTER.

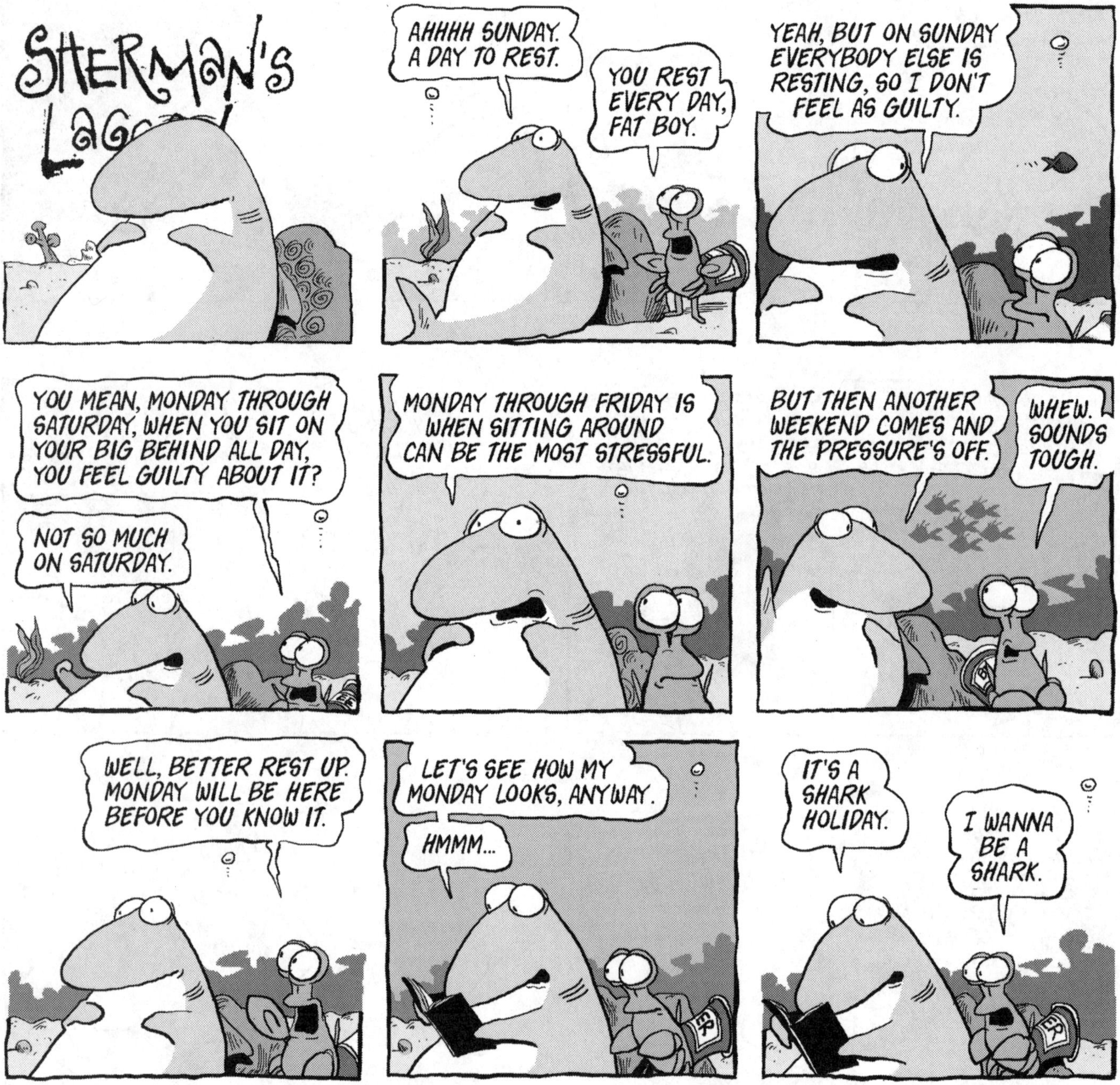
SHERMAN'S LAGOON
AHHHH SUNDAY. A DAY TO REST.
YOU REST EVERY DAY, FAT BOY.
YEAH, BUT ON SUNDAY EVERYBODY ELSE IS RESTING, SO I DON'T FEEL AS GUILTY.
YOU MEAN, MONDAY THROUGH SATURDAY, WHEN YOU SIT ON YOUR BIG BEHIND ALL DAY, YOU FEEL GUILTY ABOUT IT?
NOT SO MUCH ON SATURDAY.
MONDAY THROUGH FRIDAY IS WHEN SITTING AROUND CAN BE THE MOST STRESSFUL.
BUT THEN ANOTHER WEEKEND COMES AND THE PRESSURE'S OFF.
WHEW. SOUNDS TOUGH.
WELL, BETTER REST UP. MONDAY WILL BE HERE BEFORE YOU KNOW IT.
LET'S SEE HOW MY MONDAY LOOKS, ANYWAY.
HMMM...
IT'S A SHARK HOLIDAY.
I WANNA BE A SHARK.

MORE FOOD FOR THE MARTHA STEWART PARTY?
STRAIGHT OUT OF HER NEW COOKBOOK, WRITTEN IN PRISON.
ACTUALLY, SOME OF THE RECIPES REFLECT HER ADVERSE SURROUNDINGS WHEN SHE WROTE IT.
HOW SO?
WELL, LOOK AT HER SHRIMP COCKTAIL... "SHARPEN A SPOON HANDLE AND SNEAK UP BEHIND THE UNSUSPECTING SHRIMP..."
I'M NOT SURE MARTHA STEWART SHOULD'VE WRITTEN A COOKBOOK IN PRISON.
JUST LISTEN TO HER NEW STUFFED MUSHROOM RECIPE...
ALRIGHT.
"PLACE MUSHROOMS TOGETHER IN TIGHT, CONFINED QUARTERS..."
"LET THEM FIGHT IT OUT. SERVE THE WINNERS."
CAMP CUPCAKE CHANGED HER.
GREAT MARTHA STEWART PARTY, MEGAN.
THANKS.
ALL THE FOOD CAME FROM RECIPES SHE WROTE IN PRISON.
REALLY.
IN FACT, THERE'S A PARTY SURPRISE IN ONE OF THE CHEESECAKES.
FILE!!
WE HAVE A WINNER!

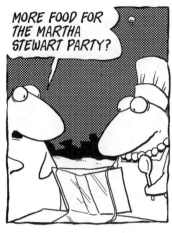

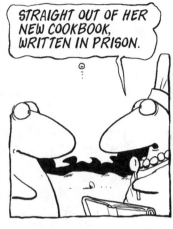

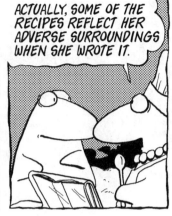

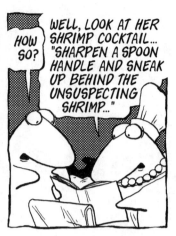

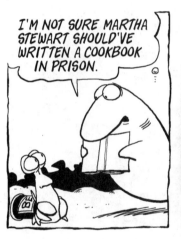

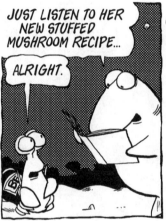

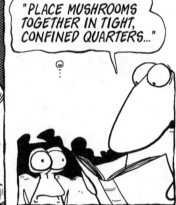

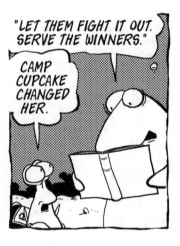

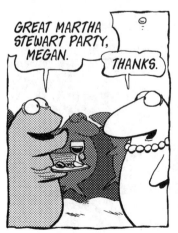

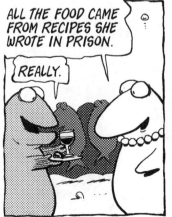

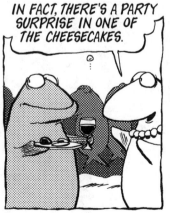

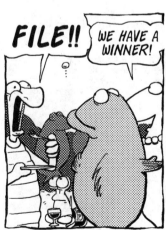

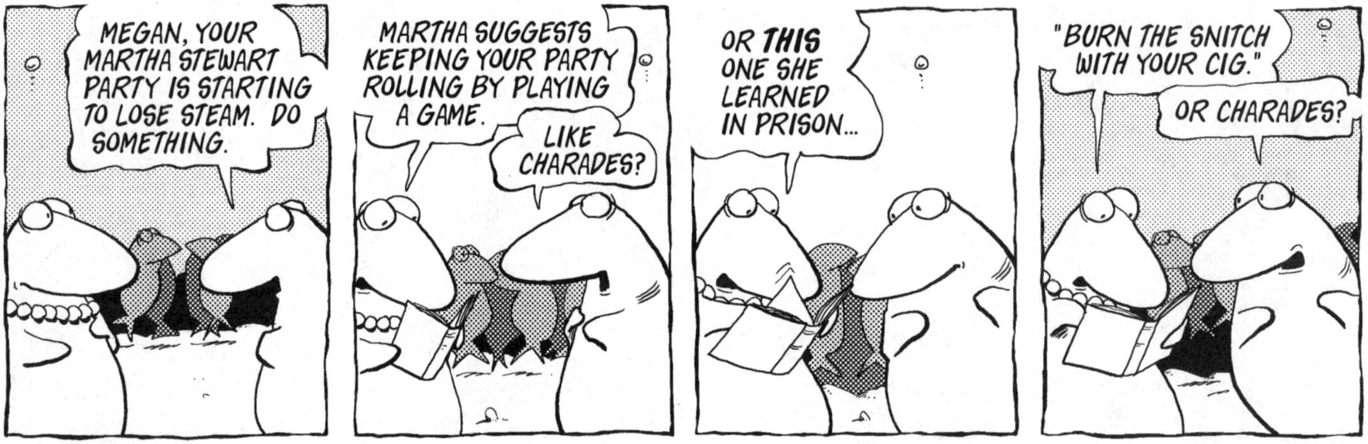
MEGAN, YOUR MARTHA STEWART PARTY IS STARTING TO LOSE STEAM. DO SOMETHING.
MARTHA SUGGESTS KEEPING YOUR PARTY ROLLING BY PLAYING A GAME.
LIKE CHARADES?
OR THIS ONE SHE LEARNED IN PRISON...
"BURN THE SNITCH WITH YOUR CIG."
OR CHARADES?

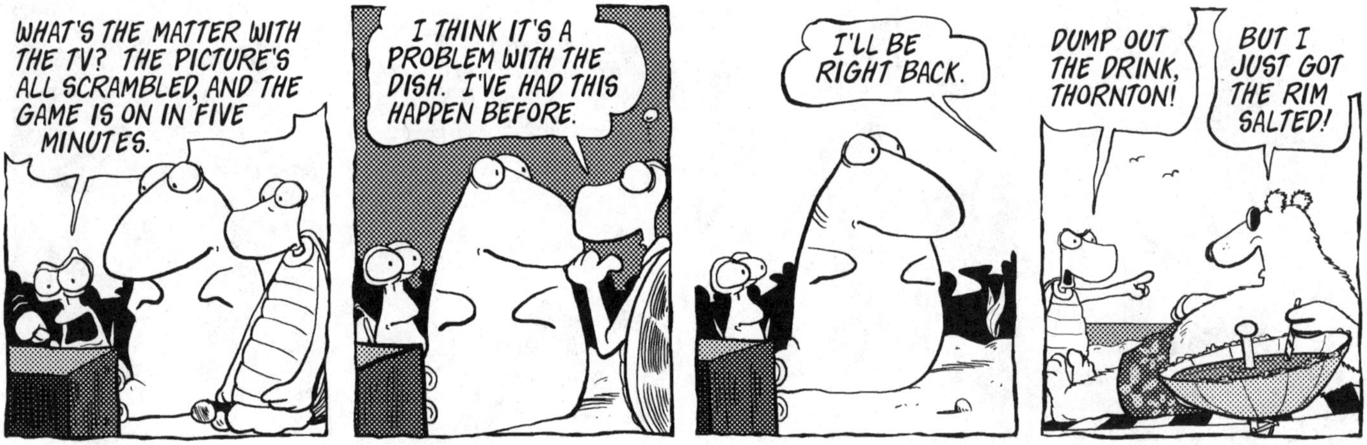
WHAT'S THE MATTER WITH THE TV? THE PICTURE'S ALL SCRAMBLED, AND THE GAME IS ON IN FIVE MINUTES.
I THINK IT'S A PROBLEM WITH THE DISH. I'VE HAD THIS HAPPEN BEFORE.
I'LL BE RIGHT BACK.
DUMP OUT THE DRINK, THORNTON!
BUT I JUST GOT THE RIM SALTED!

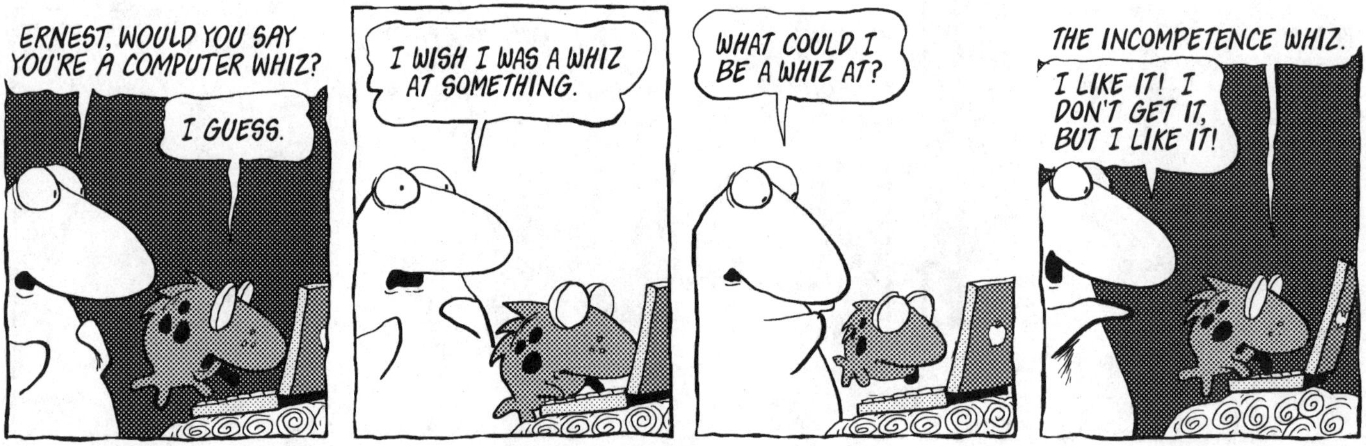
ERNEST, WOULD YOU SAY YOU'RE A COMPUTER WHIZ?
I GUESS.
I WISH I WAS A WHIZ AT SOMETHING.
WHAT COULD I BE A WHIZ AT?
THE INCOMPETENCE WHIZ.
I LIKE IT! I DON'T GET IT, BUT I LIKE IT!

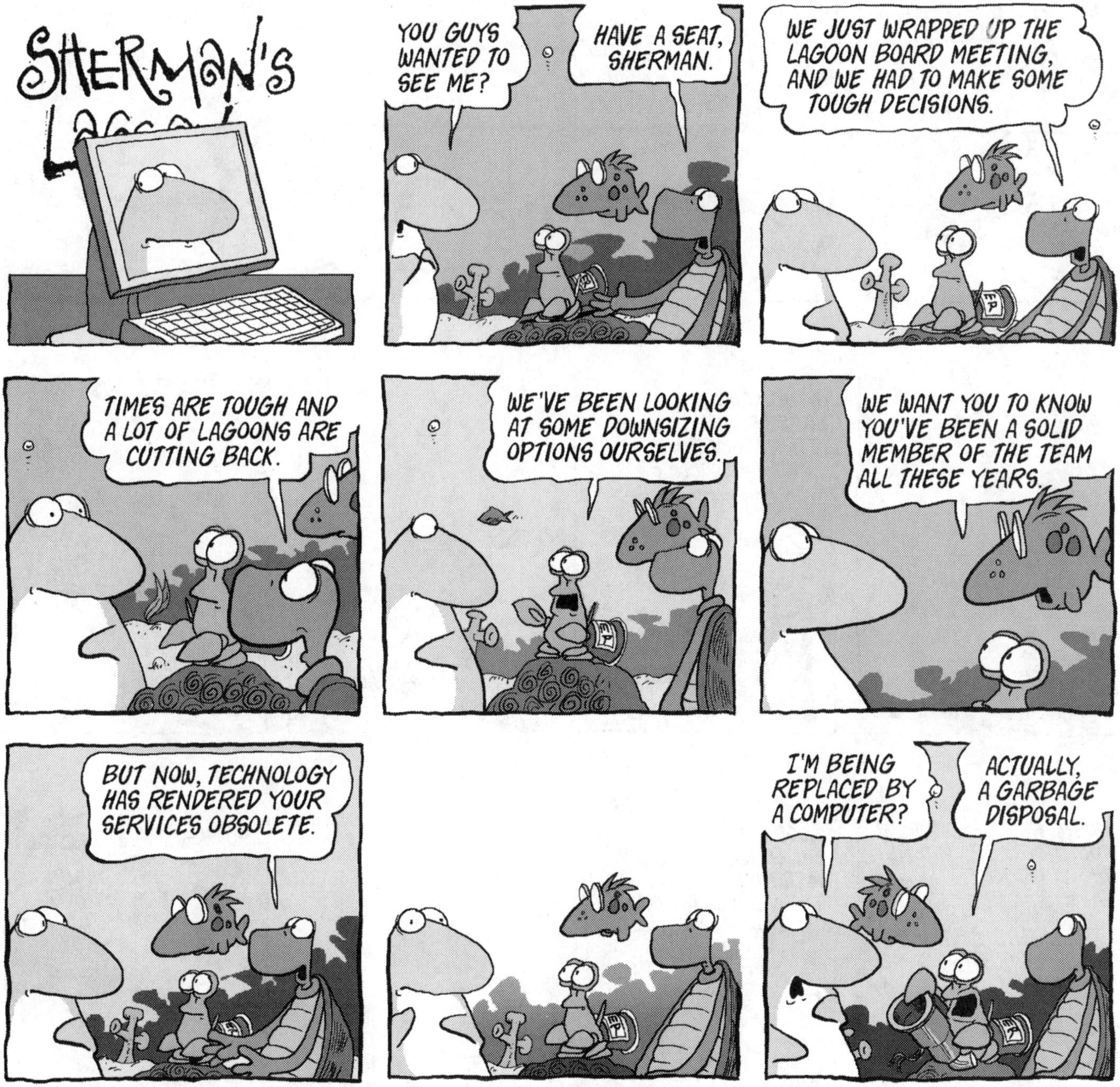
SHERMAN'S LAGOON
YOU GUYS WANTED TO SEE ME?
HAVE A SEAT, SHERMAN.
WE JUST WRAPPED UP THE LAGOON BOARD MEETING, AND WE HAD TO MAKE SOME TOUGH DECISIONS.
TIMES ARE TOUGH AND A LOT OF LAGOONS ARE CUTTING BACK.
WE'VE BEEN LOOKING AT SOME DOWNSIZING OPTIONS OURSELVES.
WE WANT YOU TO KNOW YOU'VE BEEN A SOLID MEMBER OF THE TEAM ALL THESE YEARS.
BUT NOW, TECHNOLOGY HAS RENDERED YOUR SERVICES OBSOLETE.
I'M BEING REPLACED BY A COMPUTER?
ACTUALLY, A GARBAGE DISPOSAL.

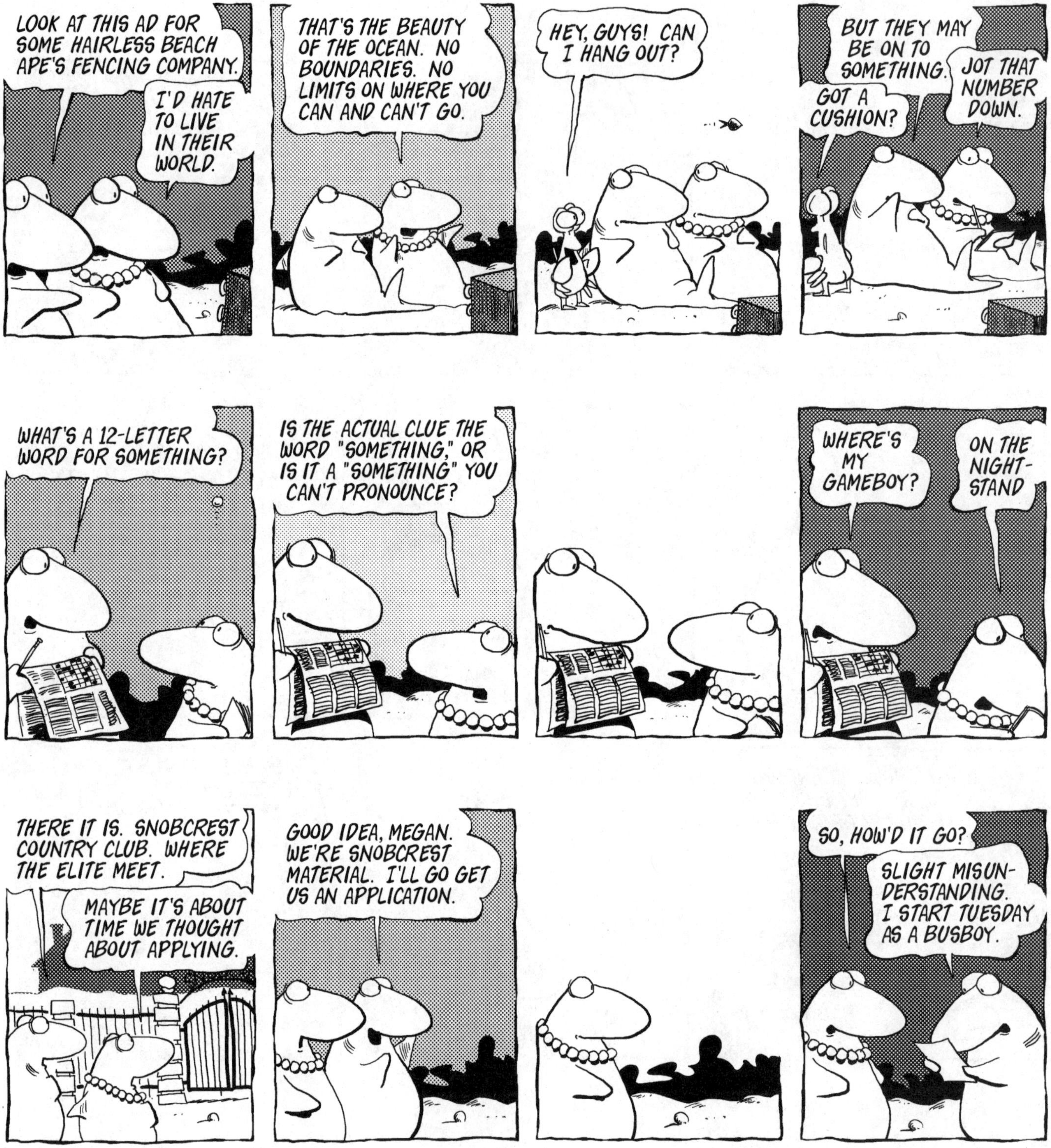
LOOK AT THIS AD FOR SOME HAIRLESS BEACH APE'S FENCING COMPANY.
I'D HATE TO LIVE IN THEIR WORLD.
THAT'S THE BEAUTY OF THE OCEAN. NO BOUNDARIES. NO LIMITS ON WHERE YOU CAN AND CAN'T GO.
HEY, GUYS! CAN I HANG OUT?
BUT THEY MAY BE ON TO SOMETHING.
GOT A CUSHION?
JOT THAT NUMBER DOWN.
WHAT'S A 12-LETTER WORD FOR SOMETHING?
IS THE ACTUAL CLUE THE WORD "SOMETHING," OR IS IT A "SOMETHING" YOU CAN'T PRONOUNCE?
WHERE'S MY GAMEBOY?
ON THE NIGHT-STAND
THERE IT IS. SNOBCREST COUNTRY CLUB. WHERE THE ELITE MEET.
MAYBE IT'S ABOUT TIME WE THOUGHT ABOUT APPLYING.
GOOD IDEA, MEGAN. WE'RE SNOBCREST MATERIAL. I'LL GO GET US AN APPLICATION.
SO, HOW'D IT GO?
SLIGHT MISUN-DERSTANDING. I START TUESDAY AS A BUSBOY.

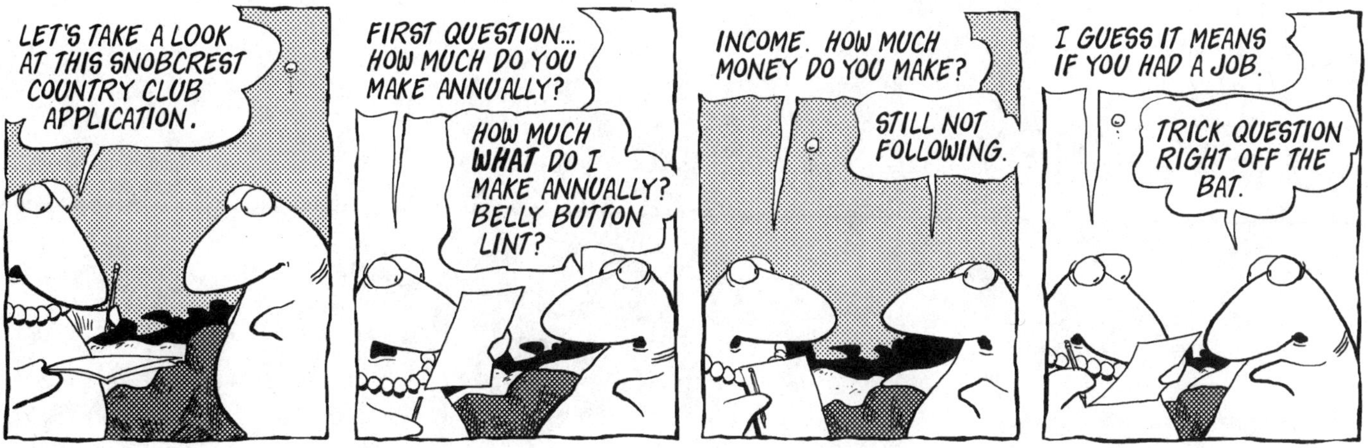
LET'S TAKE A LOOK AT THIS SNOBCREST COUNTRY CLUB APPLICATION.
FIRST QUESTION... HOW MUCH DO YOU MAKE ANNUALLY?
HOW MUCH **WHAT** DO I MAKE ANNUALLY? BELLY BUTTON LINT?
INCOME. HOW MUCH MONEY DO YOU MAKE?
STILL NOT FOLLOWING.
I GUESS IT MEANS IF YOU HAD A JOB.
TRICK QUESTION RIGHT OFF THE BAT.

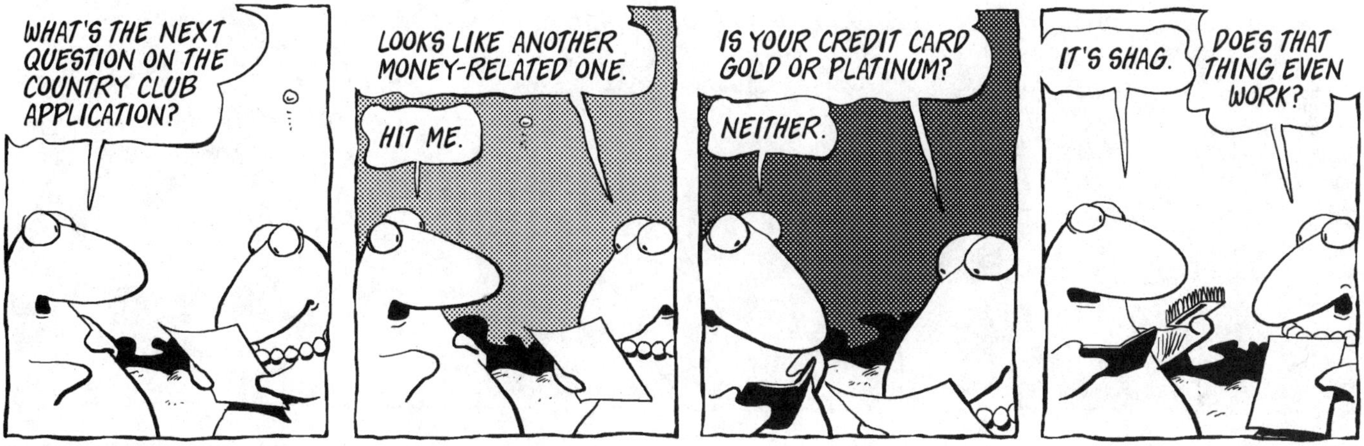
WHAT'S THE NEXT QUESTION ON THE COUNTRY CLUB APPLICATION?
LOOKS LIKE ANOTHER MONEY-RELATED ONE.
HIT ME.
IS YOUR CREDIT CARD GOLD OR PLATINUM?
NEITHER.
IT'S SHAG.
DOES THAT THING EVEN WORK?

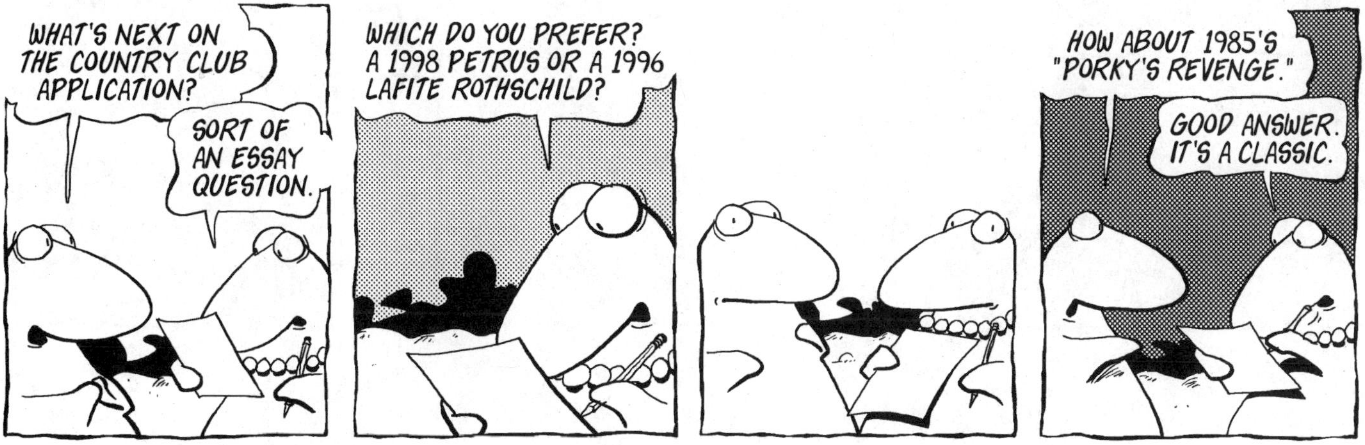
WHAT'S NEXT ON THE COUNTRY CLUB APPLICATION?
SORT OF AN ESSAY QUESTION.
WHICH DO YOU PREFER? A 1998 PETRUS OR A 1996 LAFITE ROTHSCHILD?
HOW ABOUT 1985'S "PORKY'S REVENGE."
GOOD ANSWER. IT'S A CLASSIC.

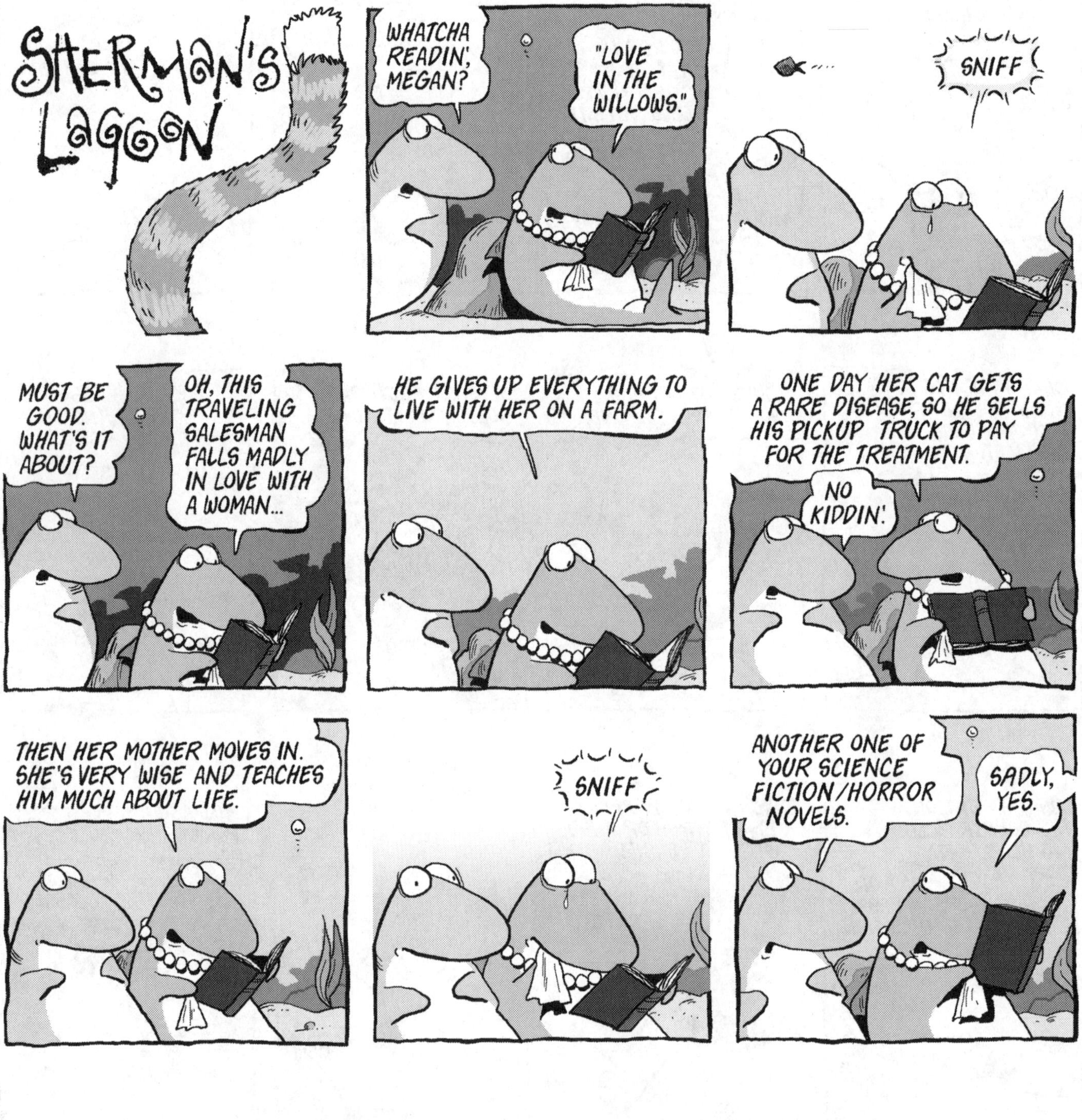
SHERMAN'S LAGOON
WHATCHA READIN', MEGAN?
"LOVE IN THE WILLOWS."
SNIFF
MUST BE GOOD. WHAT'S IT ABOUT?
OH, THIS TRAVELING SALESMAN FALLS MADLY IN LOVE WITH A WOMAN...
HE GIVES UP EVERYTHING TO LIVE WITH HER ON A FARM.
ONE DAY HER CAT GETS A RARE DISEASE, SO HE SELLS HIS PICKUP TRUCK TO PAY FOR THE TREATMENT.
NO KIDDIN'.
THEN HER MOTHER MOVES IN. SHE'S VERY WISE AND TEACHES HIM MUCH ABOUT LIFE.
SNIFF
ANOTHER ONE OF YOUR SCIENCE FICTION/HORROR NOVELS.
SADLY, YES.

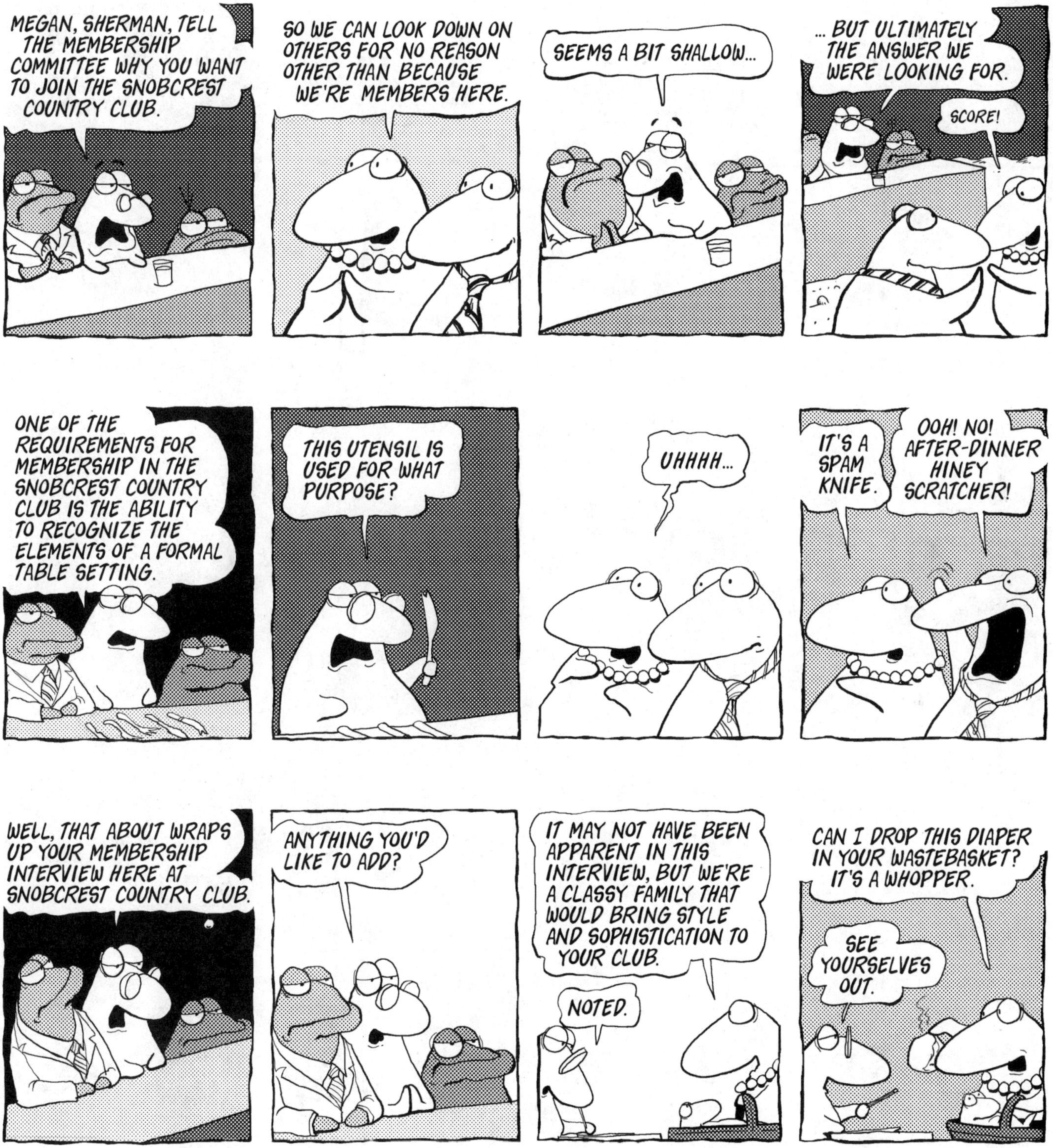
MEGAN, SHERMAN, TELL THE MEMBERSHIP COMMITTEE WHY YOU WANT TO JOIN THE SNOBCREST COUNTRY CLUB.
SO WE CAN LOOK DOWN ON OTHERS FOR NO REASON OTHER THAN BECAUSE WE'RE MEMBERS HERE.
SEEMS A BIT SHALLOW...
... BUT ULTIMATELY THE ANSWER WE WERE LOOKING FOR.
SCORE!
ONE OF THE REQUIREMENTS FOR MEMBERSHIP IN THE SNOBCREST COUNTRY CLUB IS THE ABILITY TO RECOGNIZE THE ELEMENTS OF A FORMAL TABLE SETTING.
THIS UTENSIL IS USED FOR WHAT PURPOSE?
UHHHH...
IT'S A SPAM KNIFE.
OOH! NO! AFTER-DINNER HINEY SCRATCHER!
WELL, THAT ABOUT WRAPS UP YOUR MEMBERSHIP INTERVIEW HERE AT SNOBCREST COUNTRY CLUB.
ANYTHING YOU'D LIKE TO ADD?
IT MAY NOT HAVE BEEN APPARENT IN THIS INTERVIEW, BUT WE'RE A CLASSY FAMILY THAT WOULD BRING STYLE AND SOPHISTICATION TO YOUR CLUB.
NOTED.
CAN I DROP THIS DIAPER IN YOUR WASTEBASKET? IT'S A WHOPPER.
SEE YOURSELVES OUT.

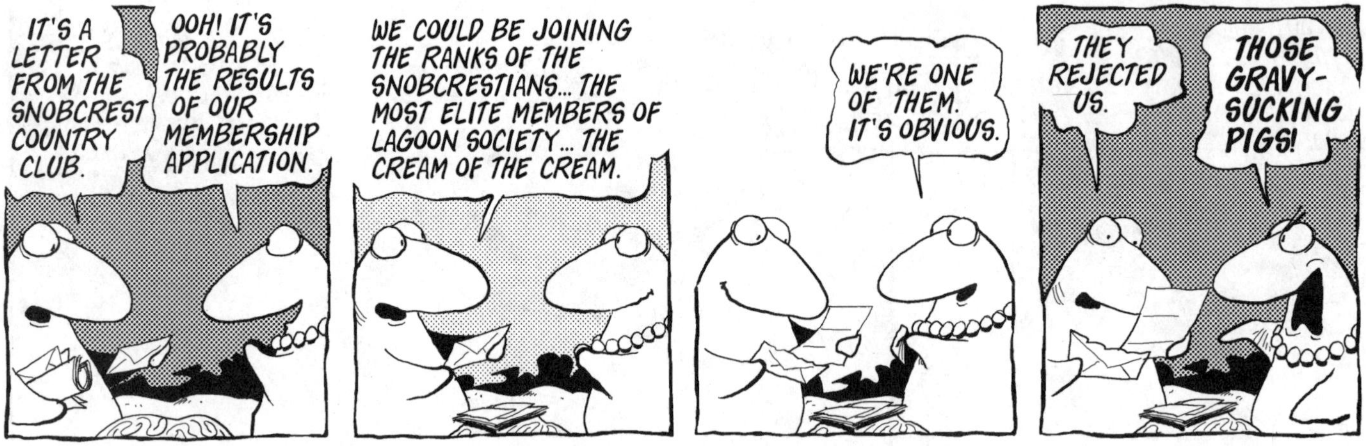
IT'S A LETTER FROM THE SNOBCREST COUNTRY CLUB.
OOH! IT'S PROBABLY THE RESULTS OF OUR MEMBERSHIP APPLICATION.
WE COULD BE JOINING THE RANKS OF THE SNOBCRESTIANS... THE MOST ELITE MEMBERS OF LAGOON SOCIETY... THE CREAM OF THE CREAM.
WE'RE ONE OF THEM. IT'S OBVIOUS.
THEY REJECTED US.
THOSE GRAVY-SUCKING PIGS!

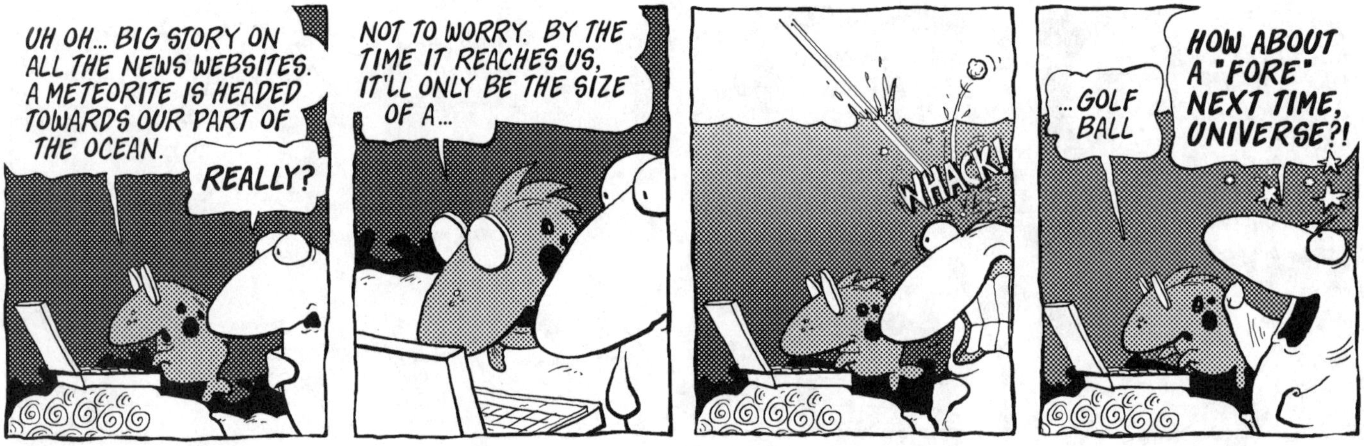
UH OH... BIG STORY ON ALL THE NEWS WEBSITES. A METEORITE IS HEADED TOWARDS OUR PART OF THE OCEAN.
REALLY?
NOT TO WORRY. BY THE TIME IT REACHES US, IT'LL ONLY BE THE SIZE OF A...
WHACK!
...GOLF BALL
HOW ABOUT A "FORE" NEXT TIME, UNIVERSE?!

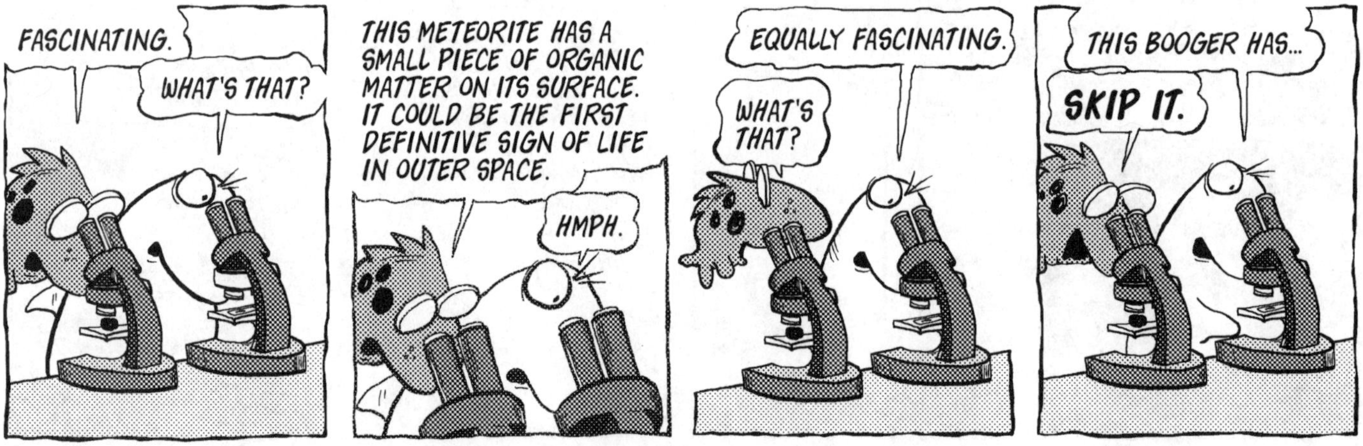
FASCINATING.
WHAT'S THAT?
THIS METEORITE HAS A SMALL PIECE OF ORGANIC MATTER ON ITS SURFACE. IT COULD BE THE FIRST DEFINITIVE SIGN OF LIFE IN OUTER SPACE.
HMPH.
EQUALLY FASCINATING.
WHAT'S THAT?
THIS BOOGER HAS...
SKIP IT.

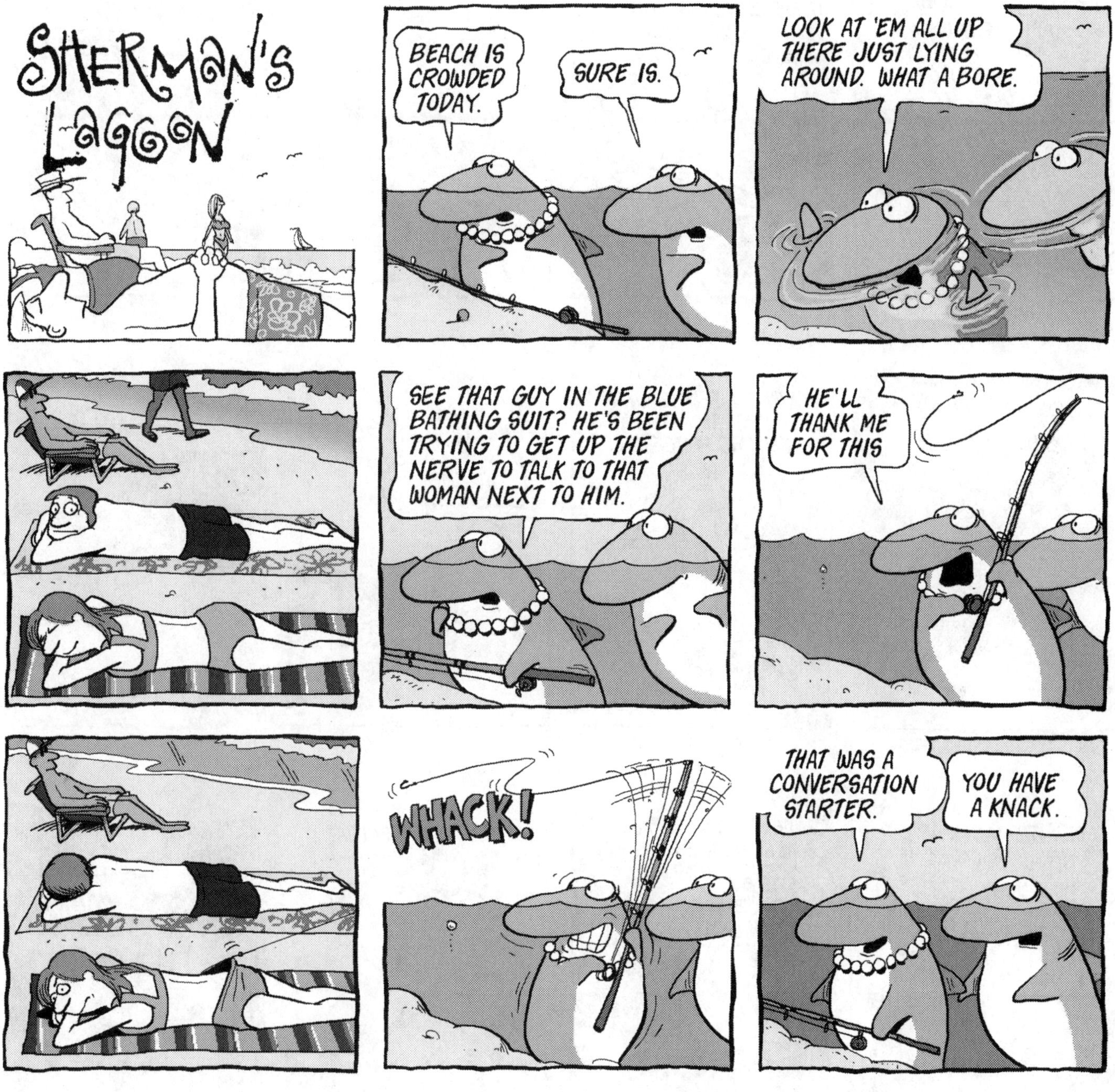
SHERMAN'S LAGOON
BEACH IS CROWDED TODAY.
SURE IS.
LOOK AT 'EM ALL UP THERE JUST LYING AROUND. WHAT A BORE.
SEE THAT GUY IN THE BLUE BATHING SUIT? HE'S BEEN TRYING TO GET UP THE NERVE TO TALK TO THAT WOMAN NEXT TO HIM.
HE'LL THANK ME FOR THIS
WHACK!
THAT WAS A CONVERSATION STARTER.
YOU HAVE A KNACK.

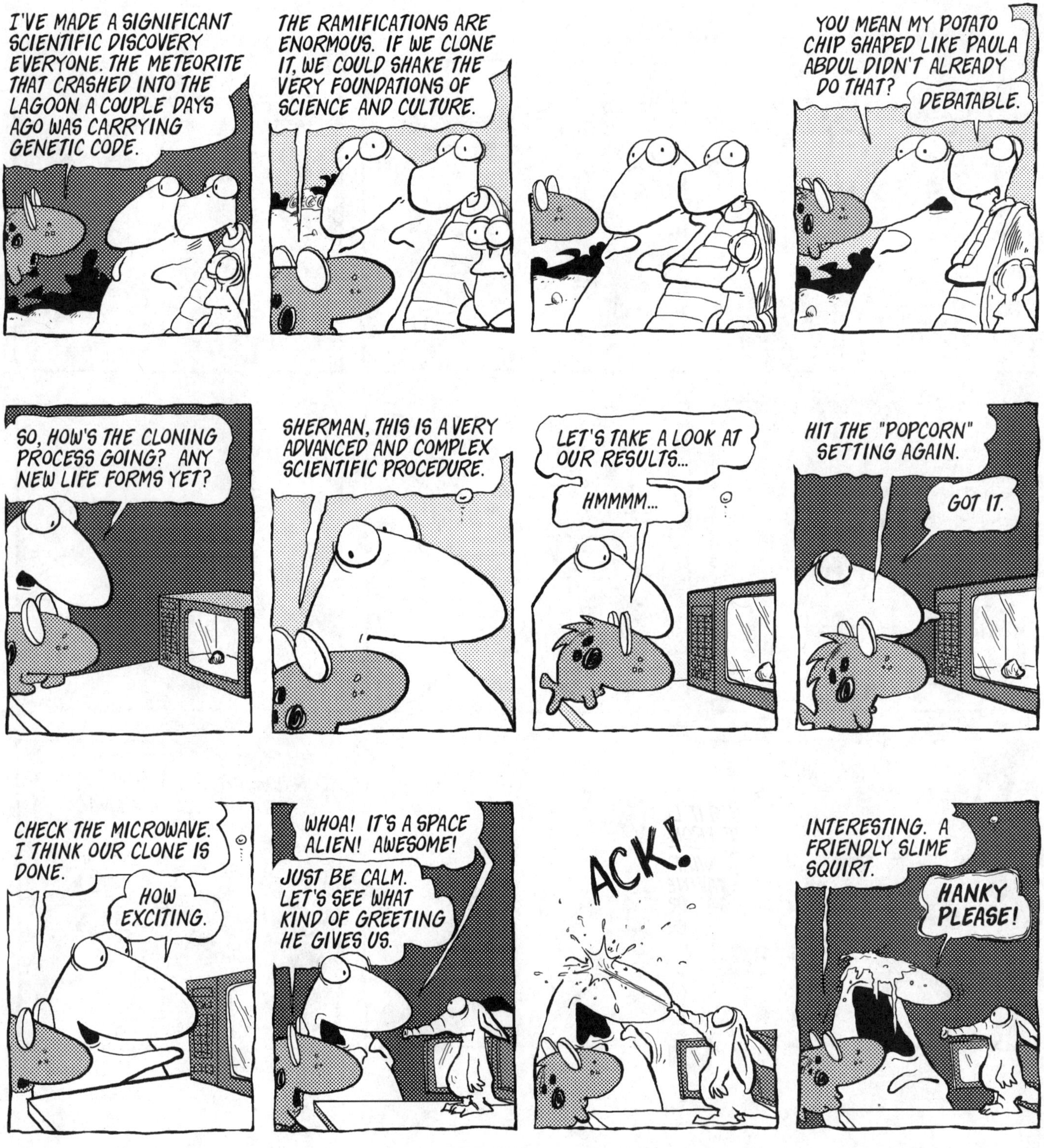
I'VE MADE A SIGNIFICANT SCIENTIFIC DISCOVERY EVERYONE. THE METEORITE THAT CRASHED INTO THE LAGOON A COUPLE DAYS AGO WAS CARRYING GENETIC CODE.
THE RAMIFICATIONS ARE ENORMOUS. IF WE CLONE IT, WE COULD SHAKE THE VERY FOUNDATIONS OF SCIENCE AND CULTURE.
YOU MEAN MY POTATO CHIP SHAPED LIKE PAULA ABDUL DIDN'T ALREADY DO THAT?
DEBATABLE.
SO, HOW'S THE CLONING PROCESS GOING? ANY NEW LIFE FORMS YET?
SHERMAN, THIS IS A VERY ADVANCED AND COMPLEX SCIENTIFIC PROCEDURE.
LET'S TAKE A LOOK AT OUR RESULTS...
HMMMM...
HIT THE "POPCORN" SETTING AGAIN.
GOT IT.
CHECK THE MICROWAVE. I THINK OUR CLONE IS DONE.
HOW EXCITING.
WHOA! IT'S A SPACE ALIEN! AWESOME!
JUST BE CALM. LET'S SEE WHAT KIND OF GREETING HE GIVES US.
ACK!
INTERESTING. A FRIENDLY SLIME SQUIRT.
HANKY PLEASE!

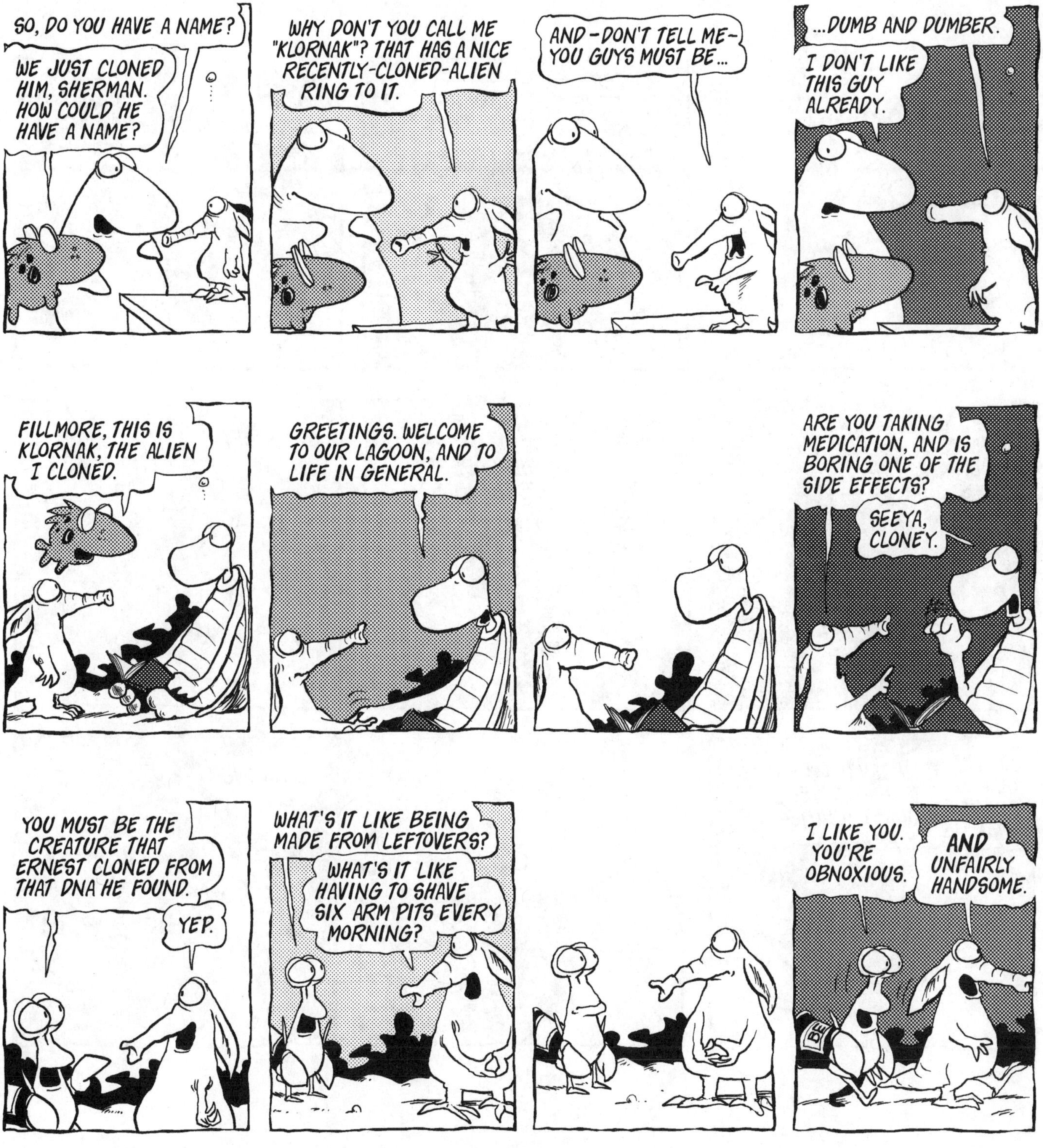

SO, DO YOU HAVE A NAME?
WE JUST CLONED HIM, SHERMAN. HOW COULD HE HAVE A NAME?
WHY DON'T YOU CALL ME "KLORNAK"? THAT HAS A NICE RECENTLY-CLONED-ALIEN RING TO IT.
AND-DON'T TELL ME-YOU GUYS MUST BE...
...DUMB AND DUMBER.
I DON'T LIKE THIS GUY ALREADY.
FILLMORE, THIS IS KLORNAK, THE ALIEN I CLONED.
GREETINGS. WELCOME TO OUR LAGOON, AND TO LIFE IN GENERAL.
ARE YOU TAKING MEDICATION, AND IS BORING ONE OF THE SIDE EFFECTS?
SEEYA, CLONEY.
YOU MUST BE THE CREATURE THAT ERNEST CLONED FROM THAT DNA HE FOUND.
YEP.
WHAT'S IT LIKE BEING MADE FROM LEFTOVERS?
WHAT'S IT LIKE HAVING TO SHAVE SIX ARM PITS EVERY MORNING?
I LIKE YOU. YOU'RE OBNOXIOUS.
AND UNFAIRLY HANDSOME.

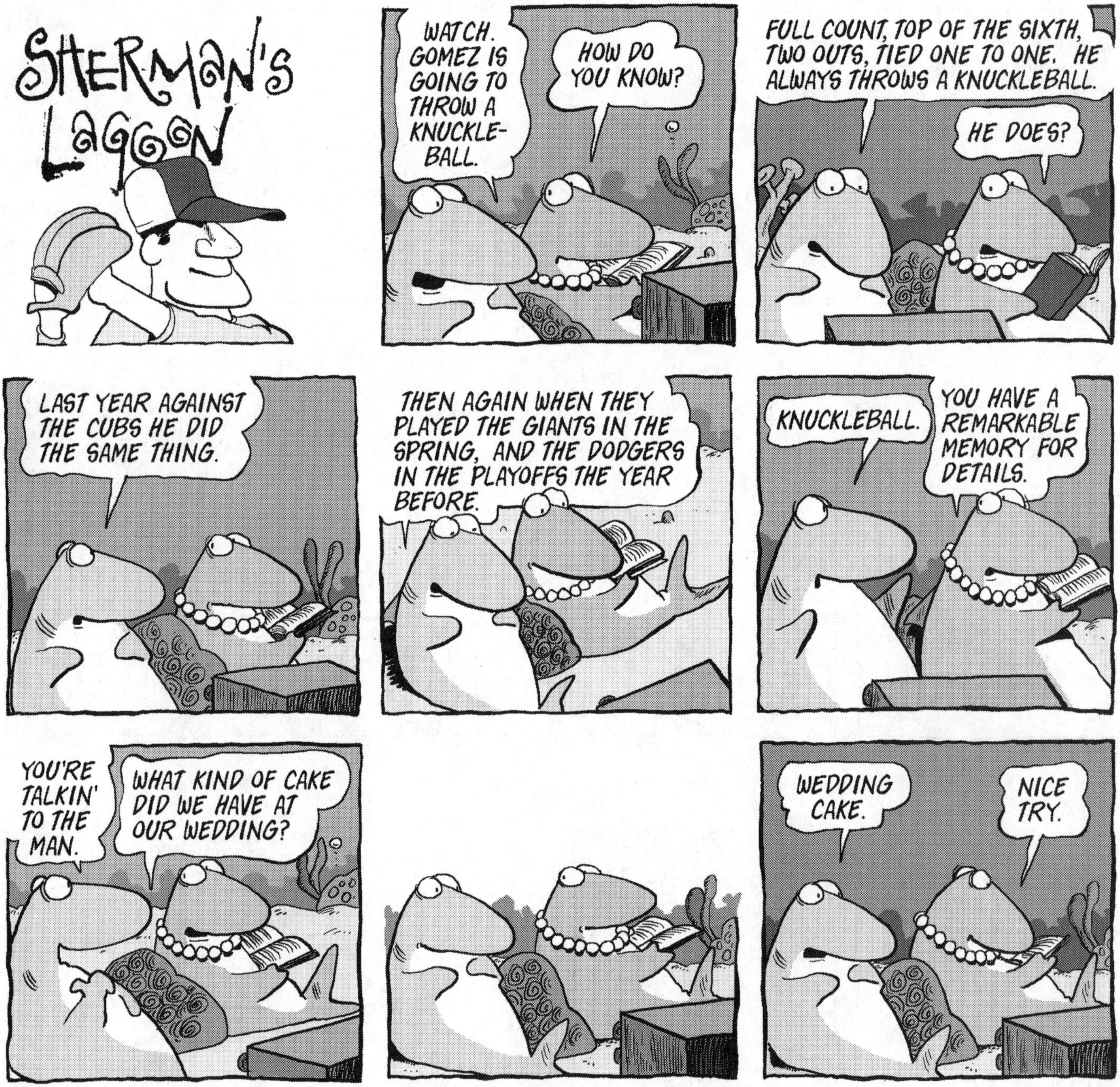
SHERMAN'S LAGOON
WATCH. GOMEZ IS GOING TO THROW A KNUCKLE-BALL.
HOW DO YOU KNOW?
FULL COUNT, TOP OF THE SIXTH, TWO OUTS, TIED ONE TO ONE. HE ALWAYS THROWS A KNUCKLEBALL.
HE DOES?
LAST YEAR AGAINST THE CUBS HE DID THE SAME THING.
THEN AGAIN WHEN THEY PLAYED THE GIANTS IN THE SPRING, AND THE DODGERS IN THE PLAYOFFS THE YEAR BEFORE.
KNUCKLEBALL.
YOU HAVE A REMARKABLE MEMORY FOR DETAILS.
YOU'RE TALKIN' TO THE MAN.
WHAT KIND OF CAKE DID WE HAVE AT OUR WEDDING?
WEDDING CAKE.
NICE TRY.

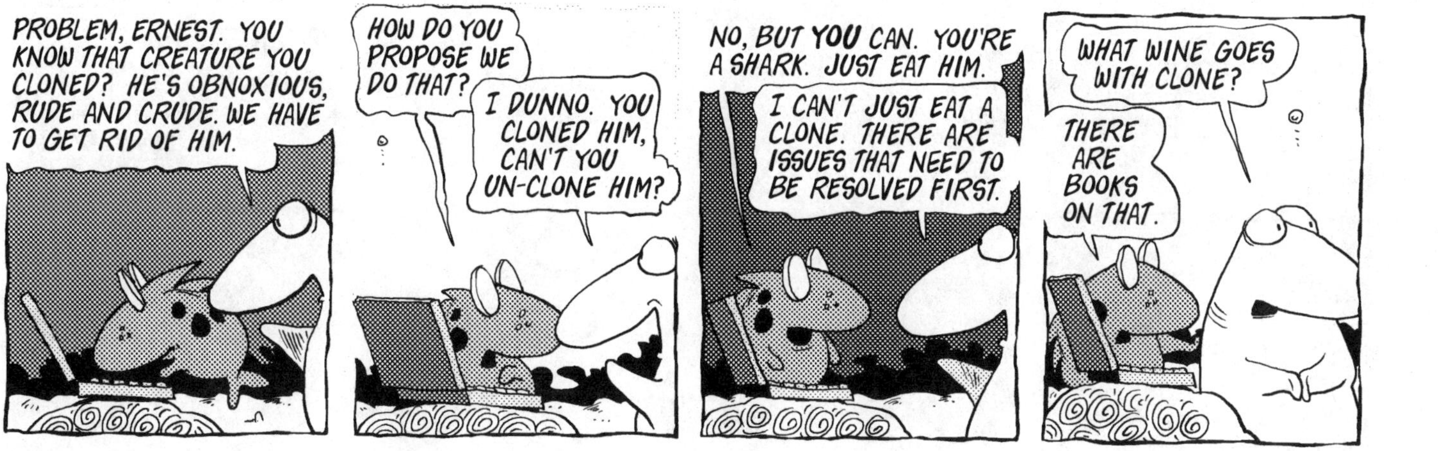
PROBLEM, ERNEST. YOU KNOW THAT CREATURE YOU CLONED? HE'S OBNOXIOUS, RUDE AND CRUDE. WE HAVE TO GET RID OF HIM.
HOW DO YOU PROPOSE WE DO THAT?
I DUNNO. YOU CLONED HIM, CAN'T YOU UN-CLONE HIM?
NO, BUT YOU CAN. YOU'RE A SHARK. JUST EAT HIM.
I CAN'T JUST EAT A CLONE. THERE ARE ISSUES THAT NEED TO BE RESOLVED FIRST.
WHAT WINE GOES WITH CLONE?
THERE ARE BOOKS ON THAT.

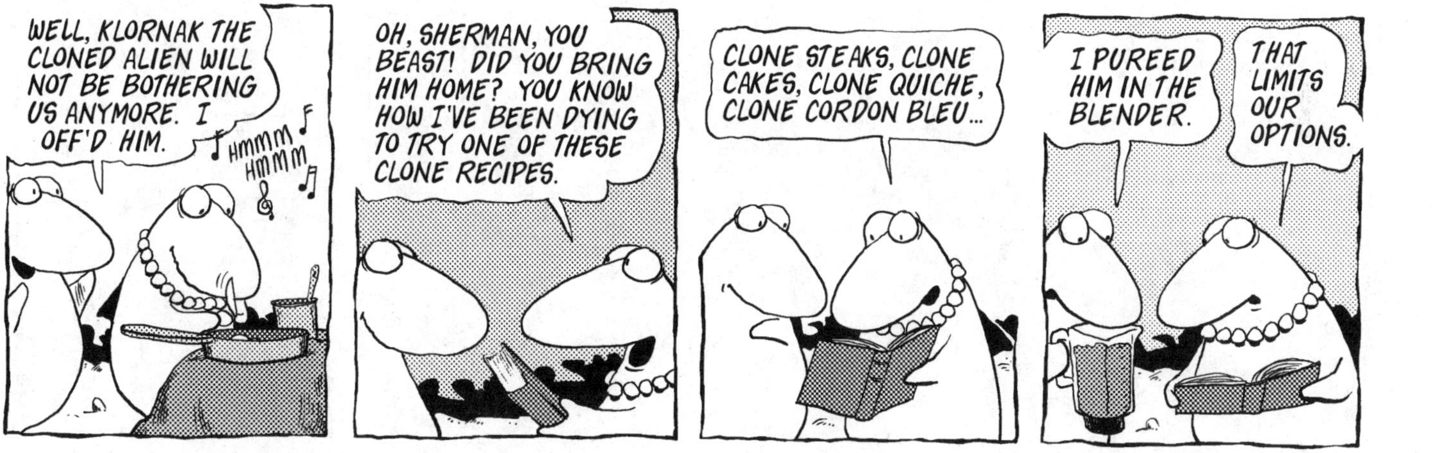
WELL, KLORNAK THE CLONED ALIEN WILL NOT BE BOTHERING US ANYMORE. I OFF'D HIM.
HMMM HMMM
OH, SHERMAN, YOU BEAST! DID YOU BRING HIM HOME? YOU KNOW HOW I'VE BEEN DYING TO TRY ONE OF THESE CLONE RECIPES.
CLONE STEAKS, CLONE CAKES, CLONE QUICHE, CLONE CORDON BLEU...
I PUREED HIM IN THE BLENDER.
THAT LIMITS OUR OPTIONS.

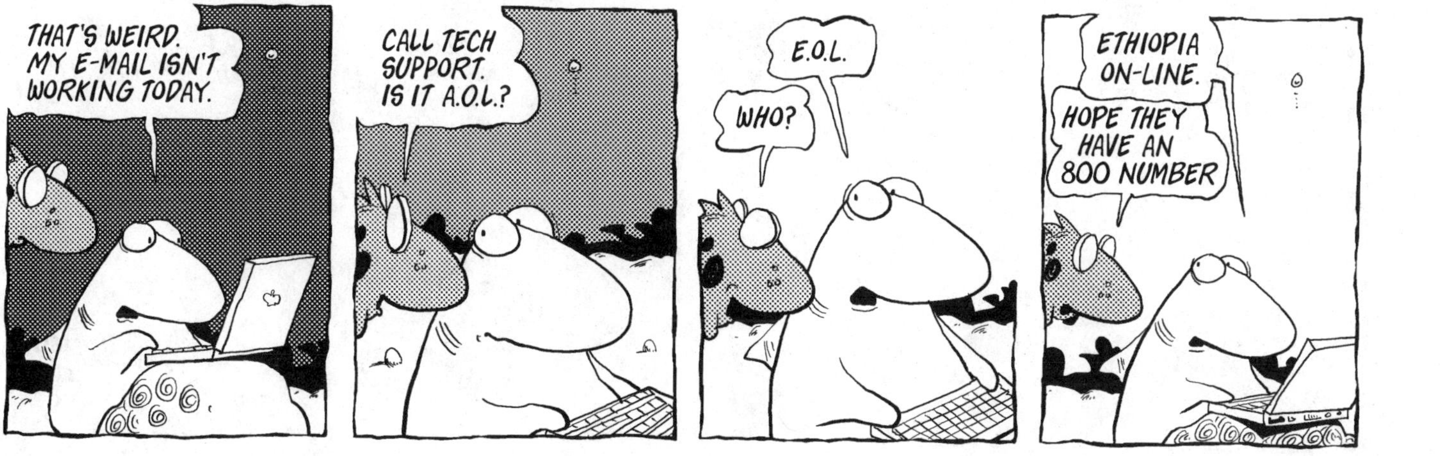
THAT'S WEIRD. MY E-MAIL ISN'T WORKING TODAY.
CALL TECH SUPPORT. IS IT A.O.L.?
E.O.L.
WHO?
ETHIOPIA ON-LINE.
HOPE THEY HAVE AN 800 NUMBER

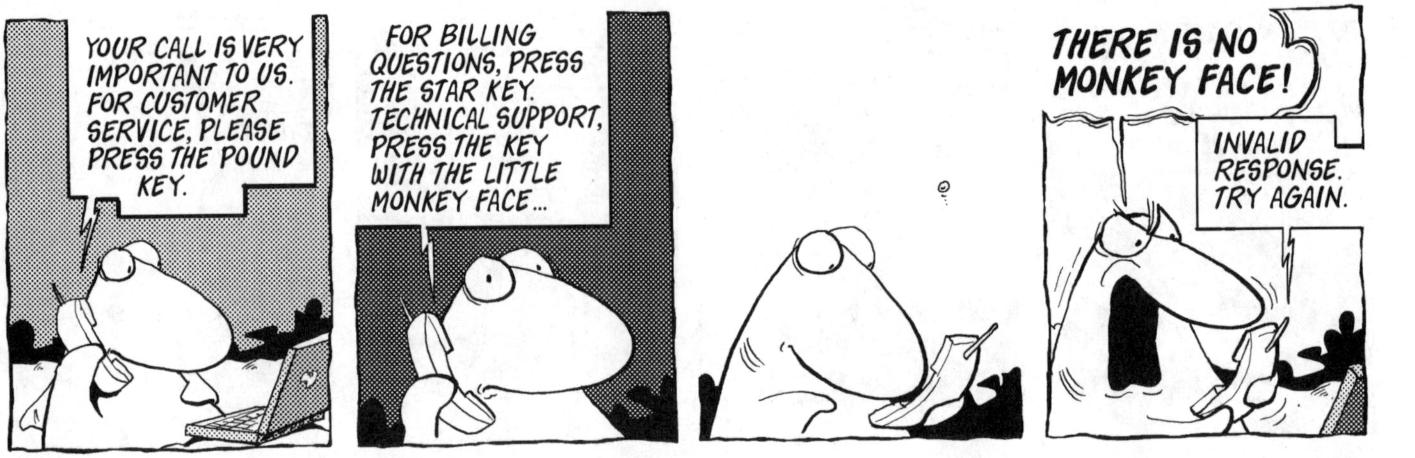
YOUR CALL IS VERY IMPORTANT TO US. FOR CUSTOMER SERVICE, PLEASE PRESS THE POUND KEY.
FOR BILLING QUESTIONS, PRESS THE STAR KEY. TECHNICAL SUPPORT, PRESS THE KEY WITH THE LITTLE MONKEY FACE...
THERE IS NO MONKEY FACE!
INVALID RESPONSE. TRY AGAIN.

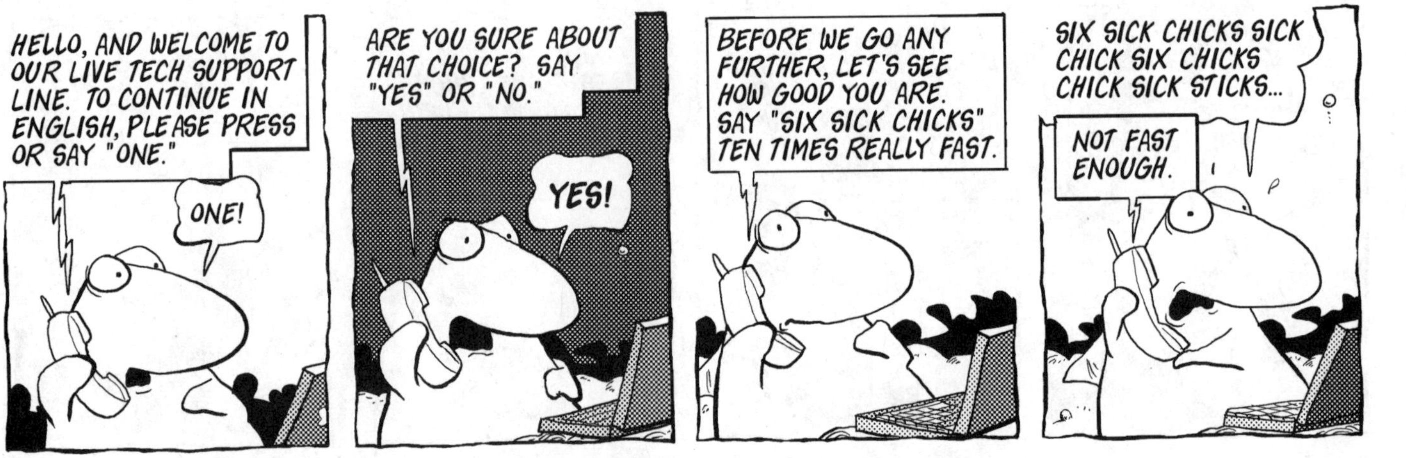
HELLO, AND WELCOME TO OUR LIVE TECH SUPPORT LINE. TO CONTINUE IN ENGLISH, PLEASE PRESS OR SAY "ONE."
ONE!
ARE YOU SURE ABOUT THAT CHOICE? SAY "YES" OR "NO."
YES!
BEFORE WE GO ANY FURTHER, LET'S SEE HOW GOOD YOU ARE. SAY "SIX SICK CHICKS" TEN TIMES REALLY FAST.
SIX SICK CHICKS SICK CHICK SIX CHICKS CHICK SICK STICKS...
NOT FAST ENOUGH.

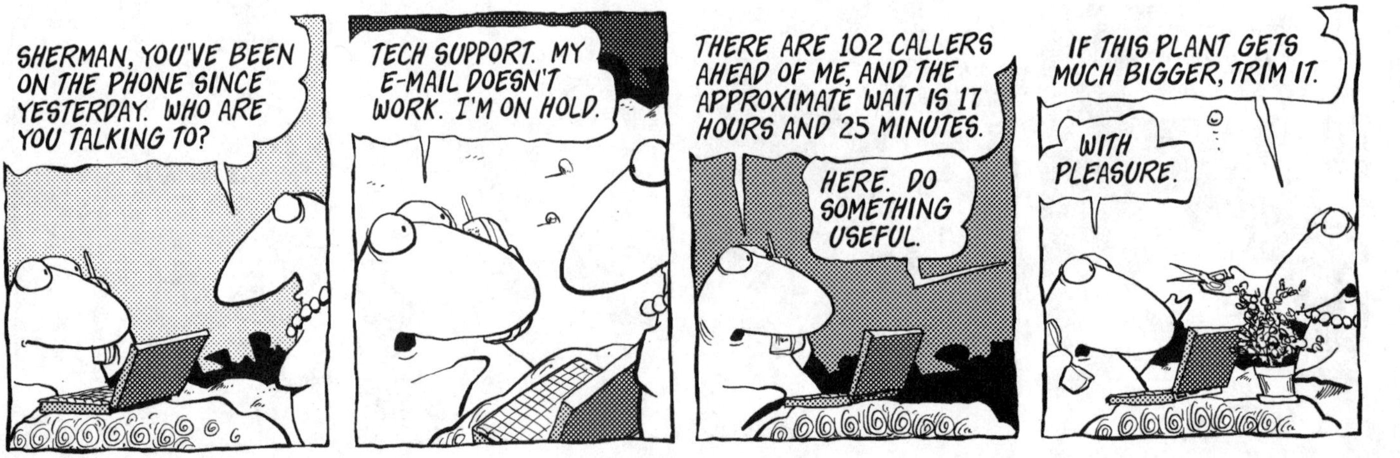
SHERMAN, YOU'VE BEEN ON THE PHONE SINCE YESTERDAY. WHO ARE YOU TALKING TO?
TECH SUPPORT. MY E-MAIL DOESN'T WORK. I'M ON HOLD.
THERE ARE 102 CALLERS AHEAD OF ME, AND THE APPROXIMATE WAIT IS 17 HOURS AND 25 MINUTES.
HERE. DO SOMETHING USEFUL.
IF THIS PLANT GETS MUCH BIGGER, TRIM IT.
WITH PLEASURE.

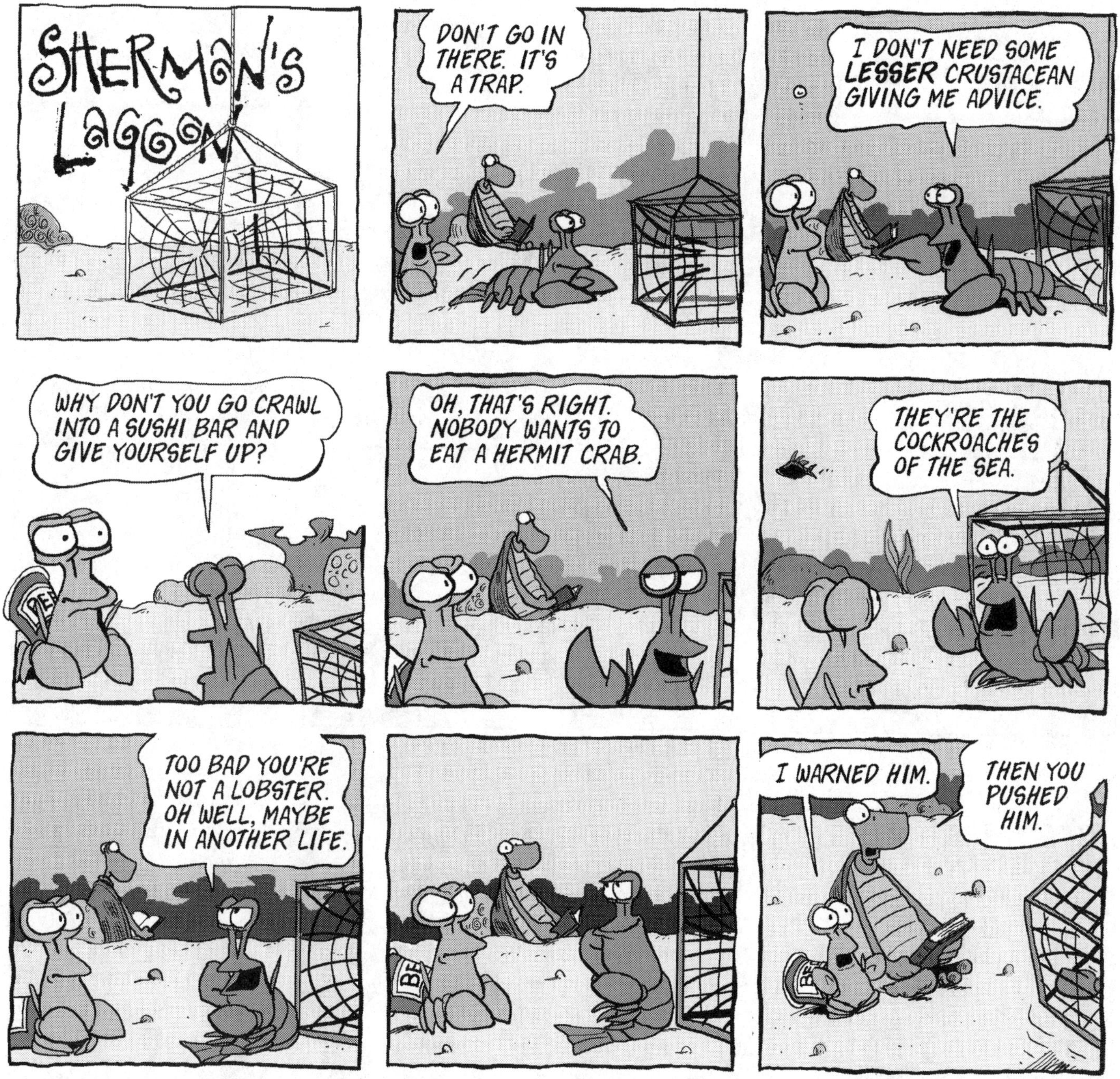
SHERMAN'S LAGOON
DON'T GO IN THERE. IT'S A TRAP.
I DON'T NEED SOME **LESSER** CRUSTACEAN GIVING ME ADVICE.
WHY DON'T YOU GO CRAWL INTO A SUSHI BAR AND GIVE YOURSELF UP?
OH, THAT'S RIGHT. NOBODY WANTS TO EAT A HERMIT CRAB.
THEY'RE THE COCKROACHES OF THE SEA.
TOO BAD YOU'RE NOT A LOBSTER. OH WELL, MAYBE IN ANOTHER LIFE.
I WARNED HIM.
THEN YOU PUSHED HIM.

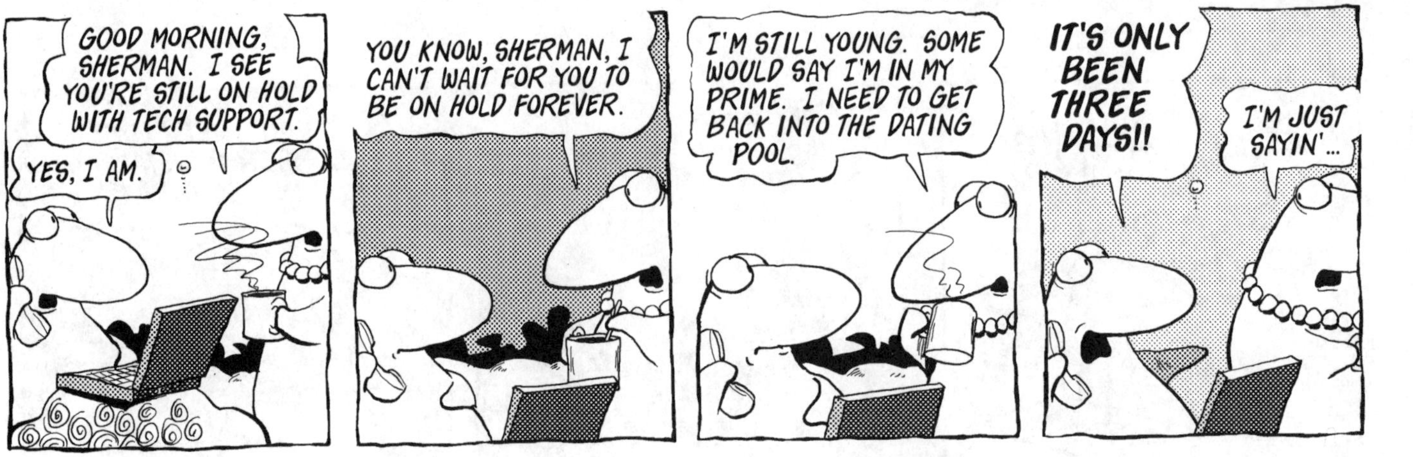
GOOD MORNING, SHERMAN. I SEE YOU'RE STILL ON HOLD WITH TECH SUPPORT.
YES, I AM.
YOU KNOW, SHERMAN, I CAN'T WAIT FOR YOU TO BE ON HOLD FOREVER.
I'M STILL YOUNG. SOME WOULD SAY I'M IN MY PRIME. I NEED TO GET BACK INTO THE DATING POOL.
IT'S ONLY BEEN THREE DAYS!!
I'M JUST SAYIN'...

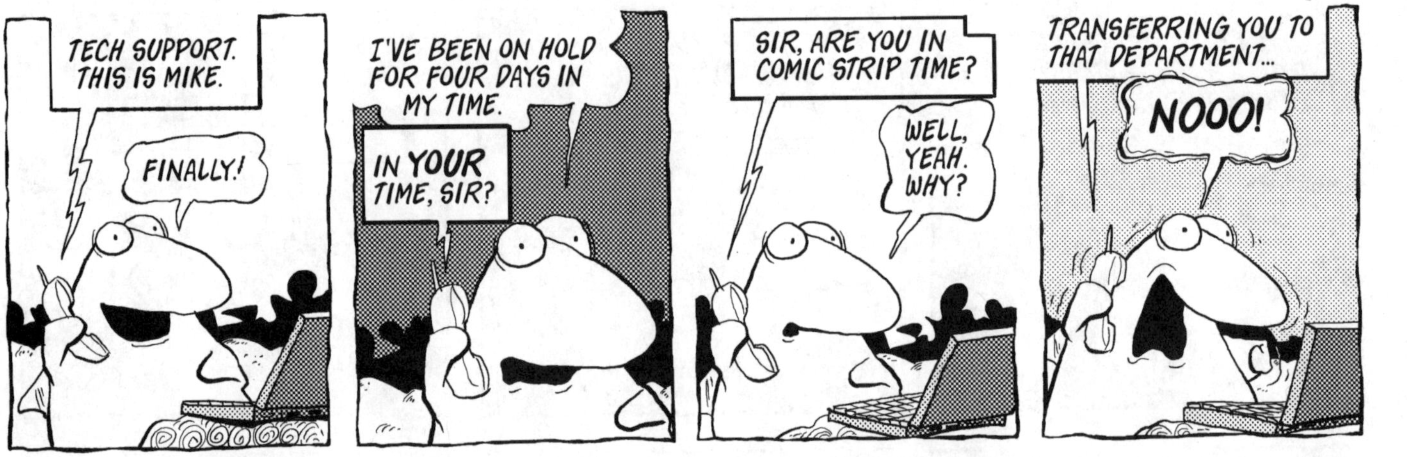
TECH SUPPORT. THIS IS MIKE.
FINALLY!
I'VE BEEN ON HOLD FOR FOUR DAYS IN MY TIME.
IN YOUR TIME, SIR?
SIR, ARE YOU IN COMIC STRIP TIME?
WELL, YEAH. WHY?
TRANSFERRING YOU TO THAT DEPARTMENT...
NOOO!

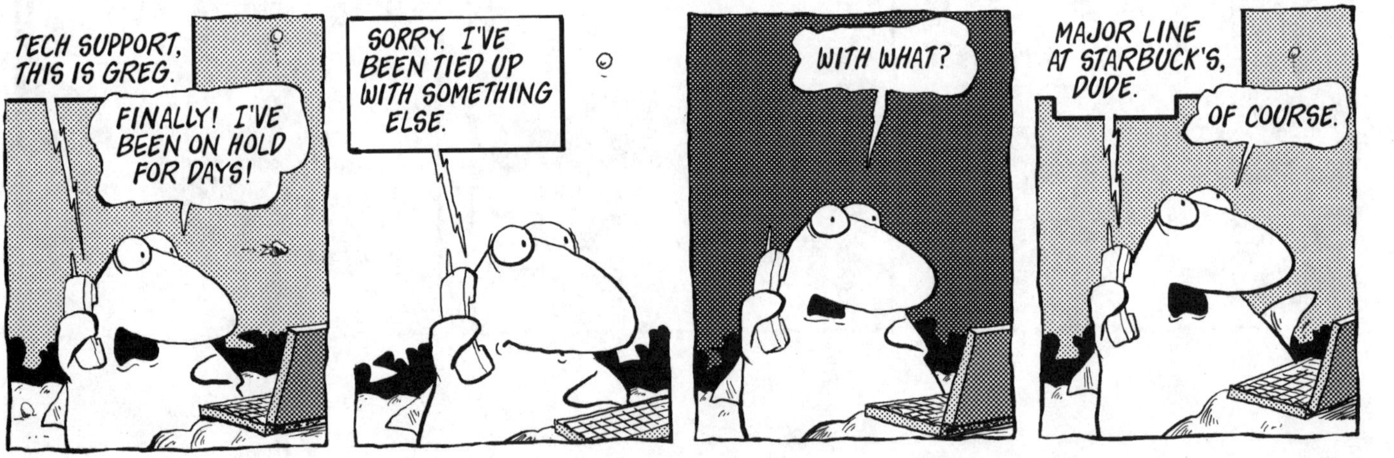
TECH SUPPORT, THIS IS GREG.
FINALLY! I'VE BEEN ON HOLD FOR DAYS!
SORRY. I'VE BEEN TIED UP WITH SOMETHING ELSE.
WITH WHAT?
MAJOR LINE AT STARBUCK'S, DUDE.
OF COURSE.

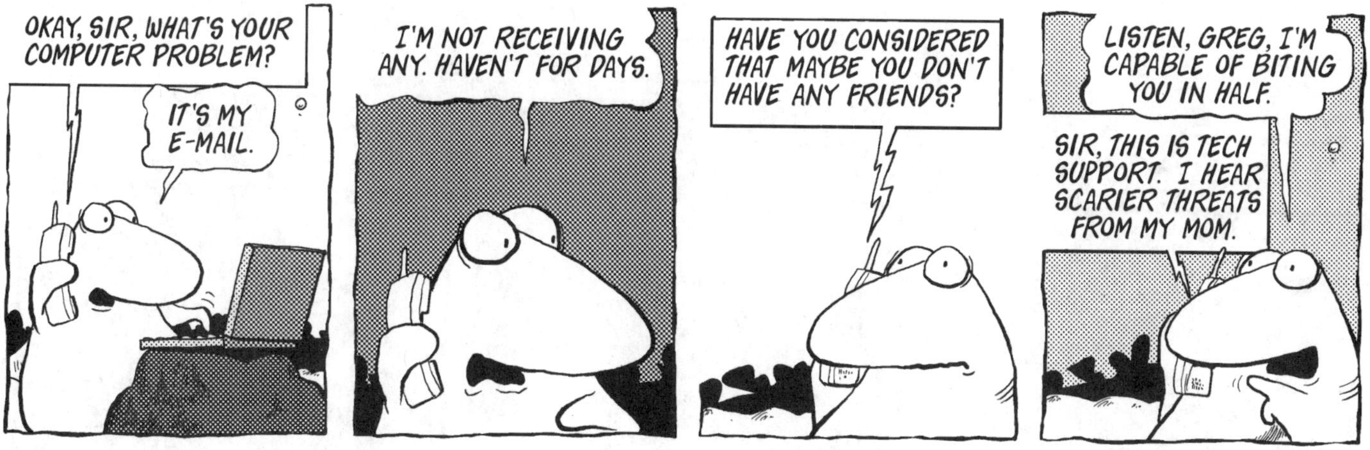
OKAY, SIR, WHAT'S YOUR COMPUTER PROBLEM?
IT'S MY E-MAIL.
I'M NOT RECEIVING ANY. HAVEN'T FOR DAYS.
HAVE YOU CONSIDERED THAT MAYBE YOU DON'T HAVE ANY FRIENDS?
LISTEN, GREG, I'M CAPABLE OF BITING YOU IN HALF.
SIR, THIS IS TECH SUPPORT. I HEAR SCARIER THREATS FROM MY MOM.

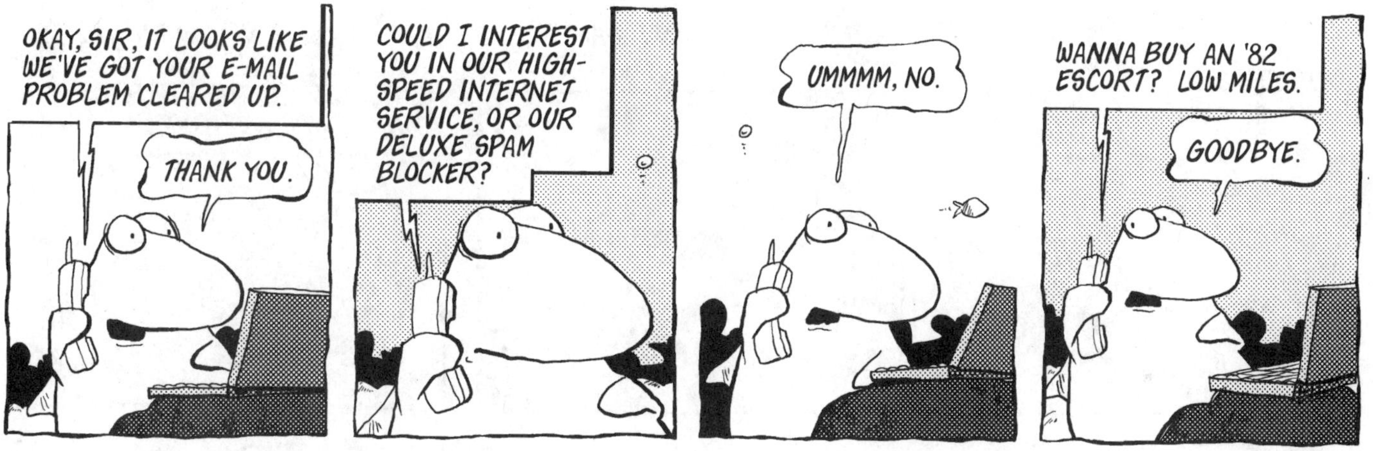
OKAY, SIR, IT LOOKS LIKE WE'VE GOT YOUR E-MAIL PROBLEM CLEARED UP.
THANK YOU.
COULD I INTEREST YOU IN OUR HIGH-SPEED INTERNET SERVICE, OR OUR DELUXE SPAM BLOCKER?
UMMMM, NO.
WANNA BUY AN '82 ESCORT? LOW MILES.
GOODBYE.

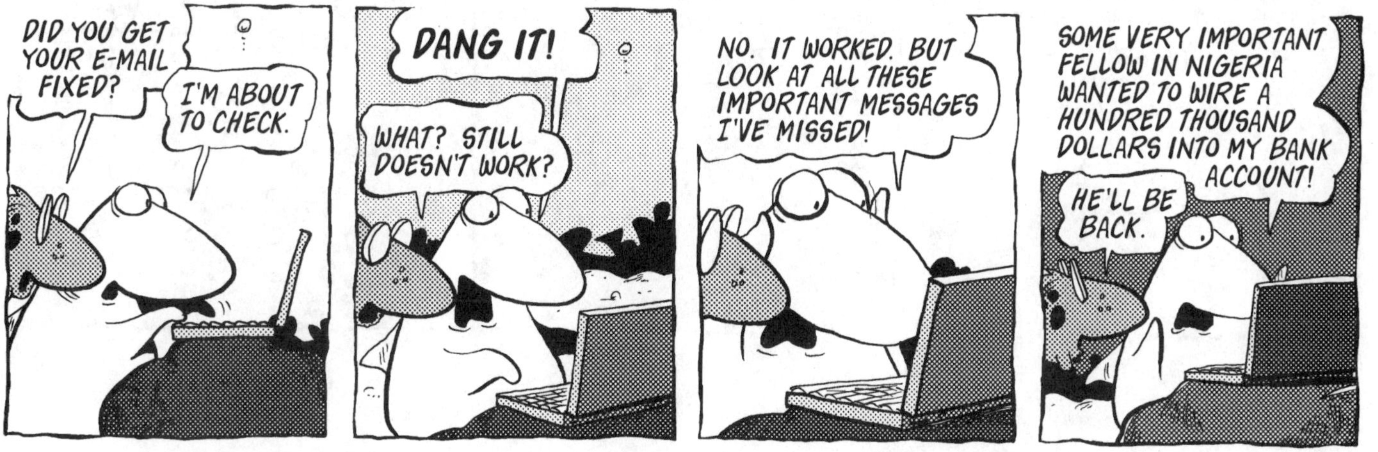
DID YOU GET YOUR E-MAIL FIXED?
I'M ABOUT TO CHECK.
DANG IT!
WHAT? STILL DOESN'T WORK?
NO. IT WORKED. BUT LOOK AT ALL THESE IMPORTANT MESSAGES I'VE MISSED!
SOME VERY IMPORTANT FELLOW IN NIGERIA WANTED TO WIRE A HUNDRED THOUSAND DOLLARS INTO MY BANK ACCOUNT!
HE'LL BE BACK.

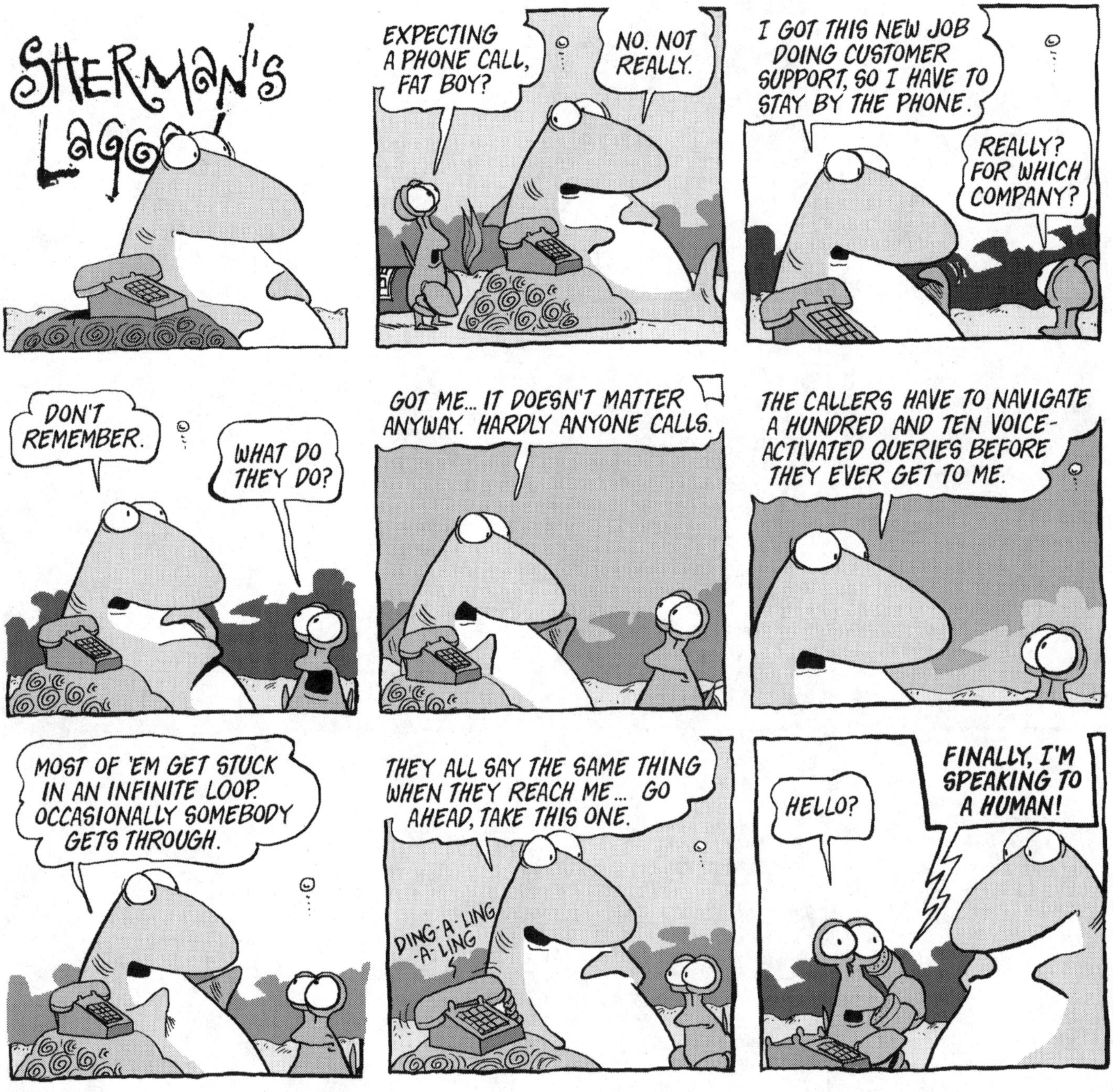
SHERMAN'S LAGOON
EXPECTING A PHONE CALL, FAT BOY?
NO. NOT REALLY.
I GOT THIS NEW JOB DOING CUSTOMER SUPPORT, SO I HAVE TO STAY BY THE PHONE.
REALLY? FOR WHICH COMPANY?
DON'T REMEMBER.
WHAT DO THEY DO?
GOT ME... IT DOESN'T MATTER ANYWAY. HARDLY ANYONE CALLS.
THE CALLERS HAVE TO NAVIGATE A HUNDRED AND TEN VOICE-ACTIVATED QUERIES BEFORE THEY EVER GET TO ME.
MOST OF 'EM GET STUCK IN AN INFINITE LOOP. OCCASIONALLY SOMEBODY GETS THROUGH.
THEY ALL SAY THE SAME THING WHEN THEY REACH ME... GO AHEAD, TAKE THIS ONE.
DING-A-LING-A-LING
HELLO?
FINALLY, I'M SPEAKING TO A HUMAN!

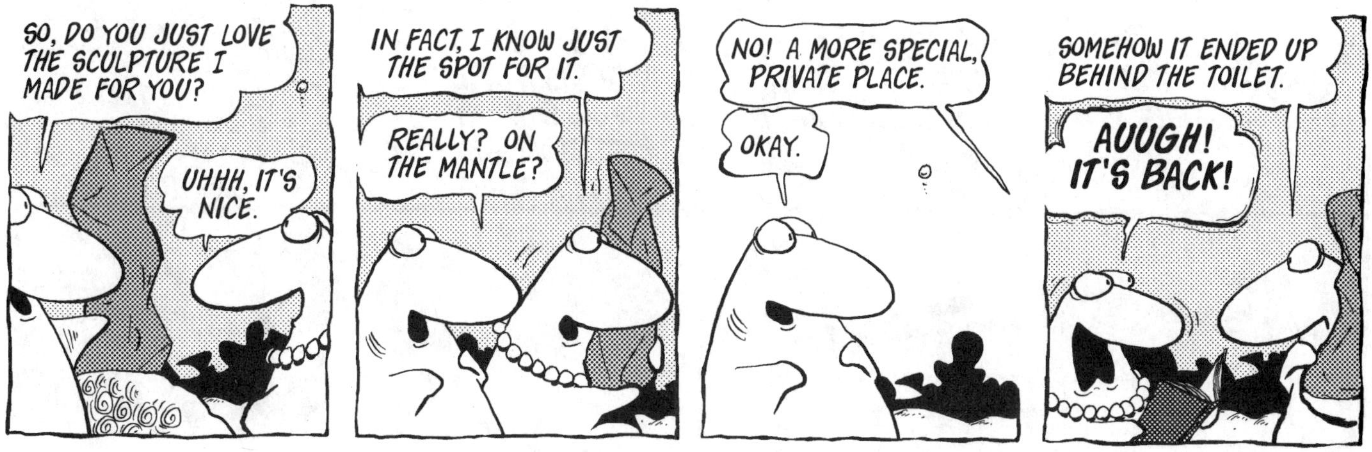
SO, DO YOU JUST LOVE THE SCULPTURE I MADE FOR YOU?
UHHH, IT'S NICE.
IN FACT, I KNOW JUST THE SPOT FOR IT.
REALLY? ON THE MANTLE?
NO! A MORE SPECIAL, PRIVATE PLACE.
OKAY.
SOMEHOW IT ENDED UP BEHIND THE TOILET.
AUUGH! IT'S BACK!

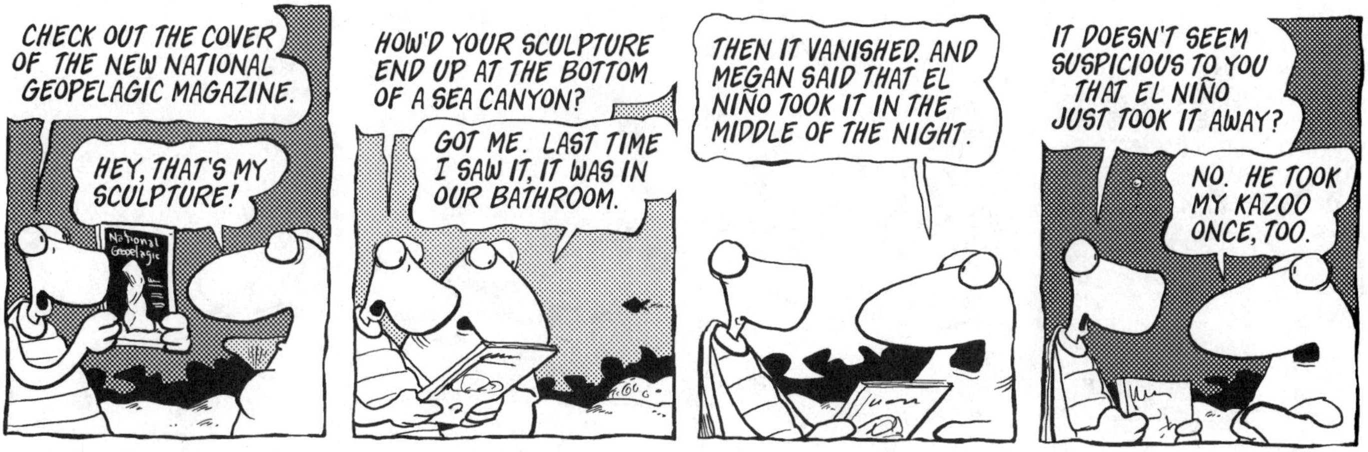
CHECK OUT THE COVER OF THE NEW NATIONAL GEOPELAGIC MAGAZINE.
HEY, THAT'S MY SCULPTURE!
National Geopelagic
HOW'D YOUR SCULPTURE END UP AT THE BOTTOM OF A SEA CANYON?
GOT ME. LAST TIME I SAW IT, IT WAS IN OUR BATHROOM.
THEN IT VANISHED. AND MEGAN SAID THAT EL NIÑO TOOK IT IN THE MIDDLE OF THE NIGHT.
IT DOESN'T SEEM SUSPICIOUS TO YOU THAT EL NIÑO JUST TOOK IT AWAY?
NO. HE TOOK MY KAZOO ONCE, TOO.

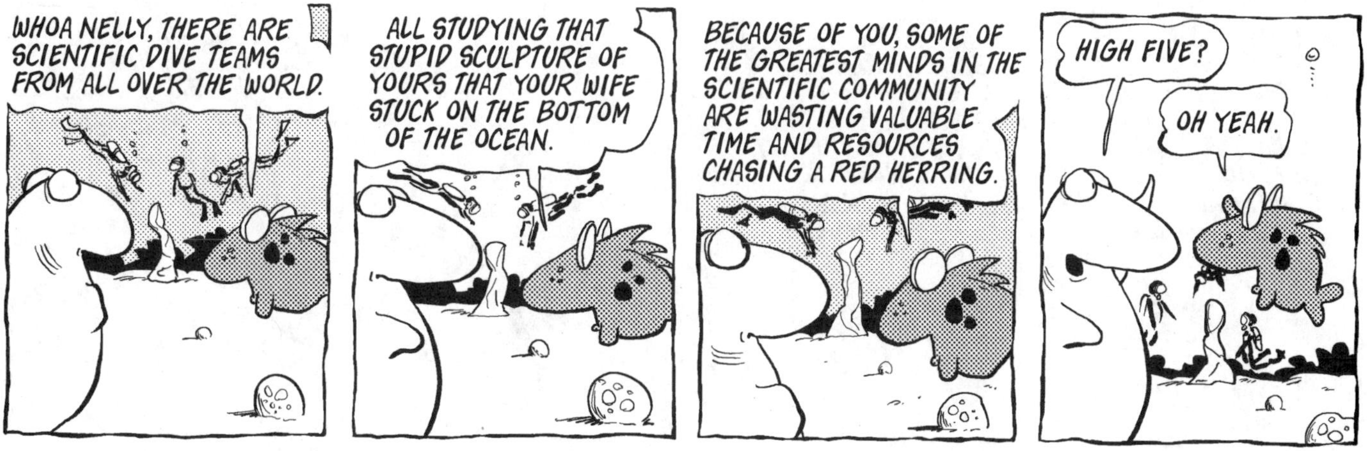
WHOA NELLY, THERE ARE SCIENTIFIC DIVE TEAMS FROM ALL OVER THE WORLD.
ALL STUDYING THAT STUPID SCULPTURE OF YOURS THAT YOUR WIFE STUCK ON THE BOTTOM OF THE OCEAN.
BECAUSE OF YOU, SOME OF THE GREATEST MINDS IN THE SCIENTIFIC COMMUNITY ARE WASTING VALUABLE TIME AND RESOURCES CHASING A RED HERRING.
HIGH FIVE?
OH YEAH.

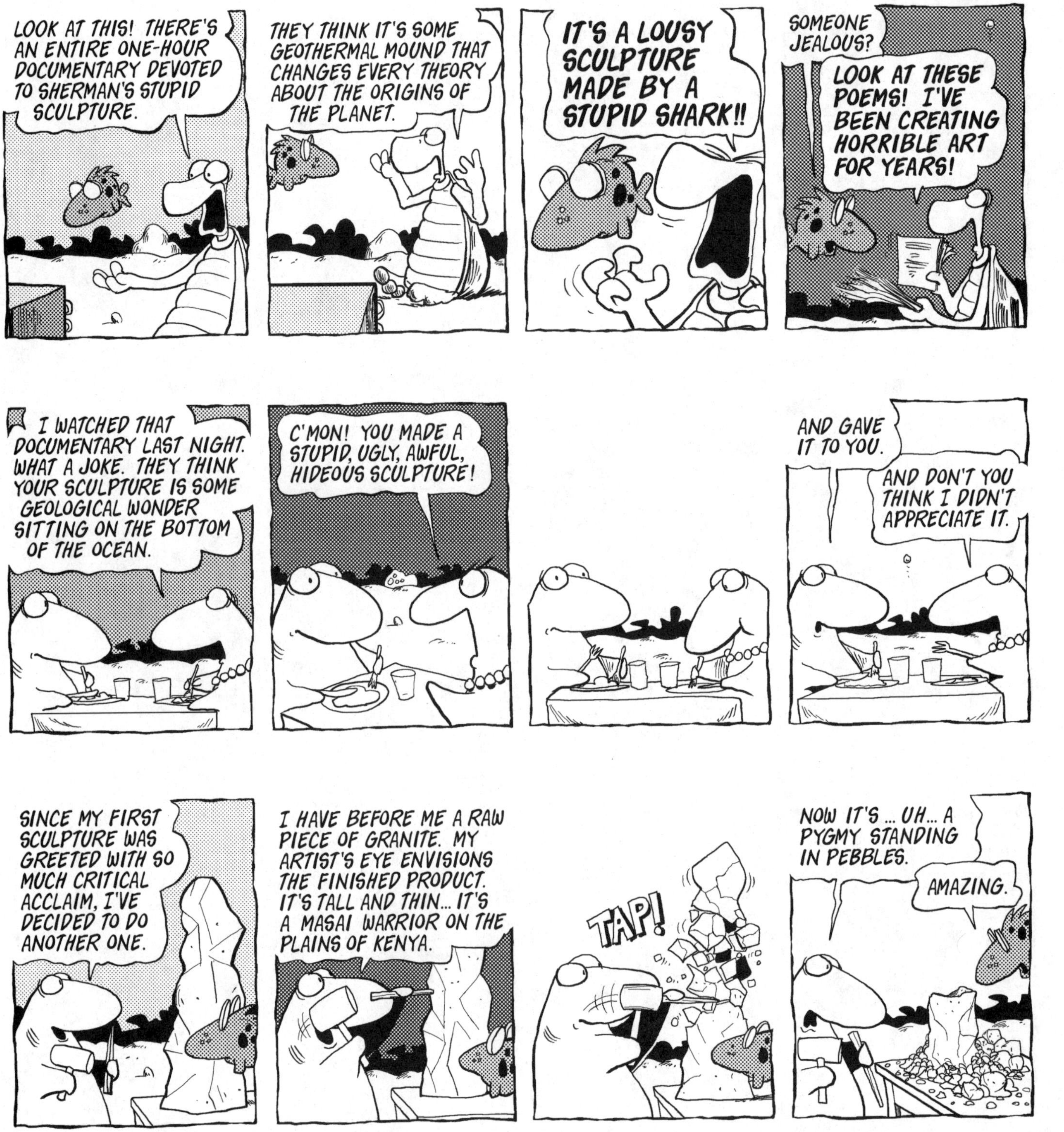
LOOK AT THIS! THERE'S AN ENTIRE ONE-HOUR DOCUMENTARY DEVOTED TO SHERMAN'S STUPID SCULPTURE.
THEY THINK IT'S SOME GEOTHERMAL MOUND THAT CHANGES EVERY THEORY ABOUT THE ORIGINS OF THE PLANET.
IT'S A LOUSY SCULPTURE MADE BY A STUPID SHARK!!
SOMEONE JEALOUS?
LOOK AT THESE POEMS! I'VE BEEN CREATING HORRIBLE ART FOR YEARS!
I WATCHED THAT DOCUMENTARY LAST NIGHT. WHAT A JOKE. THEY THINK YOUR SCULPTURE IS SOME GEOLOGICAL WONDER SITTING ON THE BOTTOM OF THE OCEAN.
C'MON! YOU MADE A STUPID, UGLY, AWFUL, HIDEOUS SCULPTURE!
AND GAVE IT TO YOU.
AND DON'T YOU THINK I DIDN'T APPRECIATE IT.
SINCE MY FIRST SCULPTURE WAS GREETED WITH SO MUCH CRITICAL ACCLAIM, I'VE DECIDED TO DO ANOTHER ONE.
I HAVE BEFORE ME A RAW PIECE OF GRANITE. MY ARTIST'S EYE ENVISIONS THE FINISHED PRODUCT. IT'S TALL AND THIN... IT'S A MASAI WARRIOR ON THE PLAINS OF KENYA.
TAP!
NOW IT'S ... UH... A PYGMY STANDING IN PEBBLES.
AMAZING.

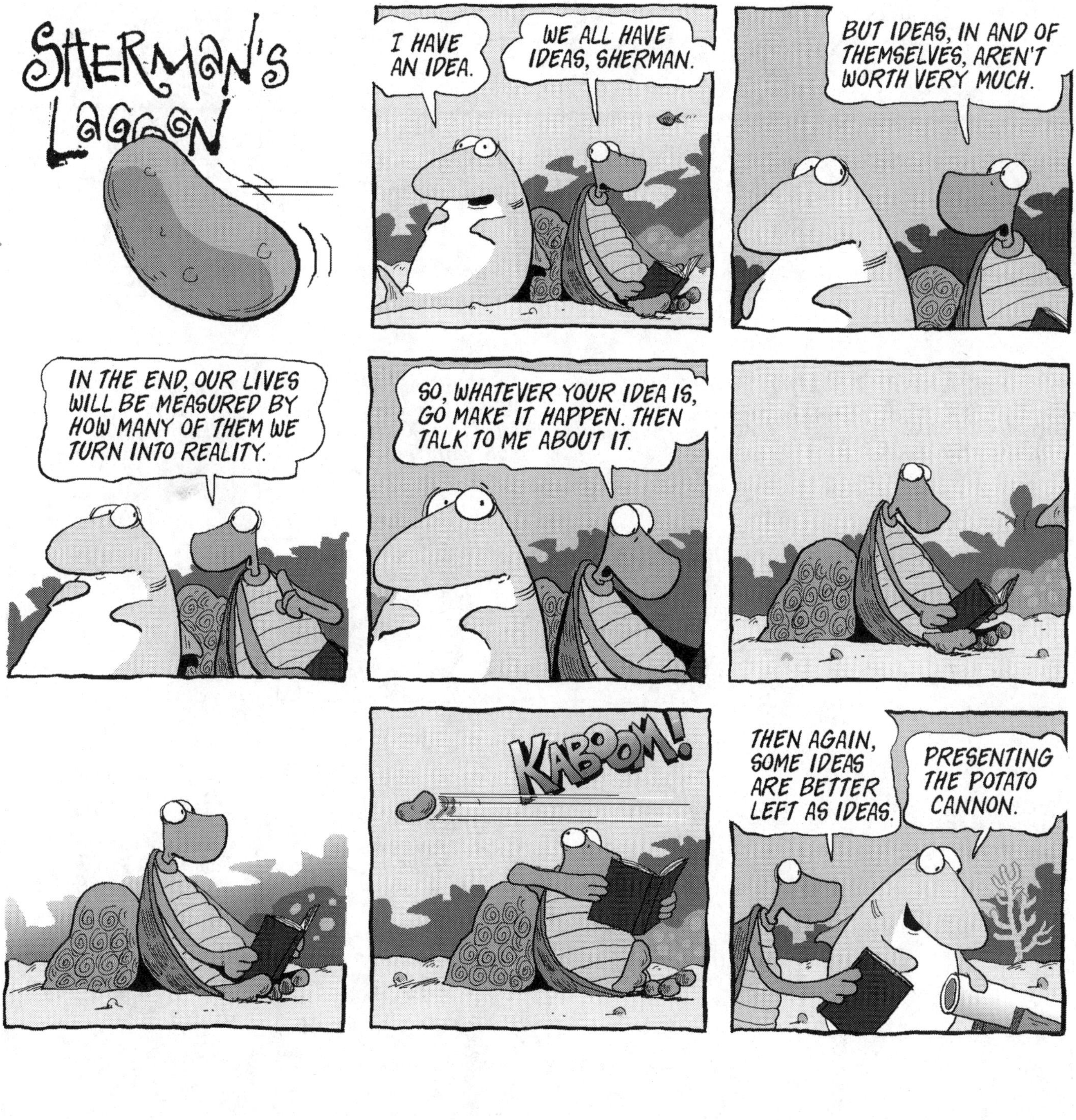
SHERMAN'S LAGOON
I HAVE AN IDEA.
WE ALL HAVE IDEAS, SHERMAN.
BUT IDEAS, IN AND OF THEMSELVES, AREN'T WORTH VERY MUCH.
IN THE END, OUR LIVES WILL BE MEASURED BY HOW MANY OF THEM WE TURN INTO REALITY.
SO, WHATEVER YOUR IDEA IS, GO MAKE IT HAPPEN. THEN TALK TO ME ABOUT IT.
KABOOM!
THEN AGAIN, SOME IDEAS ARE BETTER LEFT AS IDEAS.
PRESENTING THE POTATO CANNON.

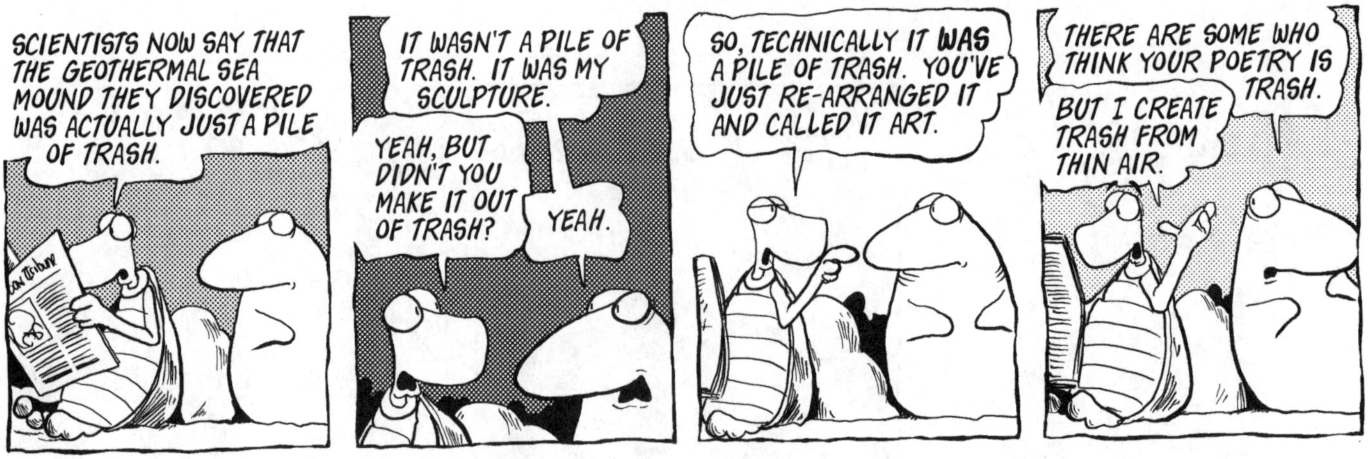
SCIENTISTS NOW SAY THAT THE GEOTHERMAL SEA MOUND THEY DISCOVERED WAS ACTUALLY JUST A PILE OF TRASH.
IT WASN'T A PILE OF TRASH. IT WAS MY SCULPTURE.
YEAH, BUT DIDN'T YOU MAKE IT OUT OF TRASH?
YEAH.
SO, TECHNICALLY IT **WAS** A PILE OF TRASH. YOU'VE JUST RE-ARRANGED IT AND CALLED IT ART.
THERE ARE SOME WHO THINK YOUR POETRY IS TRASH.
BUT I CREATE TRASH FROM THIN AIR.

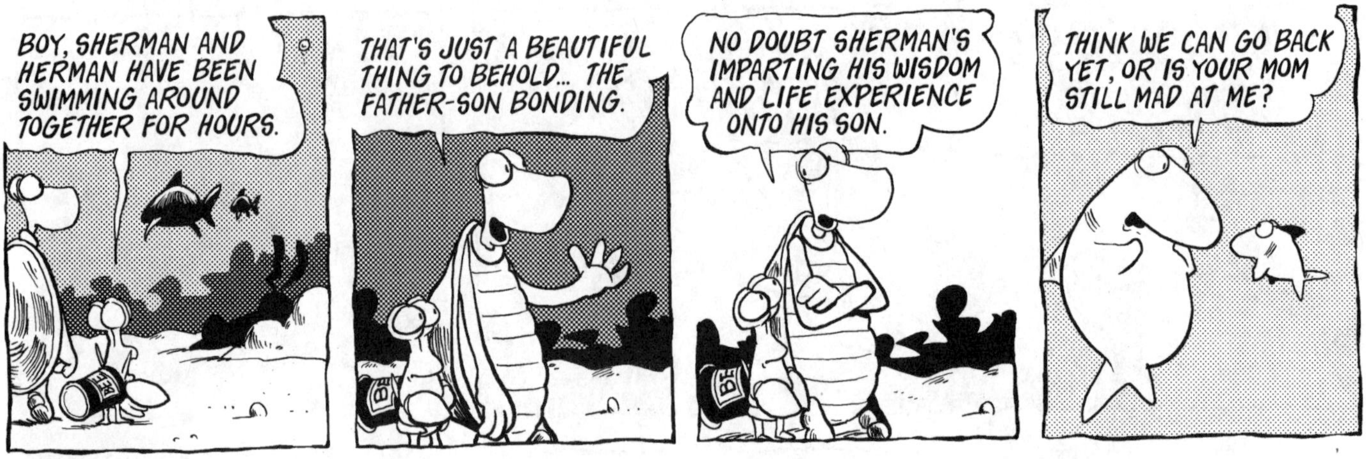
BOY, SHERMAN AND HERMAN HAVE BEEN SWIMMING AROUND TOGETHER FOR HOURS.
THAT'S JUST A BEAUTIFUL THING TO BEHOLD... THE FATHER-SON BONDING.
NO DOUBT SHERMAN'S IMPARTING HIS WISDOM AND LIFE EXPERIENCE ONTO HIS SON.
THINK WE CAN GO BACK YET, OR IS YOUR MOM STILL MAD AT ME?

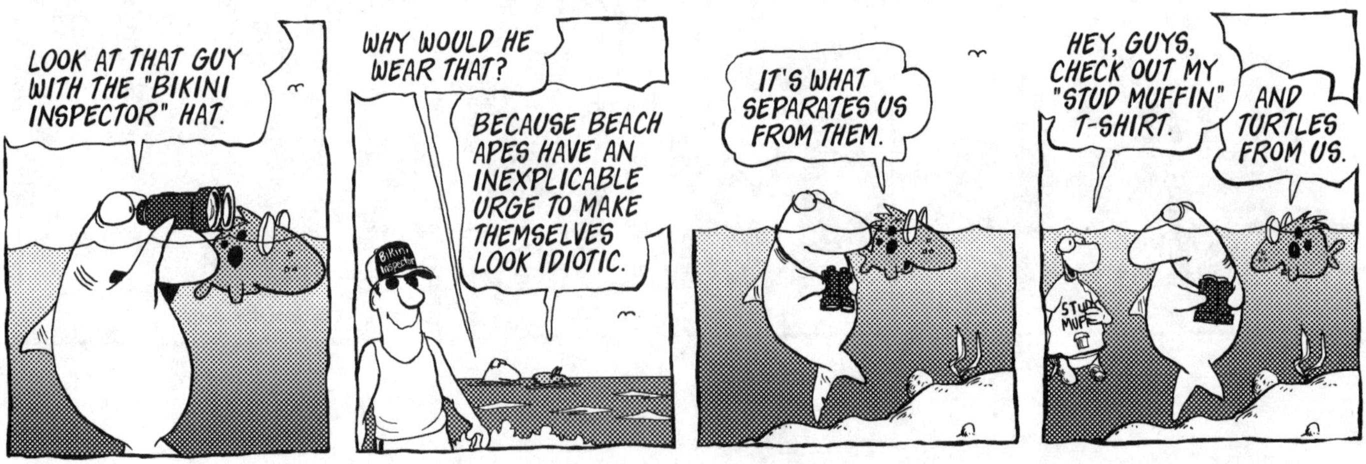
LOOK AT THAT GUY WITH THE "BIKINI INSPECTOR" HAT.
WHY WOULD HE WEAR THAT?
BECAUSE BEACH APES HAVE AN INEXPLICABLE URGE TO MAKE THEMSELVES LOOK IDIOTIC.
Bikini Inspector
IT'S WHAT SEPARATES US FROM THEM.
HEY, GUYS, CHECK OUT MY "STUD MUFFIN" T-SHIRT.
AND TURTLES FROM US.

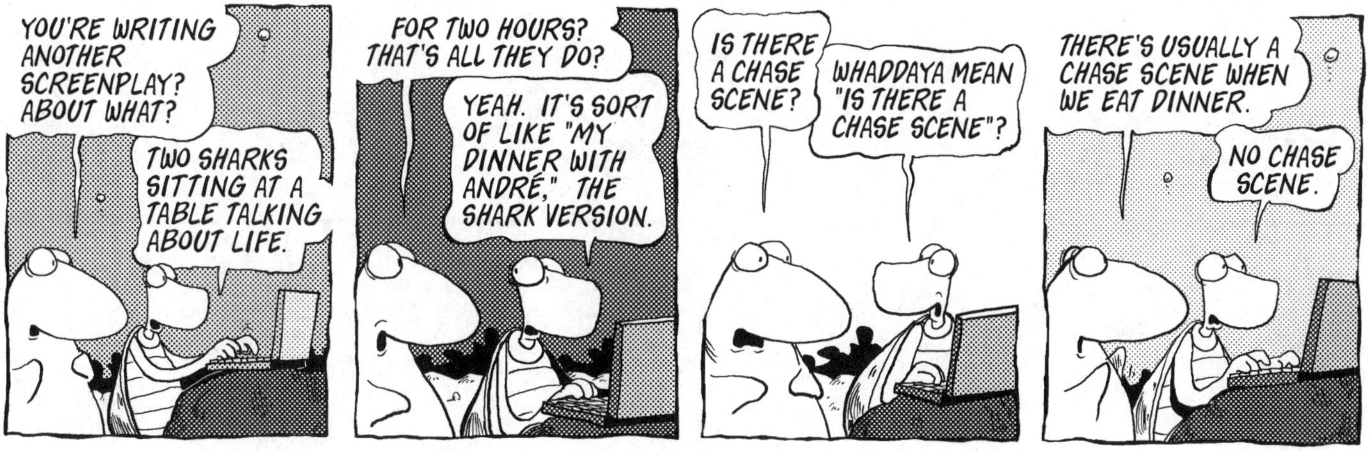
YOU'RE WRITING ANOTHER SCREENPLAY? ABOUT WHAT?
TWO SHARKS SITTING AT A TABLE TALKING ABOUT LIFE.
FOR TWO HOURS? THAT'S ALL THEY DO?
YEAH. IT'S SORT OF LIKE "MY DINNER WITH ANDRÉ," THE SHARK VERSION.
IS THERE A CHASE SCENE?
WHADDAYA MEAN "IS THERE A CHASE SCENE"?
THERE'S USUALLY A CHASE SCENE WHEN WE EAT DINNER.
NO CHASE SCENE.

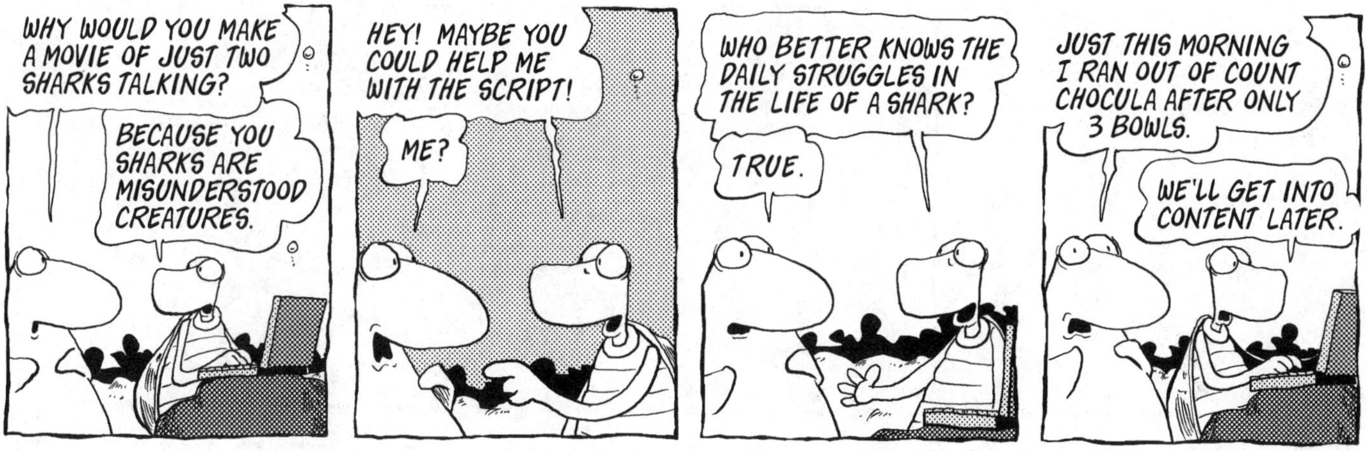
WHY WOULD YOU MAKE A MOVIE OF JUST TWO SHARKS TALKING?
BECAUSE YOU SHARKS ARE MISUNDERSTOOD CREATURES.
HEY! MAYBE YOU COULD HELP ME WITH THE SCRIPT!
ME?
WHO BETTER KNOWS THE DAILY STRUGGLES IN THE LIFE OF A SHARK?
TRUE.
JUST THIS MORNING I RAN OUT OF COUNT CHOCULA AFTER ONLY 3 BOWLS.
WE'LL GET INTO CONTENT LATER.

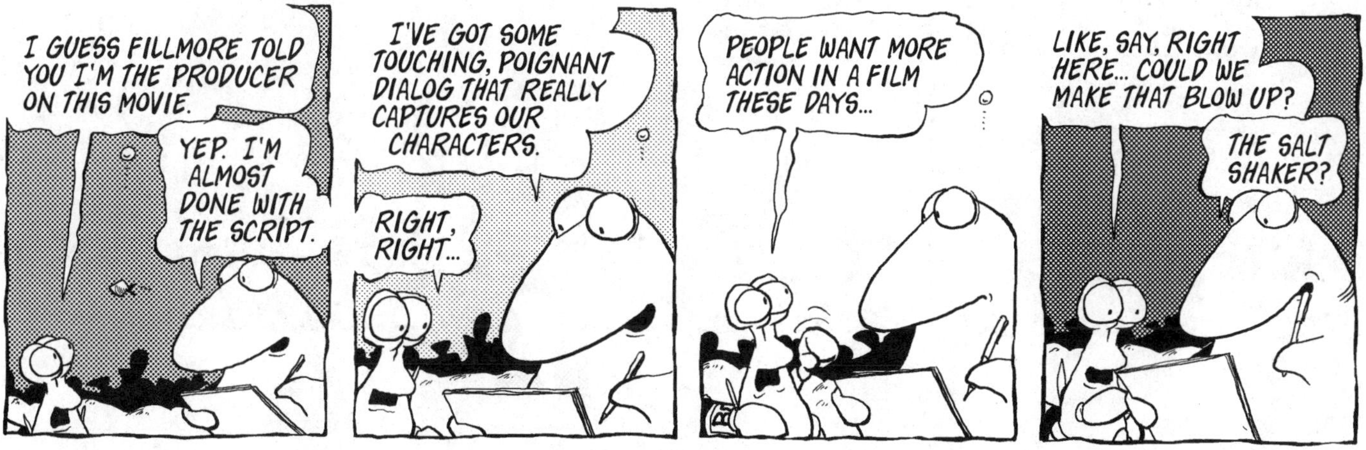
I GUESS FILLMORE TOLD YOU I'M THE PRODUCER ON THIS MOVIE.
YEP. I'M ALMOST DONE WITH THE SCRIPT.
I'VE GOT SOME TOUCHING, POIGNANT DIALOG THAT REALLY CAPTURES OUR CHARACTERS.
RIGHT, RIGHT...
PEOPLE WANT MORE ACTION IN A FILM THESE DAYS...
LIKE, SAY, RIGHT HERE... COULD WE MAKE THAT BLOW UP?
THE SALT SHAKER?

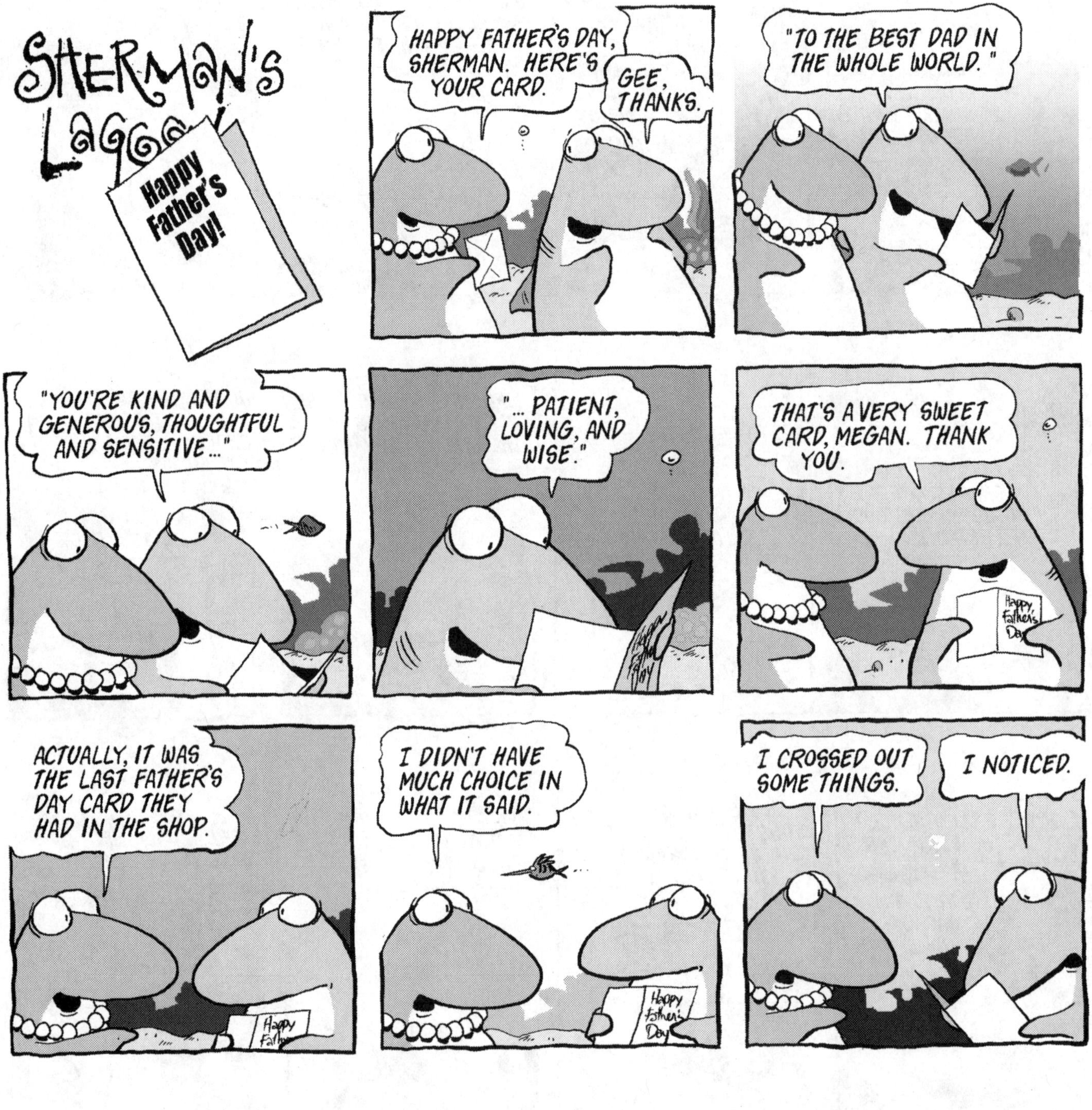
Sherman's Lagoon
Happy Father's Day!
HAPPY FATHER'S DAY, SHERMAN. HERE'S YOUR CARD.
GEE, THANKS.
"TO THE BEST DAD IN THE WHOLE WORLD."
"YOU'RE KIND AND GENEROUS, THOUGHTFUL AND SENSITIVE..."
"... PATIENT, LOVING, AND WISE."
THAT'S A VERY SWEET CARD, MEGAN. THANK YOU.
Happy Father's Day
ACTUALLY, IT WAS THE LAST FATHER'S DAY CARD THEY HAD IN THE SHOP.
I DIDN'T HAVE MUCH CHOICE IN WHAT IT SAID.
Happy Father's Day
I CROSSED OUT SOME THINGS.
I NOTICED.

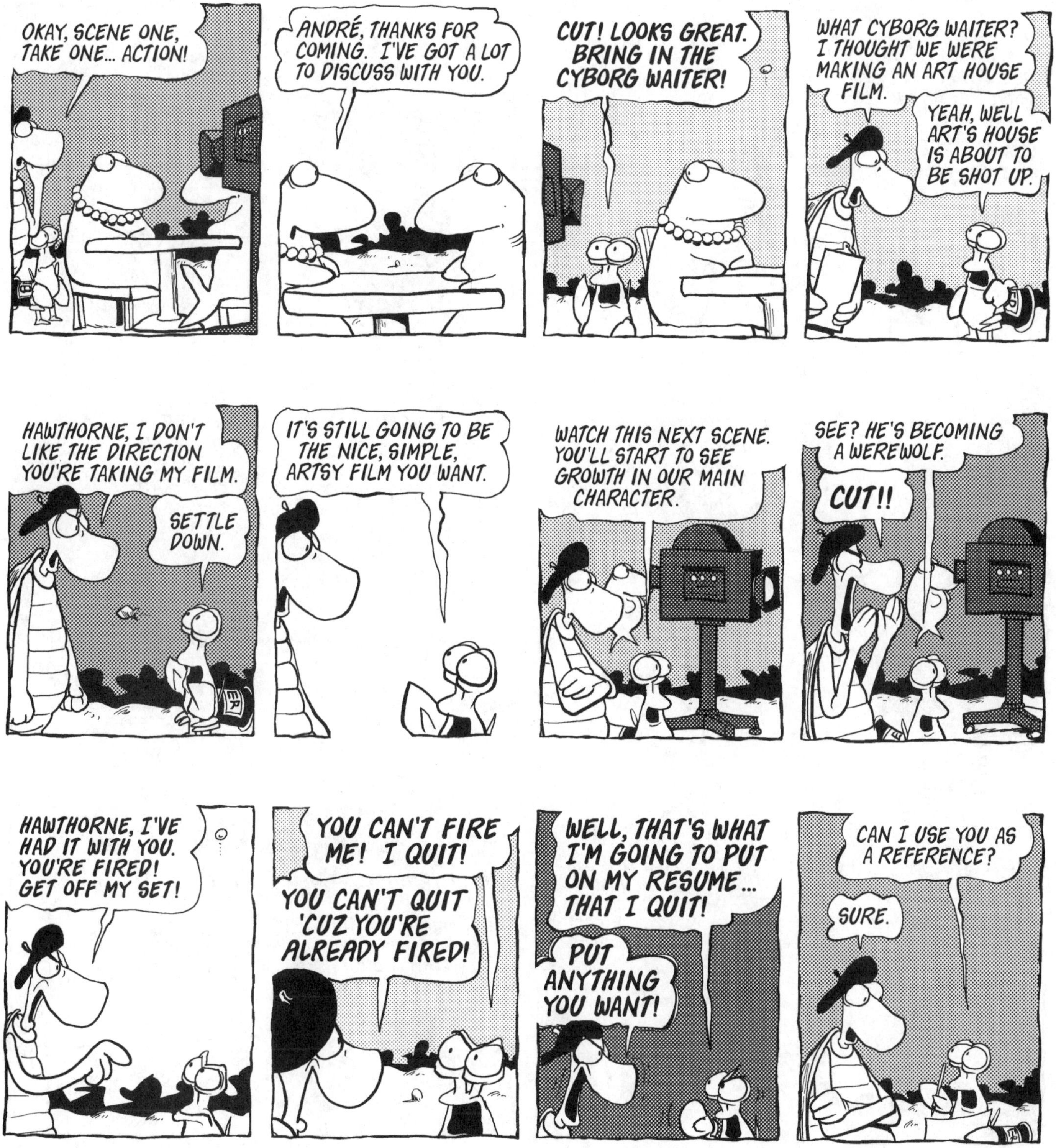
OKAY, SCENE ONE, TAKE ONE... ACTION!
ANDRÉ, THANKS FOR COMING. I'VE GOT A LOT TO DISCUSS WITH YOU.
CUT! LOOKS GREAT. BRING IN THE CYBORG WAITER!
WHAT CYBORG WAITER? I THOUGHT WE WERE MAKING AN ART HOUSE FILM.
YEAH, WELL ART'S HOUSE IS ABOUT TO BE SHOT UP.
HAWTHORNE, I DON'T LIKE THE DIRECTION YOU'RE TAKING MY FILM.
SETTLE DOWN.
IT'S STILL GOING TO BE THE NICE, SIMPLE, ARTSY FILM YOU WANT.
WATCH THIS NEXT SCENE. YOU'LL START TO SEE GROWTH IN OUR MAIN CHARACTER.
SEE? HE'S BECOMING A WEREWOLF.
CUT!!
HAWTHORNE, I'VE HAD IT WITH YOU. YOU'RE FIRED! GET OFF MY SET!
YOU CAN'T FIRE ME! I QUIT!
YOU CAN'T QUIT 'CUZ YOU'RE ALREADY FIRED!
WELL, THAT'S WHAT I'M GOING TO PUT ON MY RESUME... THAT I QUIT!
PUT ANYTHING YOU WANT!
CAN I USE YOU AS A REFERENCE?
SURE.

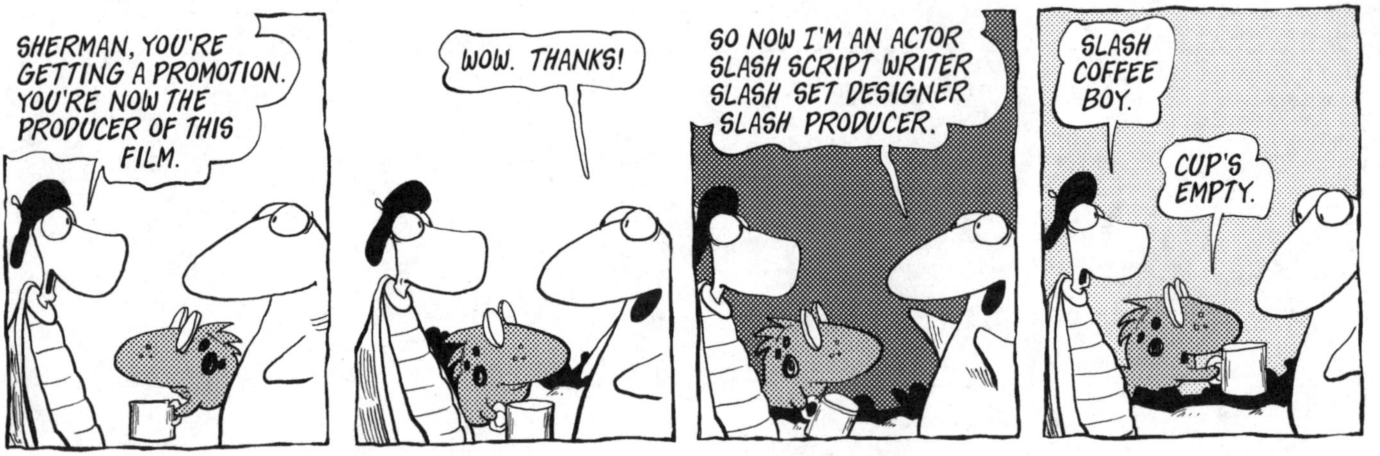
SHERMAN, YOU'RE GETTING A PROMOTION. YOU'RE NOW THE PRODUCER OF THIS FILM.
WOW. THANKS!
SO NOW I'M AN ACTOR SLASH SCRIPT WRITER SLASH SET DESIGNER SLASH PRODUCER.
SLASH COFFEE BOY.
CUP'S EMPTY.

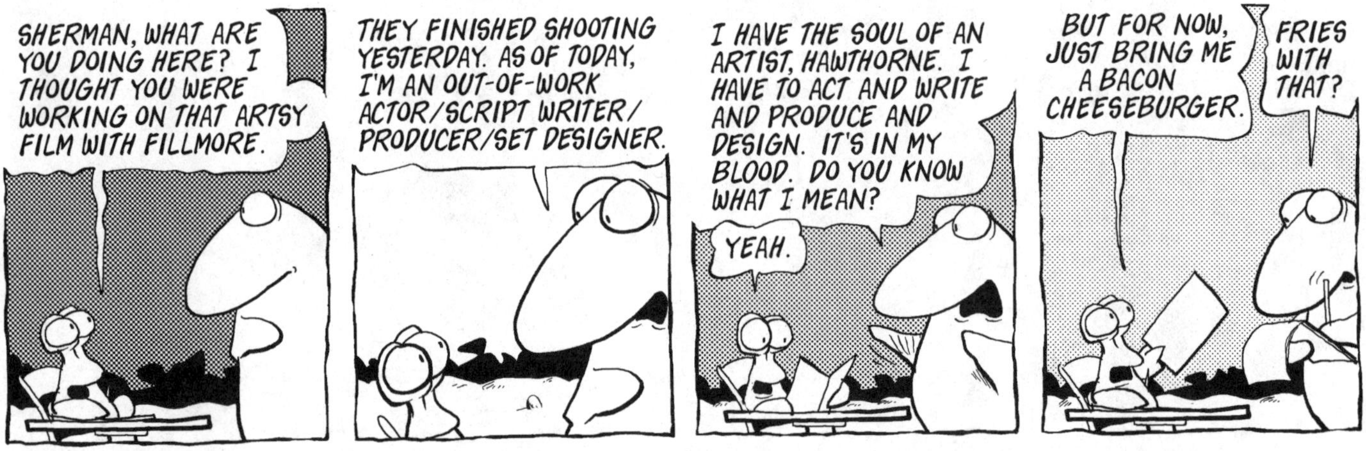
SHERMAN, WHAT ARE YOU DOING HERE? I THOUGHT YOU WERE WORKING ON THAT ARTSY FILM WITH FILLMORE.
THEY FINISHED SHOOTING YESTERDAY. AS OF TODAY, I'M AN OUT-OF-WORK ACTOR/SCRIPT WRITER/PRODUCER/SET DESIGNER.
I HAVE THE SOUL OF AN ARTIST, HAWTHORNE. I HAVE TO ACT AND WRITE AND PRODUCE AND DESIGN. IT'S IN MY BLOOD. DO YOU KNOW WHAT I MEAN?
YEAH.
BUT FOR NOW, JUST BRING ME A BACON CHEESEBURGER.
FRIES WITH THAT?

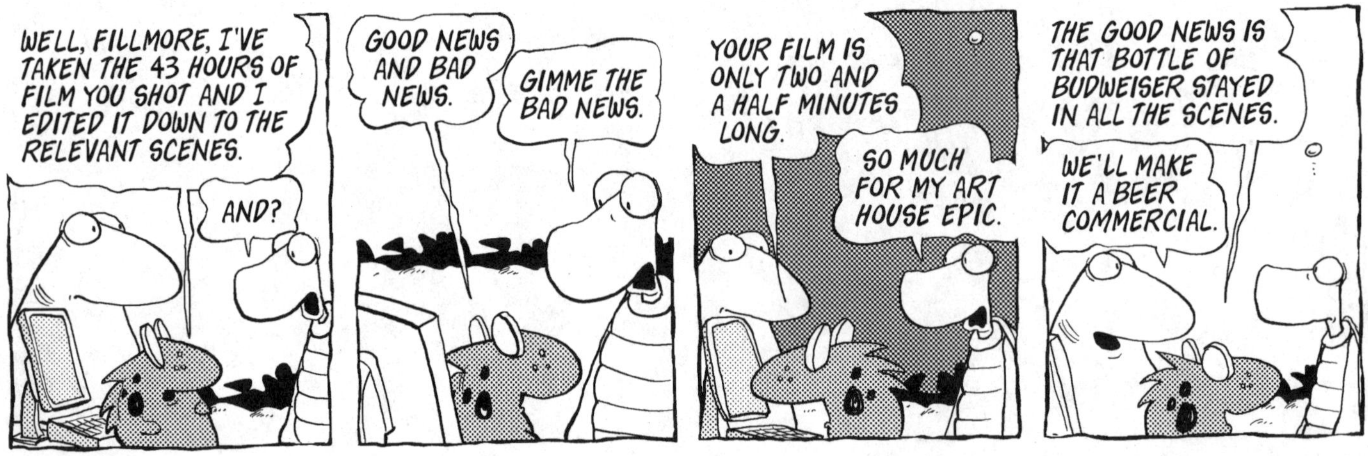
WELL, FILLMORE, I'VE TAKEN THE 43 HOURS OF FILM YOU SHOT AND I EDITED IT DOWN TO THE RELEVANT SCENES.
AND?
GOOD NEWS AND BAD NEWS.
GIMME THE BAD NEWS.
YOUR FILM IS ONLY TWO AND A HALF MINUTES LONG.
SO MUCH FOR MY ART HOUSE EPIC.
THE GOOD NEWS IS THAT BOTTLE OF BUDWEISER STAYED IN ALL THE SCENES.
WE'LL MAKE IT A BEER COMMERCIAL.

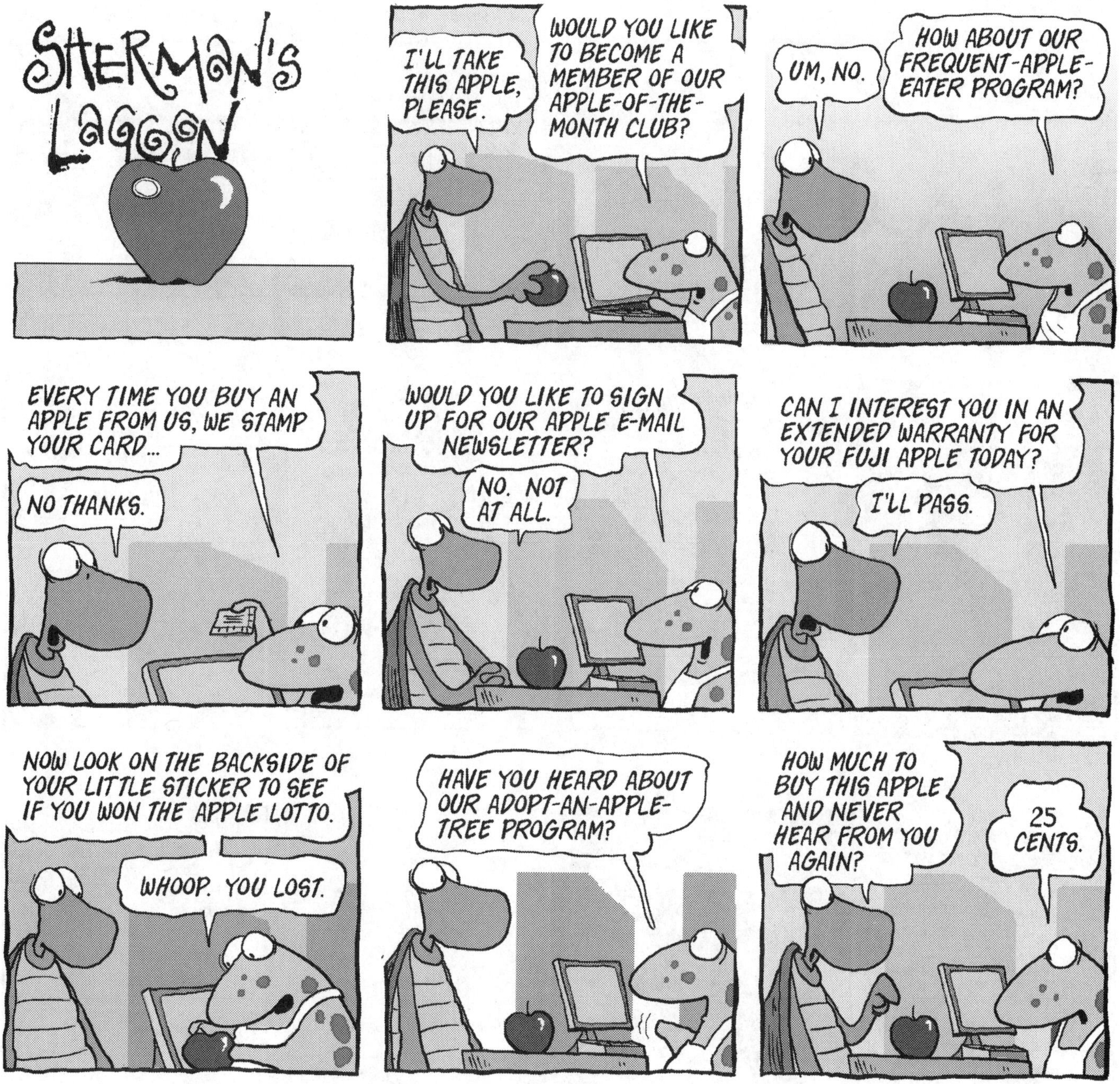
SHERMAN'S LAGOON
I'LL TAKE THIS APPLE, PLEASE.
WOULD YOU LIKE TO BECOME A MEMBER OF OUR APPLE-OF-THE-MONTH CLUB?
UM, NO.
HOW ABOUT OUR FREQUENT-APPLE-EATER PROGRAM?
EVERY TIME YOU BUY AN APPLE FROM US, WE STAMP YOUR CARD...
NO THANKS.
WOULD YOU LIKE TO SIGN UP FOR OUR APPLE E-MAIL NEWSLETTER?
NO. NOT AT ALL.
CAN I INTEREST YOU IN AN EXTENDED WARRANTY FOR YOUR FUJI APPLE TODAY?
I'LL PASS.
NOW LOOK ON THE BACKSIDE OF YOUR LITTLE STICKER TO SEE IF YOU WON THE APPLE LOTTO.
WHOOP. YOU LOST.
HAVE YOU HEARD ABOUT OUR ADOPT-AN-APPLE-TREE PROGRAM?
HOW MUCH TO BUY THIS APPLE AND NEVER HEAR FROM YOU AGAIN?
25 CENTS.

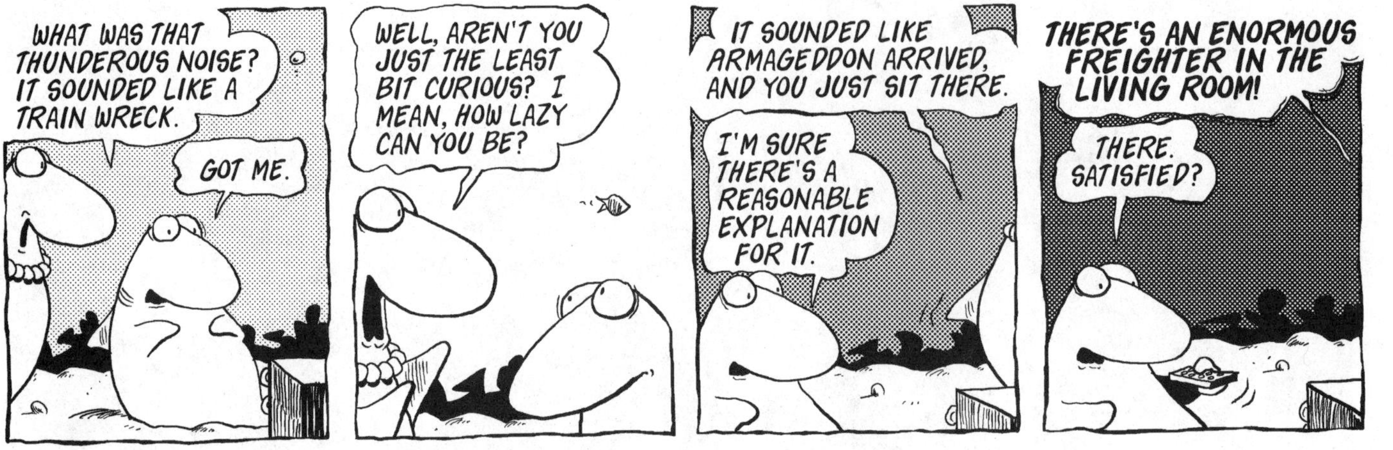
WHAT WAS THAT THUNDEROUS NOISE? IT SOUNDED LIKE A TRAIN WRECK.
GOT ME.
WELL, AREN'T YOU JUST THE LEAST BIT CURIOUS? I MEAN, HOW LAZY CAN YOU BE?
IT SOUNDED LIKE ARMAGEDDON ARRIVED, AND YOU JUST SIT THERE.
I'M SURE THERE'S A REASONABLE EXPLANATION FOR IT.
THERE'S AN ENORMOUS FREIGHTER IN THE LIVING ROOM!
THERE. SATISFIED?

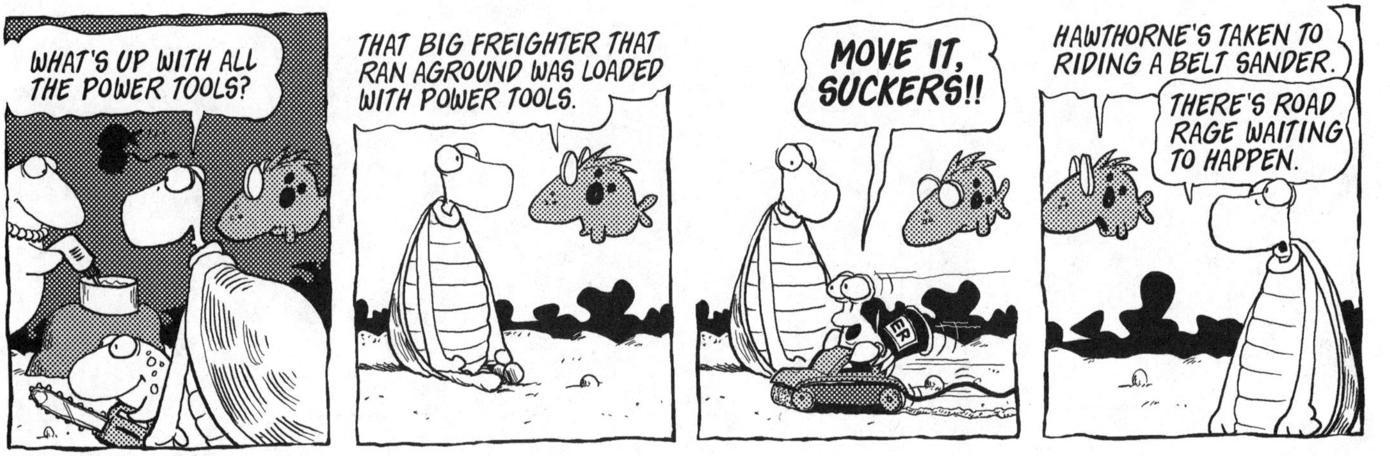
WHAT'S UP WITH ALL THE POWER TOOLS?
THAT BIG FREIGHTER THAT RAN AGROUND WAS LOADED WITH POWER TOOLS.
MOVE IT, SUCKERS!!
HAWTHORNE'S TAKEN TO RIDING A BELT SANDER.
THERE'S ROAD RAGE WAITING TO HAPPEN.

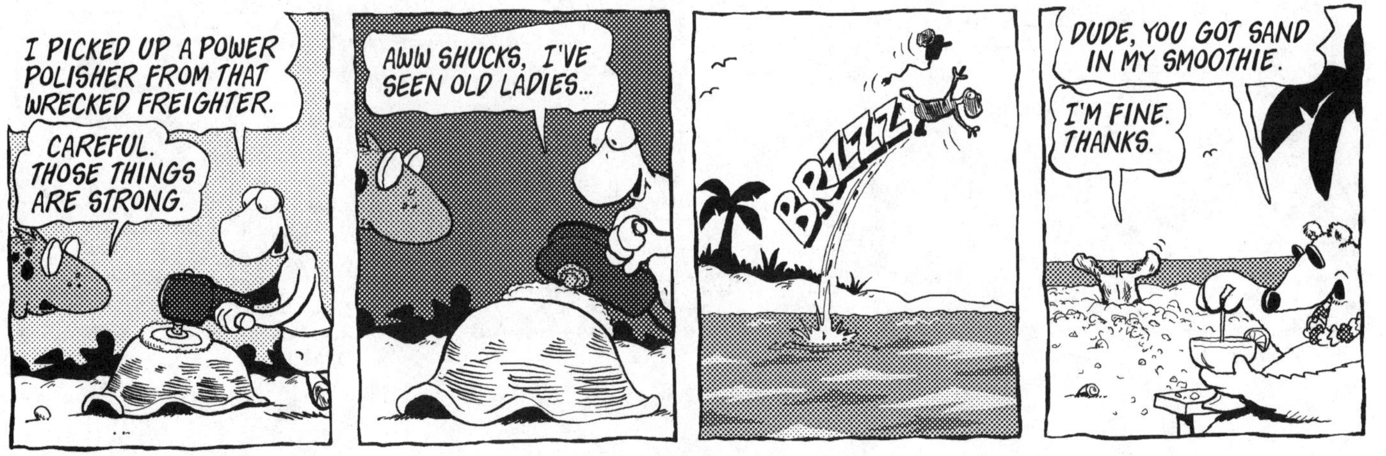
I PICKED UP A POWER POLISHER FROM THAT WRECKED FREIGHTER.
CAREFUL. THOSE THINGS ARE STRONG.
AWW SHUCKS, I'VE SEEN OLD LADIES...
BRZZZZ
DUDE, YOU GOT SAND IN MY SMOOTHIE.
I'M FINE. THANKS.

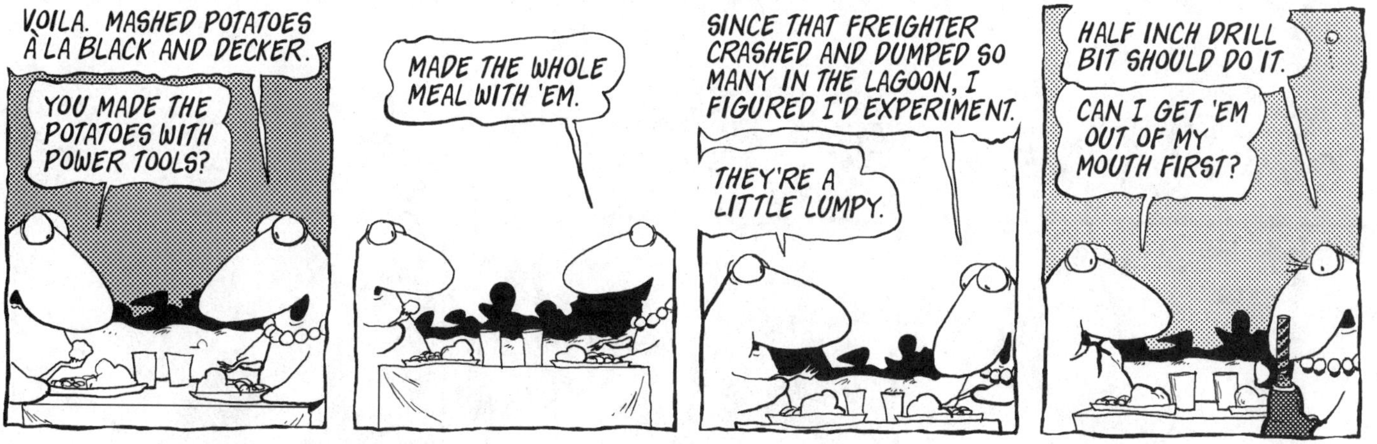
VOILA. MASHED POTATOES À LA BLACK AND DECKER.
YOU MADE THE POTATOES WITH POWER TOOLS?
MADE THE WHOLE MEAL WITH 'EM.
SINCE THAT FREIGHTER CRASHED AND DUMPED SO MANY IN THE LAGOON, I FIGURED I'D EXPERIMENT.
THEY'RE A LITTLE LUMPY.
HALF INCH DRILL BIT SHOULD DO IT.
CAN I GET 'EM OUT OF MY MOUTH FIRST?

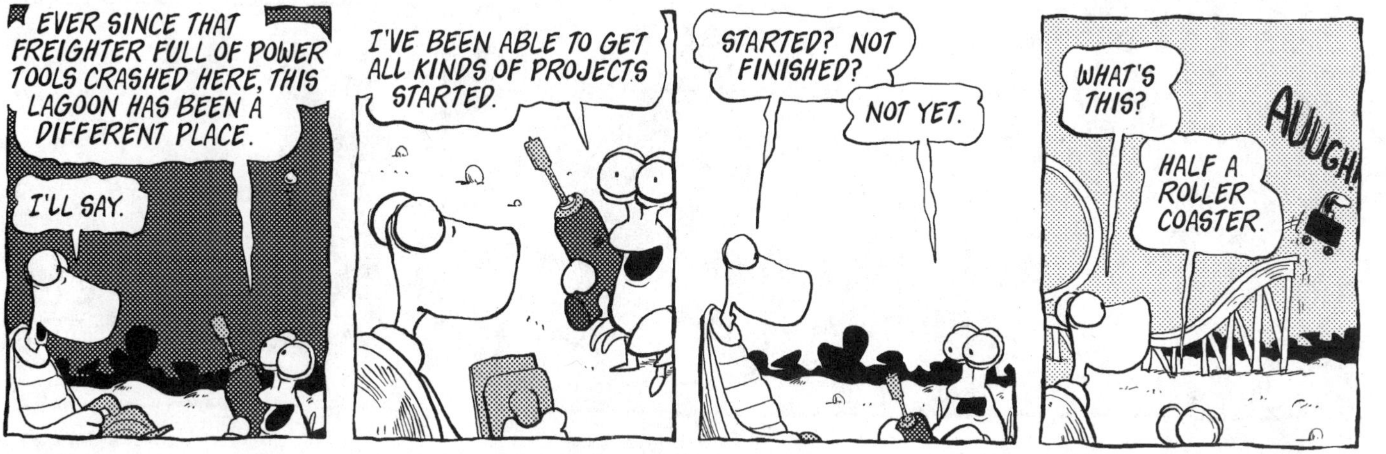
EVER SINCE THAT FREIGHTER FULL OF POWER TOOLS CRASHED HERE, THIS LAGOON HAS BEEN A DIFFERENT PLACE.
I'LL SAY.
I'VE BEEN ABLE TO GET ALL KINDS OF PROJECTS STARTED.
STARTED? NOT FINISHED?
NOT YET.
WHAT'S THIS?
HALF A ROLLER COASTER.
AUUGH!

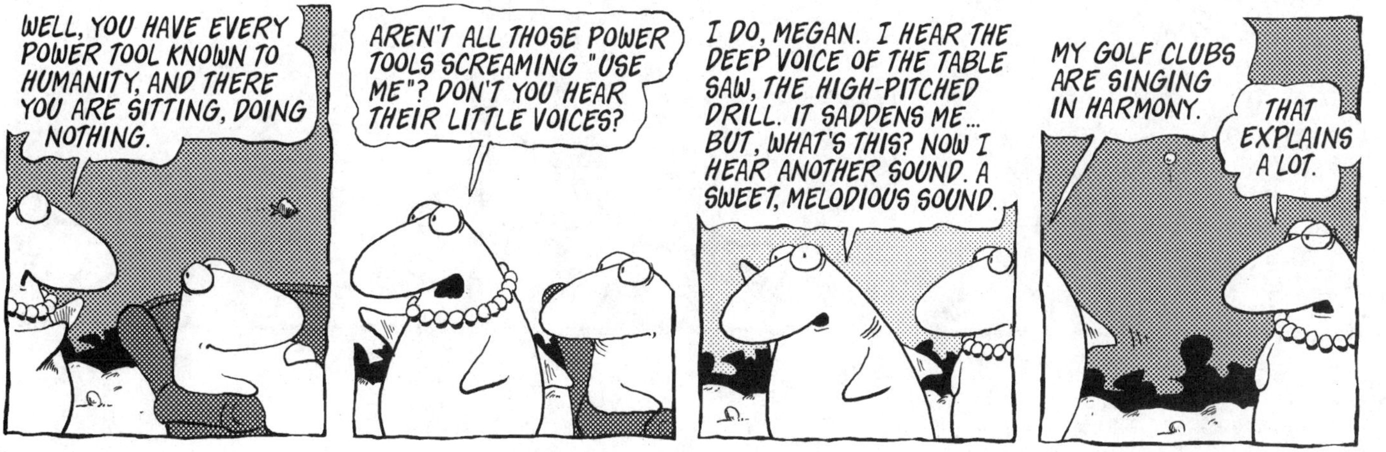
WELL, YOU HAVE EVERY POWER TOOL KNOWN TO HUMANITY, AND THERE YOU ARE SITTING, DOING NOTHING.
AREN'T ALL THOSE POWER TOOLS SCREAMING "USE ME"? DON'T YOU HEAR THEIR LITTLE VOICES?
I DO, MEGAN. I HEAR THE DEEP VOICE OF THE TABLE SAW, THE HIGH-PITCHED DRILL. IT SADDENS ME... BUT, WHAT'S THIS? NOW I HEAR ANOTHER SOUND. A SWEET, MELODIOUS SOUND.
MY GOLF CLUBS ARE SINGING IN HARMONY.
THAT EXPLAINS A LOT.

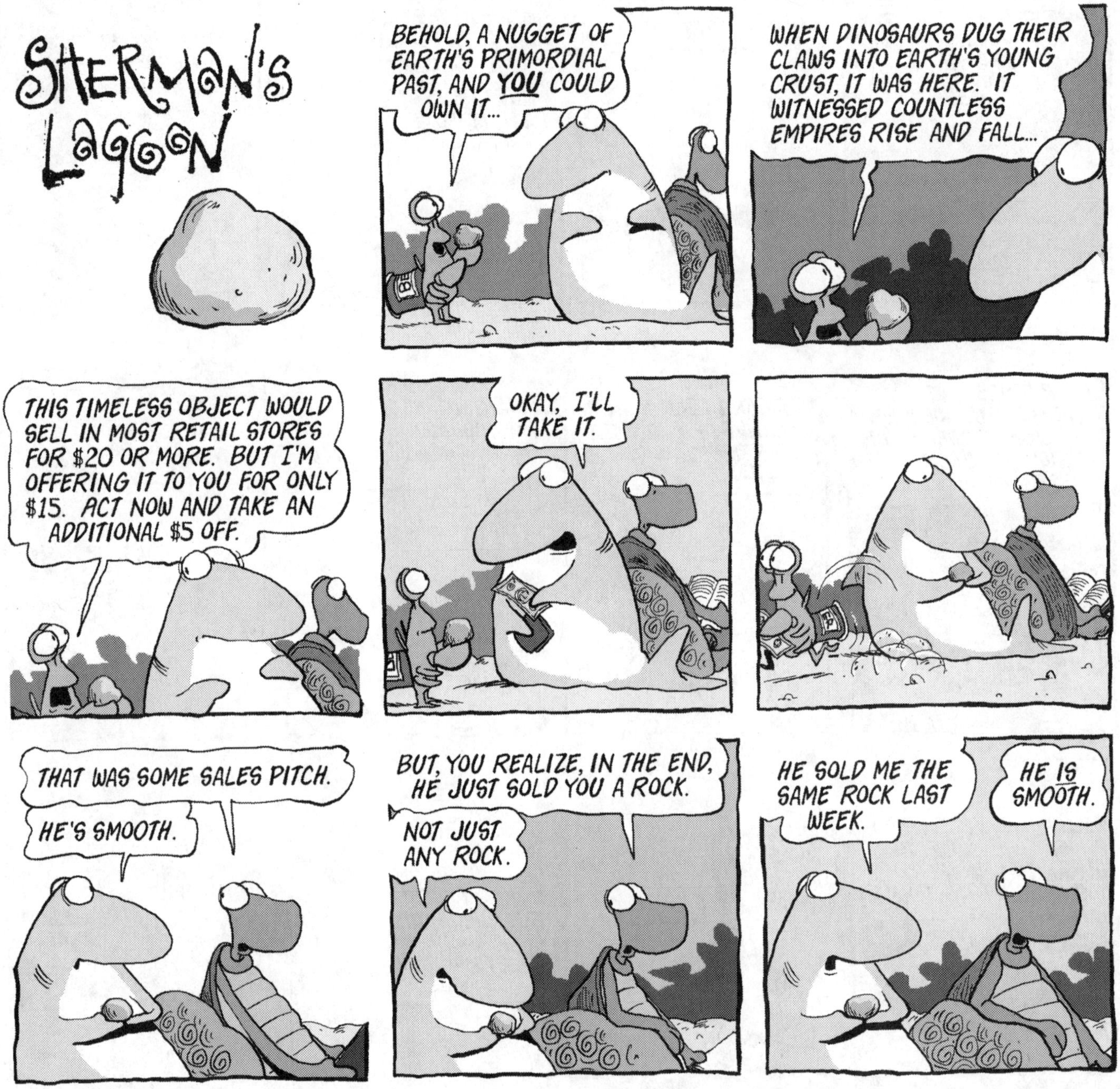
SHERMAN'S LAGOON
BEHOLD, A NUGGET OF EARTH'S PRIMORDIAL PAST, AND YOU COULD OWN IT...
WHEN DINOSAURS DUG THEIR CLAWS INTO EARTH'S YOUNG CRUST, IT WAS HERE. IT WITNESSED COUNTLESS EMPIRES RISE AND FALL...
THIS TIMELESS OBJECT WOULD SELL IN MOST RETAIL STORES FOR $20 OR MORE. BUT I'M OFFERING IT TO YOU FOR ONLY $15. ACT NOW AND TAKE AN ADDITIONAL $5 OFF.
OKAY, I'LL TAKE IT.
THAT WAS SOME SALES PITCH.
HE'S SMOOTH.
BUT, YOU REALIZE, IN THE END, HE JUST SOLD YOU A ROCK.
NOT JUST ANY ROCK.
HE SOLD ME THE SAME ROCK LAST WEEK.
HE IS SMOOTH.

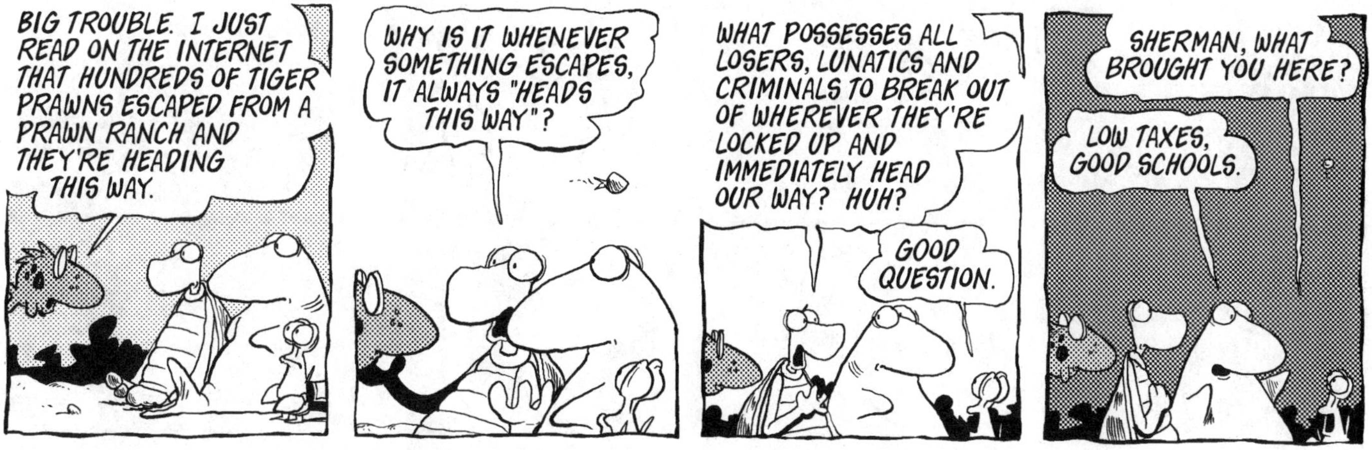
BIG TROUBLE. I JUST READ ON THE INTERNET THAT HUNDREDS OF TIGER PRAWNS ESCAPED FROM A PRAWN RANCH AND THEY'RE HEADING THIS WAY.
WHY IS IT WHENEVER SOMETHING ESCAPES, IT ALWAYS "HEADS THIS WAY"?
WHAT POSSESSES ALL LOSERS, LUNATICS AND CRIMINALS TO BREAK OUT OF WHEREVER THEY'RE LOCKED UP AND IMMEDIATELY HEAD OUR WAY? HUH?
GOOD QUESTION.
SHERMAN, WHAT BROUGHT YOU HERE?
LOW TAXES, GOOD SCHOOLS.

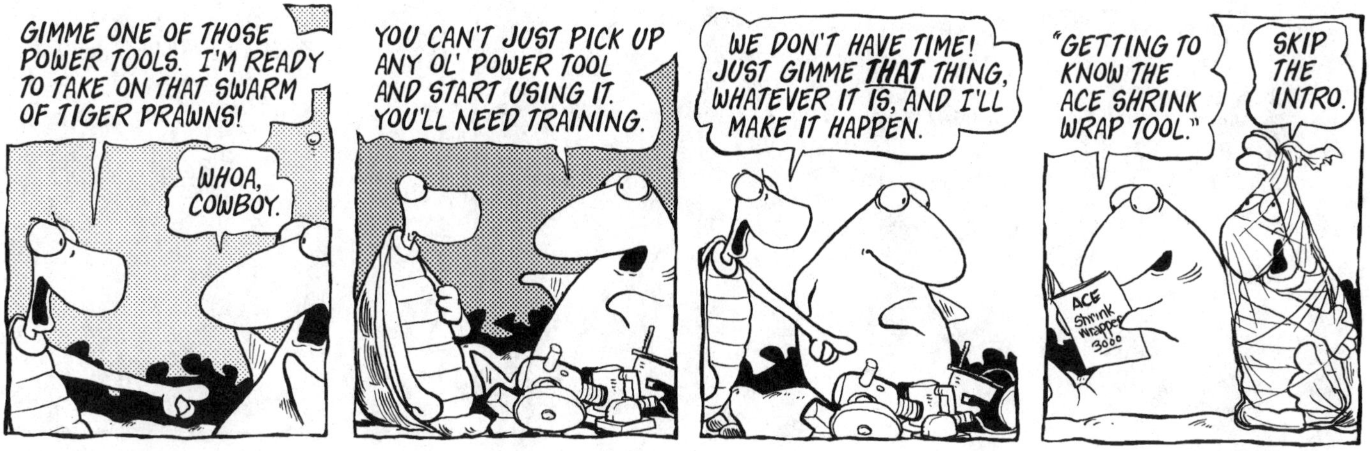
GIMME ONE OF THOSE POWER TOOLS. I'M READY TO TAKE ON THAT SWARM OF TIGER PRAWNS!
WHOA, COWBOY.
YOU CAN'T JUST PICK UP ANY OL' POWER TOOL AND START USING IT. YOU'LL NEED TRAINING.
WE DON'T HAVE TIME! JUST GIMME THAT THING, WHATEVER IT IS, AND I'LL MAKE IT HAPPEN.
"GETTING TO KNOW THE ACE SHRINK WRAP TOOL."
SKIP THE INTRO.
ACE Shrink Wrapper 3000

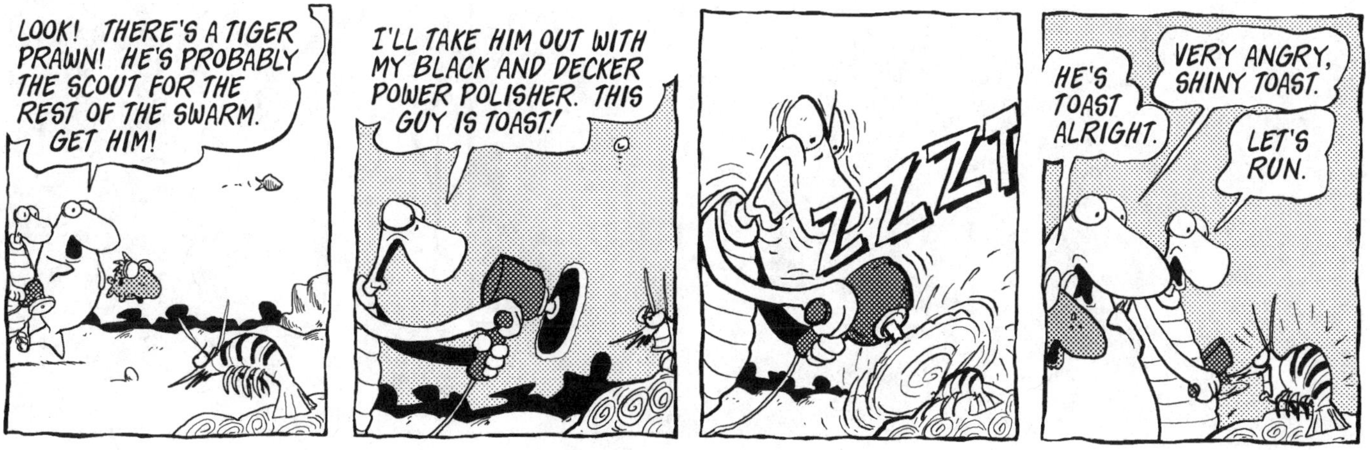
LOOK! THERE'S A TIGER PRAWN! HE'S PROBABLY THE SCOUT FOR THE REST OF THE SWARM. GET HIM!
I'LL TAKE HIM OUT WITH MY BLACK AND DECKER POWER POLISHER. THIS GUY IS TOAST!
ZZZZT
HE'S TOAST ALRIGHT.
VERY ANGRY, SHINY TOAST.
LET'S RUN.

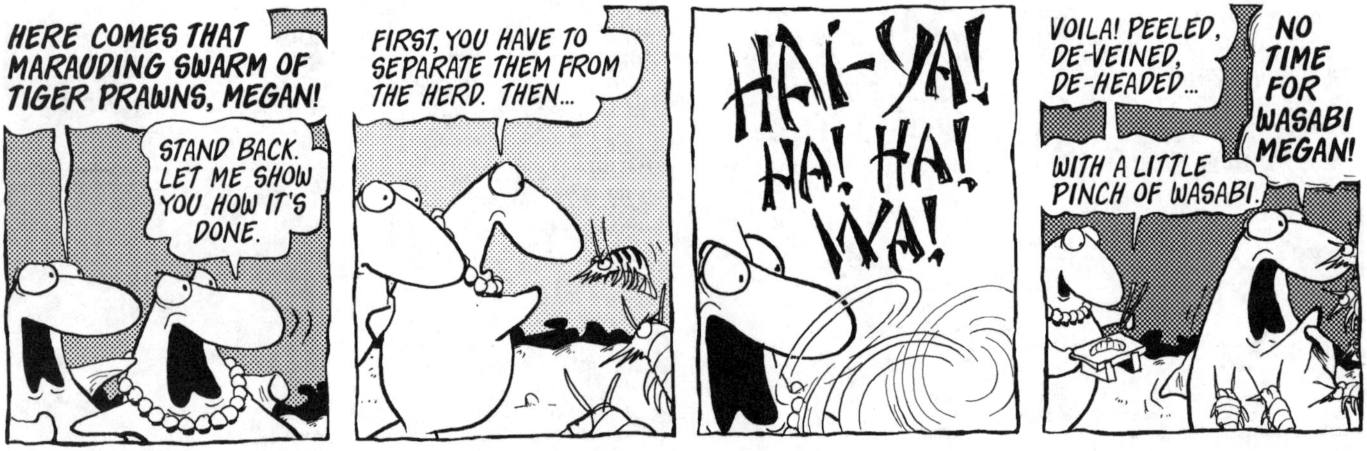
HERE COMES THAT MARAUDING SWARM OF TIGER PRAWNS, MEGAN!
STAND BACK. LET ME SHOW YOU HOW IT'S DONE.
FIRST, YOU HAVE TO SEPARATE THEM FROM THE HERD. THEN...
HAI-YA! HA! HA! WA!
VOILA! PEELED, DE-VEINED, DE-HEADED...
WITH A LITTLE PINCH OF WASABI.
NO TIME FOR WASABI MEGAN!

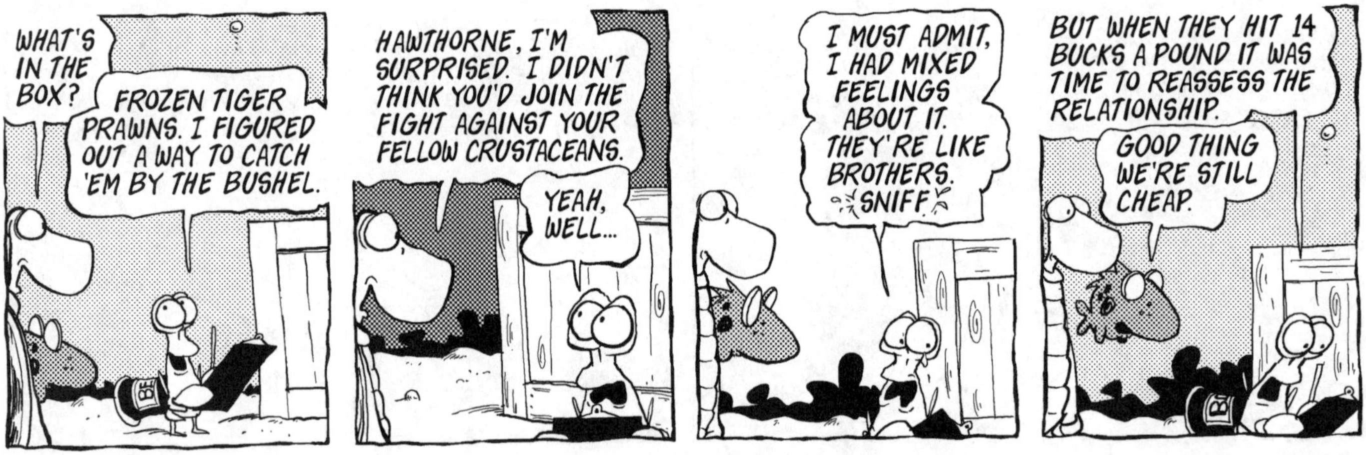
WHAT'S IN THE BOX?
FROZEN TIGER PRAWNS. I FIGURED OUT A WAY TO CATCH 'EM BY THE BUSHEL.
HAWTHORNE, I'M SURPRISED. I DIDN'T THINK YOU'D JOIN THE FIGHT AGAINST YOUR FELLOW CRUSTACEANS.
YEAH, WELL...
I MUST ADMIT, I HAD MIXED FEELINGS ABOUT IT. THEY'RE LIKE BROTHERS. SNIFF
BUT WHEN THEY HIT 14 BUCKS A POUND IT WAS TIME TO REASSESS THE RELATIONSHIP.
GOOD THING WE'RE STILL CHEAP.

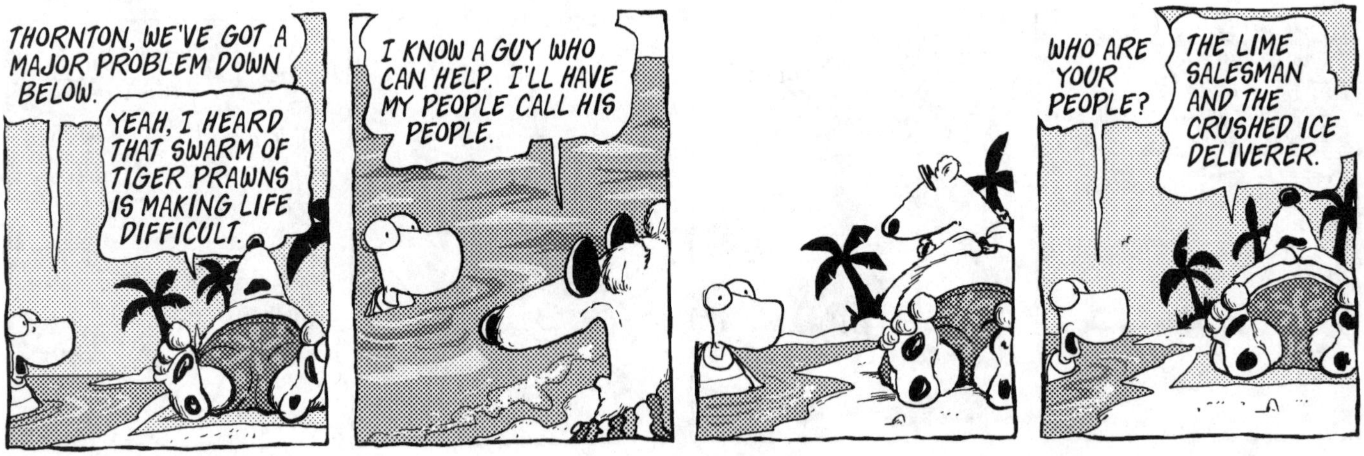
THORNTON, WE'VE GOT A MAJOR PROBLEM DOWN BELOW.
YEAH, I HEARD THAT SWARM OF TIGER PRAWNS IS MAKING LIFE DIFFICULT.
I KNOW A GUY WHO CAN HELP. I'LL HAVE MY PEOPLE CALL HIS PEOPLE.
WHO ARE YOUR PEOPLE?
THE LIME SALESMAN AND THE CRUSHED ICE DELIVERER.

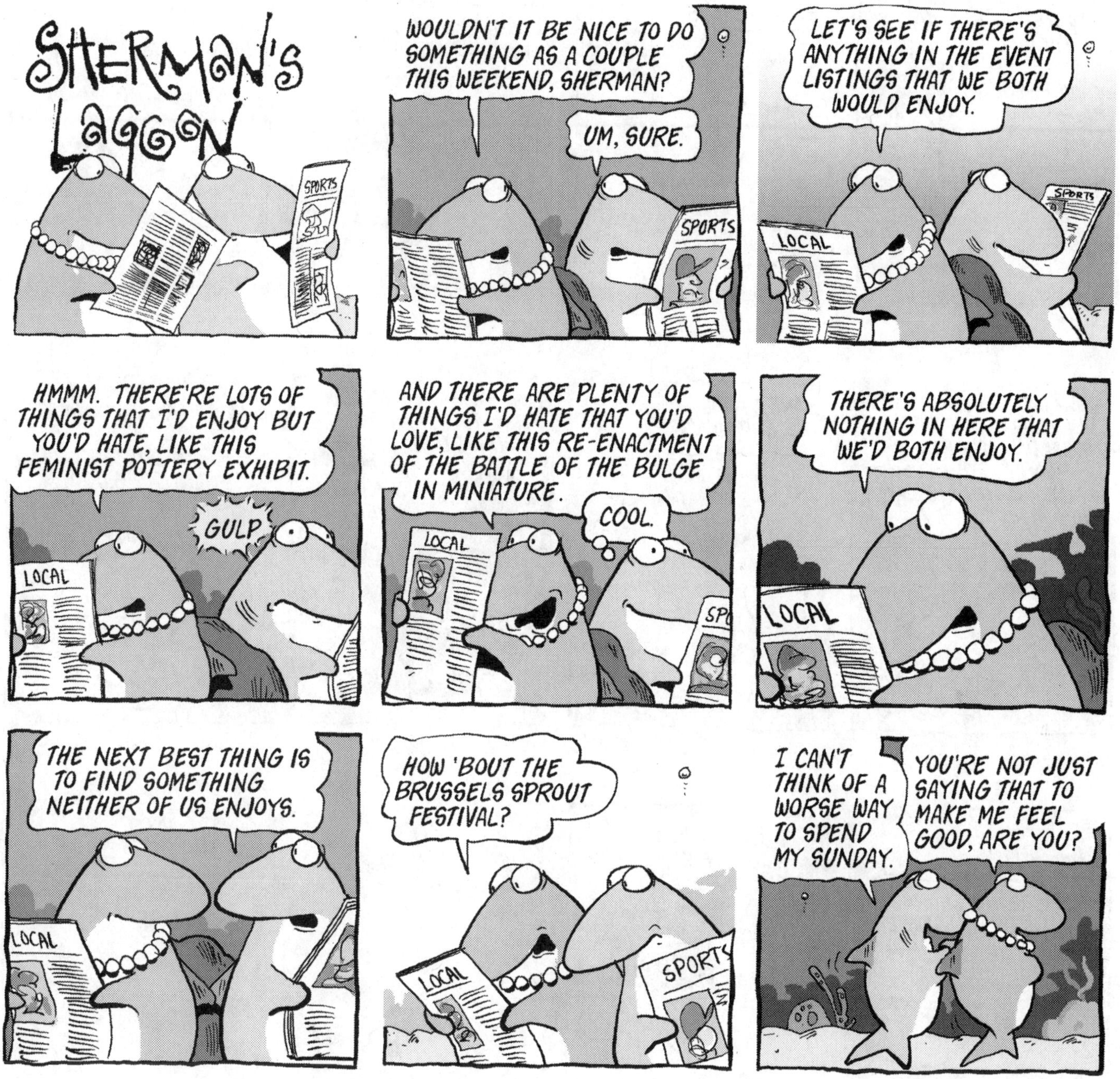
SHERMAN'S LAGOON
SPORTS
WOULDN'T IT BE NICE TO DO SOMETHING AS A COUPLE THIS WEEKEND, SHERMAN?
UM, SURE.
SPORTS
LET'S SEE IF THERE'S ANYTHING IN THE EVENT LISTINGS THAT WE BOTH WOULD ENJOY.
LOCAL
SPORTS
HMMM. THERE'RE LOTS OF THINGS THAT I'D ENJOY BUT YOU'D HATE, LIKE THIS FEMINIST POTTERY EXHIBIT.
GULP
LOCAL
AND THERE ARE PLENTY OF THINGS I'D HATE THAT YOU'D LOVE, LIKE THIS RE-ENACTMENT OF THE BATTLE OF THE BULGE IN MINIATURE.
COOL.
LOCAL
THERE'S ABSOLUTELY NOTHING IN HERE THAT WE'D BOTH ENJOY.
LOCAL
THE NEXT BEST THING IS TO FIND SOMETHING NEITHER OF US ENJOYS.
LOCAL
HOW 'BOUT THE BRUSSELS SPROUT FESTIVAL?
LOCAL
SPORTS
I CAN'T THINK OF A WORSE WAY TO SPEND MY SUNDAY.
YOU'RE NOT JUST SAYING THAT TO MAKE ME FEEL GOOD, ARE YOU?

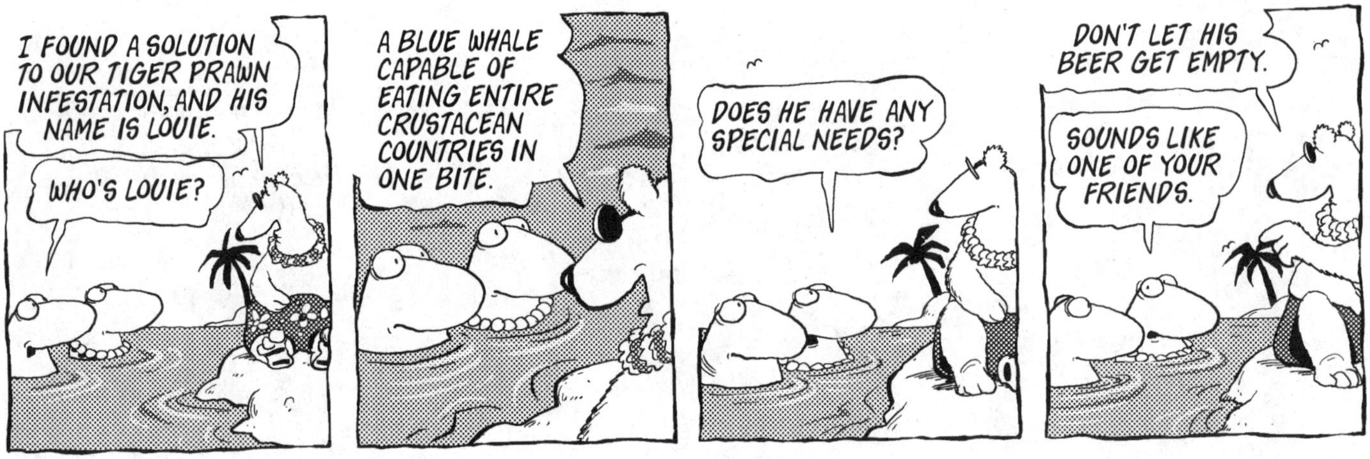
I FOUND A SOLUTION TO OUR TIGER PRAWN INFESTATION, AND HIS NAME IS LOUIE.
WHO'S LOUIE?
A BLUE WHALE CAPABLE OF EATING ENTIRE CRUSTACEAN COUNTRIES IN ONE BITE.
DOES HE HAVE ANY SPECIAL NEEDS?
DON'T LET HIS BEER GET EMPTY.
SOUNDS LIKE ONE OF YOUR FRIENDS.

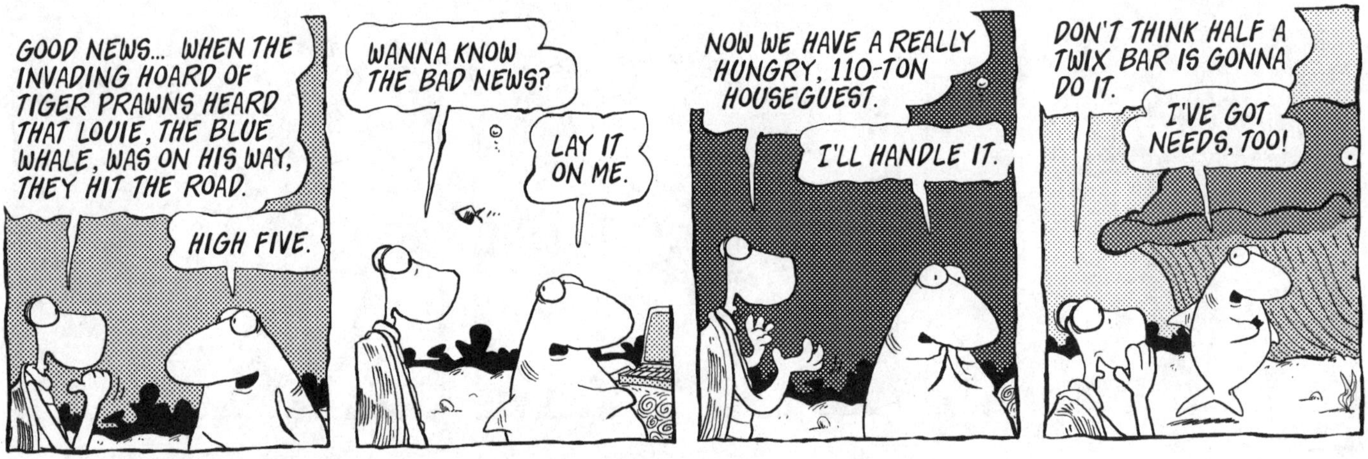
GOOD NEWS... WHEN THE INVADING HOARD OF TIGER PRAWNS HEARD THAT LOUIE, THE BLUE WHALE, WAS ON HIS WAY, THEY HIT THE ROAD.
HIGH FIVE.
WANNA KNOW THE BAD NEWS?
LAY IT ON ME.
NOW WE HAVE A REALLY HUNGRY, 110-TON HOUSEGUEST.
I'LL HANDLE IT.
DON'T THINK HALF A TWIX BAR IS GONNA DO IT.
I'VE GOT NEEDS, TOO!

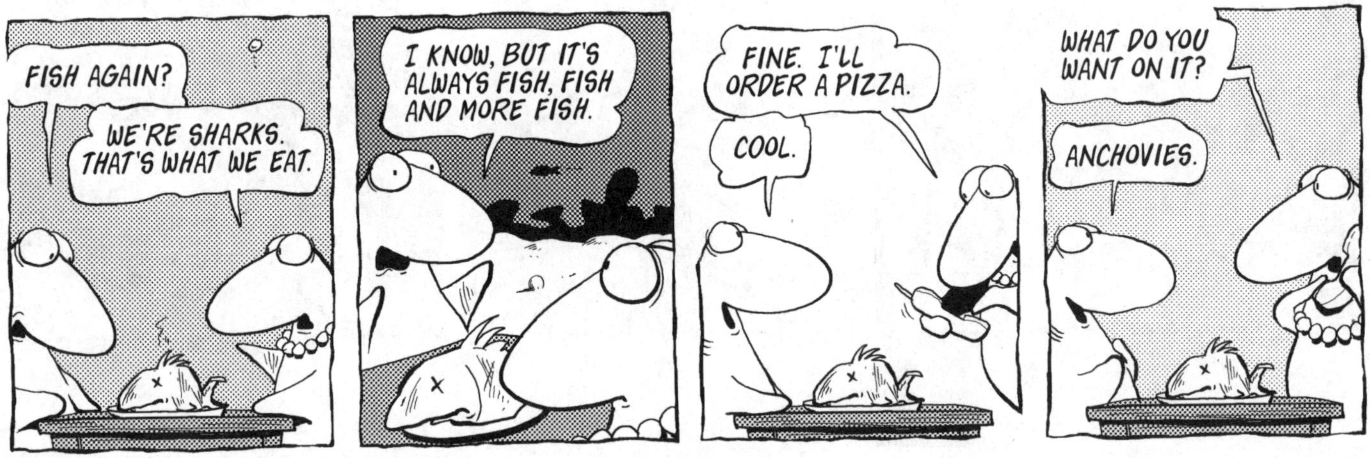
FISH AGAIN?
WE'RE SHARKS. THAT'S WHAT WE EAT.
I KNOW, BUT IT'S ALWAYS FISH, FISH AND MORE FISH.
FINE. I'LL ORDER A PIZZA.
COOL.
WHAT DO YOU WANT ON IT?
ANCHOVIES.

YA KNOW, I WAS THINKING ABOUT OUR CONVERSATION YESTERDAY.
YEAH.
IT'S NOT JUST OUR DINNER CHOICES THAT ARE LIMITED BECAUSE WE'RE SHARKS. IT'S EVERYTHING.
HUMANS HAVE IT MADE. THEY HAVE ALL KINDS OF FUN CHOICES AND ACTIVITIES TO CHOOSE FROM.
JUST ONCE I'D LIKE TO HAVE NAILS I COULD GET MANICURED.
NAILS. YEAH. THINK OF THE SCRATCHING POSSIBILITIES.
KAHUNA, CAN YOU USE YOUR MAGICAL POWERS TO CHANGE US INTO HUMANS?
KAHUNA CAN. BUT TRANSMOGRIFICATION IS VERY SERIOUS UNDERTAKING.
KAHUNA NOT TAKE LIGHTLY, NOR CHANGE THINGS ON WHIM.
LAST WEEK YOU CHANGED ME INTO A Q-TIP!
KAHUNA HAVE EAR WAX.
ARE YOU READY TO BE TRANSFORMED INTO HUMANS?
READY.
DO IT.
POOF!
WHOA NELLY! CHECK IT OUT, MEGAN! WE'RE HUMANS!
BUT APPARENTLY YOUR BELT DIDN'T MAKE IT THROUGH.
GOOD THING I WORE BOXERS.

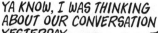

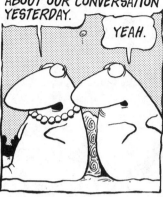

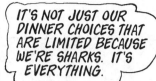

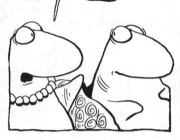

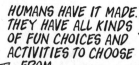

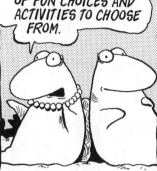

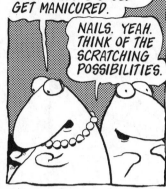

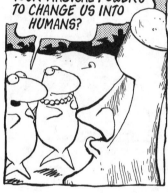

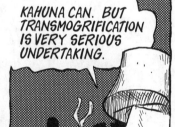

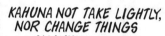

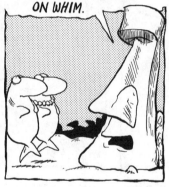

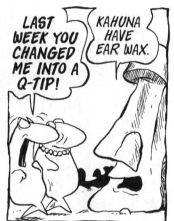

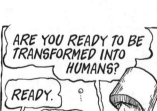

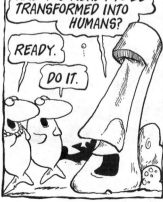

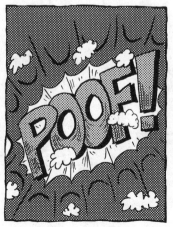

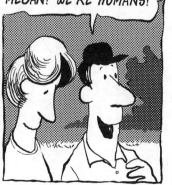

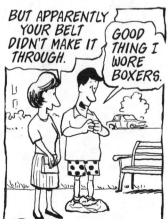

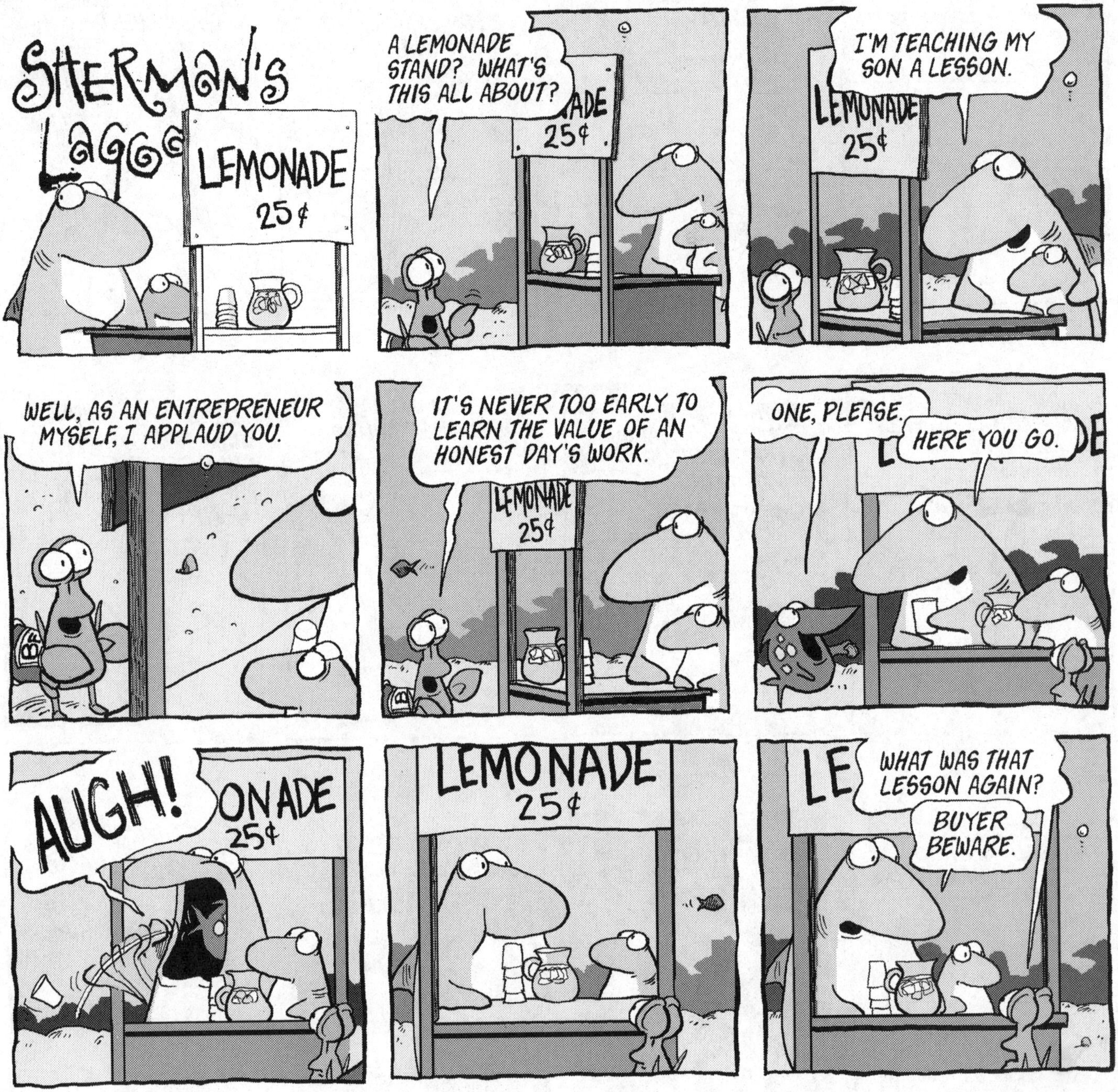
SHERMAN'S LAGOON
LEMONADE
25¢
A LEMONADE STAND? WHAT'S THIS ALL ABOUT?
I'M TEACHING MY SON A LESSON.
WELL, AS AN ENTREPRENEUR MYSELF, I APPLAUD YOU.
IT'S NEVER TOO EARLY TO LEARN THE VALUE OF AN HONEST DAY'S WORK.
ONE, PLEASE.
HERE YOU GO.
AUGH!
LEMONADE
25¢
WHAT WAS THAT LESSON AGAIN?
BUYER BEWARE.

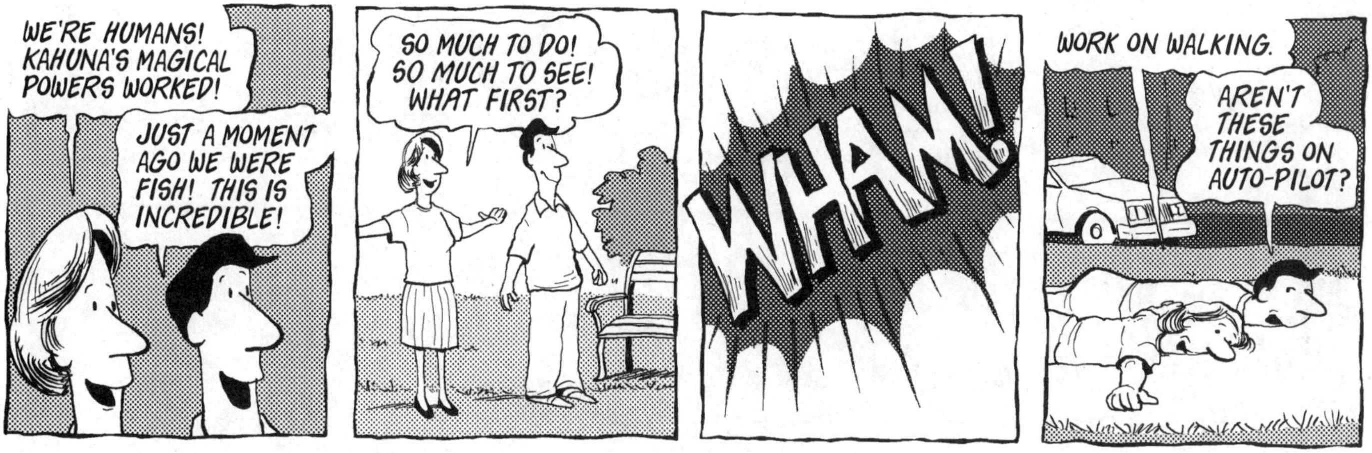
WE'RE HUMANS! KAHUNA'S MAGICAL POWERS WORKED!
JUST A MOMENT AGO WE WERE FISH! THIS IS INCREDIBLE!
SO MUCH TO DO! SO MUCH TO SEE! WHAT FIRST?
WHAM!
WORK ON WALKING.
AREN'T THESE THINGS ON AUTO-PILOT?

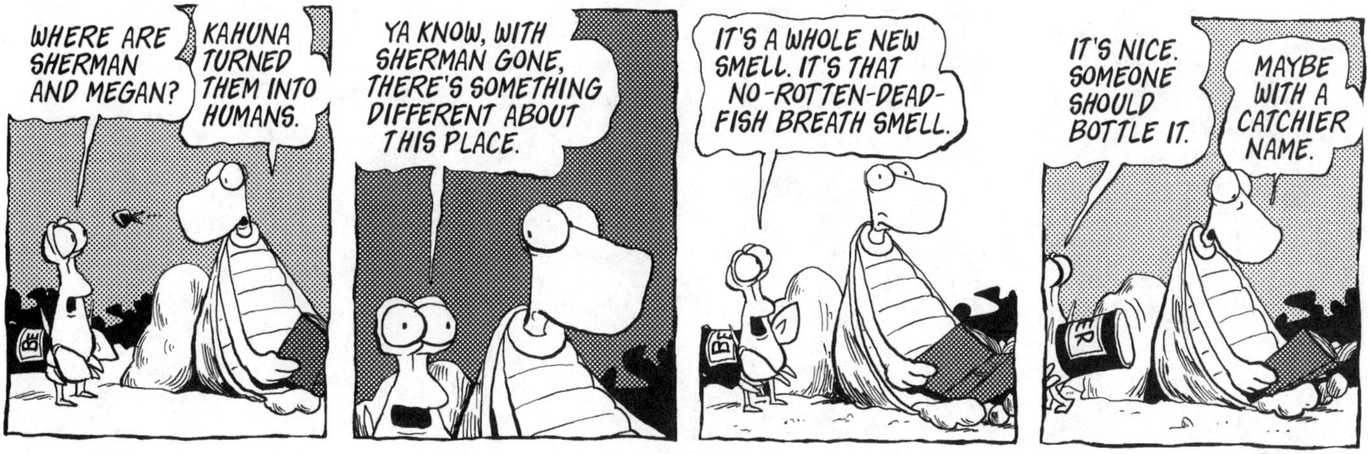
WHERE ARE SHERMAN AND MEGAN?
KAHUNA TURNED THEM INTO HUMANS.
YA KNOW, WITH SHERMAN GONE, THERE'S SOMETHING DIFFERENT ABOUT THIS PLACE.
IT'S A WHOLE NEW SMELL. IT'S THAT NO-ROTTEN-DEAD-FISH BREATH SMELL.
IT'S NICE. SOMEONE SHOULD BOTTLE IT.
MAYBE WITH A CATCHIER NAME.

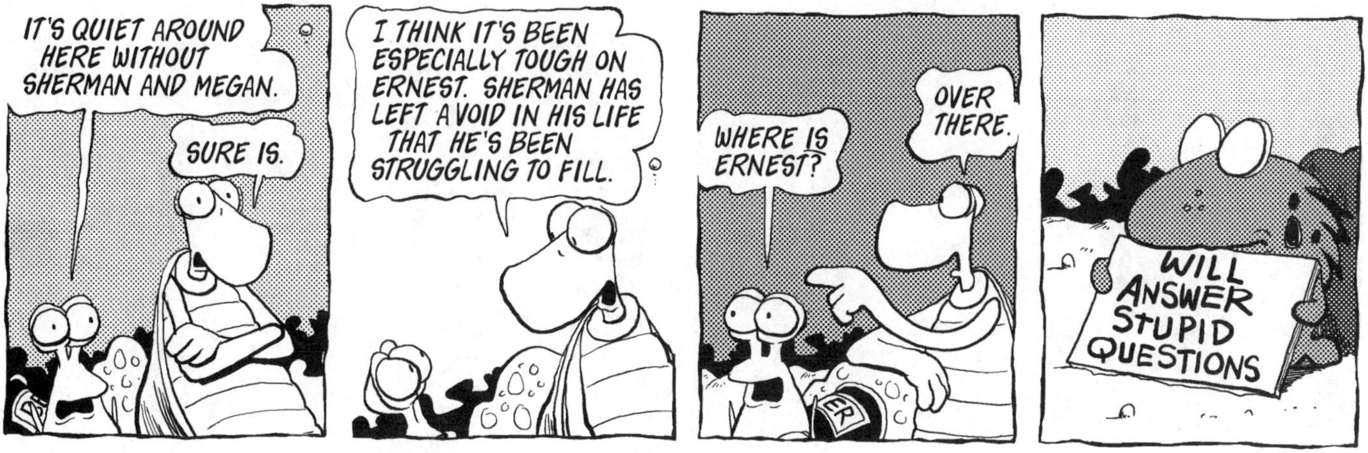
IT'S QUIET AROUND HERE WITHOUT SHERMAN AND MEGAN.
SURE IS.
I THINK IT'S BEEN ESPECIALLY TOUGH ON ERNEST. SHERMAN HAS LEFT A VOID IN HIS LIFE THAT HE'S BEEN STRUGGLING TO FILL.
WHERE IS ERNEST?
OVER THERE.
WILL ANSWER STUPID QUESTIONS

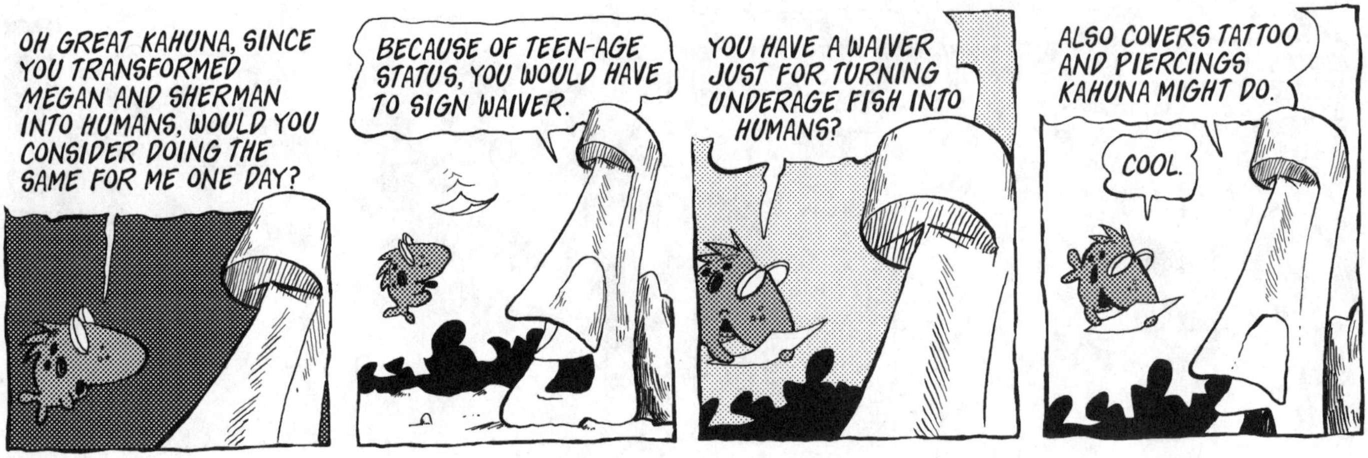

OH GREAT KAHUNA, SINCE YOU TRANSFORMED MEGAN AND SHERMAN INTO HUMANS, WOULD YOU CONSIDER DOING THE SAME FOR ME ONE DAY?
BECAUSE OF TEEN-AGE STATUS, YOU WOULD HAVE TO SIGN WAIVER.
YOU HAVE A WAIVER JUST FOR TURNING UNDERAGE FISH INTO HUMANS?
ALSO COVERS TATTOO AND PIERCINGS KAHUNA MIGHT DO.
COOL.

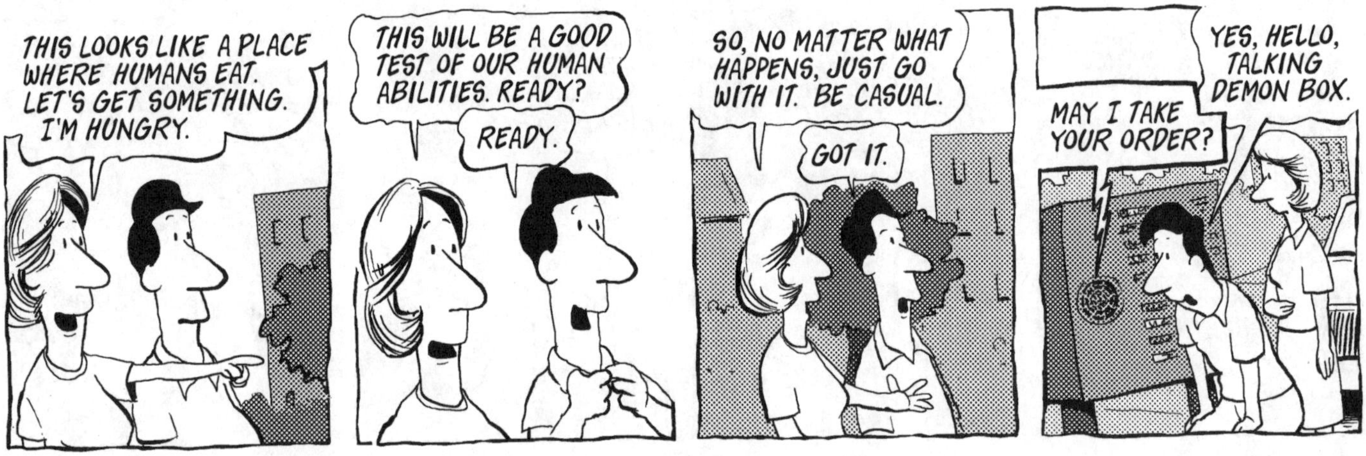

THIS LOOKS LIKE A PLACE WHERE HUMANS EAT. LET'S GET SOMETHING. I'M HUNGRY.
THIS WILL BE A GOOD TEST OF OUR HUMAN ABILITIES. READY?
READY.
SO, NO MATTER WHAT HAPPENS, JUST GO WITH IT. BE CASUAL.
GOT IT.
MAY I TAKE YOUR ORDER?
YES, HELLO, TALKING DEMON BOX.

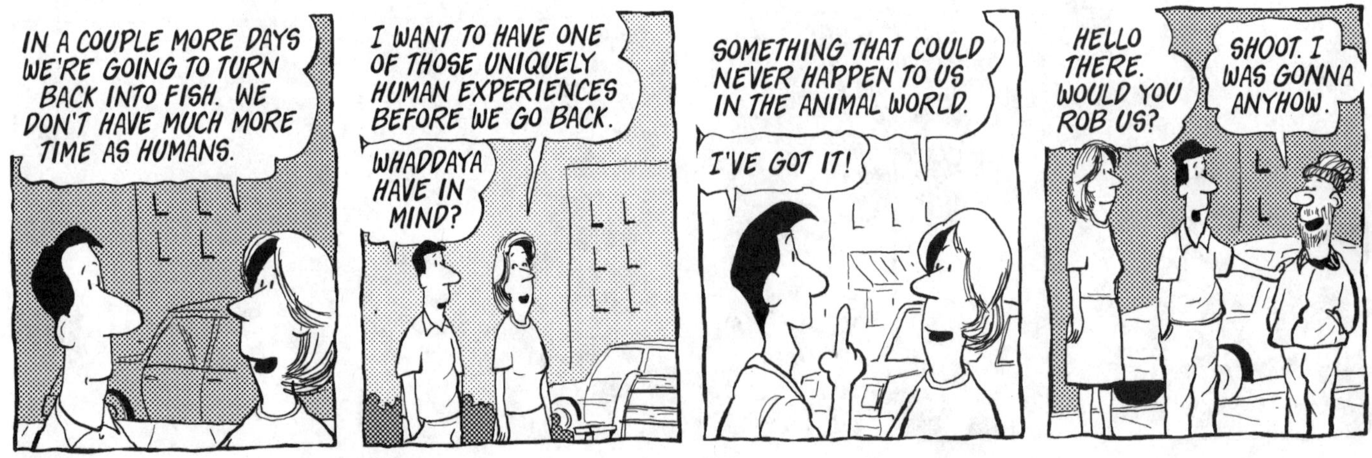

IN A COUPLE MORE DAYS WE'RE GOING TO TURN BACK INTO FISH. WE DON'T HAVE MUCH MORE TIME AS HUMANS.
I WANT TO HAVE ONE OF THOSE UNIQUELY HUMAN EXPERIENCES BEFORE WE GO BACK.
WHADDAYA HAVE IN MIND?
SOMETHING THAT COULD NEVER HAPPEN TO US IN THE ANIMAL WORLD.
I'VE GOT IT!
HELLO THERE. WOULD YOU ROB US?
SHOOT. I WAS GONNA ANYHOW.

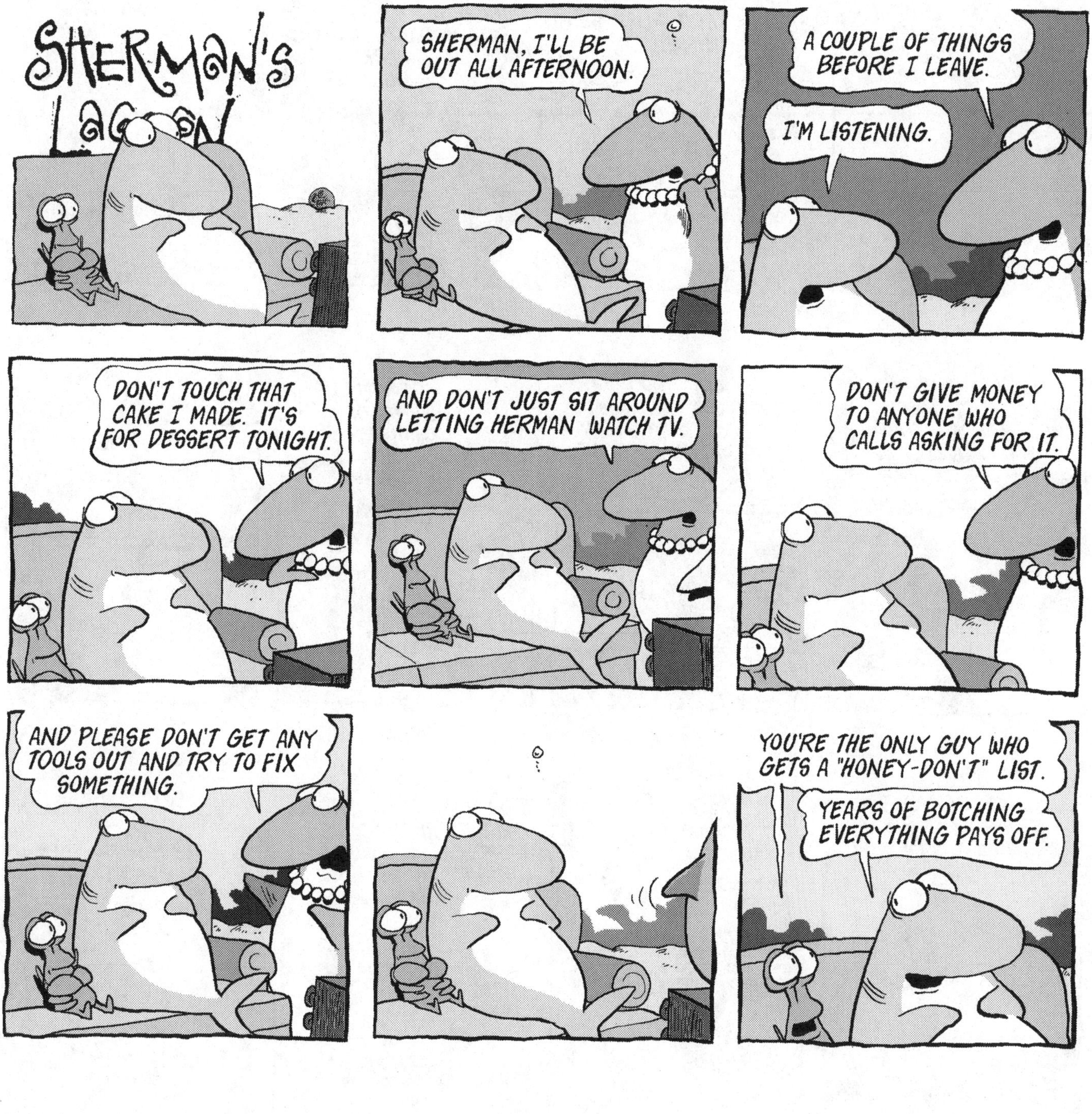
SHERMAN'S LAGOON
SHERMAN, I'LL BE OUT ALL AFTERNOON.
A COUPLE OF THINGS BEFORE I LEAVE.
I'M LISTENING.
DON'T TOUCH THAT CAKE I MADE. IT'S FOR DESSERT TONIGHT.
AND DON'T JUST SIT AROUND LETTING HERMAN WATCH TV.
DON'T GIVE MONEY TO ANYONE WHO CALLS ASKING FOR IT.
AND PLEASE DON'T GET ANY TOOLS OUT AND TRY TO FIX SOMETHING.
YOU'RE THE ONLY GUY WHO GETS A "HONEY-DON'T" LIST.
YEARS OF BOTCHING EVERYTHING PAYS OFF.

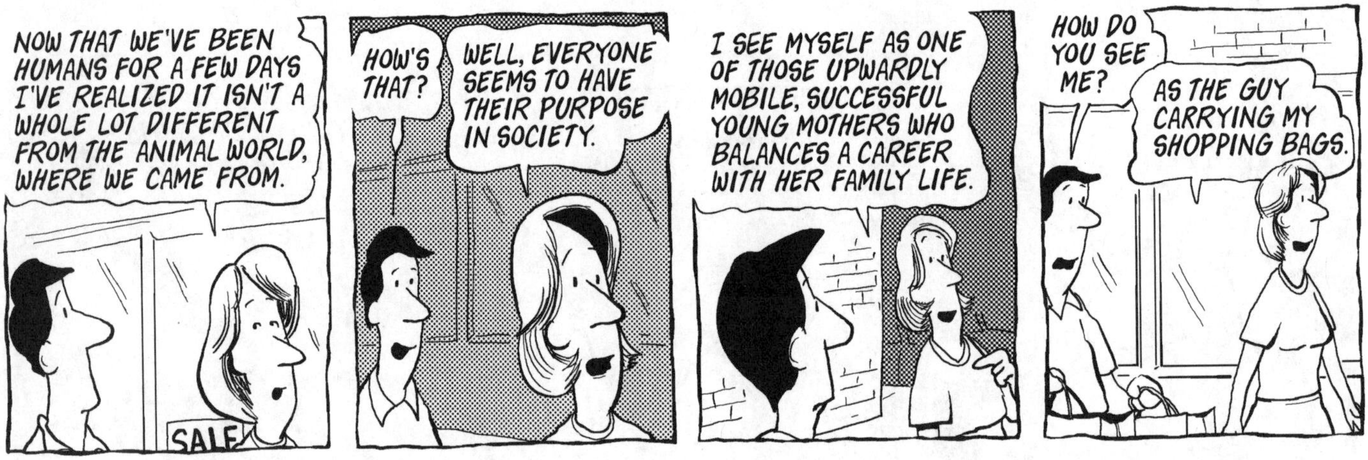
NOW THAT WE'VE BEEN HUMANS FOR A FEW DAYS I'VE REALIZED IT ISN'T A WHOLE LOT DIFFERENT FROM THE ANIMAL WORLD, WHERE WE CAME FROM.
SALE
HOW'S THAT?
WELL, EVERYONE SEEMS TO HAVE THEIR PURPOSE IN SOCIETY.
I SEE MYSELF AS ONE OF THOSE UPWARDLY MOBILE, SUCCESSFUL YOUNG MOTHERS WHO BALANCES A CAREER WITH HER FAMILY LIFE.
HOW DO YOU SEE ME?
AS THE GUY CARRYING MY SHOPPING BAGS.

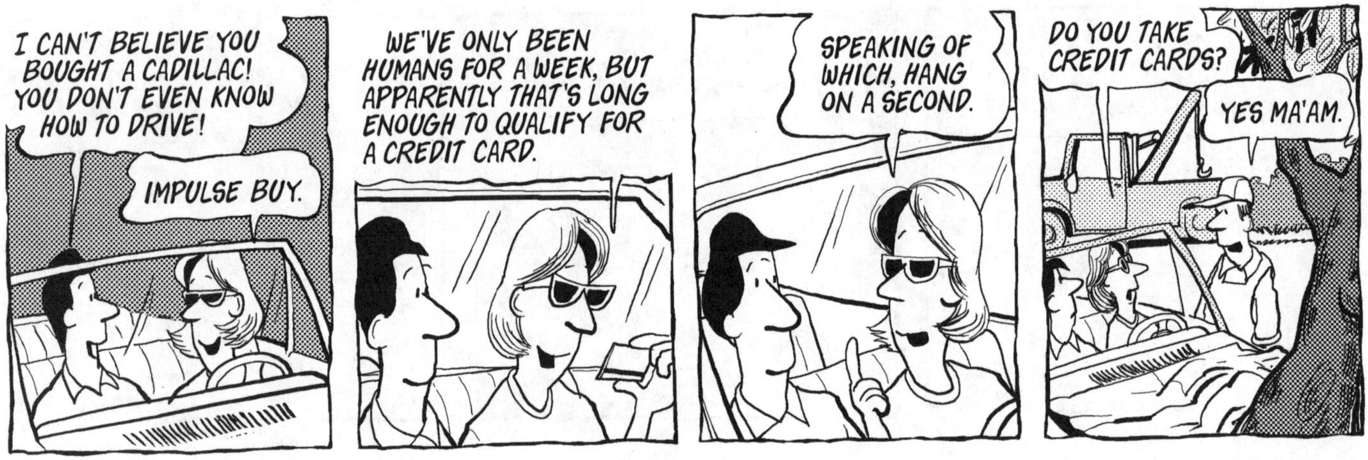
I CAN'T BELIEVE YOU BOUGHT A CADILLAC! YOU DON'T EVEN KNOW HOW TO DRIVE!
IMPULSE BUY.
WE'VE ONLY BEEN HUMANS FOR A WEEK, BUT APPARENTLY THAT'S LONG ENOUGH TO QUALIFY FOR A CREDIT CARD.
SPEAKING OF WHICH, HANG ON A SECOND.
DO YOU TAKE CREDIT CARDS?
YES MA'AM.

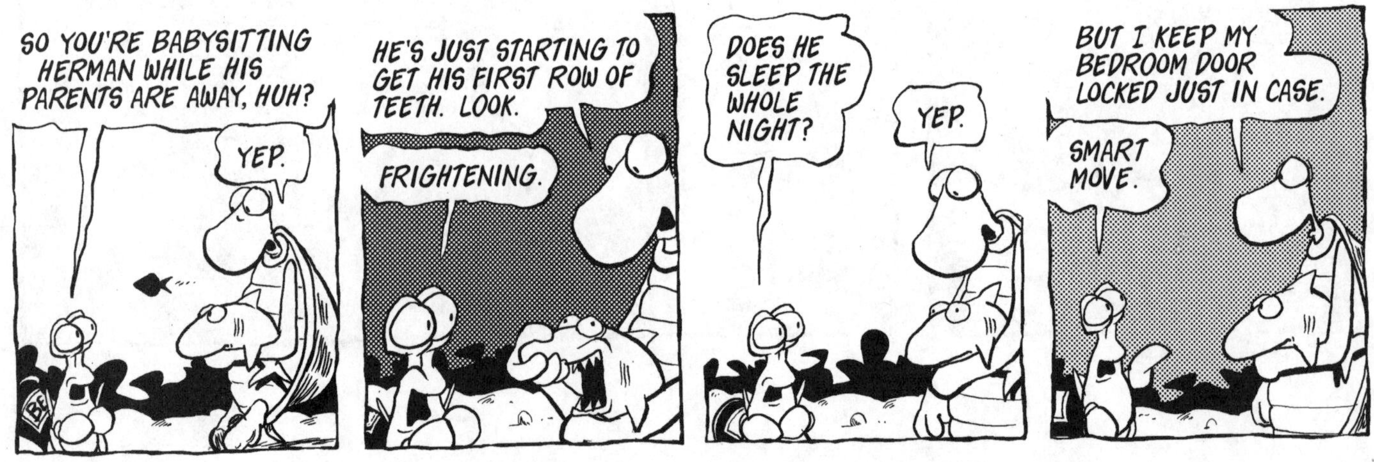
SO YOU'RE BABYSITTING HERMAN WHILE HIS PARENTS ARE AWAY, HUH?
YEP.
HE'S JUST STARTING TO GET HIS FIRST ROW OF TEETH. LOOK.
FRIGHTENING.
DOES HE SLEEP THE WHOLE NIGHT?
YEP.
BUT I KEEP MY BEDROOM DOOR LOCKED JUST IN CASE.
SMART MOVE.

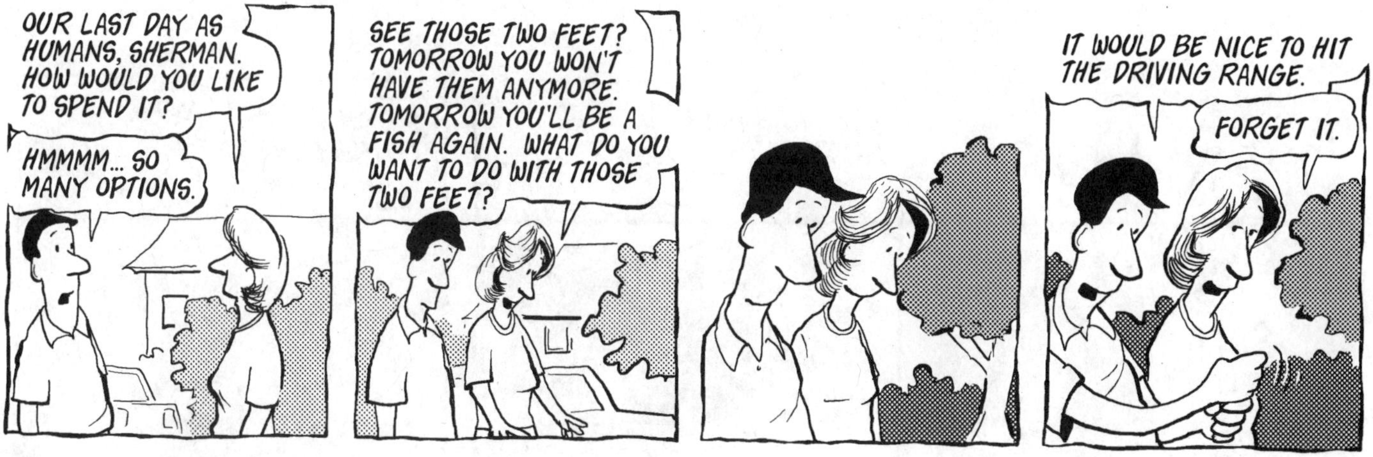
OUR LAST DAY AS HUMANS, SHERMAN. HOW WOULD YOU LIKE TO SPEND IT?
HMMMM... SO MANY OPTIONS.
SEE THOSE TWO FEET? TOMORROW YOU WON'T HAVE THEM ANYMORE. TOMORROW YOU'LL BE A FISH AGAIN. WHAT DO YOU WANT TO DO WITH THOSE TWO FEET?
IT WOULD BE NICE TO HIT THE DRIVING RANGE.
FORGET IT.

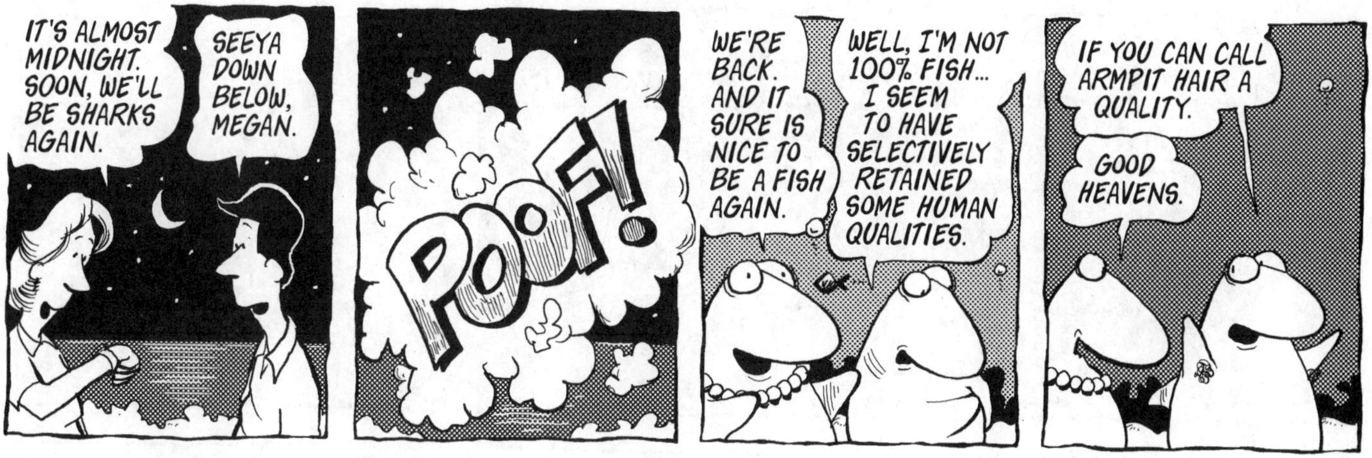
IT'S ALMOST MIDNIGHT. SOON, WE'LL BE SHARKS AGAIN.
SEEYA DOWN BELOW, MEGAN.
POOF!
WE'RE BACK. AND IT SURE IS NICE TO BE A FISH AGAIN.
WELL, I'M NOT 100% FISH... I SEEM TO HAVE SELECTIVELY RETAINED SOME HUMAN QUALITIES.
IF YOU CAN CALL ARMPIT HAIR A QUALITY.
GOOD HEAVENS.

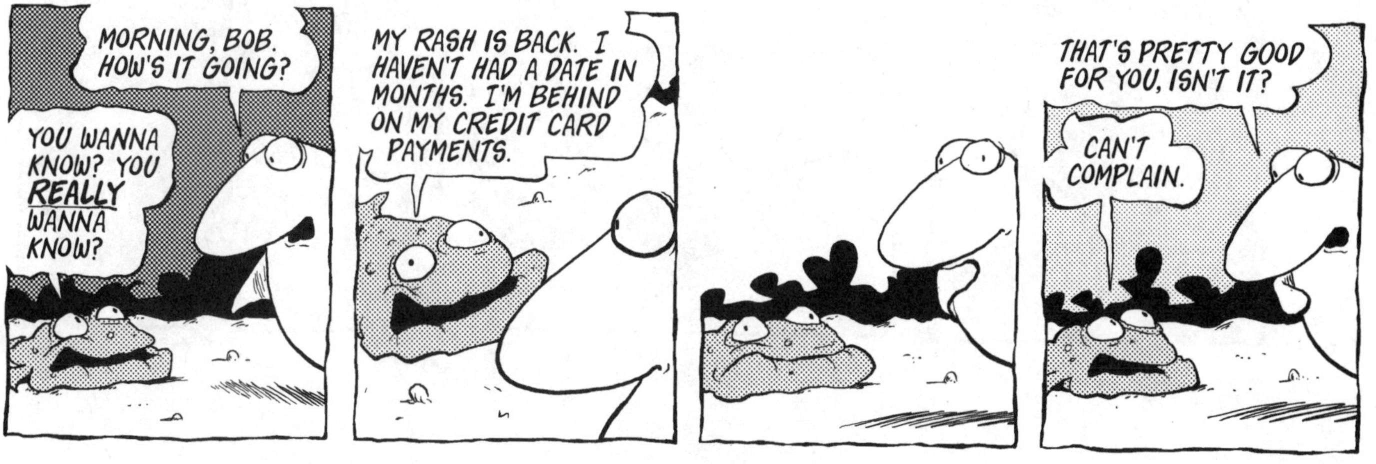
MORNING, BOB. HOW'S IT GOING?
YOU WANNA KNOW? YOU REALLY WANNA KNOW?
MY RASH IS BACK. I HAVEN'T HAD A DATE IN MONTHS. I'M BEHIND ON MY CREDIT CARD PAYMENTS.
THAT'S PRETTY GOOD FOR YOU, ISN'T IT?
CAN'T COMPLAIN.

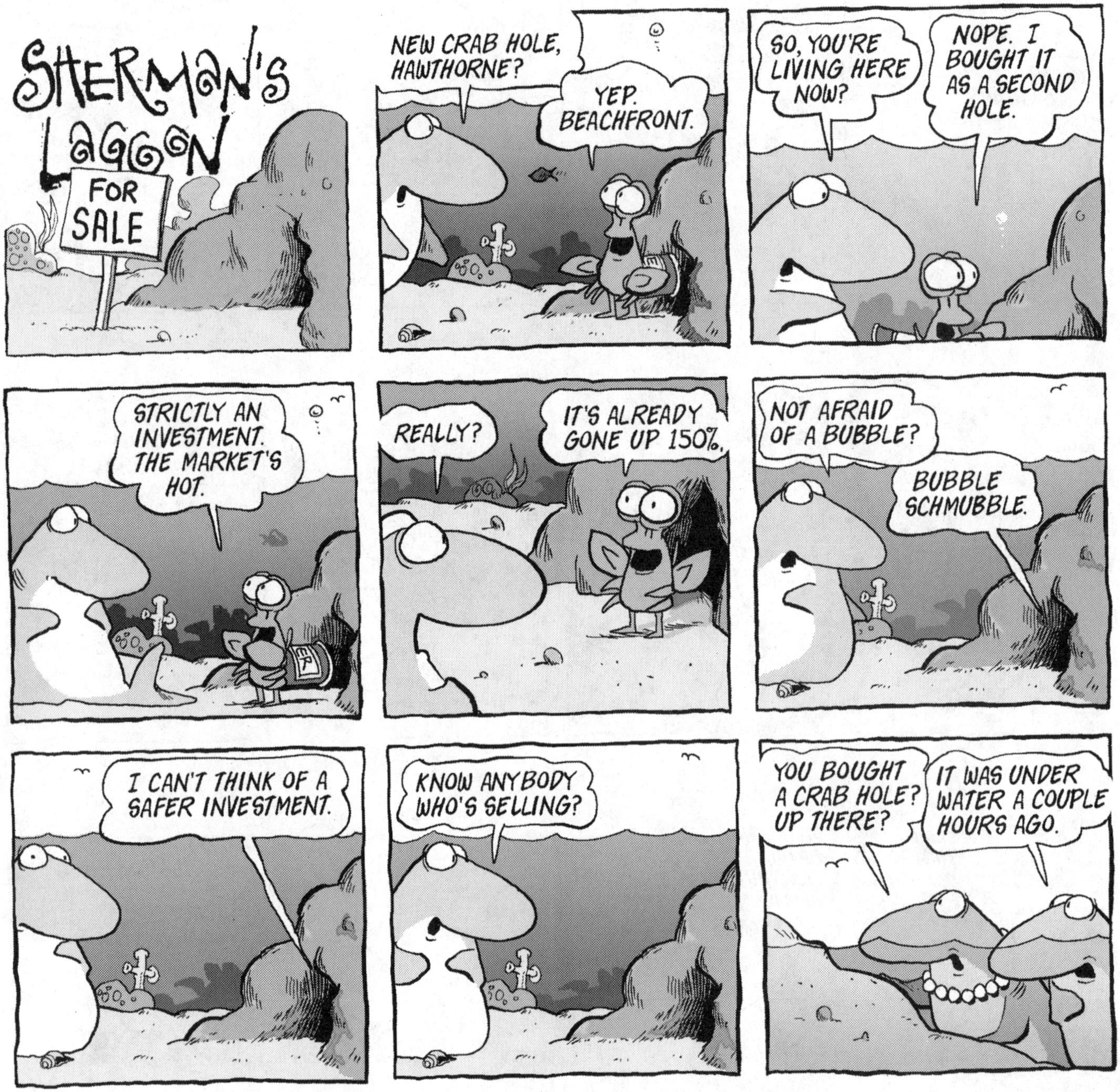
SHERMAN'S LAGOON
FOR SALE
NEW CRAB HOLE, HAWTHORNE?
YEP. BEACHFRONT.
SO, YOU'RE LIVING HERE NOW?
NOPE. I BOUGHT IT AS A SECOND HOLE.
STRICTLY AN INVESTMENT. THE MARKET'S HOT.
REALLY?
IT'S ALREADY GONE UP 150%.
NOT AFRAID OF A BUBBLE?
BUBBLE SCHMUBBLE.
I CAN'T THINK OF A SAFER INVESTMENT.
KNOW ANYBODY WHO'S SELLING?
YOU BOUGHT A CRAB HOLE? UP THERE?
IT WAS UNDER WATER A COUPLE HOURS AGO.

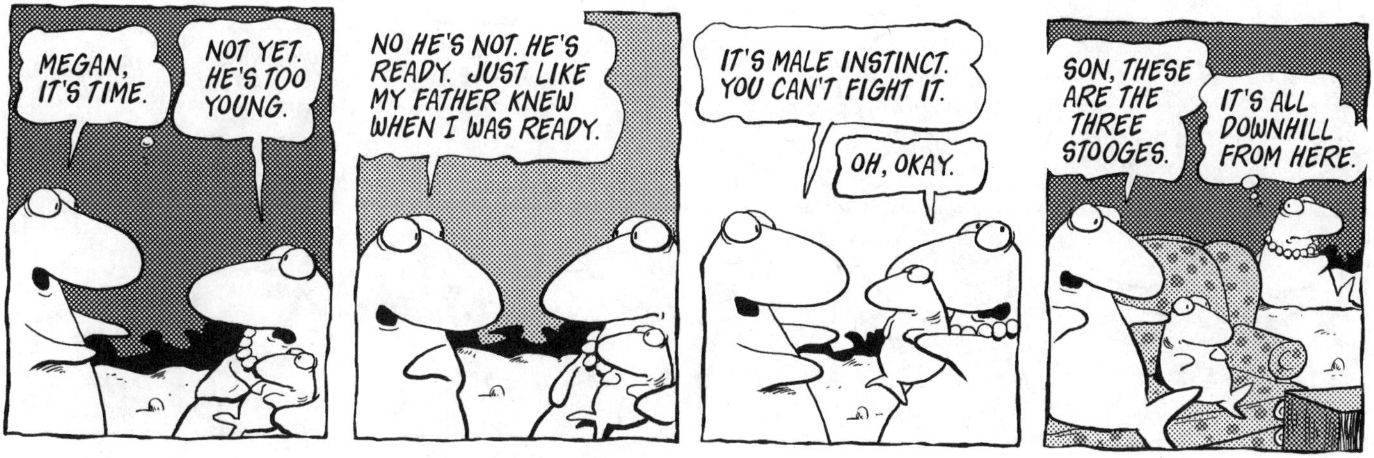

MEGAN, IT'S TIME.
NOT YET. HE'S TOO YOUNG.
NO HE'S NOT. HE'S READY. JUST LIKE MY FATHER KNEW WHEN I WAS READY.
IT'S MALE INSTINCT. YOU CAN'T FIGHT IT.
OH, OKAY.
SON, THESE ARE THE THREE STOOGES.
IT'S ALL DOWNHILL FROM HERE.

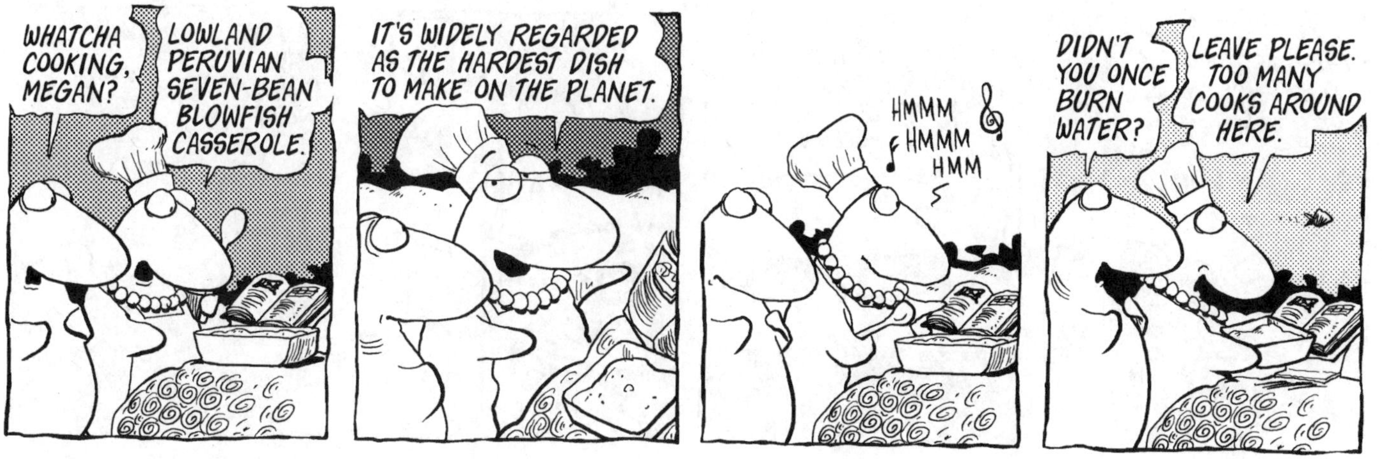

WHATCHA COOKING, MEGAN?
LOWLAND PERUVIAN SEVEN-BEAN BLOWFISH CASSEROLE.
IT'S WIDELY REGARDED AS THE HARDEST DISH TO MAKE ON THE PLANET.
HMMM HMMM HMM
DIDN'T YOU ONCE BURN WATER?
LEAVE PLEASE. TOO MANY COOKS AROUND HERE.

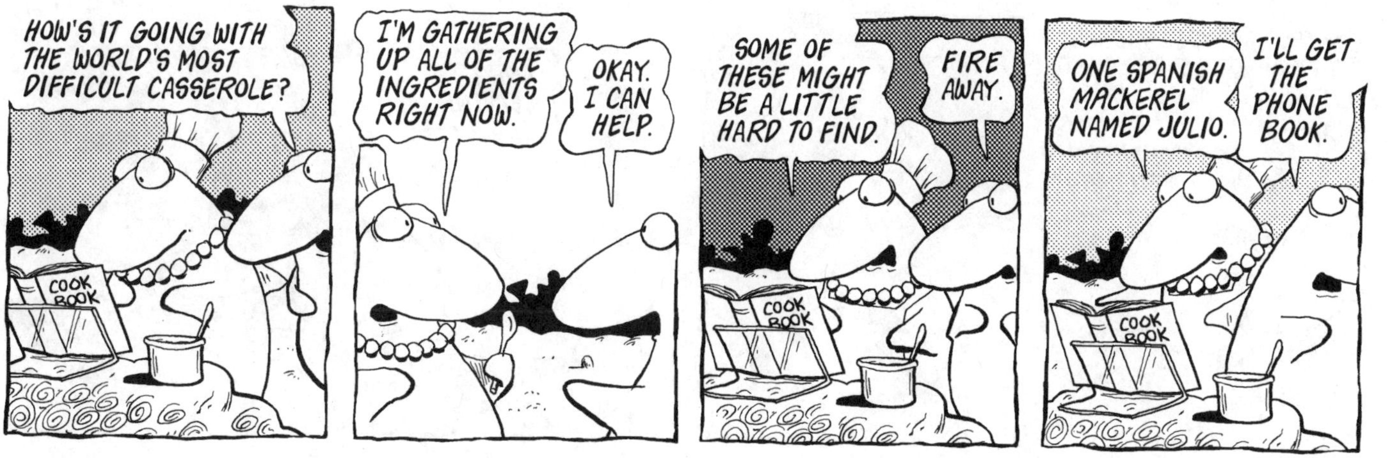

HOW'S IT GOING WITH THE WORLD'S MOST DIFFICULT CASSEROLE?
COOK BOOK
I'M GATHERING UP ALL OF THE INGREDIENTS RIGHT NOW.
OKAY. I CAN HELP.
SOME OF THESE MIGHT BE A LITTLE HARD TO FIND.
FIRE AWAY.
COOK BOOK
ONE SPANISH MACKEREL NAMED JULIO.
I'LL GET THE PHONE BOOK.
COOK BOOK

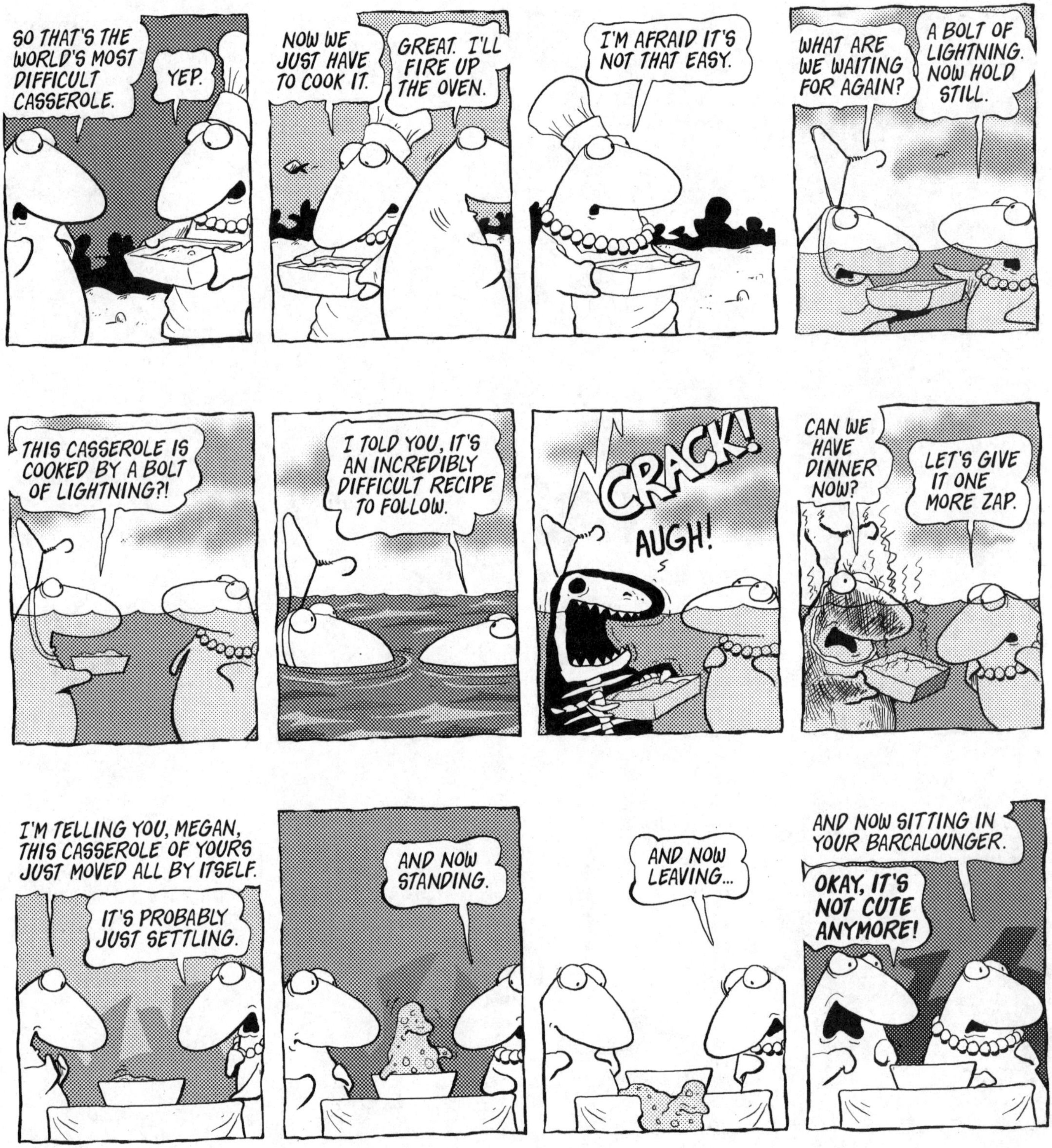
SO THAT'S THE WORLD'S MOST DIFFICULT CASSEROLE.
YEP.
NOW WE JUST HAVE TO COOK IT.
GREAT. I'LL FIRE UP THE OVEN.
I'M AFRAID IT'S NOT THAT EASY.
WHAT ARE WE WAITING FOR AGAIN?
A BOLT OF LIGHTNING. NOW HOLD STILL.
THIS CASSEROLE IS COOKED BY A BOLT OF LIGHTNING?!
I TOLD YOU, IT'S AN INCREDIBLY DIFFICULT RECIPE TO FOLLOW.
CRACK!
AUGH!
CAN WE HAVE DINNER NOW?
LET'S GIVE IT ONE MORE ZAP.
I'M TELLING YOU, MEGAN, THIS CASSEROLE OF YOURS JUST MOVED ALL BY ITSELF.
IT'S PROBABLY JUST SETTLING.
AND NOW STANDING.
AND NOW LEAVING...
AND NOW SITTING IN YOUR BARCALOUNGER.
OKAY, IT'S NOT CUTE ANYMORE!

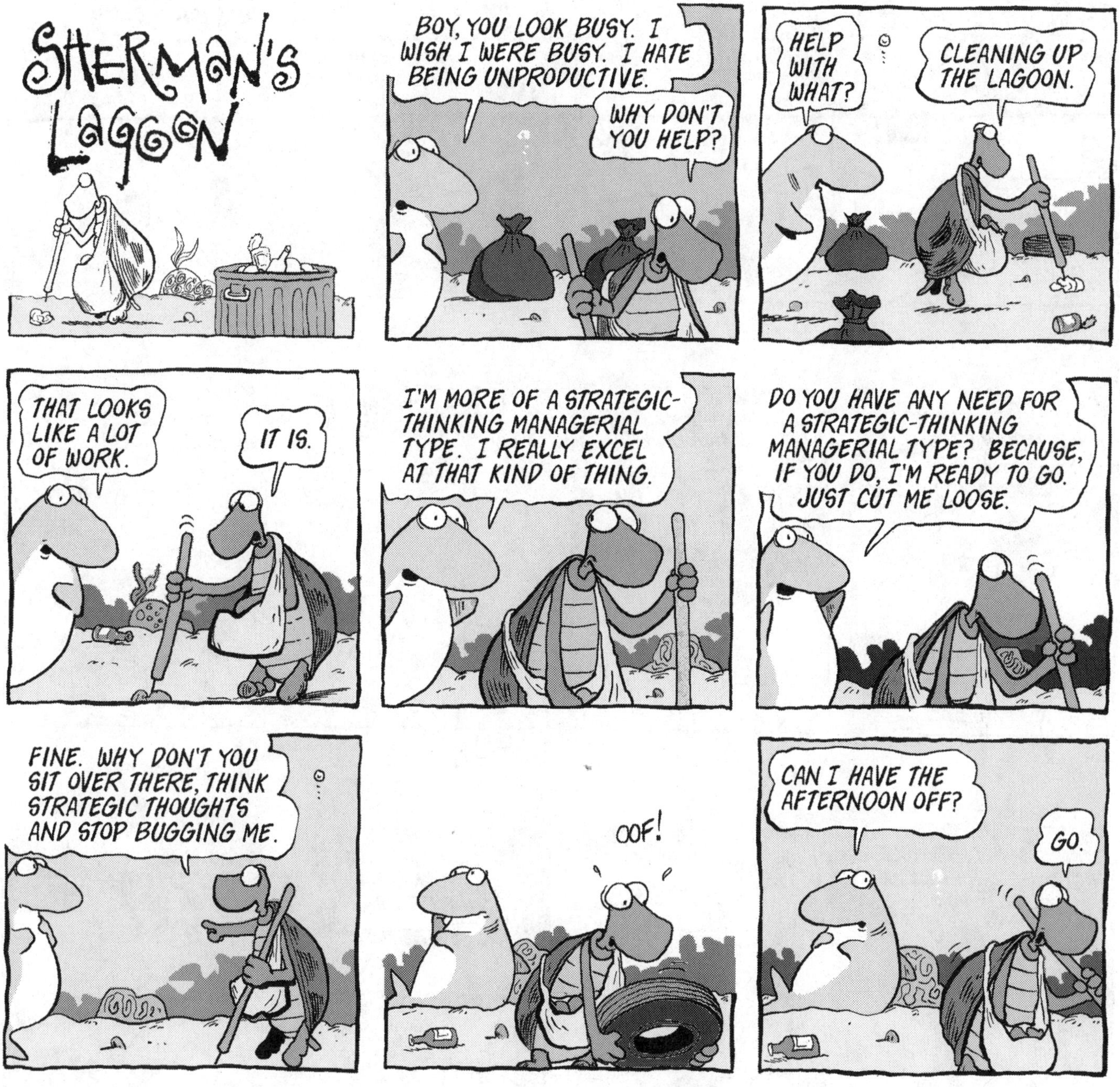
SHERMAN'S LAGOON
BOY, YOU LOOK BUSY. I WISH I WERE BUSY. I HATE BEING UNPRODUCTIVE.
WHY DON'T YOU HELP?
HELP WITH WHAT?
CLEANING UP THE LAGOON.
THAT LOOKS LIKE A LOT OF WORK.
IT IS.
I'M MORE OF A STRATEGIC-THINKING MANAGERIAL TYPE. I REALLY EXCEL AT THAT KIND OF THING.
DO YOU HAVE ANY NEED FOR A STRATEGIC-THINKING MANAGERIAL TYPE? BECAUSE, IF YOU DO, I'M READY TO GO. JUST CUT ME LOOSE.
FINE. WHY DON'T YOU SIT OVER THERE, THINK STRATEGIC THOUGHTS AND STOP BUGGING ME.
OOF!
CAN I HAVE THE AFTERNOON OFF?
GO.

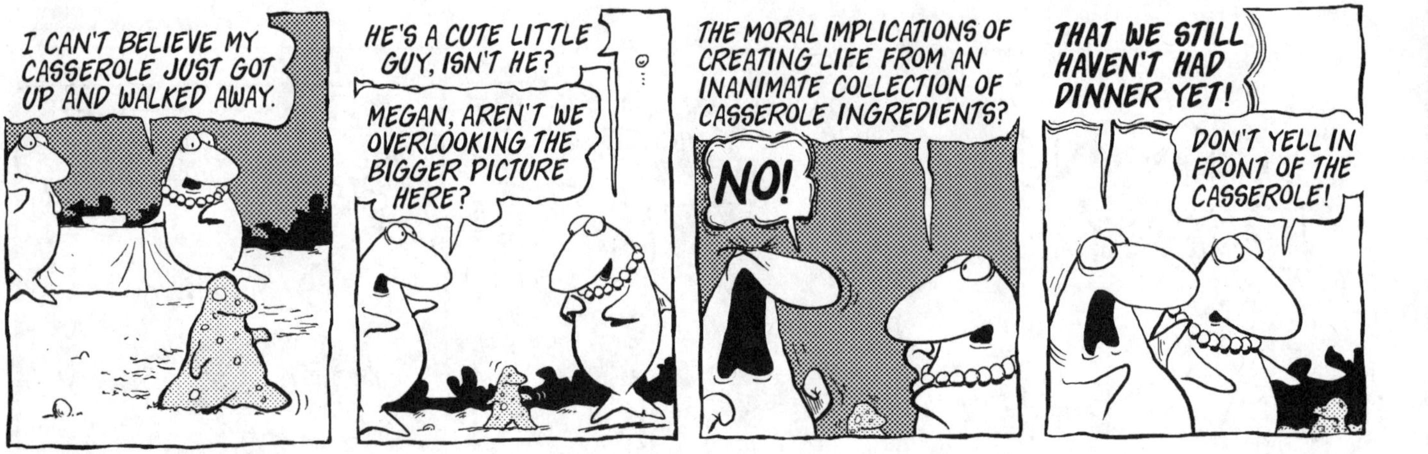
I CAN'T BELIEVE MY CASSEROLE JUST GOT UP AND WALKED AWAY.
HE'S A CUTE LITTLE GUY, ISN'T HE?
MEGAN, AREN'T WE OVERLOOKING THE BIGGER PICTURE HERE?
THE MORAL IMPLICATIONS OF CREATING LIFE FROM AN INANIMATE COLLECTION OF CASSEROLE INGREDIENTS?
NO!
THAT WE STILL HAVEN'T HAD DINNER YET!
DON'T YELL IN FRONT OF THE CASSEROLE!

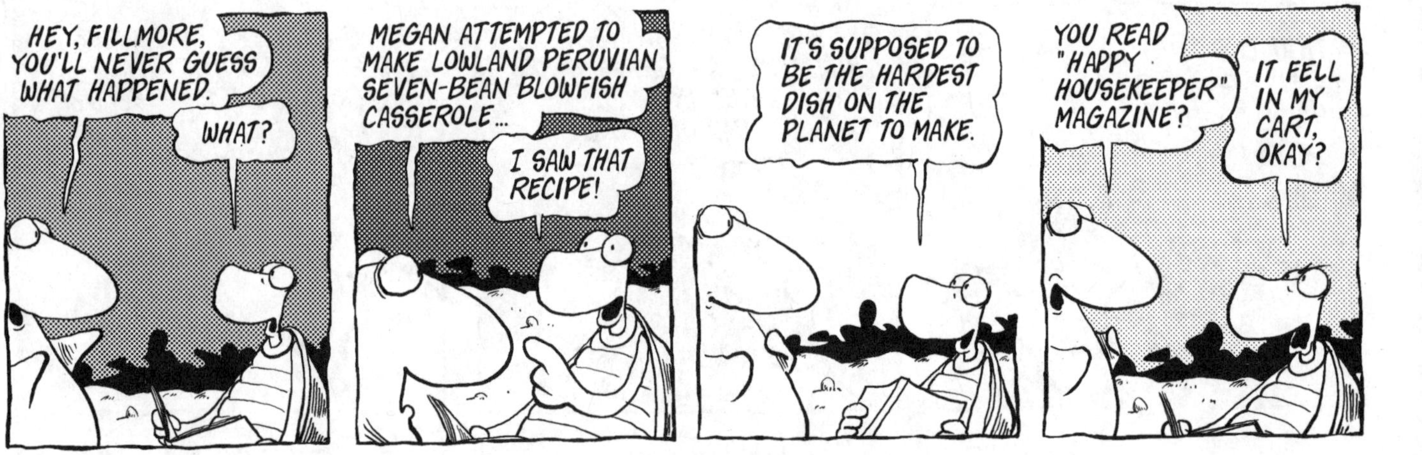
HEY, FILLMORE, YOU'LL NEVER GUESS WHAT HAPPENED.
WHAT?
MEGAN ATTEMPTED TO MAKE LOWLAND PERUVIAN SEVEN-BEAN BLOWFISH CASSEROLE...
I SAW THAT RECIPE!
IT'S SUPPOSED TO BE THE HARDEST DISH ON THE PLANET TO MAKE.
YOU READ "HAPPY HOUSEKEEPER" MAGAZINE?
IT FELL IN MY CART, OKAY?

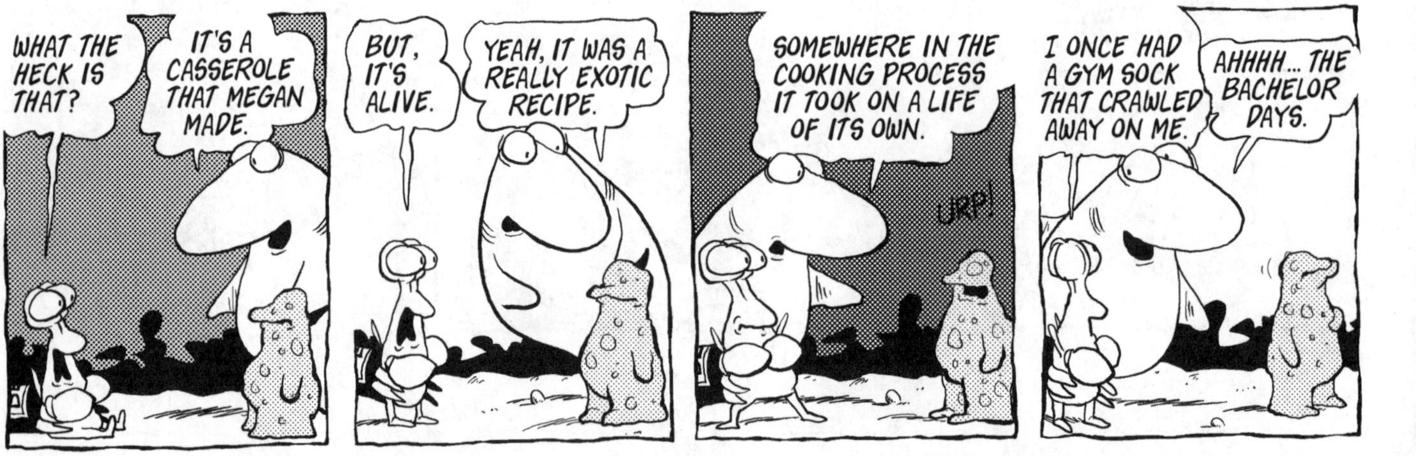
WHAT THE HECK IS THAT?
IT'S A CASSEROLE THAT MEGAN MADE.
BUT, IT'S ALIVE.
YEAH, IT WAS A REALLY EXOTIC RECIPE.
SOMEWHERE IN THE COOKING PROCESS IT TOOK ON A LIFE OF ITS OWN.
URP!
I ONCE HAD A GYM SOCK THAT CRAWLED AWAY ON ME.
AHHHH... THE BACHELOR DAYS.

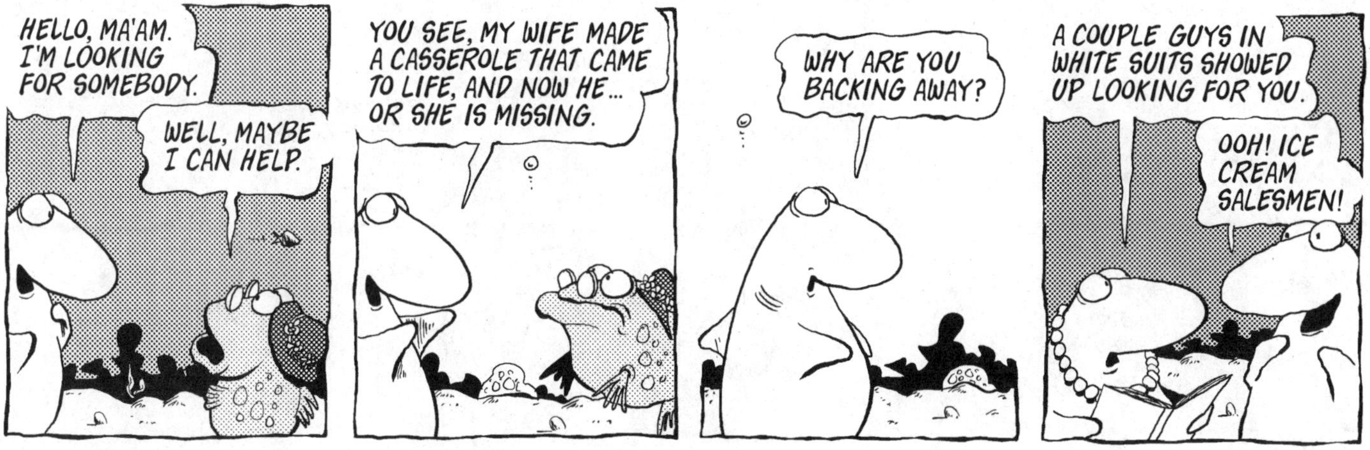
HELLO, MA'AM. I'M LOOKING FOR SOMEBODY.
WELL, MAYBE I CAN HELP.
YOU SEE, MY WIFE MADE A CASSEROLE THAT CAME TO LIFE, AND NOW HE... OR SHE IS MISSING.
WHY ARE YOU BACKING AWAY?
A COUPLE GUYS IN WHITE SUITS SHOWED UP LOOKING FOR YOU.
OOH! ICE CREAM SALESMEN!

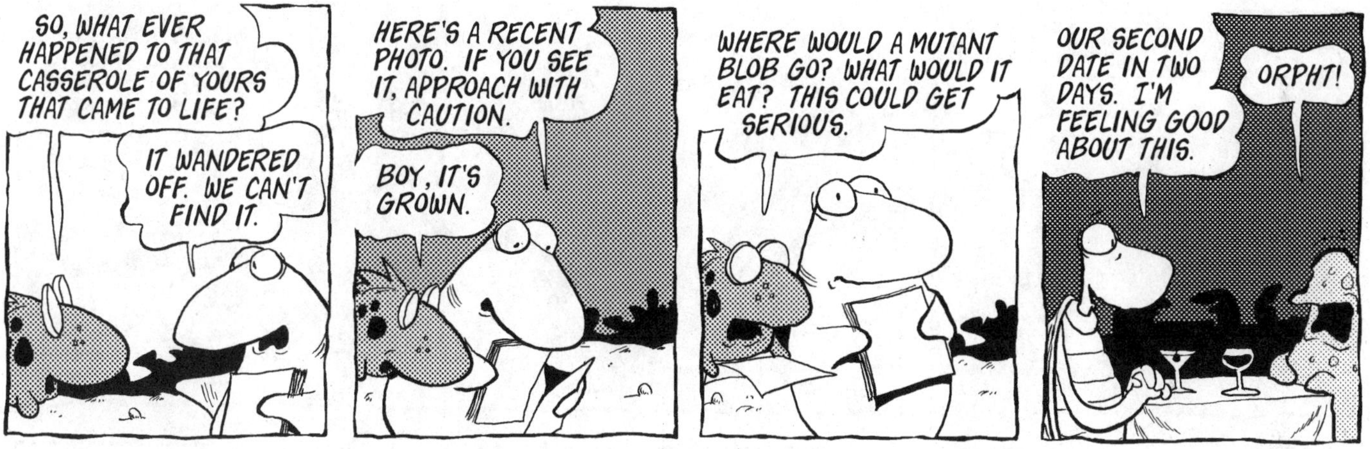
SO, WHAT EVER HAPPENED TO THAT CASSEROLE OF YOURS THAT CAME TO LIFE?
IT WANDERED OFF. WE CAN'T FIND IT.
HERE'S A RECENT PHOTO. IF YOU SEE IT, APPROACH WITH CAUTION.
BOY, IT'S GROWN.
WHERE WOULD A MUTANT BLOB GO? WHAT WOULD IT EAT? THIS COULD GET SERIOUS.
OUR SECOND DATE IN TWO DAYS. I'M FEELING GOOD ABOUT THIS.
ORPHT!

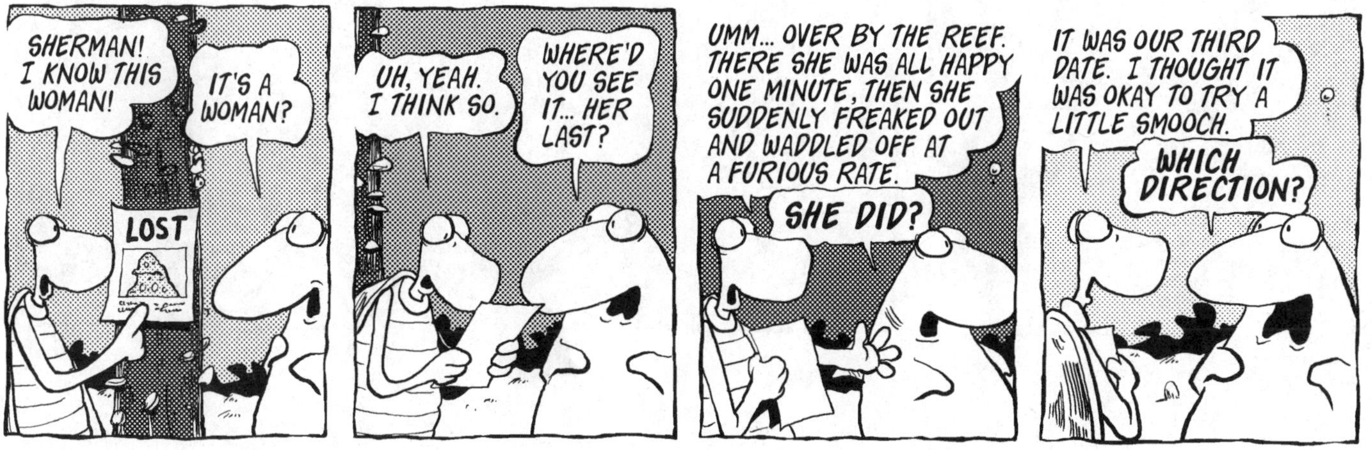
SHERMAN! I KNOW THIS WOMAN!
IT'S A WOMAN?
LOST
UH, YEAH. I THINK SO.
WHERE'D YOU SEE IT... HER LAST?
UMM... OVER BY THE REEF. THERE SHE WAS ALL HAPPY ONE MINUTE, THEN SHE SUDDENLY FREAKED OUT AND WADDLED OFF AT A FURIOUS RATE.
SHE DID?
IT WAS OUR THIRD DATE. I THOUGHT IT WAS OKAY TO TRY A LITTLE SMOOCH.
WHICH DIRECTION?

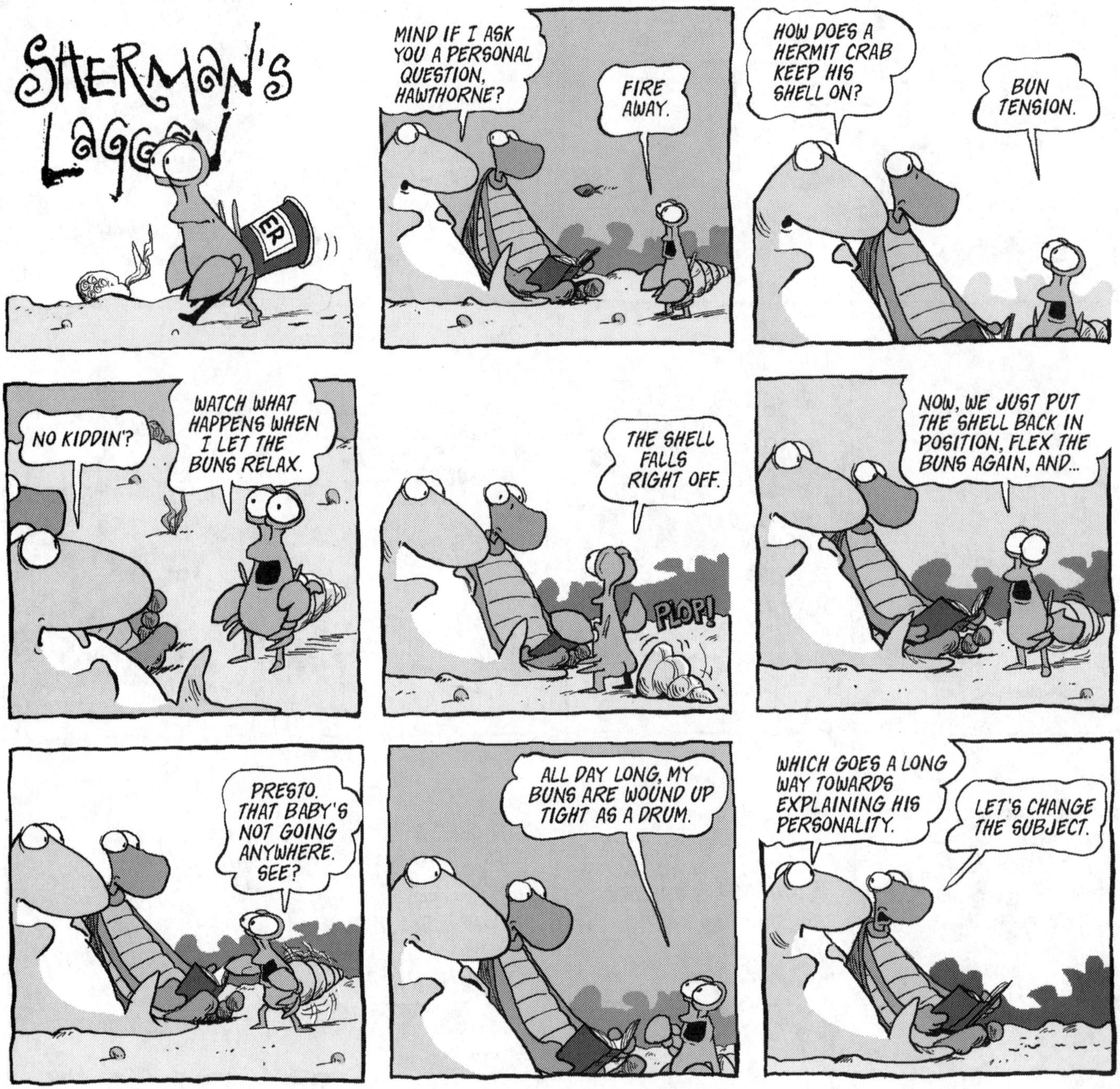
SHERMAN'S LAGOON
MIND IF I ASK YOU A PERSONAL QUESTION, HAWTHORNE?
FIRE AWAY.
HOW DOES A HERMIT CRAB KEEP HIS SHELL ON?
BUN TENSION.
NO KIDDIN'?
WATCH WHAT HAPPENS WHEN I LET THE BUNS RELAX.
THE SHELL FALLS RIGHT OFF.
PLOP!
NOW, WE JUST PUT THE SHELL BACK IN POSITION, FLEX THE BUNS AGAIN, AND...
PRESTO. THAT BABY'S NOT GOING ANYWHERE. SEE?
ALL DAY LONG, MY BUNS ARE WOUND UP TIGHT AS A DRUM.
WHICH GOES A LONG WAY TOWARDS EXPLAINING HIS PERSONALITY.
LET'S CHANGE THE SUBJECT.

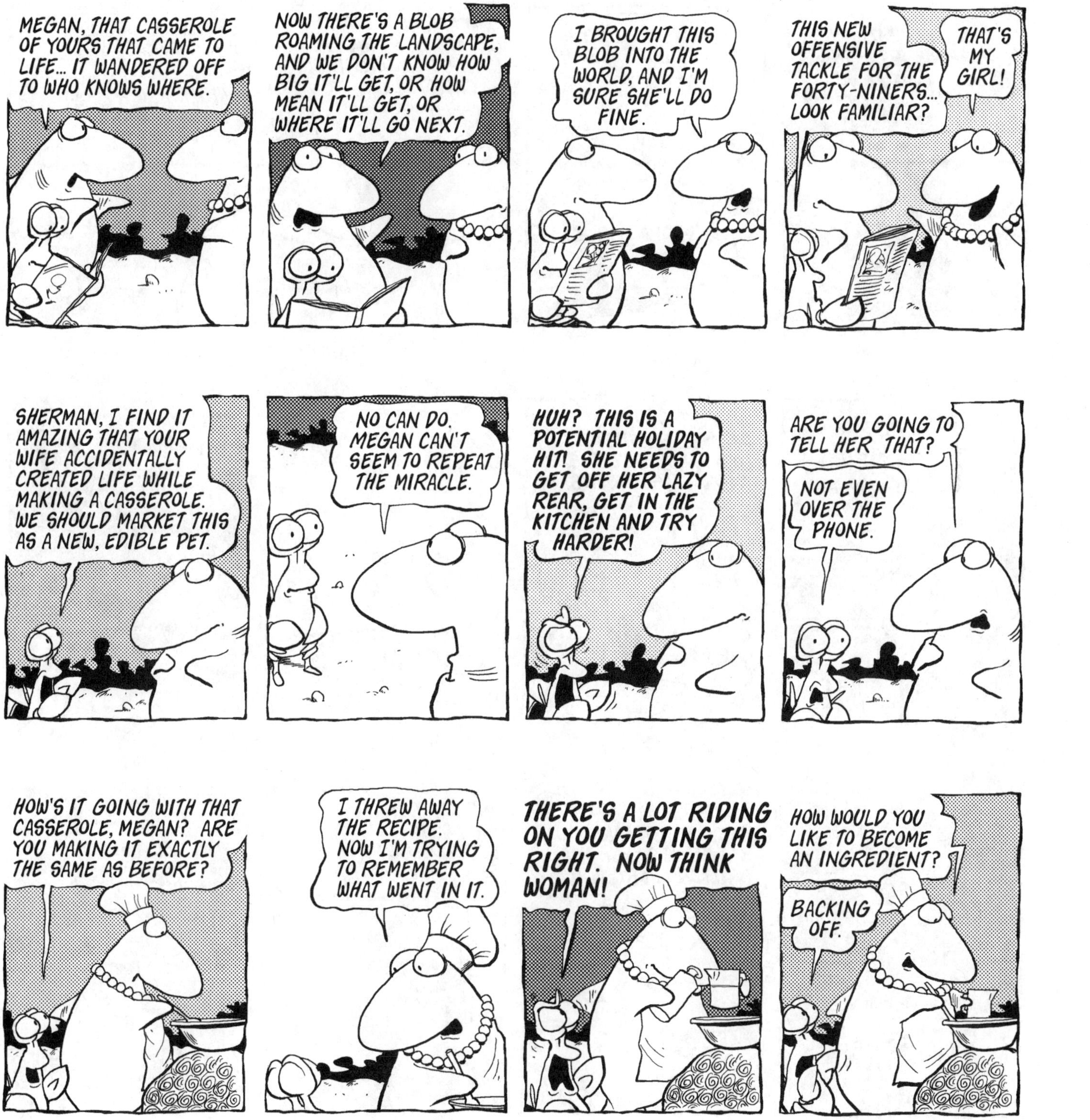
MEGAN, THAT CASSEROLE OF YOURS THAT CAME TO LIFE... IT WANDERED OFF TO WHO KNOWS WHERE.
NOW THERE'S A BLOB ROAMING THE LANDSCAPE, AND WE DON'T KNOW HOW BIG IT'LL GET, OR HOW MEAN IT'LL GET, OR WHERE IT'LL GO NEXT.
I BROUGHT THIS BLOB INTO THE WORLD, AND I'M SURE SHE'LL DO FINE.
THIS NEW OFFENSIVE TACKLE FOR THE FORTY-NINERS... LOOK FAMILIAR?
THAT'S MY GIRL!
SHERMAN, I FIND IT AMAZING THAT YOUR WIFE ACCIDENTALLY CREATED LIFE WHILE MAKING A CASSEROLE. WE SHOULD MARKET THIS AS A NEW, EDIBLE PET.
NO CAN DO. MEGAN CAN'T SEEM TO REPEAT THE MIRACLE.
HUH? THIS IS A POTENTIAL HOLIDAY HIT! SHE NEEDS TO GET OFF HER LAZY REAR, GET IN THE KITCHEN AND TRY HARDER!
ARE YOU GOING TO TELL HER THAT?
NOT EVEN OVER THE PHONE.
HOW'S IT GOING WITH THAT CASSEROLE, MEGAN? ARE YOU MAKING IT EXACTLY THE SAME AS BEFORE?
I THREW AWAY THE RECIPE. NOW I'M TRYING TO REMEMBER WHAT WENT IN IT.
THERE'S A LOT RIDING ON YOU GETTING THIS RIGHT. NOW THINK WOMAN!
HOW WOULD YOU LIKE TO BECOME AN INGREDIENT?
BACKING OFF.

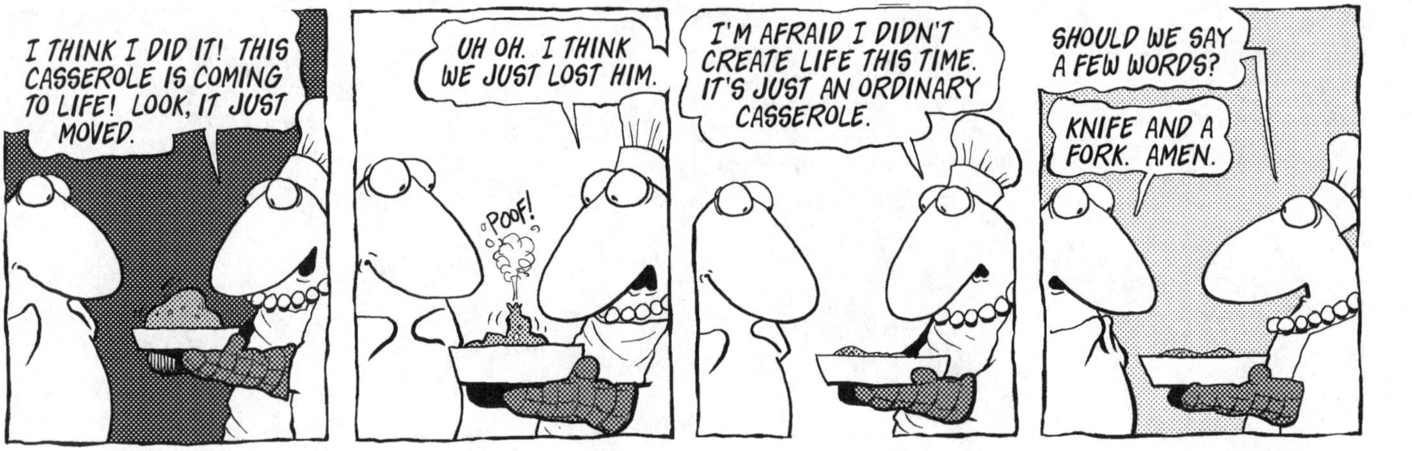
I THINK I DID IT! THIS CASSEROLE IS COMING TO LIFE! LOOK, IT JUST MOVED.
UH OH. I THINK WE JUST LOST HIM.
POOF!
I'M AFRAID I DIDN'T CREATE LIFE THIS TIME. IT'S JUST AN ORDINARY CASSEROLE.
SHOULD WE SAY A FEW WORDS?
KNIFE AND A FORK. AMEN.

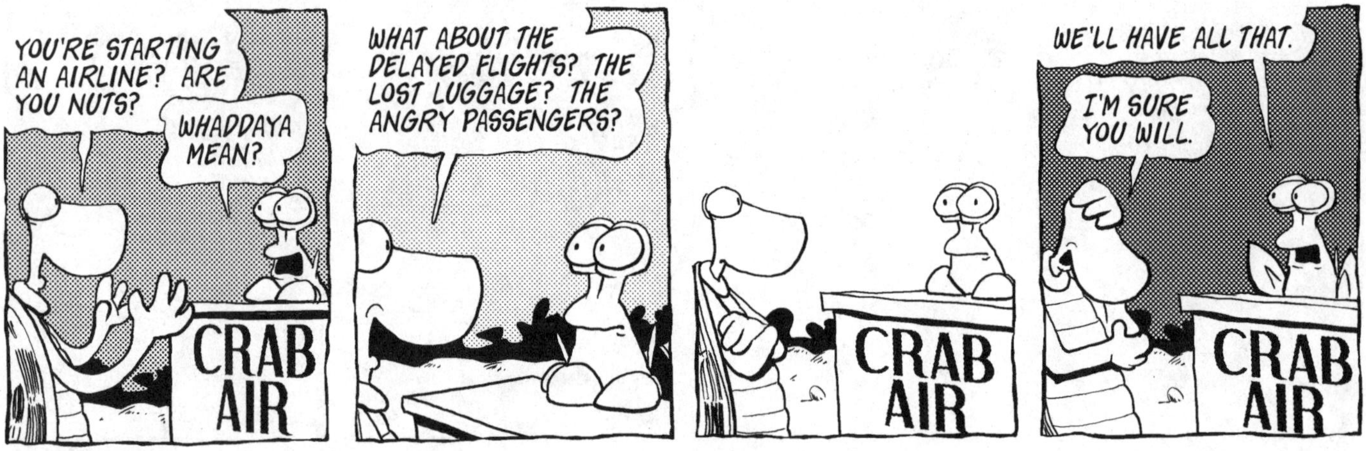
YOU'RE STARTING AN AIRLINE? ARE YOU NUTS?
WHADDAYA MEAN?
CRAB AIR
WHAT ABOUT THE DELAYED FLIGHTS? THE LOST LUGGAGE? THE ANGRY PASSENGERS?
CRAB AIR
WE'LL HAVE ALL THAT.
I'M SURE YOU WILL.
CRAB AIR

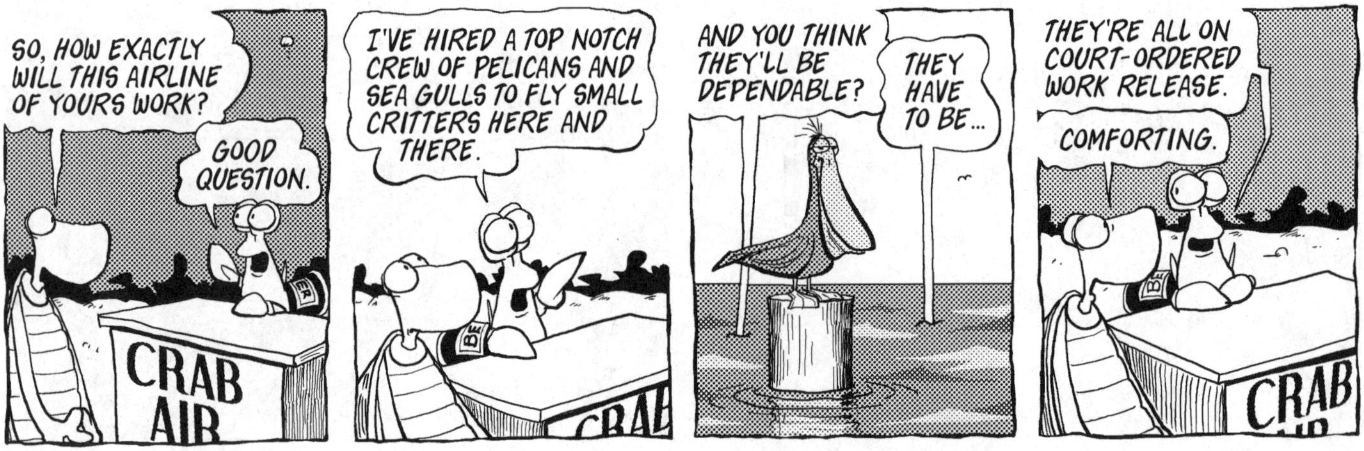
SO, HOW EXACTLY WILL THIS AIRLINE OF YOURS WORK?
GOOD QUESTION.
CRAB AIR
I'VE HIRED A TOP NOTCH CREW OF PELICANS AND SEA GULLS TO FLY SMALL CRITTERS HERE AND THERE.
AND YOU THINK THEY'LL BE DEPENDABLE?
THEY HAVE TO BE...
THEY'RE ALL ON COURT-ORDERED WORK RELEASE.
COMFORTING.
CRAB

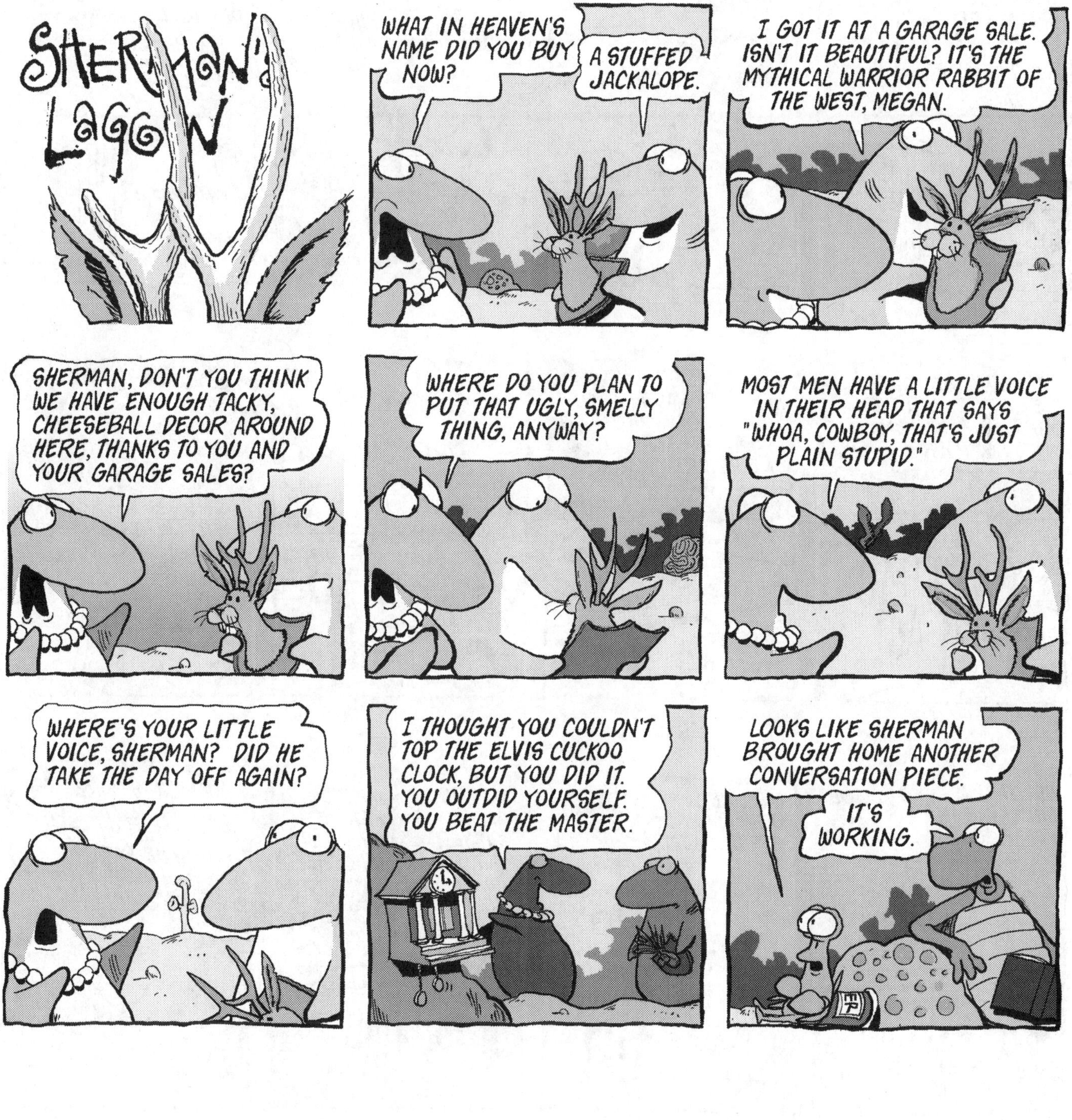
SHERMAN'S LAGOON
WHAT IN HEAVEN'S NAME DID YOU BUY NOW?
A STUFFED JACKALOPE.
I GOT IT AT A GARAGE SALE. ISN'T IT BEAUTIFUL? IT'S THE MYTHICAL WARRIOR RABBIT OF THE WEST, MEGAN.
SHERMAN, DON'T YOU THINK WE HAVE ENOUGH TACKY, CHEESEBALL DECOR AROUND HERE, THANKS TO YOU AND YOUR GARAGE SALES?
WHERE DO YOU PLAN TO PUT THAT UGLY, SMELLY THING, ANYWAY?
MOST MEN HAVE A LITTLE VOICE IN THEIR HEAD THAT SAYS "WHOA, COWBOY, THAT'S JUST PLAIN STUPID."
WHERE'S YOUR LITTLE VOICE, SHERMAN? DID HE TAKE THE DAY OFF AGAIN?
I THOUGHT YOU COULDN'T TOP THE ELVIS CUCKOO CLOCK, BUT YOU DID IT. YOU OUTDID YOURSELF. YOU BEAT THE MASTER.
LOOKS LIKE SHERMAN BROUGHT HOME ANOTHER CONVERSATION PIECE.
IT'S WORKING.

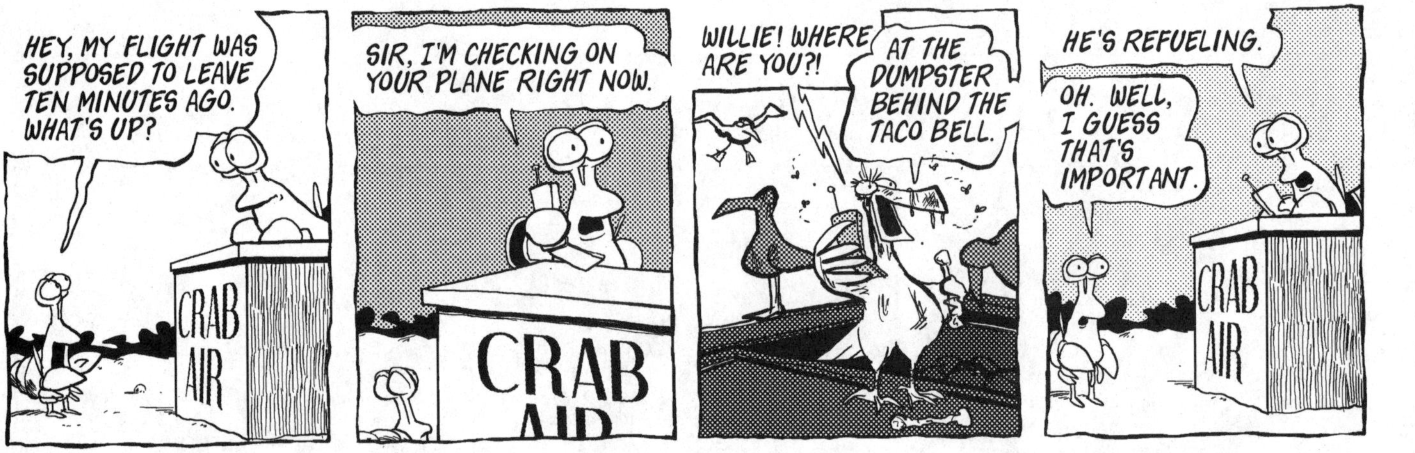
HEY, MY FLIGHT WAS SUPPOSED TO LEAVE TEN MINUTES AGO. WHAT'S UP?
CRAB AIR
SIR, I'M CHECKING ON YOUR PLANE RIGHT NOW.
CRAB
WILLIE! WHERE ARE YOU?!
AT THE DUMPSTER BEHIND THE TACO BELL.
HE'S REFUELING.
OH. WELL, I GUESS THAT'S IMPORTANT.
CRAB AIR

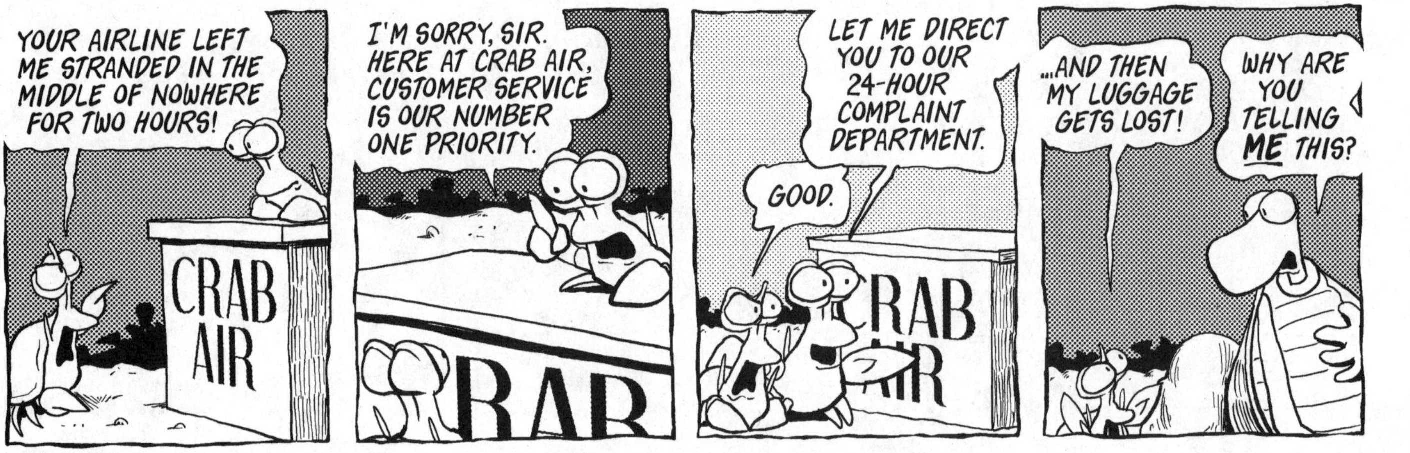
YOUR AIRLINE LEFT ME STRANDED IN THE MIDDLE OF NOWHERE FOR TWO HOURS!
CRAB AIR
I'M SORRY, SIR. HERE AT CRAB AIR, CUSTOMER SERVICE IS OUR NUMBER ONE PRIORITY.
LET ME DIRECT YOU TO OUR 24-HOUR COMPLAINT DEPARTMENT.
GOOD.
...AND THEN MY LUGGAGE GETS LOST!
WHY ARE YOU TELLING **ME** THIS?

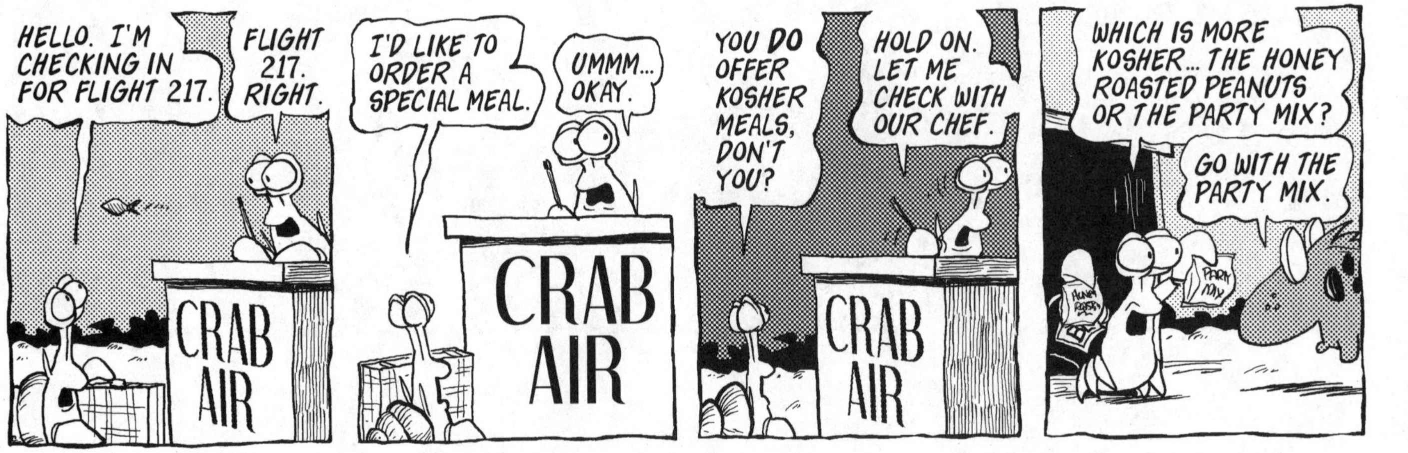
HELLO. I'M CHECKING IN FOR FLIGHT 217.
FLIGHT 217. RIGHT.
CRAB AIR
I'D LIKE TO ORDER A SPECIAL MEAL.
UMMM... OKAY.
CRAB AIR
YOU **DO** OFFER KOSHER MEALS, DON'T YOU?
HOLD ON. LET ME CHECK WITH OUR CHEF.
CRAB AIR
WHICH IS MORE KOSHER... THE HONEY ROASTED PEANUTS OR THE PARTY MIX?
GO WITH THE PARTY MIX.

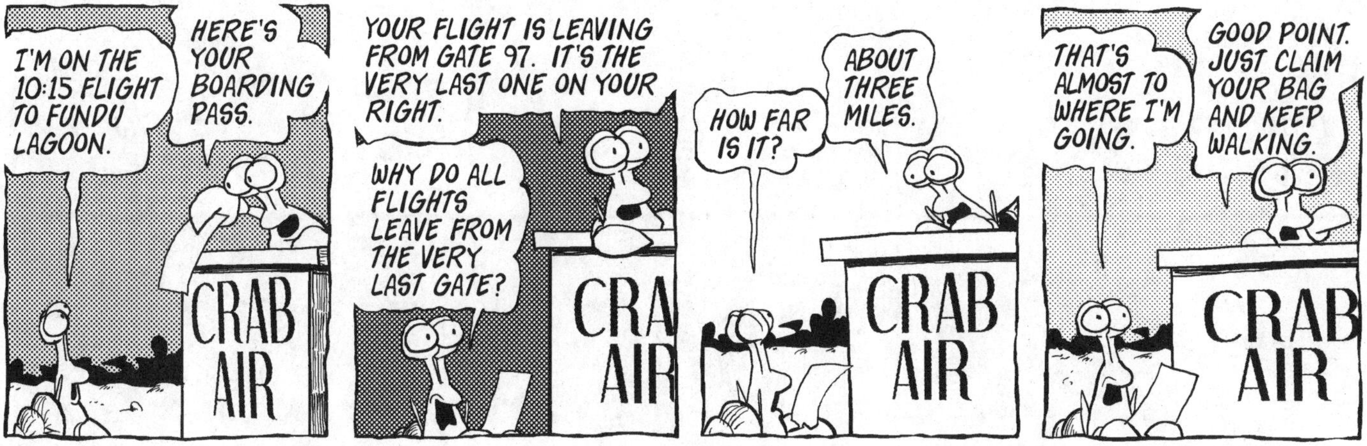
I'M ON THE 10:15 FLIGHT TO FUNDU LAGOON.
HERE'S YOUR BOARDING PASS.
CRAB AIR
YOUR FLIGHT IS LEAVING FROM GATE 97. IT'S THE VERY LAST ONE ON YOUR RIGHT.
WHY DO ALL FLIGHTS LEAVE FROM THE VERY LAST GATE?
HOW FAR IS IT?
ABOUT THREE MILES.
THAT'S ALMOST TO WHERE I'M GOING.
GOOD POINT. JUST CLAIM YOUR BAG AND KEEP WALKING.

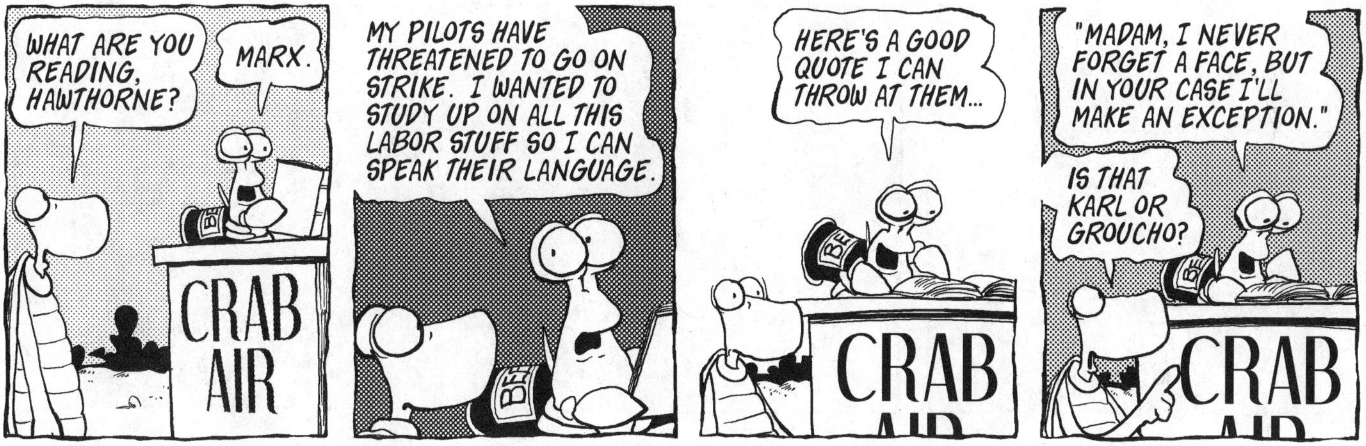
WHAT ARE YOU READING, HAWTHORNE?
MARX.
CRAB AIR
MY PILOTS HAVE THREATENED TO GO ON STRIKE. I WANTED TO STUDY UP ON ALL THIS LABOR STUFF SO I CAN SPEAK THEIR LANGUAGE.
HERE'S A GOOD QUOTE I CAN THROW AT THEM...
"MADAM, I NEVER FORGET A FACE, BUT IN YOUR CASE I'LL MAKE AN EXCEPTION."
IS THAT KARL OR GROUCHO?

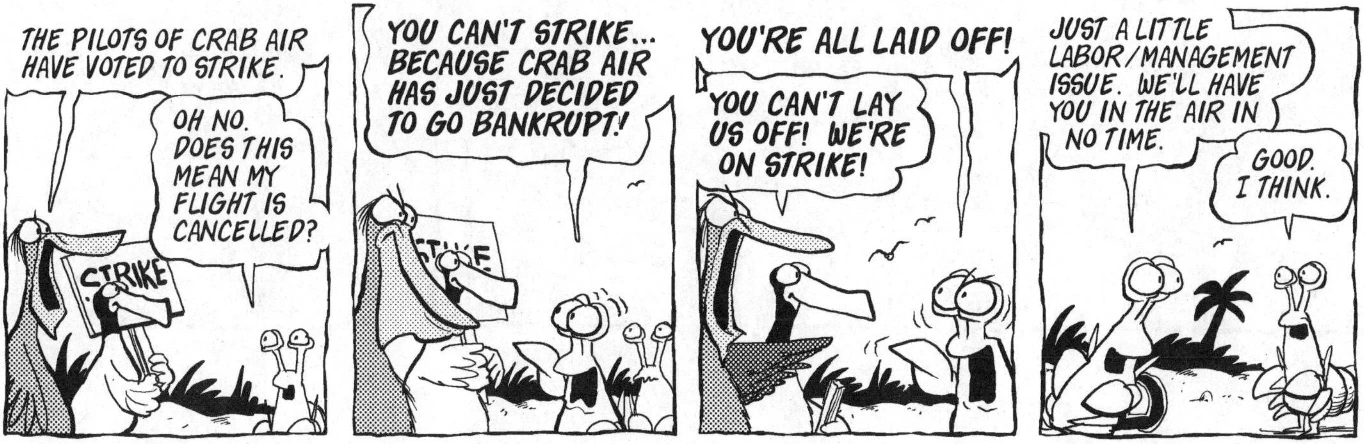
THE PILOTS OF CRAB AIR HAVE VOTED TO STRIKE.
OH NO. DOES THIS MEAN MY FLIGHT IS CANCELLED?
STRIKE
YOU CAN'T STRIKE... BECAUSE CRAB AIR HAS JUST DECIDED TO GO BANKRUPT!
YOU'RE ALL LAID OFF!
YOU CAN'T LAY US OFF! WE'RE ON STRIKE!
JUST A LITTLE LABOR/MANAGEMENT ISSUE. WE'LL HAVE YOU IN THE AIR IN NO TIME.
GOOD. I THINK.

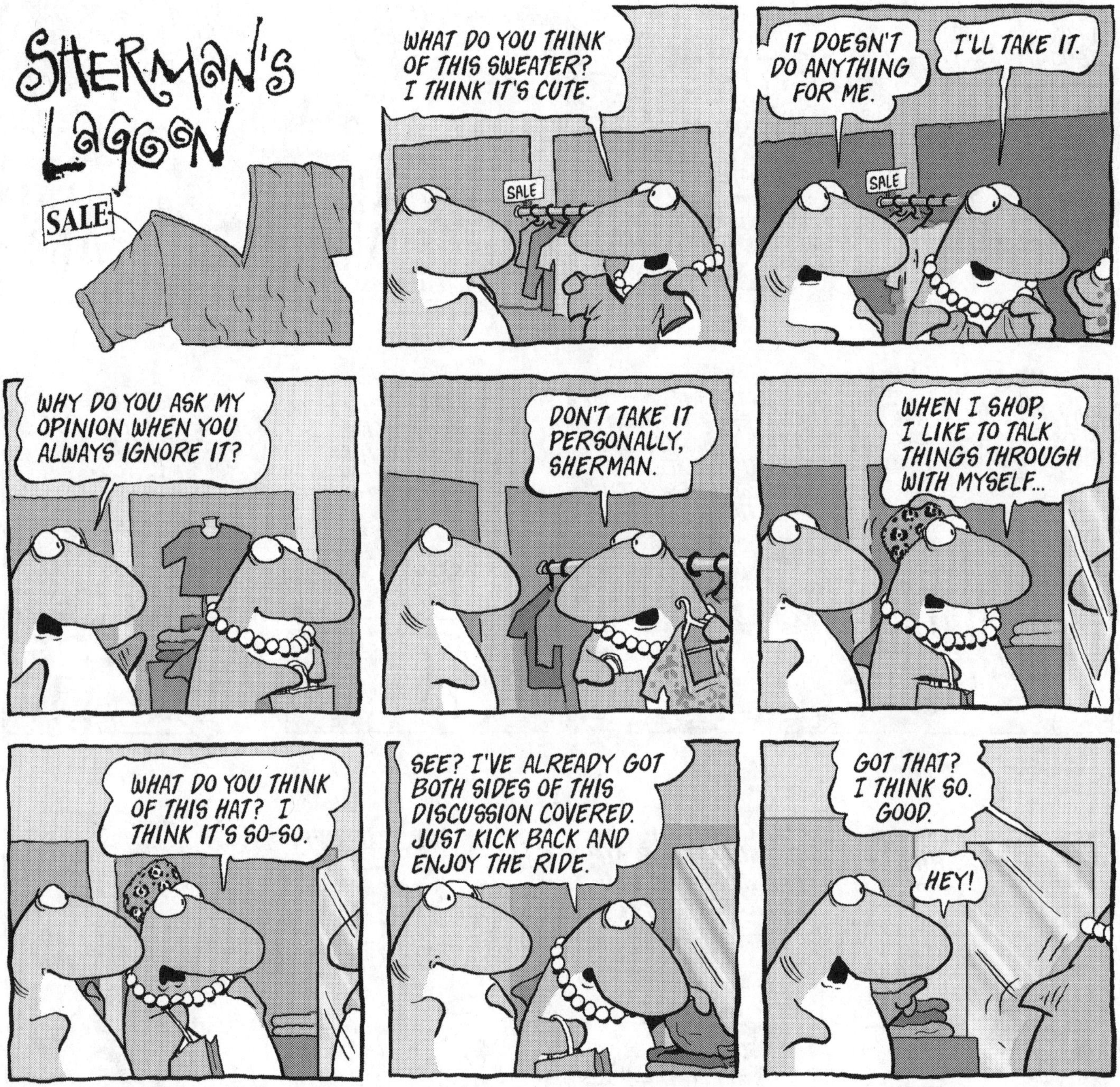
SHERMAN'S LAGOON
SALE
WHAT DO YOU THINK OF THIS SWEATER? I THINK IT'S CUTE.
SALE
IT DOESN'T DO ANYTHING FOR ME.
I'LL TAKE IT.
SALE
WHY DO YOU ASK MY OPINION WHEN YOU ALWAYS IGNORE IT?
DON'T TAKE IT PERSONALLY, SHERMAN.
WHEN I SHOP, I LIKE TO TALK THINGS THROUGH WITH MYSELF...
WHAT DO YOU THINK OF THIS HAT? I THINK IT'S SO-SO.
SEE? I'VE ALREADY GOT BOTH SIDES OF THIS DISCUSSION COVERED. JUST KICK BACK AND ENJOY THE RIDE.
GOT THAT? I THINK SO. GOOD.
HEY!

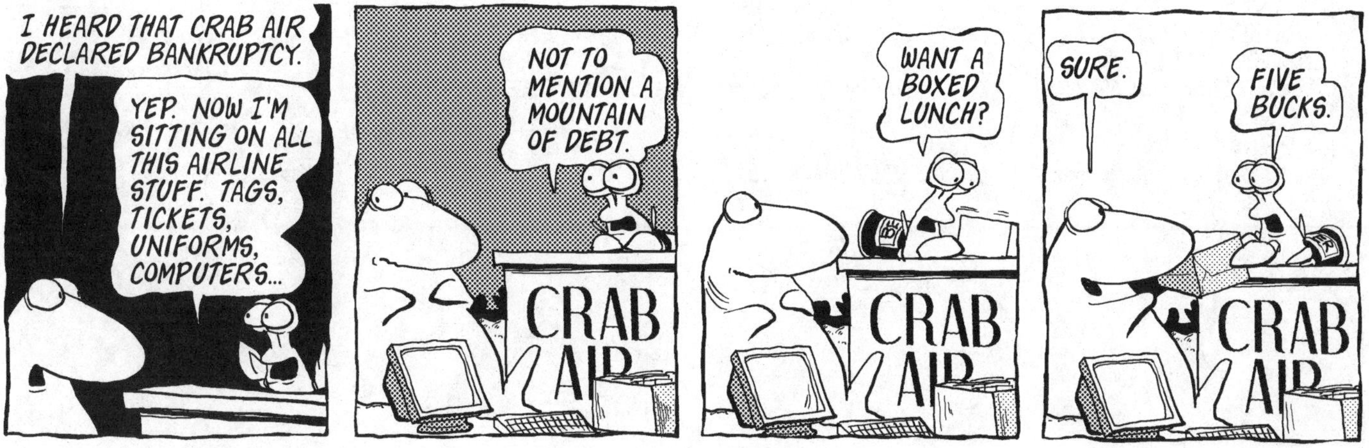
I HEARD THAT CRAB AIR DECLARED BANKRUPTCY.
YEP. NOW I'M SITTING ON ALL THIS AIRLINE STUFF. TAGS, TICKETS, UNIFORMS, COMPUTERS...
NOT TO MENTION A MOUNTAIN OF DEBT.
CRAB AIR
WANT A BOXED LUNCH?
SURE.
FIVE BUCKS.

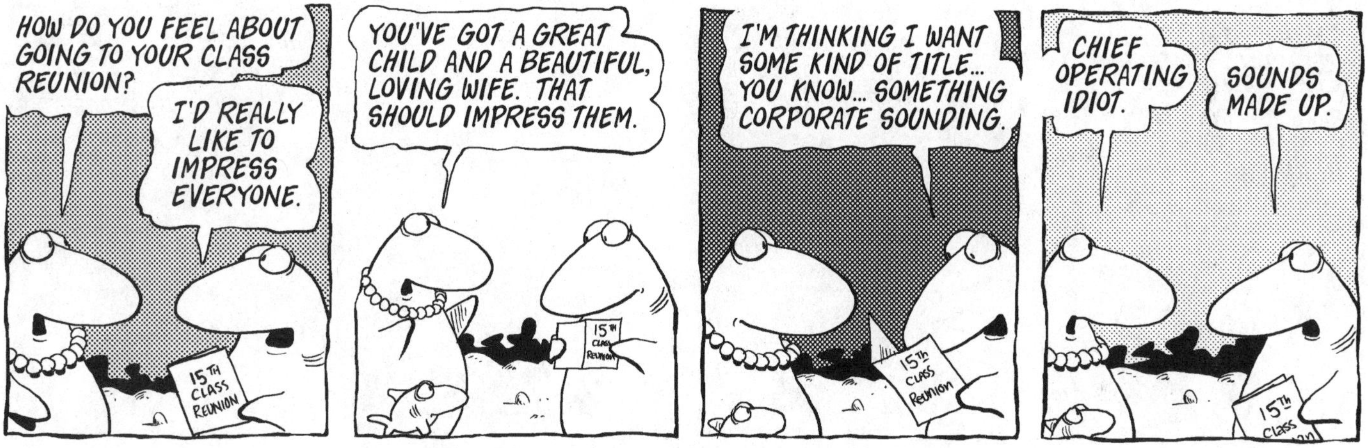
HOW DO YOU FEEL ABOUT GOING TO YOUR CLASS REUNION?
I'D REALLY LIKE TO IMPRESS EVERYONE.
15TH CLASS REUNION
YOU'VE GOT A GREAT CHILD AND A BEAUTIFUL, LOVING WIFE. THAT SHOULD IMPRESS THEM.
I'M THINKING I WANT SOME KIND OF TITLE... YOU KNOW... SOMETHING CORPORATE SOUNDING.
CHIEF OPERATING IDIOT.
SOUNDS MADE UP.

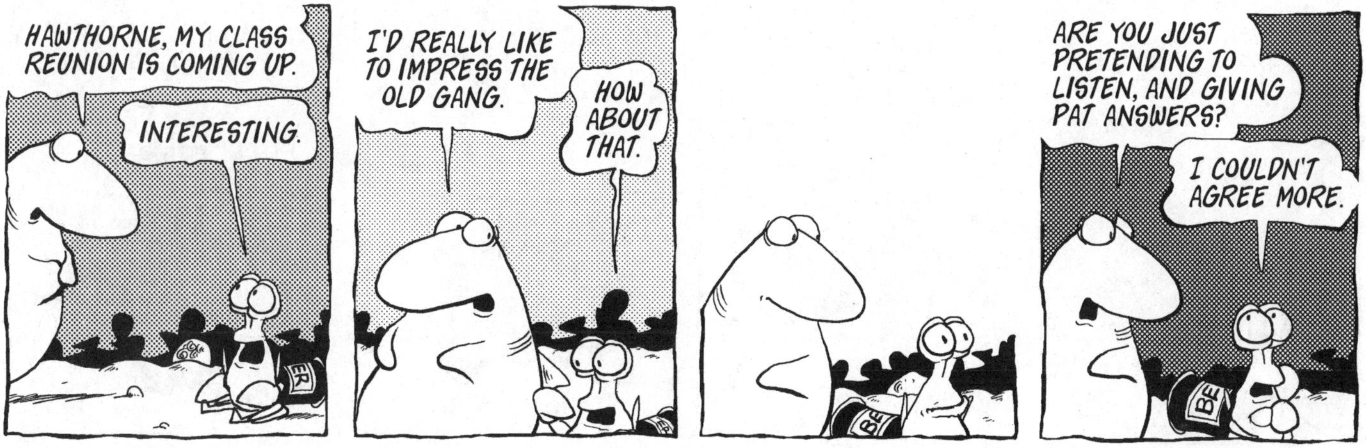
HAWTHORNE, MY CLASS REUNION IS COMING UP.
INTERESTING.
I'D REALLY LIKE TO IMPRESS THE OLD GANG.
HOW ABOUT THAT.
ARE YOU JUST PRETENDING TO LISTEN, AND GIVING PAT ANSWERS?
I COULDN'T AGREE MORE.

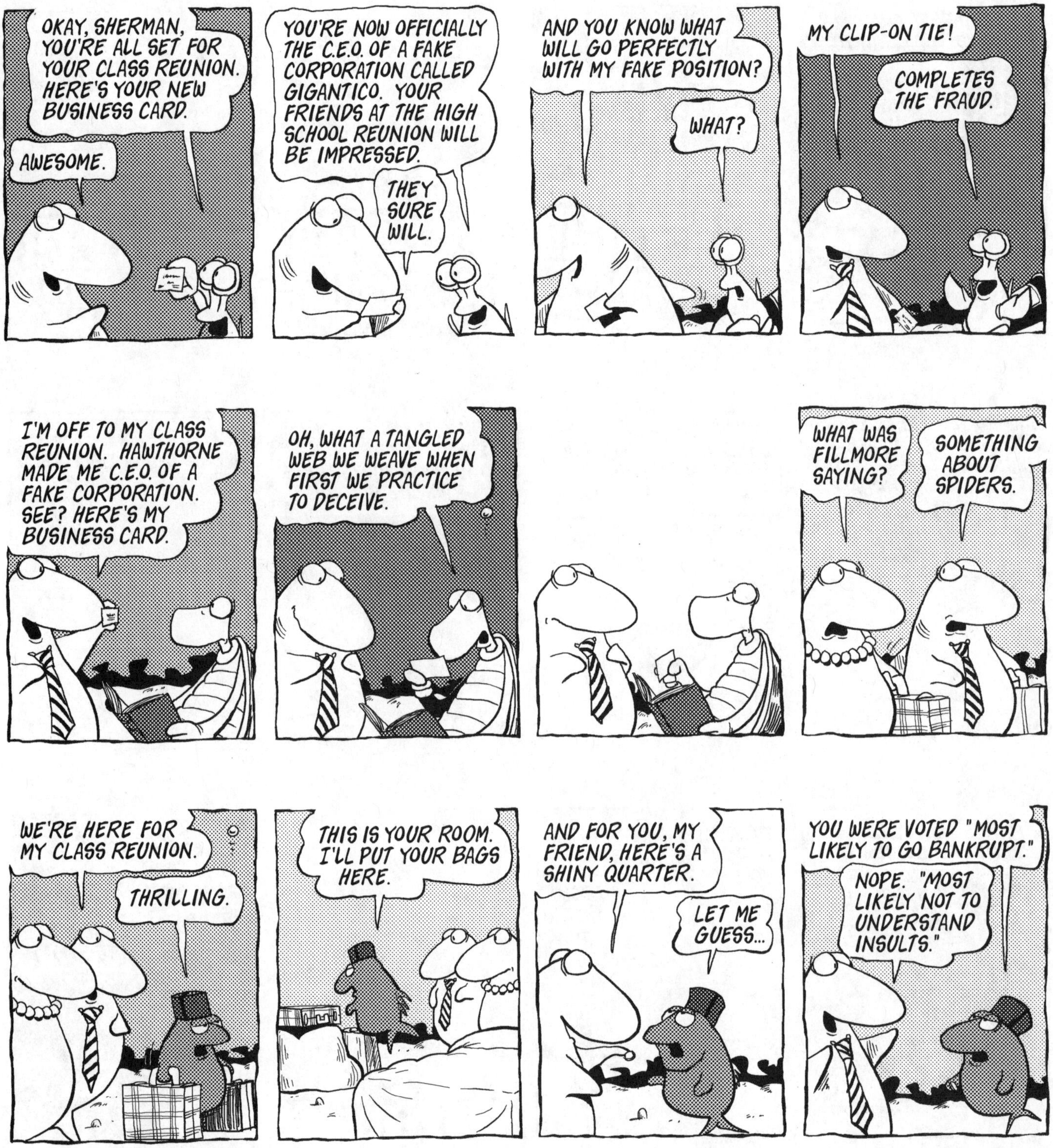
OKAY, SHERMAN, YOU'RE ALL SET FOR YOUR CLASS REUNION. HERE'S YOUR NEW BUSINESS CARD.
AWESOME.
YOU'RE NOW OFFICIALLY THE C.E.O. OF A FAKE CORPORATION CALLED GIGANTICO. YOUR FRIENDS AT THE HIGH SCHOOL REUNION WILL BE IMPRESSED.
THEY SURE WILL.
AND YOU KNOW WHAT WILL GO PERFECTLY WITH MY FAKE POSITION?
WHAT?
MY CLIP-ON TIE!
COMPLETES THE FRAUD.
I'M OFF TO MY CLASS REUNION. HAWTHORNE MADE ME C.E.O. OF A FAKE CORPORATION. SEE? HERE'S MY BUSINESS CARD.
OH, WHAT A TANGLED WEB WE WEAVE WHEN FIRST WE PRACTICE TO DECEIVE.
WHAT WAS FILLMORE SAYING?
SOMETHING ABOUT SPIDERS.
WE'RE HERE FOR MY CLASS REUNION.
THRILLING.
THIS IS YOUR ROOM. I'LL PUT YOUR BAGS HERE.
AND FOR YOU, MY FRIEND, HERE'S A SHINY QUARTER.
LET ME GUESS...
YOU WERE VOTED "MOST LIKELY TO GO BANKRUPT."
NOPE. "MOST LIKELY NOT TO UNDERSTAND INSULTS."

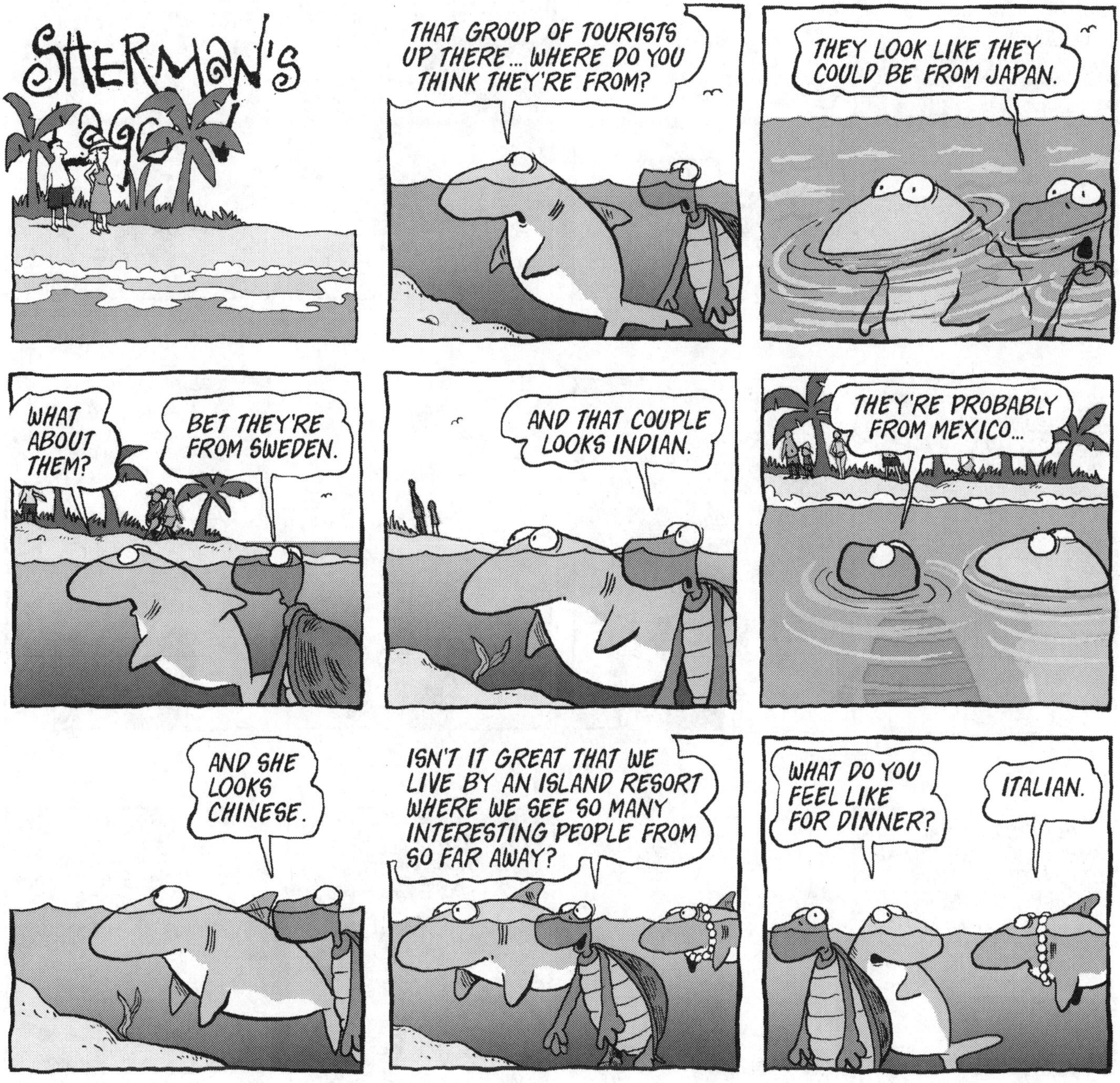
SHERMAN'S LAGOON
THAT GROUP OF TOURISTS UP THERE... WHERE DO YOU THINK THEY'RE FROM?
THEY LOOK LIKE THEY COULD BE FROM JAPAN.
WHAT ABOUT THEM?
BET THEY'RE FROM SWEDEN.
AND THAT COUPLE LOOKS INDIAN.
THEY'RE PROBABLY FROM MEXICO...
AND SHE LOOKS CHINESE.
ISN'T IT GREAT THAT WE LIVE BY AN ISLAND RESORT WHERE WE SEE SO MANY INTERESTING PEOPLE FROM SO FAR AWAY?
WHAT DO YOU FEEL LIKE FOR DINNER?
ITALIAN.

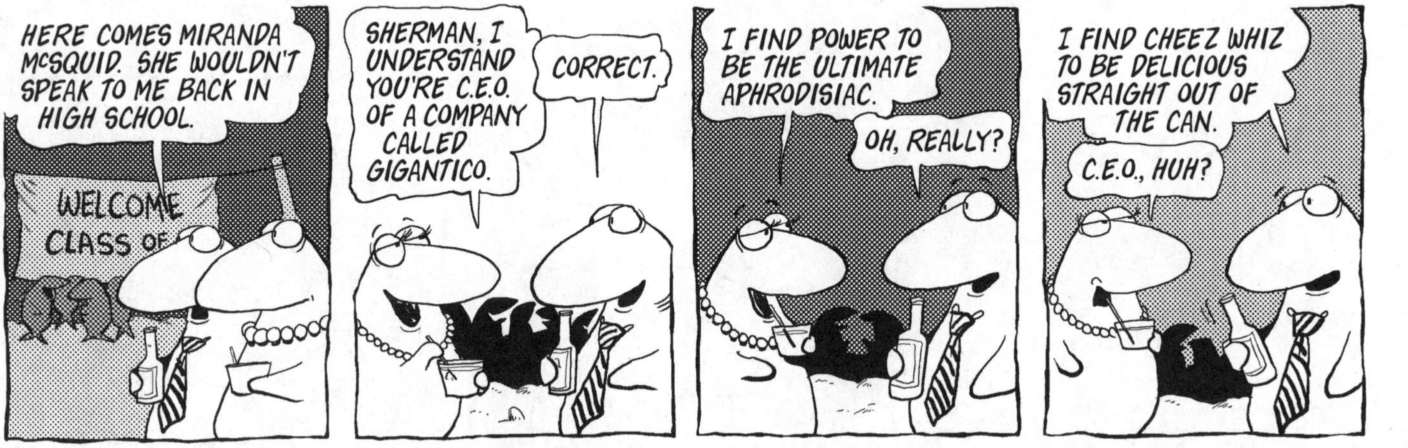
HERE COMES MIRANDA McSQUID. SHE WOULDN'T SPEAK TO ME BACK IN HIGH SCHOOL.
WELCOME CLASS OF
SHERMAN, I UNDERSTAND YOU'RE C.E.O. OF A COMPANY CALLED GIGANTICO.
CORRECT.
I FIND POWER TO BE THE ULTIMATE APHRODISIAC.
OH, REALLY?
I FIND CHEEZ WHIZ TO BE DELICIOUS STRAIGHT OUT OF THE CAN.
C.E.O., HUH?

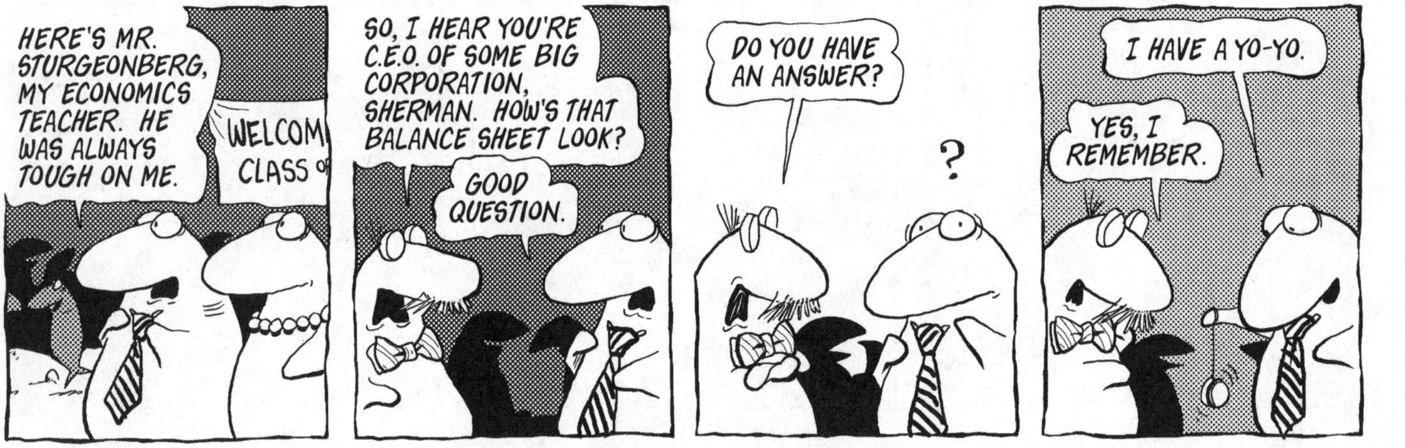
HERE'S MR. STURGEONBERG, MY ECONOMICS TEACHER. HE WAS ALWAYS TOUGH ON ME.
WELCOM CLASS OF
SO, I HEAR YOU'RE C.E.O. OF SOME BIG CORPORATION, SHERMAN. HOW'S THAT BALANCE SHEET LOOK?
GOOD QUESTION.
DO YOU HAVE AN ANSWER?
?
I HAVE A YO-YO.
YES, I REMEMBER.

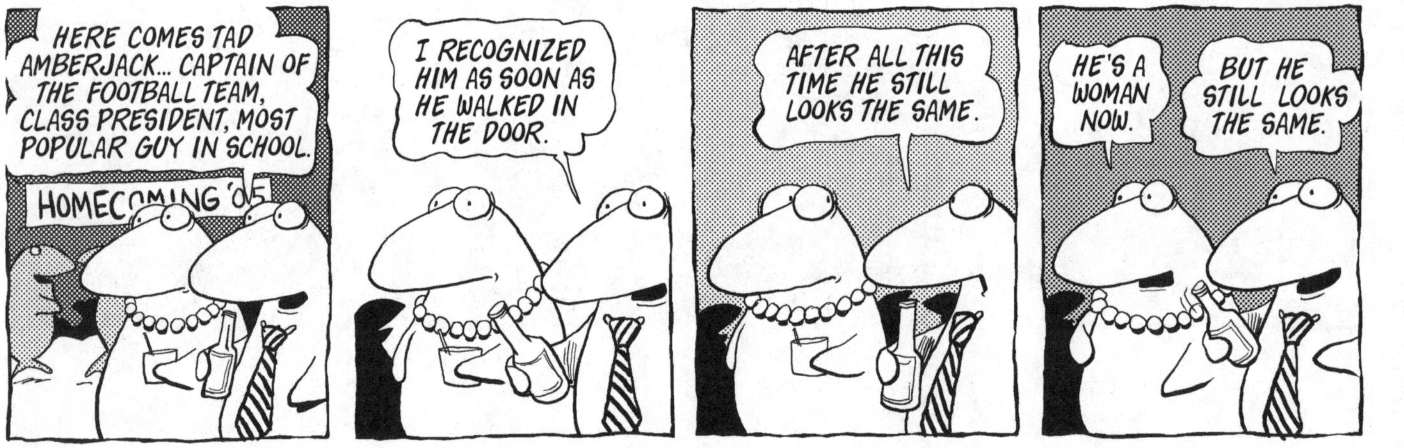
HERE COMES TAD AMBERJACK... CAPTAIN OF THE FOOTBALL TEAM, CLASS PRESIDENT, MOST POPULAR GUY IN SCHOOL.
HOMECOMING '05
I RECOGNIZED HIM AS SOON AS HE WALKED IN THE DOOR.
AFTER ALL THIS TIME HE STILL LOOKS THE SAME.
HE'S A WOMAN NOW.
BUT HE STILL LOOKS THE SAME.

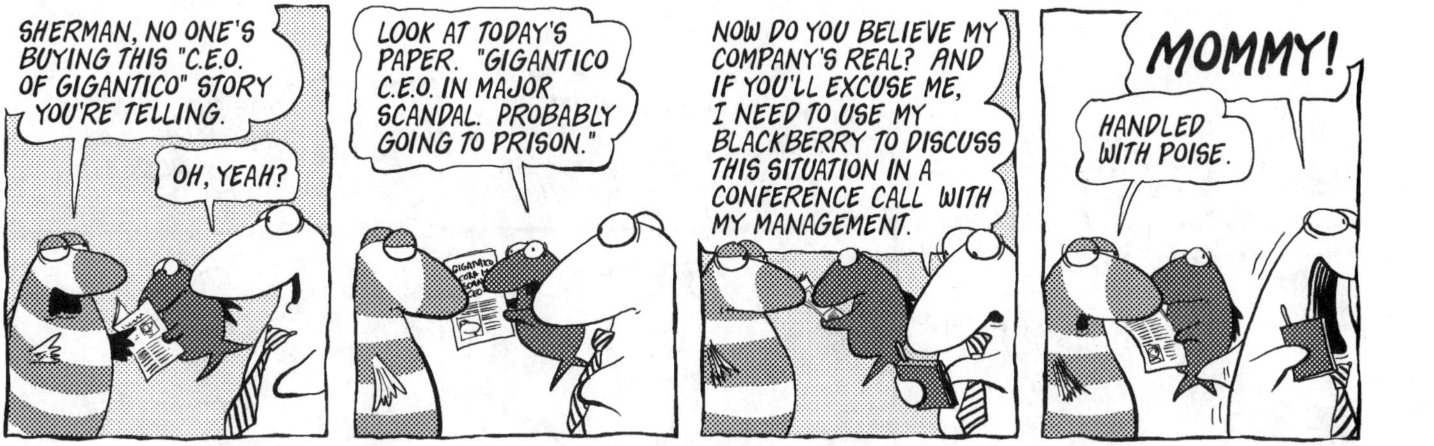
SHERMAN, NO ONE'S BUYING THIS "C.E.O. OF GIGANTICO" STORY YOU'RE TELLING.
OH, YEAH?
LOOK AT TODAY'S PAPER. "GIGANTICO C.E.O. IN MAJOR SCANDAL. PROBABLY GOING TO PRISON."
NOW DO YOU BELIEVE MY COMPANY'S REAL? AND IF YOU'LL EXCUSE ME, I NEED TO USE MY BLACKBERRY TO DISCUSS THIS SITUATION IN A CONFERENCE CALL WITH MY MANAGEMENT.
MOMMY!
HANDLED WITH POISE.

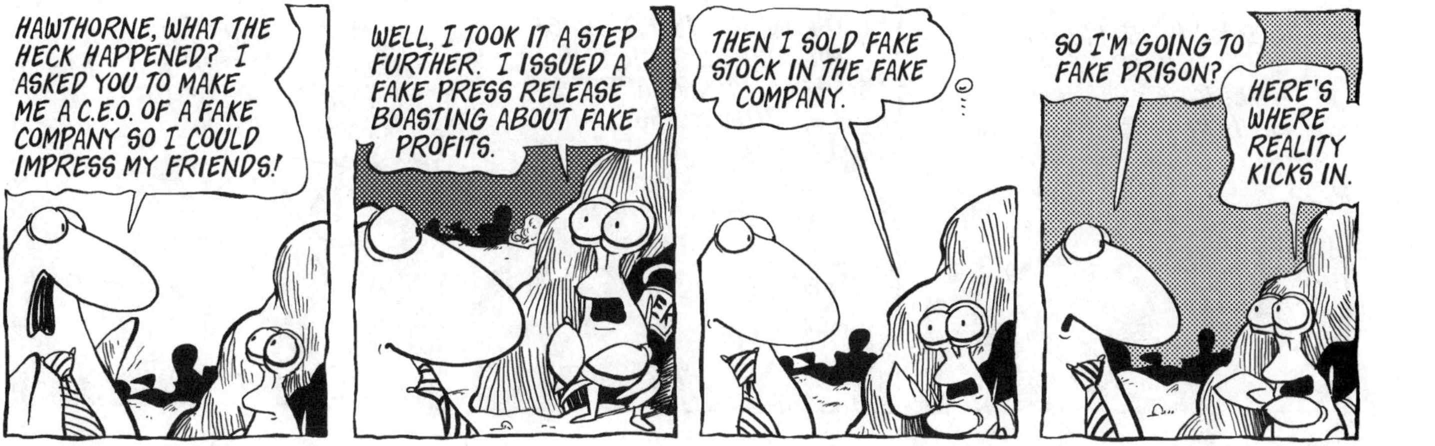
HAWTHORNE, WHAT THE HECK HAPPENED? I ASKED YOU TO MAKE ME A C.E.O. OF A FAKE COMPANY SO I COULD IMPRESS MY FRIENDS!
WELL, I TOOK IT A STEP FURTHER. I ISSUED A FAKE PRESS RELEASE BOASTING ABOUT FAKE PROFITS.
THEN I SOLD FAKE STOCK IN THE FAKE COMPANY.
SO I'M GOING TO FAKE PRISON?
HERE'S WHERE REALITY KICKS IN.

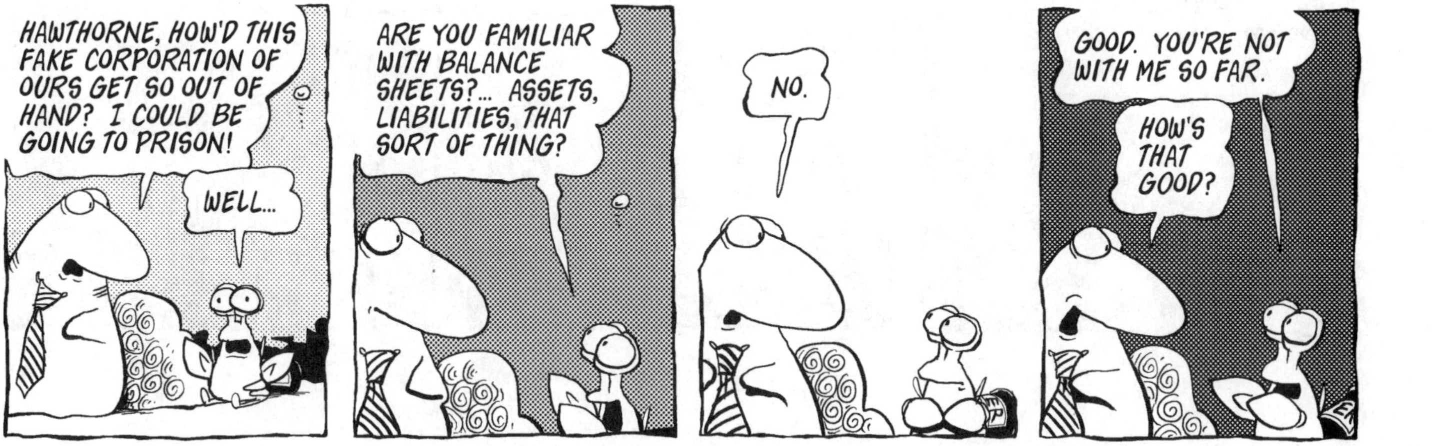
HAWTHORNE, HOW'D THIS FAKE CORPORATION OF OURS GET SO OUT OF HAND? I COULD BE GOING TO PRISON!
WELL...
ARE YOU FAMILIAR WITH BALANCE SHEETS?... ASSETS, LIABILITIES, THAT SORT OF THING?
NO.
GOOD. YOU'RE NOT WITH ME SO FAR.
HOW'S THAT GOOD?

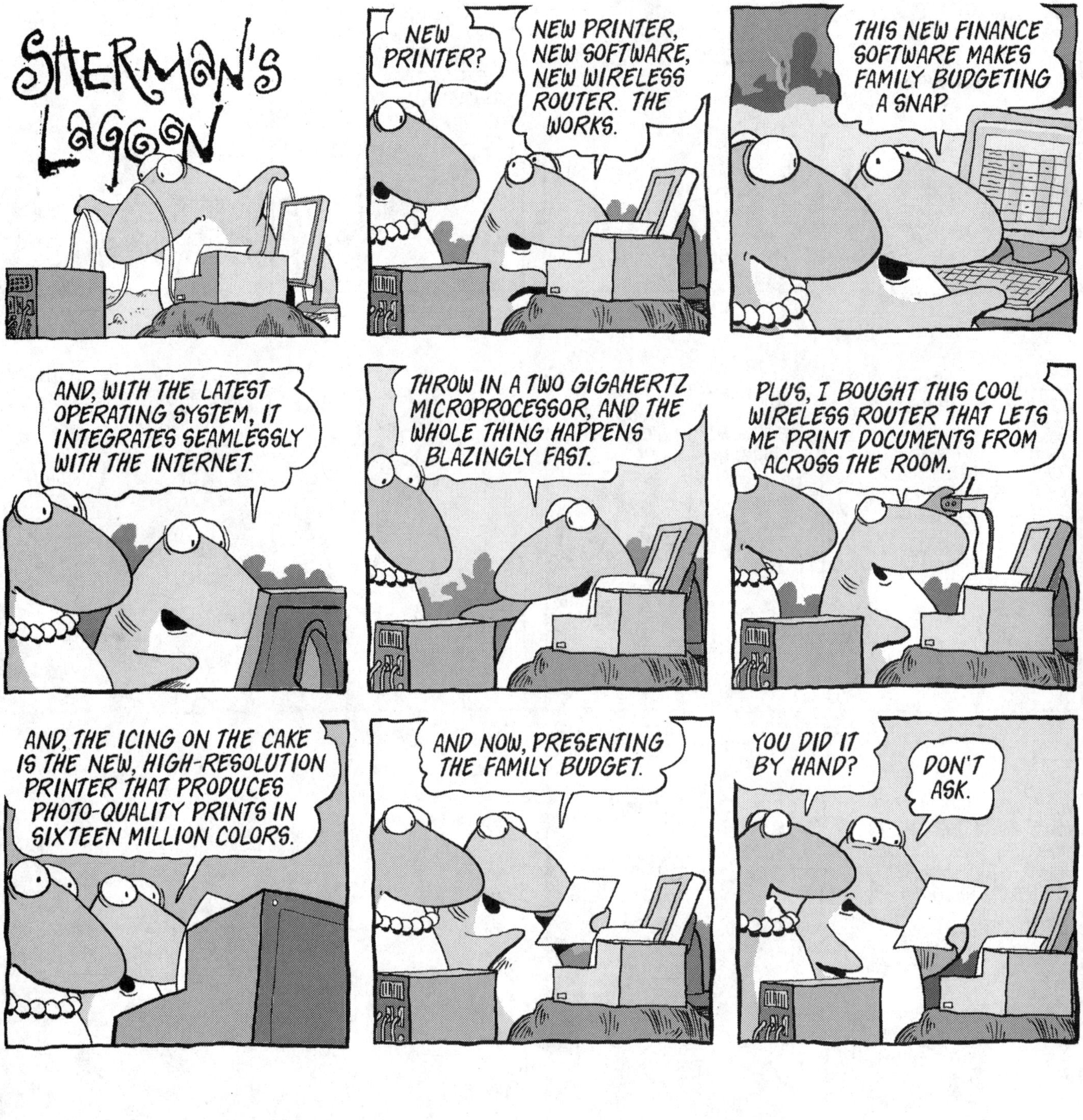
SHERMAN'S LAGOON
NEW PRINTER?
NEW PRINTER, NEW SOFTWARE, NEW WIRELESS ROUTER. THE WORKS.
THIS NEW FINANCE SOFTWARE MAKES FAMILY BUDGETING A SNAP.
AND, WITH THE LATEST OPERATING SYSTEM, IT INTEGRATES SEAMLESSLY WITH THE INTERNET.
THROW IN A TWO GIGAHERTZ MICROPROCESSOR, AND THE WHOLE THING HAPPENS BLAZINGLY FAST.
PLUS, I BOUGHT THIS COOL WIRELESS ROUTER THAT LETS ME PRINT DOCUMENTS FROM ACROSS THE ROOM.
AND, THE ICING ON THE CAKE IS THE NEW, HIGH-RESOLUTION PRINTER THAT PRODUCES PHOTO-QUALITY PRINTS IN SIXTEEN MILLION COLORS.
AND NOW, PRESENTING THE FAMILY BUDGET.
YOU DID IT BY HAND?
DON'T ASK.

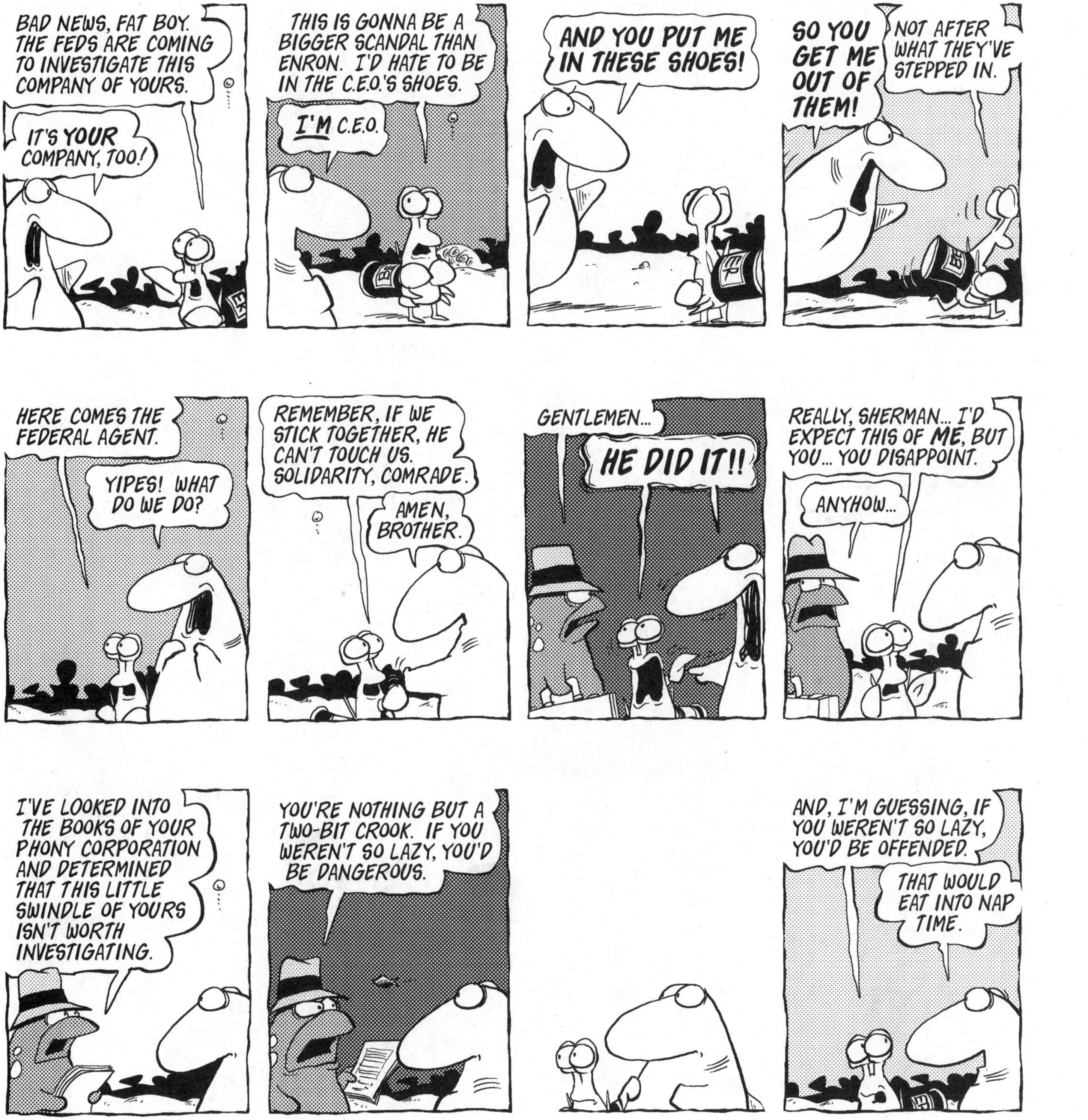
BAD NEWS, FAT BOY. THE FEDS ARE COMING TO INVESTIGATE THIS COMPANY OF YOURS.
IT'S YOUR COMPANY, TOO!
THIS IS GONNA BE A BIGGER SCANDAL THAN ENRON. I'D HATE TO BE IN THE C.E.O.'S SHOES.
I'M C.E.O.
AND YOU PUT ME IN THESE SHOES!
SO YOU GET ME OUT OF THEM!
NOT AFTER WHAT THEY'VE STEPPED IN.
HERE COMES THE FEDERAL AGENT.
YIPES! WHAT DO WE DO?
REMEMBER, IF WE STICK TOGETHER, HE CAN'T TOUCH US. SOLIDARITY, COMRADE.
AMEN, BROTHER.
GENTLEMEN...
HE DID IT!!
REALLY, SHERMAN... I'D EXPECT THIS OF ME, BUT YOU... YOU DISAPPOINT.
ANYHOW...
I'VE LOOKED INTO THE BOOKS OF YOUR PHONY CORPORATION AND DETERMINED THAT THIS LITTLE SWINDLE OF YOURS ISN'T WORTH INVESTIGATING.
YOU'RE NOTHING BUT A TWO-BIT CROOK. IF YOU WEREN'T SO LAZY, YOU'D BE DANGEROUS.
AND, I'M GUESSING, IF YOU WEREN'T SO LAZY, YOU'D BE OFFENDED.
THAT WOULD EAT INTO NAP TIME.

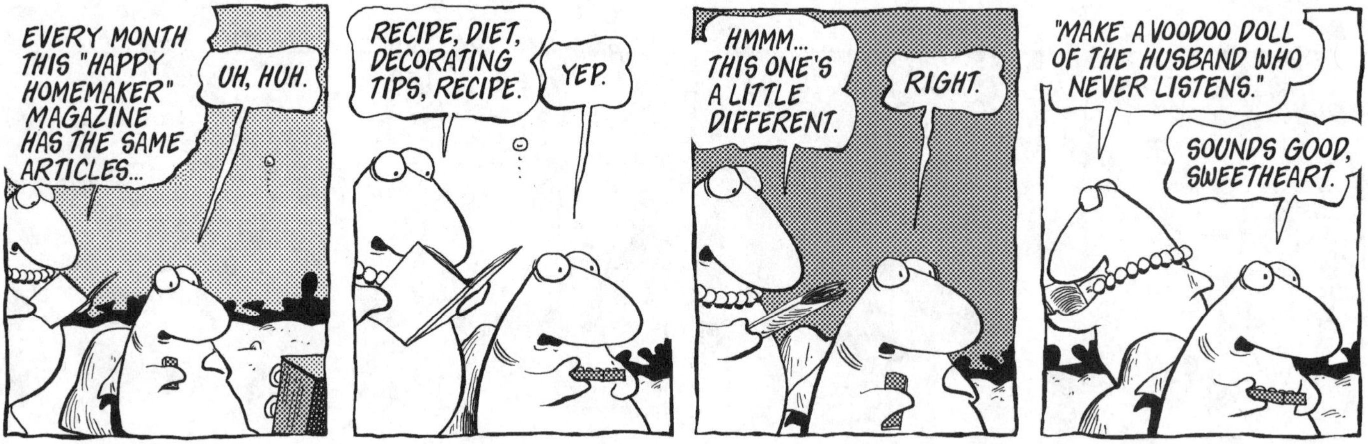
EVERY MONTH THIS "HAPPY HOMEMAKER" MAGAZINE HAS THE SAME ARTICLES...
UH, HUH.
RECIPE, DIET, DECORATING TIPS, RECIPE.
YEP.
HMMM... THIS ONE'S A LITTLE DIFFERENT.
RIGHT.
"MAKE A VOODOO DOLL OF THE HUSBAND WHO NEVER LISTENS."
SOUNDS GOOD, SWEETHEART.

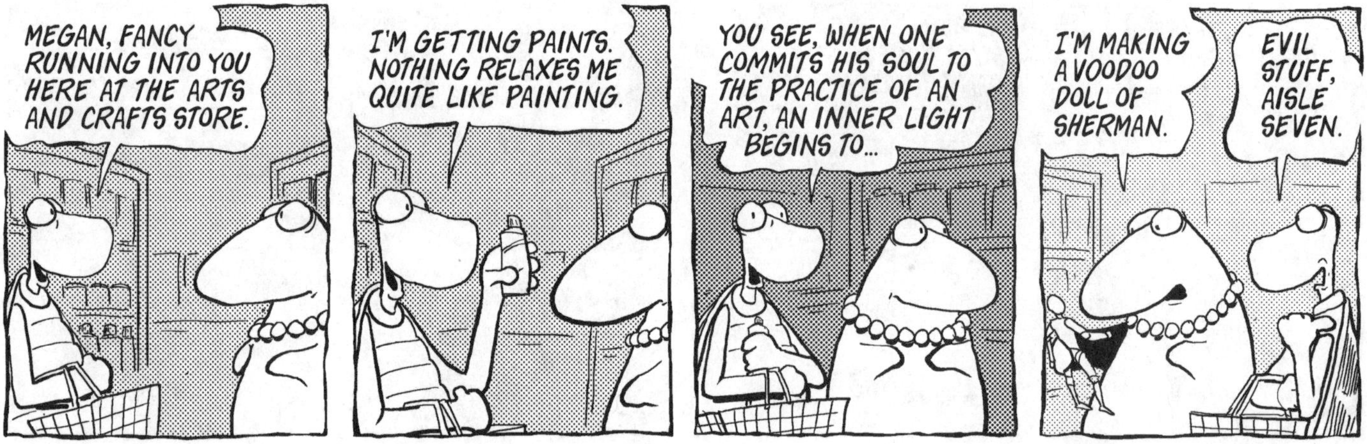
MEGAN, FANCY RUNNING INTO YOU HERE AT THE ARTS AND CRAFTS STORE.
I'M GETTING PAINTS. NOTHING RELAXES ME QUITE LIKE PAINTING.
YOU SEE, WHEN ONE COMMITS HIS SOUL TO THE PRACTICE OF AN ART, AN INNER LIGHT BEGINS TO...
I'M MAKING A VOODOO DOLL OF SHERMAN.
EVIL STUFF, AISLE SEVEN.

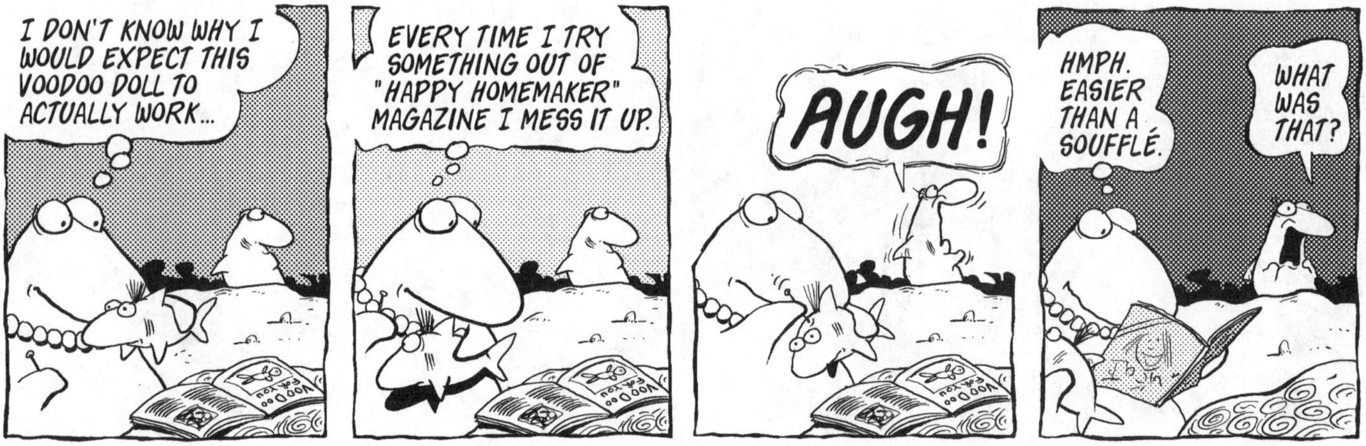
I DON'T KNOW WHY I WOULD EXPECT THIS VOODOO DOLL TO ACTUALLY WORK...
EVERY TIME I TRY SOMETHING OUT OF "HAPPY HOMEMAKER" MAGAZINE I MESS IT UP.
AUGH!
HMPH. EASIER THAN A SOUFFLÉ.
WHAT WAS THAT?

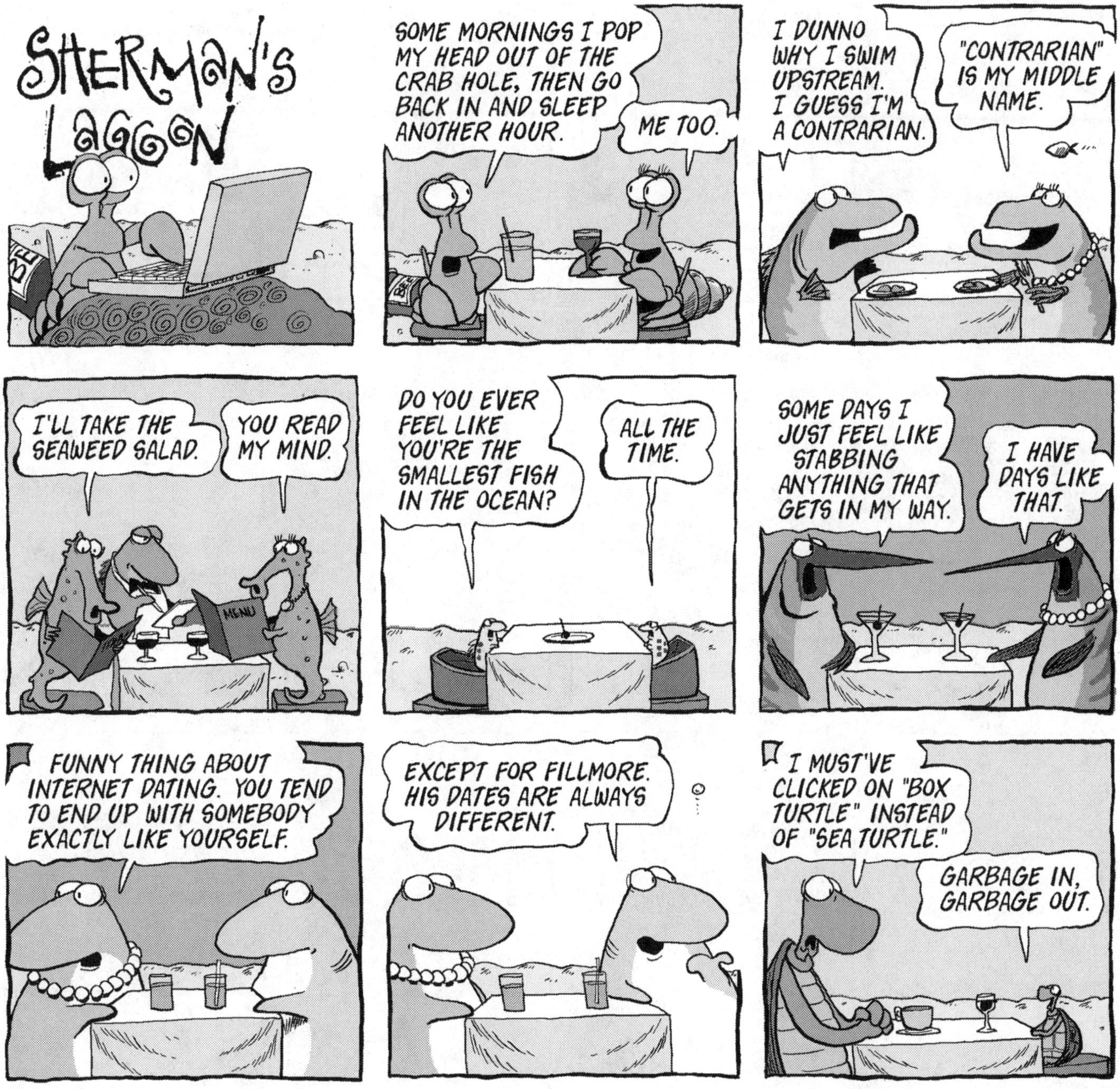
SHERMAN'S LAGOON
SOME MORNINGS I POP MY HEAD OUT OF THE CRAB HOLE, THEN GO BACK IN AND SLEEP ANOTHER HOUR.
ME TOO.
I DUNNO WHY I SWIM UPSTREAM. I GUESS I'M A CONTRARIAN.
"CONTRARIAN" IS MY MIDDLE NAME.
I'LL TAKE THE SEAWEED SALAD.
YOU READ MY MIND.
MENU
DO YOU EVER FEEL LIKE YOU'RE THE SMALLEST FISH IN THE OCEAN?
ALL THE TIME.
SOME DAYS I JUST FEEL LIKE STABBING ANYTHING THAT GETS IN MY WAY.
I HAVE DAYS LIKE THAT.
FUNNY THING ABOUT INTERNET DATING. YOU TEND TO END UP WITH SOMEBODY EXACTLY LIKE YOURSELF.
EXCEPT FOR FILLMORE. HIS DATES ARE ALWAYS DIFFERENT.
I MUST'VE CLICKED ON "BOX TURTLE" INSTEAD OF "SEA TURTLE."
GARBAGE IN, GARBAGE OUT.

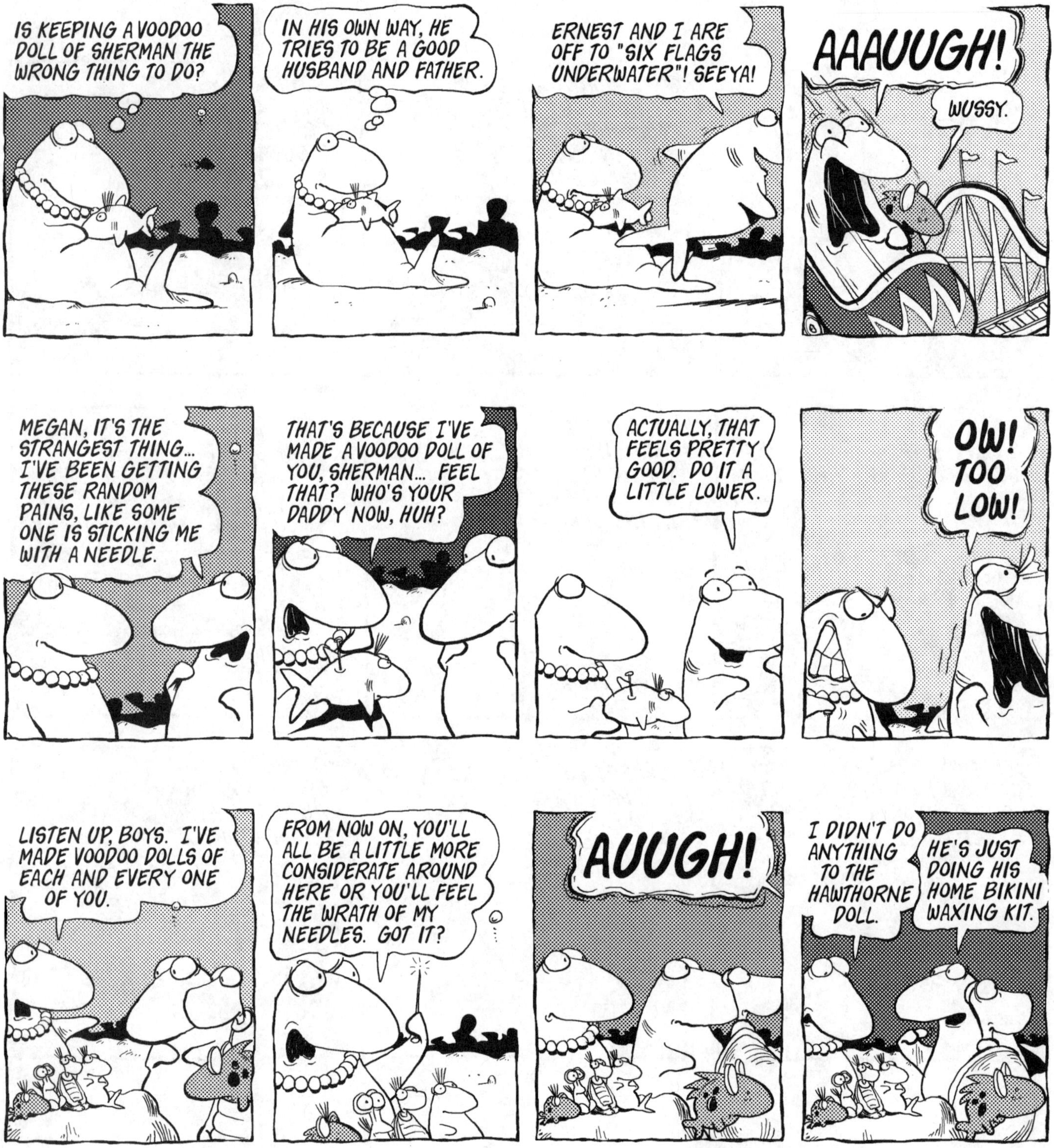
IS KEEPING A VOODOO DOLL OF SHERMAN THE WRONG THING TO DO?
IN HIS OWN WAY, HE TRIES TO BE A GOOD HUSBAND AND FATHER.
ERNEST AND I ARE OFF TO "SIX FLAGS UNDERWATER"! SEEYA!
AAAUUGH!
WUSSY.
MEGAN, IT'S THE STRANGEST THING... I'VE BEEN GETTING THESE RANDOM PAINS, LIKE SOME ONE IS STICKING ME WITH A NEEDLE.
THAT'S BECAUSE I'VE MADE A VOODOO DOLL OF YOU, SHERMAN... FEEL THAT? WHO'S YOUR DADDY NOW, HUH?
ACTUALLY, THAT FEELS PRETTY GOOD. DO IT A LITTLE LOWER.
OW! TOO LOW!
LISTEN UP, BOYS. I'VE MADE VOODOO DOLLS OF EACH AND EVERY ONE OF YOU.
FROM NOW ON, YOU'LL ALL BE A LITTLE MORE CONSIDERATE AROUND HERE OR YOU'LL FEEL THE WRATH OF MY NEEDLES. GOT IT?
AUUGH!
I DIDN'T DO ANYTHING TO THE HAWTHORNE DOLL.
HE'S JUST DOING HIS HOME BIKINI WAXING KIT.

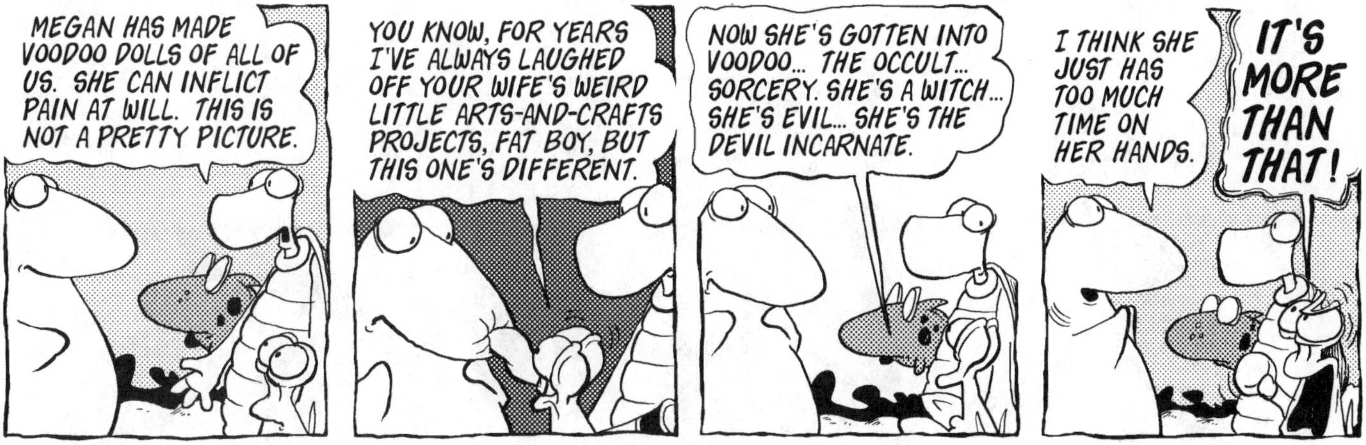

MEGAN HAS MADE VOODOO DOLLS OF ALL OF US. SHE CAN INFLICT PAIN AT WILL. THIS IS NOT A PRETTY PICTURE.
YOU KNOW, FOR YEARS I'VE ALWAYS LAUGHED OFF YOUR WIFE'S WEIRD LITTLE ARTS-AND-CRAFTS PROJECTS, FAT BOY, BUT THIS ONE'S DIFFERENT.
NOW SHE'S GOTTEN INTO VOODOO... THE OCCULT... SORCERY. SHE'S A WITCH... SHE'S EVIL... SHE'S THE DEVIL INCARNATE.
I THINK SHE JUST HAS TOO MUCH TIME ON HER HANDS.
IT'S MORE THAN THAT!

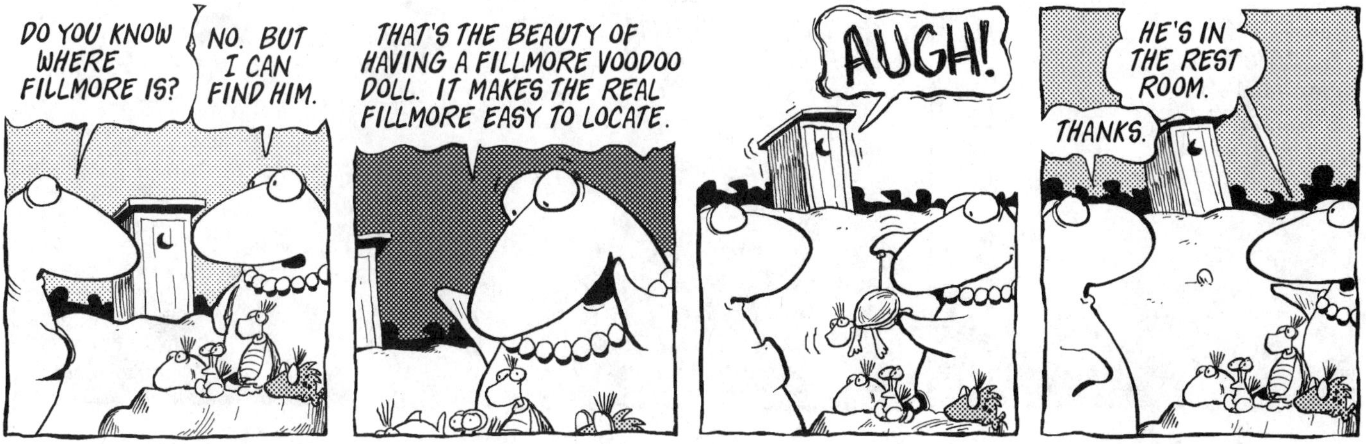

DO YOU KNOW WHERE FILLMORE IS?
NO. BUT I CAN FIND HIM.
THAT'S THE BEAUTY OF HAVING A FILLMORE VOODOO DOLL. IT MAKES THE REAL FILLMORE EASY TO LOCATE.
AUGH!
HE'S IN THE REST ROOM.
THANKS.

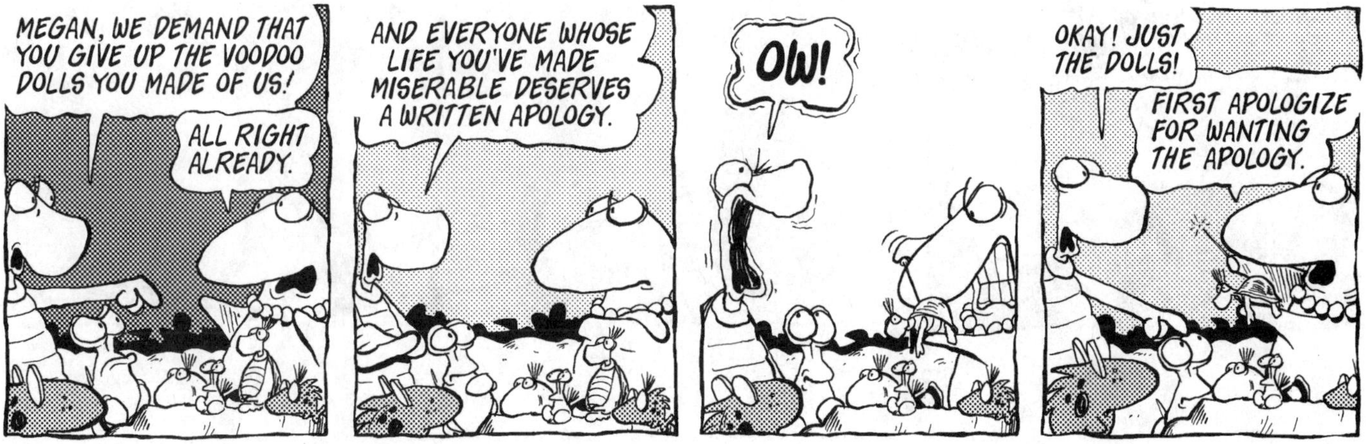

MEGAN, WE DEMAND THAT YOU GIVE UP THE VOODOO DOLLS YOU MADE OF US!
ALL RIGHT ALREADY.
AND EVERYONE WHOSE LIFE YOU'VE MADE MISERABLE DESERVES A WRITTEN APOLOGY.
OW!
OKAY! JUST THE DOLLS!
FIRST APOLOGIZE FOR WANTING THE APOLOGY.

SHERMAN'S LAGOON

"HOW'RE YA DOIN'?"

"ME? I'M OKAY, I GUESS."

"REALLY?"

"WELL, NO... NOW THAT YOU MENTION IT, NOT REALLY."

"YEAH?"

"YEAH... THAT SHE-TURTLE I WENT OUT WITH DUMPED ME AFTER ONE DATE..."

"SHE SAID I WASN'T MAN ENOUGH FOR HER."

"HMPH."

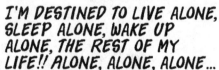

"I'M DESTINED TO LIVE ALONE, SLEEP ALONE, WAKE UP ALONE, THE REST OF MY LIFE!! ALONE, ALONE, ALONE..."

SNORT!

"AND YOU'RE THE FIRST ONE TO LISTEN!"

"LEMME CALL YOU BACK."

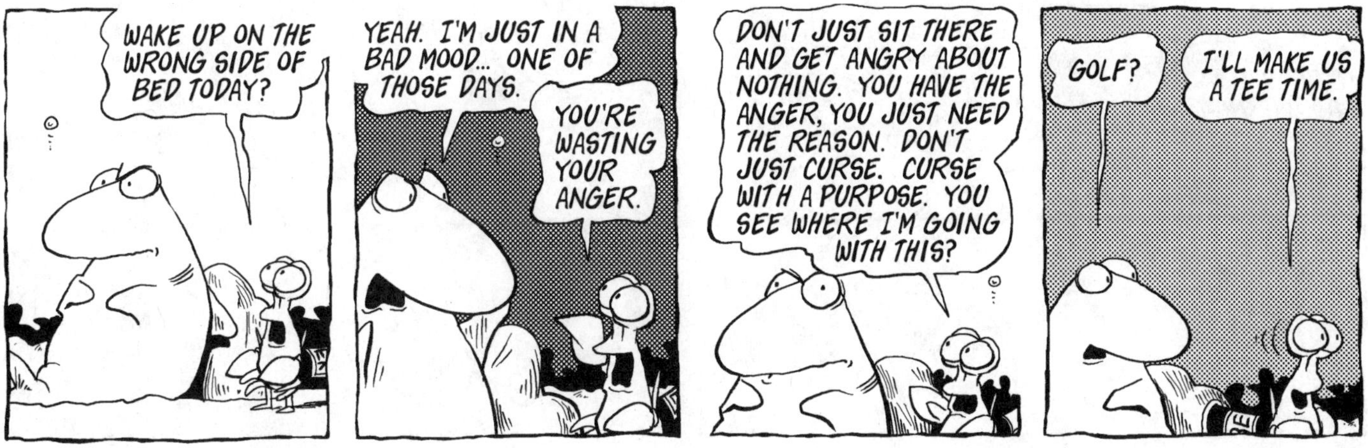
WAKE UP ON THE WRONG SIDE OF BED TODAY?
YEAH. I'M JUST IN A BAD MOOD... ONE OF THOSE DAYS.
YOU'RE WASTING YOUR ANGER.
DON'T JUST SIT THERE AND GET ANGRY ABOUT NOTHING. YOU HAVE THE ANGER, YOU JUST NEED THE REASON. DON'T JUST CURSE. CURSE WITH A PURPOSE. YOU SEE WHERE I'M GOING WITH THIS?
GOLF?
I'LL MAKE US A TEE TIME.

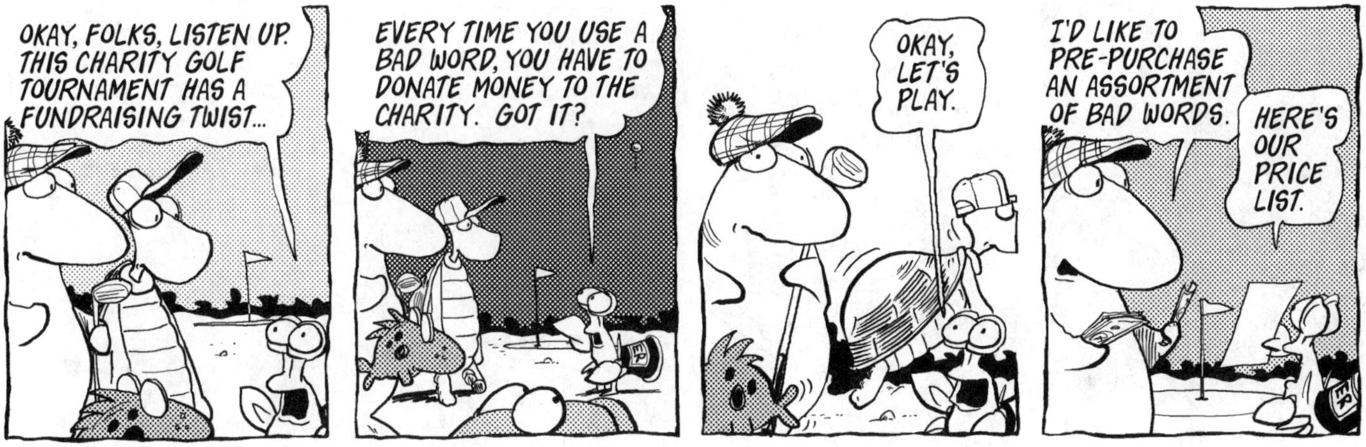
OKAY, FOLKS, LISTEN UP. THIS CHARITY GOLF TOURNAMENT HAS A FUNDRAISING TWIST...
EVERY TIME YOU USE A BAD WORD, YOU HAVE TO DONATE MONEY TO THE CHARITY. GOT IT?
OKAY, LET'S PLAY.
I'D LIKE TO PRE-PURCHASE AN ASSORTMENT OF BAD WORDS.
HERE'S OUR PRICE LIST.

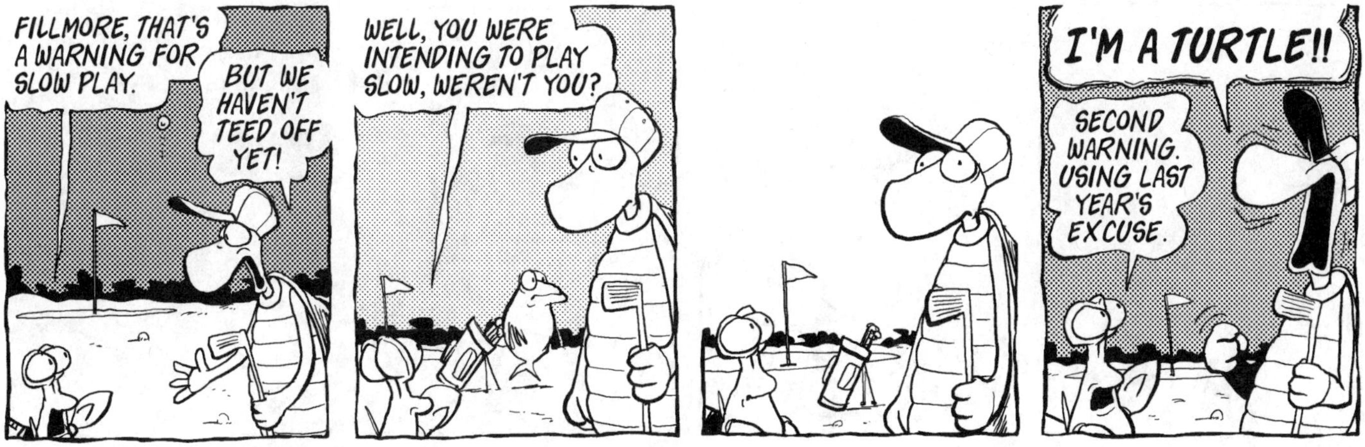
FILLMORE, THAT'S A WARNING FOR SLOW PLAY.
BUT WE HAVEN'T TEED OFF YET!
WELL, YOU WERE INTENDING TO PLAY SLOW, WEREN'T YOU?
I'M A TURTLE!!
SECOND WARNING. USING LAST YEAR'S EXCUSE.

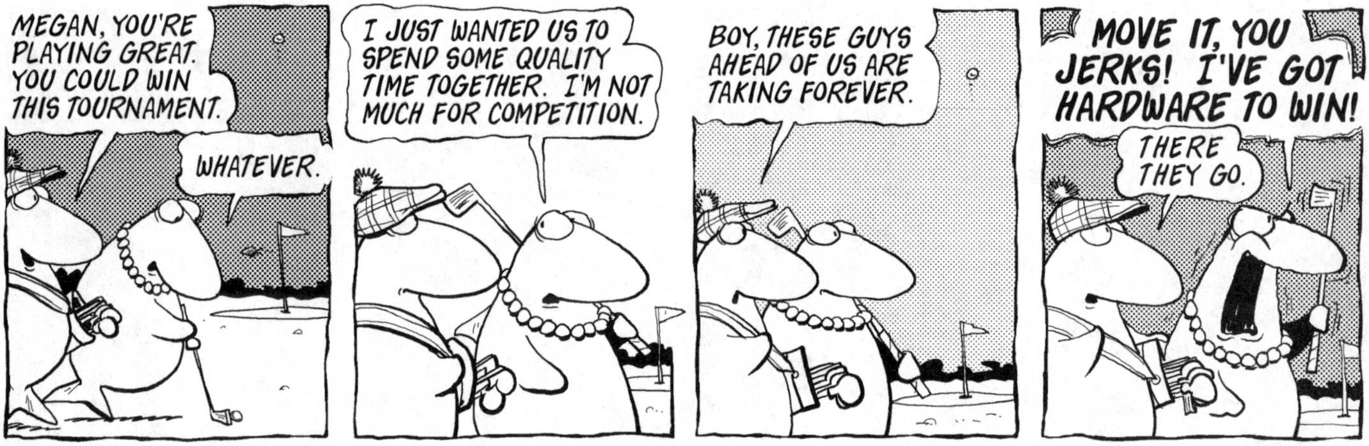
MEGAN, YOU'RE PLAYING GREAT. YOU COULD WIN THIS TOURNAMENT.
WHATEVER.
I JUST WANTED US TO SPEND SOME QUALITY TIME TOGETHER. I'M NOT MUCH FOR COMPETITION.
BOY, THESE GUYS AHEAD OF US ARE TAKING FOREVER.
MOVE IT, YOU JERKS! I'VE GOT HARDWARE TO WIN!
THERE THEY GO.

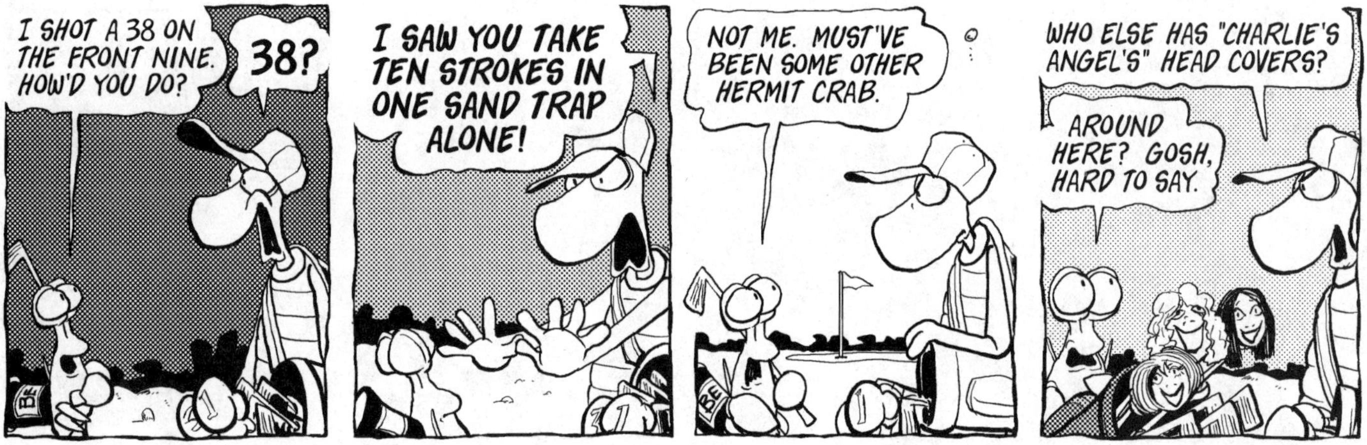
I SHOT A 38 ON THE FRONT NINE. HOW'D YOU DO?
38?
I SAW YOU TAKE TEN STROKES IN ONE SAND TRAP ALONE!
NOT ME. MUST'VE BEEN SOME OTHER HERMIT CRAB.
WHO ELSE HAS "CHARLIE'S ANGEL'S" HEAD COVERS?
AROUND HERE? GOSH, HARD TO SAY.

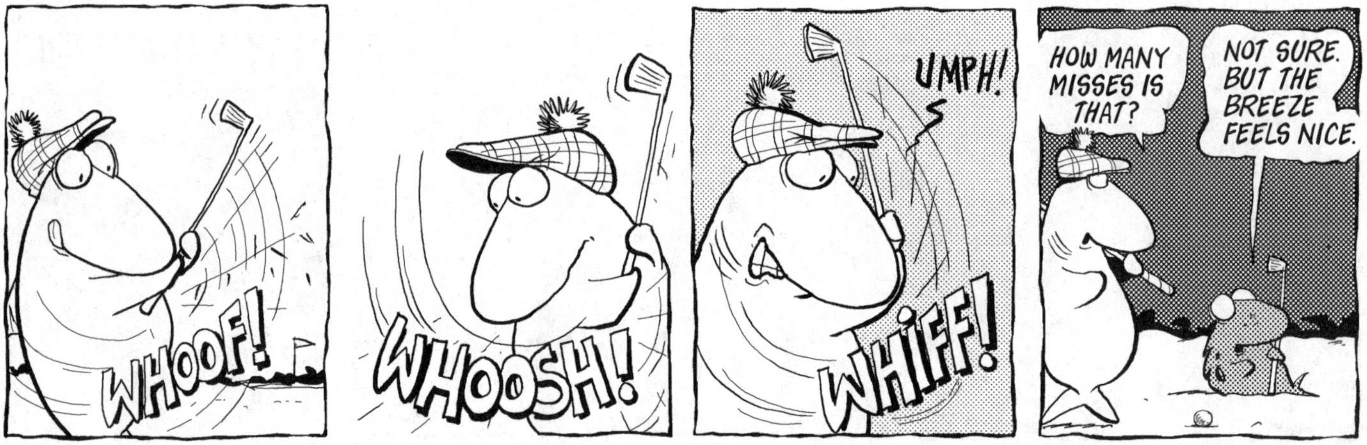
WHOOF!
WHOOSH!
UMPH!
WHIFF!
HOW MANY MISSES IS THAT?
NOT SURE. BUT THE BREEZE FEELS NICE.

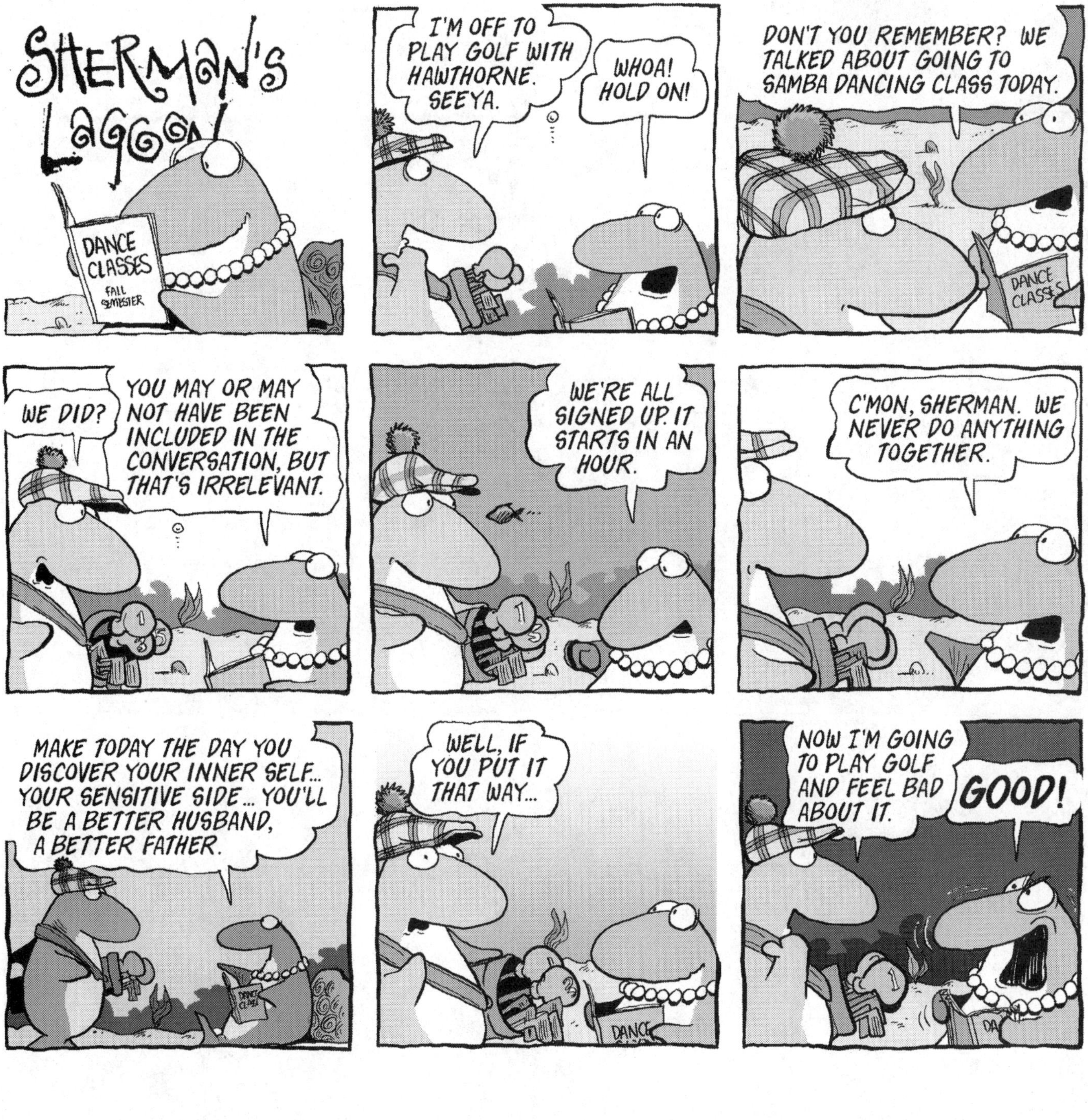
SHERMAN'S LAGOON
DANCE CLASSES FALL SEMESTER
I'M OFF TO PLAY GOLF WITH HAWTHORNE. SEEYA.
WHOA! HOLD ON!
DON'T YOU REMEMBER? WE TALKED ABOUT GOING TO SAMBA DANCING CLASS TODAY.
DANCE CLASSES
WE DID?
YOU MAY OR MAY NOT HAVE BEEN INCLUDED IN THE CONVERSATION, BUT THAT'S IRRELEVANT.
WE'RE ALL SIGNED UP. IT STARTS IN AN HOUR.
C'MON, SHERMAN. WE NEVER DO ANYTHING TOGETHER.
MAKE TODAY THE DAY YOU DISCOVER YOUR INNER SELF... YOUR SENSITIVE SIDE... YOU'LL BE A BETTER HUSBAND, A BETTER FATHER.
WELL, IF YOU PUT IT THAT WAY...
NOW I'M GOING TO PLAY GOLF AND FEEL BAD ABOUT IT.
GOOD!

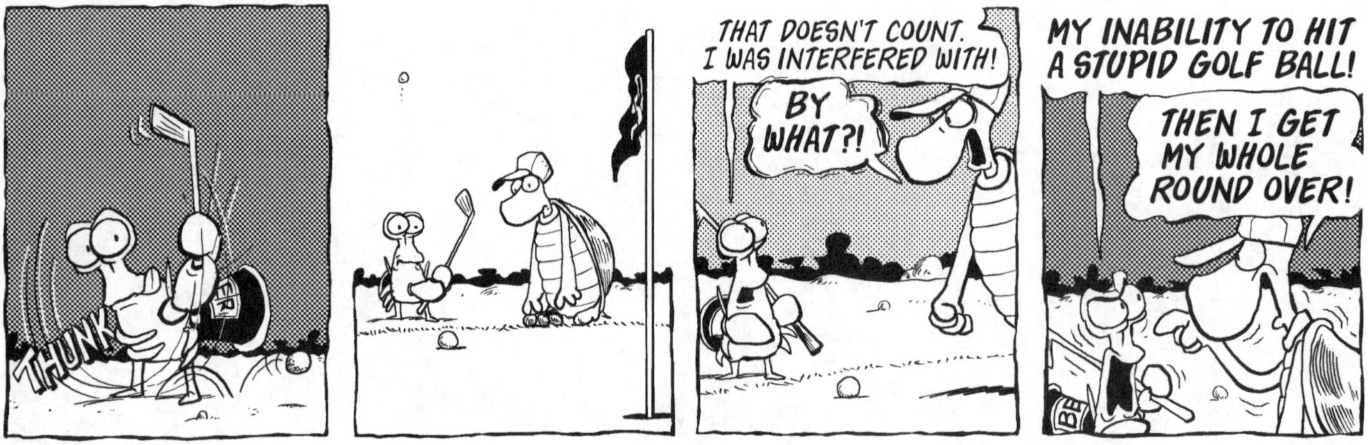
THUNK
THAT DOESN'T COUNT. I WAS INTERFERED WITH!
BY WHAT?!
MY INABILITY TO HIT A STUPID GOLF BALL!
THEN I GET MY WHOLE ROUND OVER!

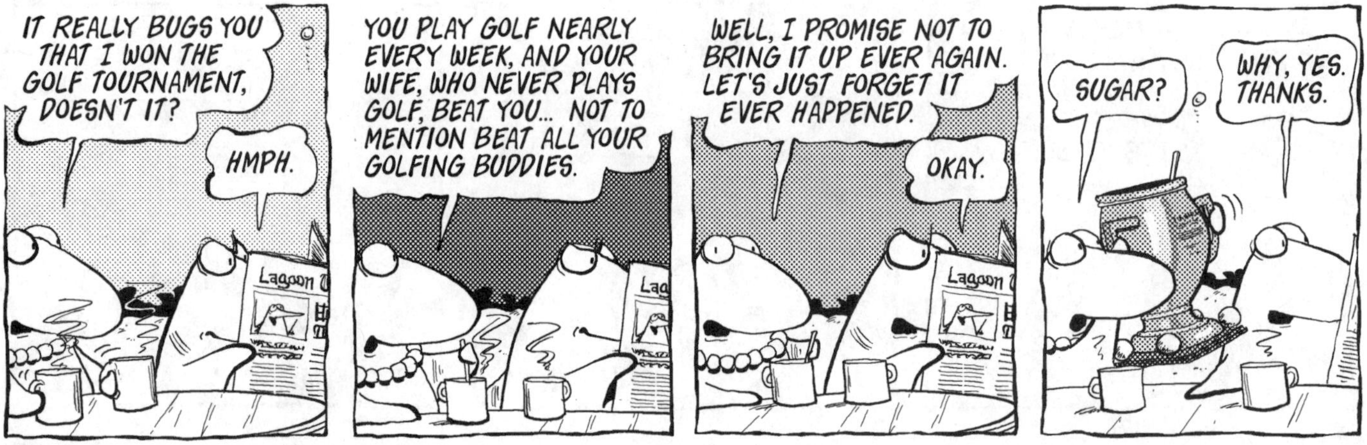
IT REALLY BUGS YOU THAT I WON THE GOLF TOURNAMENT, DOESN'T IT?
HMPH.
YOU PLAY GOLF NEARLY EVERY WEEK, AND YOUR WIFE, WHO NEVER PLAYS GOLF, BEAT YOU... NOT TO MENTION BEAT ALL YOUR GOLFING BUDDIES.
WELL, I PROMISE NOT TO BRING IT UP EVER AGAIN. LET'S JUST FORGET IT EVER HAPPENED.
OKAY.
SUGAR?
WHY, YES. THANKS.

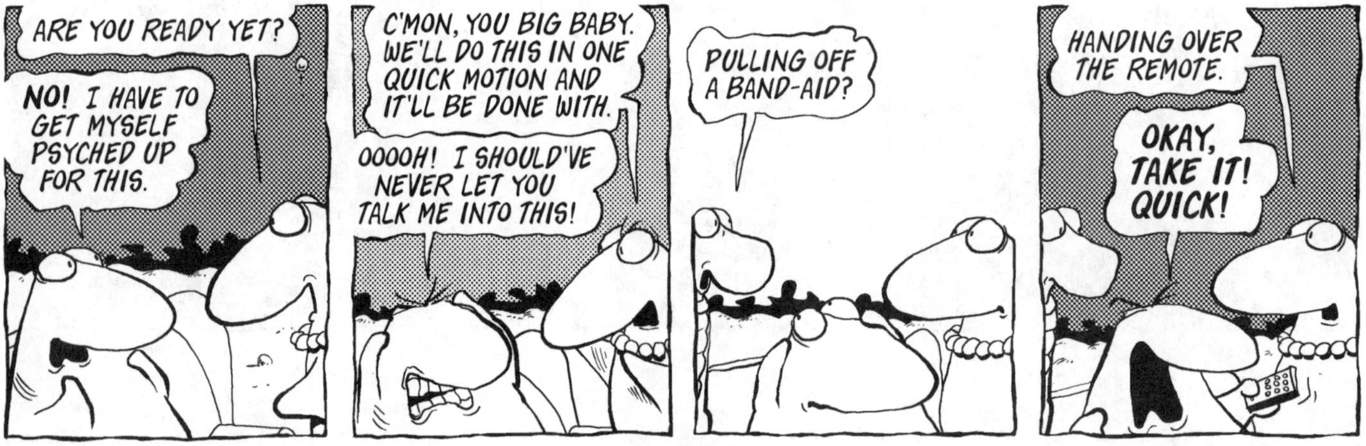
ARE YOU READY YET?
NO! I HAVE TO GET MYSELF PSYCHED UP FOR THIS.
C'MON, YOU BIG BABY. WE'LL DO THIS IN ONE QUICK MOTION AND IT'LL BE DONE WITH.
OOOOH! I SHOULD'VE NEVER LET YOU TALK ME INTO THIS!
PULLING OFF A BAND-AID?
HANDING OVER THE REMOTE.
OKAY, TAKE IT! QUICK!

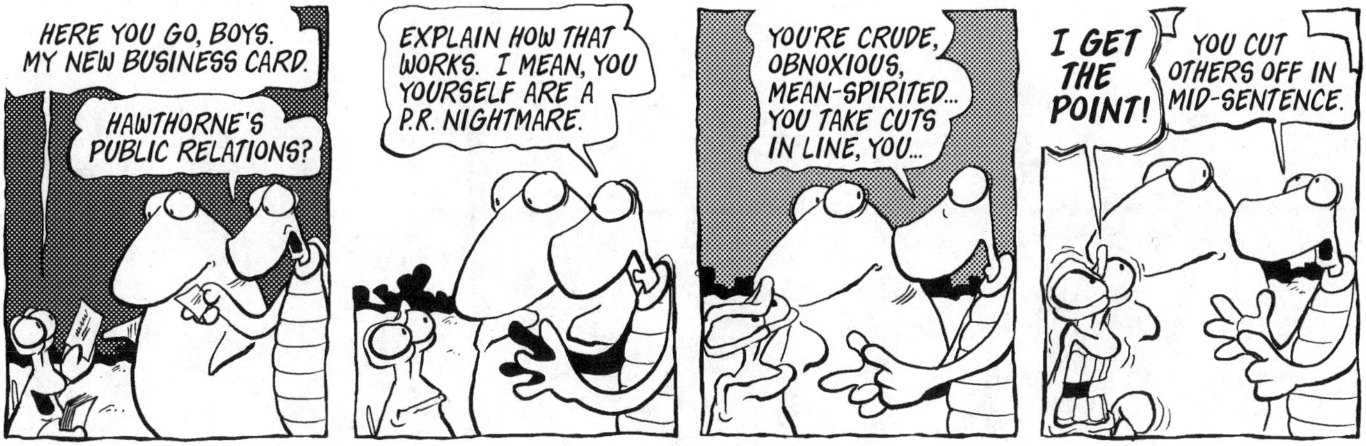
HERE YOU GO, BOYS. MY NEW BUSINESS CARD.
HAWTHORNE'S PUBLIC RELATIONS?
EXPLAIN HOW THAT WORKS. I MEAN, YOU YOURSELF ARE A P.R. NIGHTMARE.
YOU'RE CRUDE, OBNOXIOUS, MEAN-SPIRITED... YOU TAKE CUTS IN LINE, YOU...
I GET THE POINT!
YOU CUT OTHERS OFF IN MID-SENTENCE.

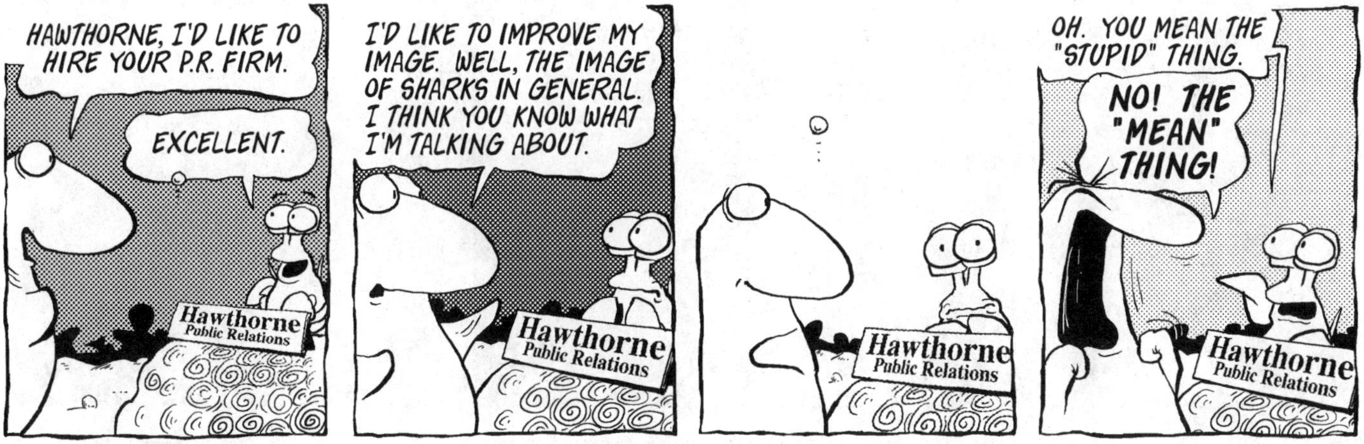
HAWTHORNE, I'D LIKE TO HIRE YOUR P.R. FIRM.
EXCELLENT.
Hawthorne Public Relations
I'D LIKE TO IMPROVE MY IMAGE. WELL, THE IMAGE OF SHARKS IN GENERAL. I THINK YOU KNOW WHAT I'M TALKING ABOUT.
Hawthorne Public Relations
Hawthorne Public Relations
OH. YOU MEAN THE "STUPID" THING.
NO! THE "MEAN" THING!
Hawthorne Public Relations

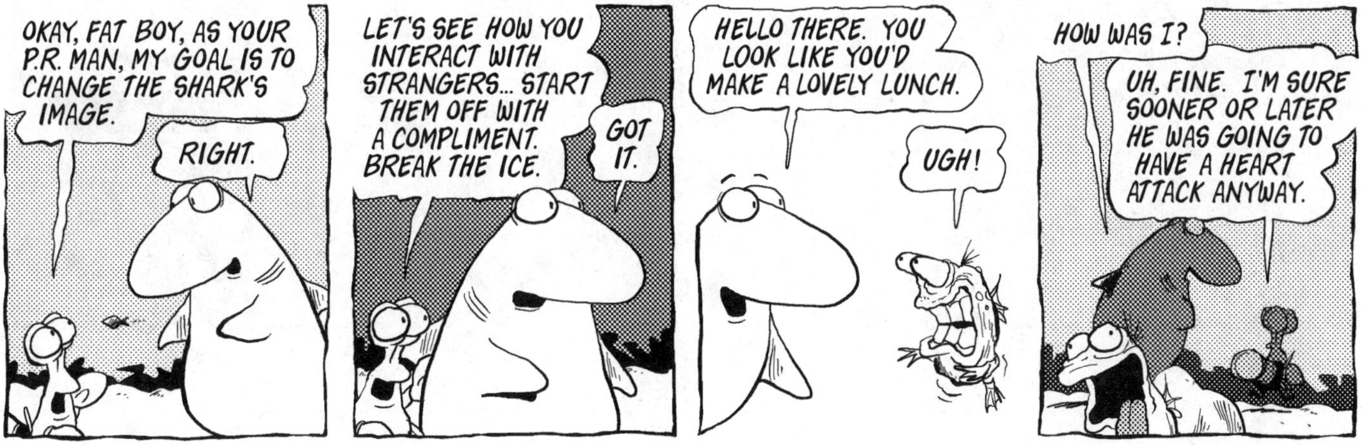
OKAY, FAT BOY, AS YOUR P.R. MAN, MY GOAL IS TO CHANGE THE SHARK'S IMAGE.
RIGHT.
LET'S SEE HOW YOU INTERACT WITH STRANGERS... START THEM OFF WITH A COMPLIMENT. BREAK THE ICE.
GOT IT.
HELLO THERE. YOU LOOK LIKE YOU'D MAKE A LOVELY LUNCH.
UGH!
HOW WAS I?
UH, FINE. I'M SURE SOONER OR LATER HE WAS GOING TO HAVE A HEART ATTACK ANYWAY.

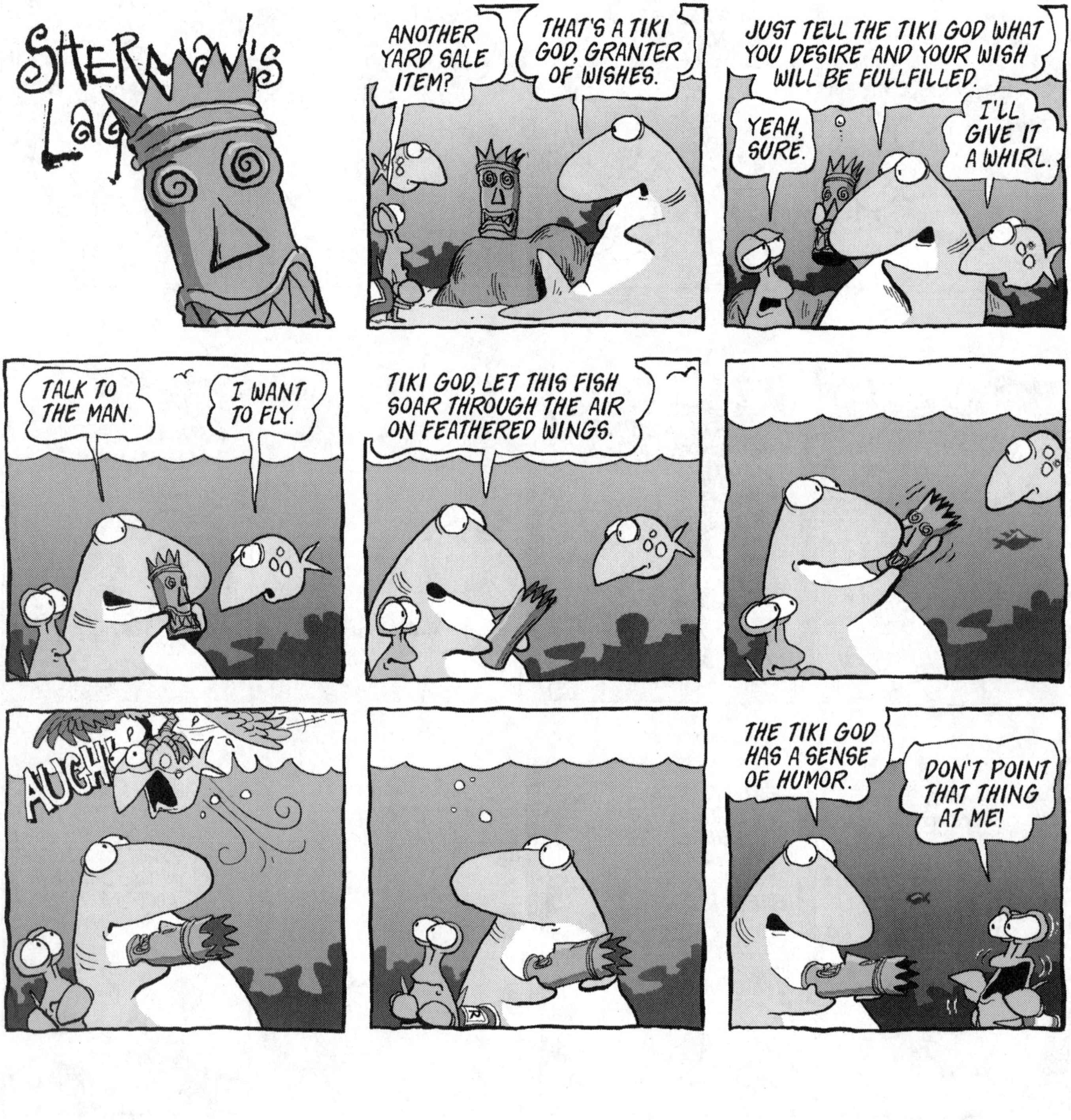
SHERMAN'S LAG
ANOTHER YARD SALE ITEM?
THAT'S A TIKI GOD, GRANTER OF WISHES.
JUST TELL THE TIKI GOD WHAT YOU DESIRE AND YOUR WISH WILL BE FULLFILLED.
YEAH, SURE.
I'LL GIVE IT A WHIRL.
TALK TO THE MAN.
I WANT TO FLY.
TIKI GOD, LET THIS FISH SOAR THROUGH THE AIR ON FEATHERED WINGS.
AUGH!
THE TIKI GOD HAS A SENSE OF HUMOR.
DON'T POINT THAT THING AT ME!

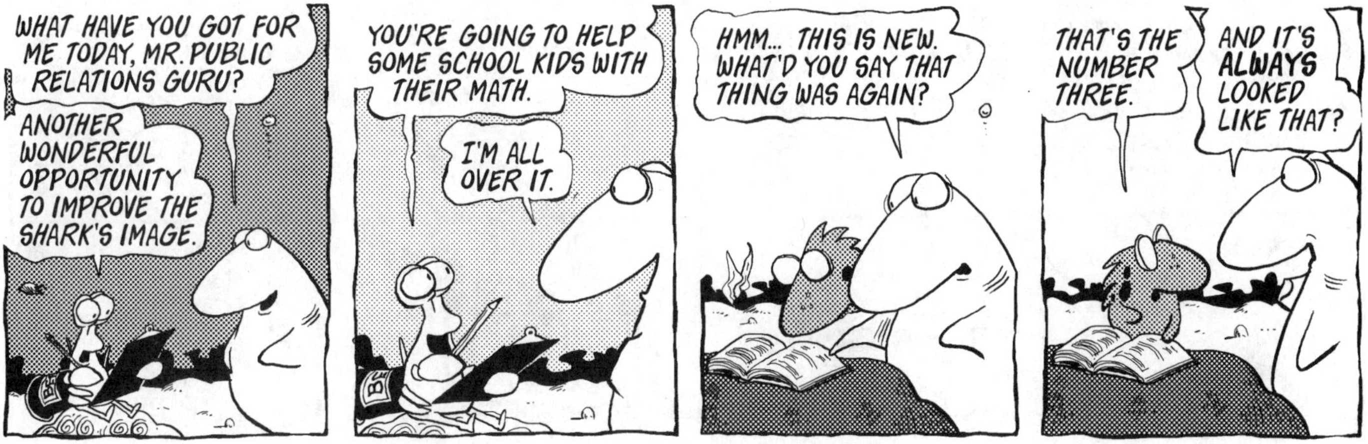
WHAT HAVE YOU GOT FOR ME TODAY, MR. PUBLIC RELATIONS GURU?
ANOTHER WONDERFUL OPPORTUNITY TO IMPROVE THE SHARK'S IMAGE.
YOU'RE GOING TO HELP SOME SCHOOL KIDS WITH THEIR MATH.
I'M ALL OVER IT.
HMM... THIS IS NEW. WHAT'D YOU SAY THAT THING WAS AGAIN?
THAT'S THE NUMBER THREE.
AND IT'S ALWAYS LOOKED LIKE THAT?

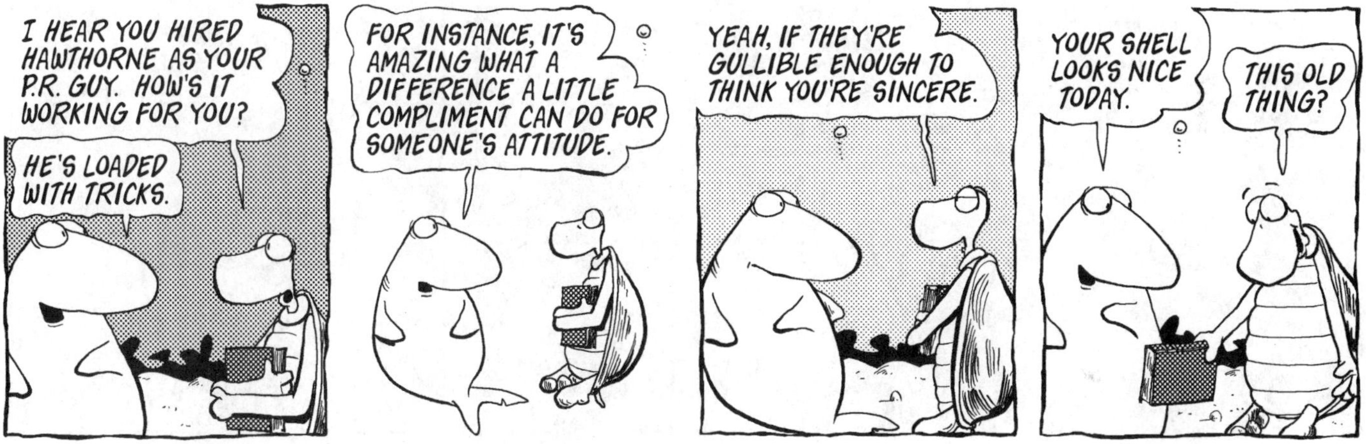
I HEAR YOU HIRED HAWTHORNE AS YOUR P.R. GUY. HOW'S IT WORKING FOR YOU?
HE'S LOADED WITH TRICKS.
FOR INSTANCE, IT'S AMAZING WHAT A DIFFERENCE A LITTLE COMPLIMENT CAN DO FOR SOMEONE'S ATTITUDE.
YEAH, IF THEY'RE GULLIBLE ENOUGH TO THINK YOU'RE SINCERE.
YOUR SHELL LOOKS NICE TODAY.
THIS OLD THING?

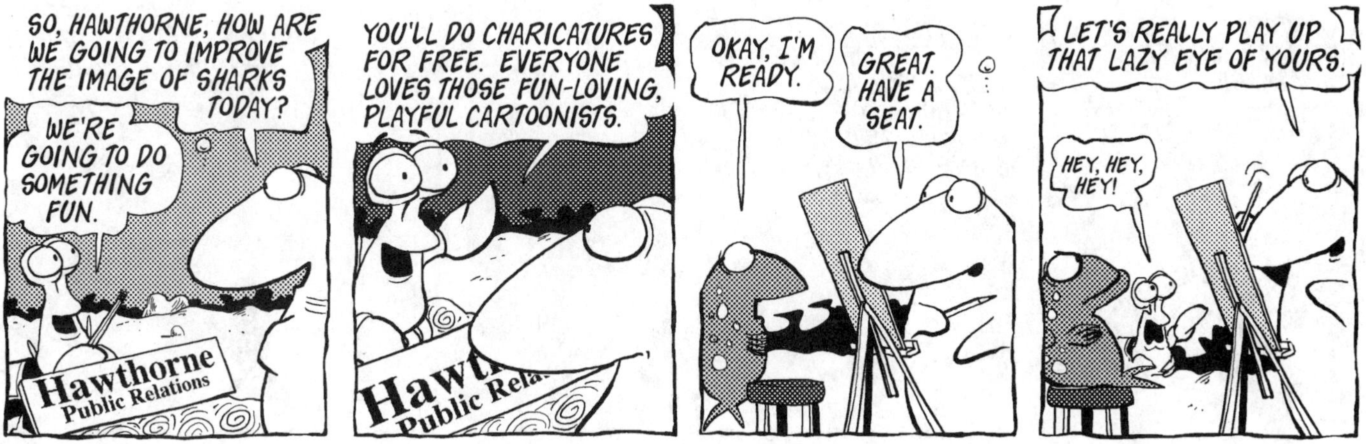
SO, HAWTHORNE, HOW ARE WE GOING TO IMPROVE THE IMAGE OF SHARKS TODAY?
WE'RE GOING TO DO SOMETHING FUN.
Hawthorne Public Relations
YOU'LL DO CHARICATURES FOR FREE. EVERYONE LOVES THOSE FUN-LOVING, PLAYFUL CARTOONISTS.
OKAY, I'M READY.
GREAT. HAVE A SEAT.
LET'S REALLY PLAY UP THAT LAZY EYE OF YOURS.
HEY, HEY, HEY!

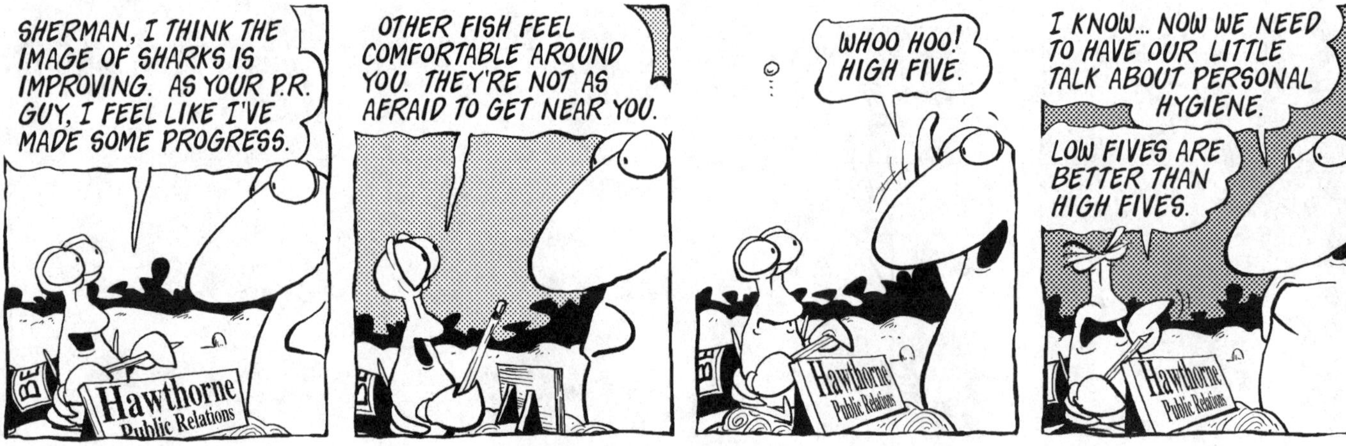
SHERMAN, I THINK THE IMAGE OF SHARKS IS IMPROVING. AS YOUR P.R. GUY, I FEEL LIKE I'VE MADE SOME PROGRESS.
Hawthorne Public Relations
OTHER FISH FEEL COMFORTABLE AROUND YOU. THEY'RE NOT AS AFRAID TO GET NEAR YOU.
WHOO HOO! HIGH FIVE.
Hawthorne Public Relations
I KNOW... NOW WE NEED TO HAVE OUR LITTLE TALK ABOUT PERSONAL HYGIENE.
LOW FIVES ARE BETTER THAN HIGH FIVES.
Hawthorne Public Relations

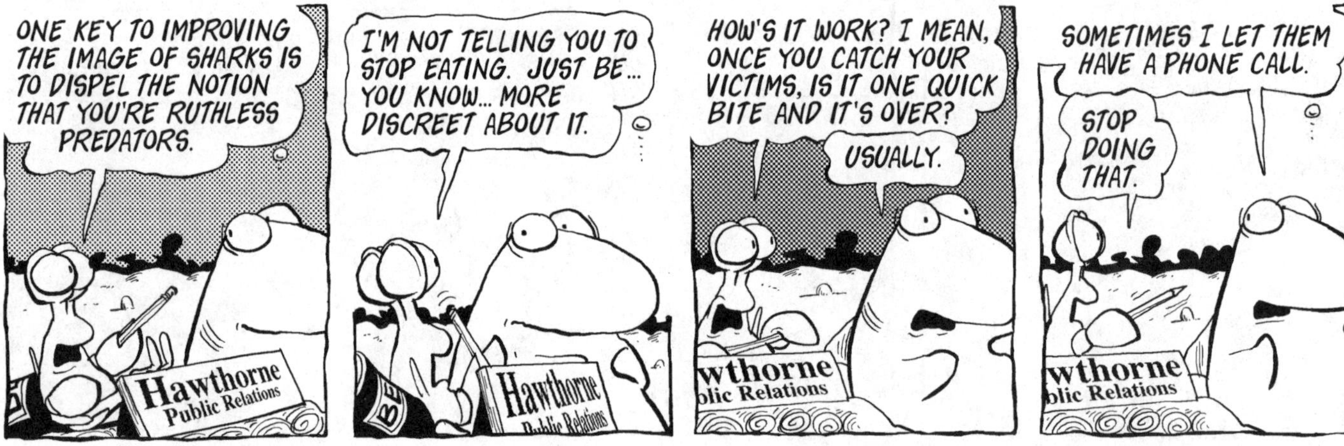
ONE KEY TO IMPROVING THE IMAGE OF SHARKS IS TO DISPEL THE NOTION THAT YOU'RE RUTHLESS PREDATORS.
Hawthorne Public Relations
I'M NOT TELLING YOU TO STOP EATING. JUST BE... YOU KNOW... MORE DISCREET ABOUT IT.
Hawthorne
HOW'S IT WORK? I MEAN, ONCE YOU CATCH YOUR VICTIMS, IS IT ONE QUICK BITE AND IT'S OVER?
USUALLY.
SOMETIMES I LET THEM HAVE A PHONE CALL.
STOP DOING THAT.

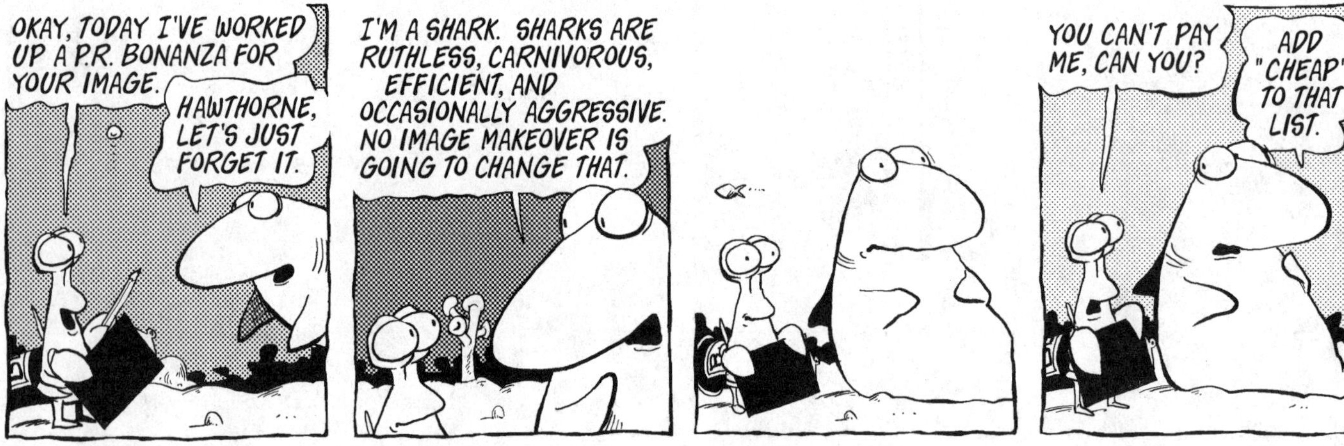
OKAY, TODAY I'VE WORKED UP A P.R. BONANZA FOR YOUR IMAGE.
HAWTHORNE, LET'S JUST FORGET IT.
I'M A SHARK. SHARKS ARE RUTHLESS, CARNIVOROUS, EFFICIENT, AND OCCASIONALLY AGGRESSIVE. NO IMAGE MAKEOVER IS GOING TO CHANGE THAT.
YOU CAN'T PAY ME, CAN YOU?
ADD "CHEAP" TO THAT LIST.

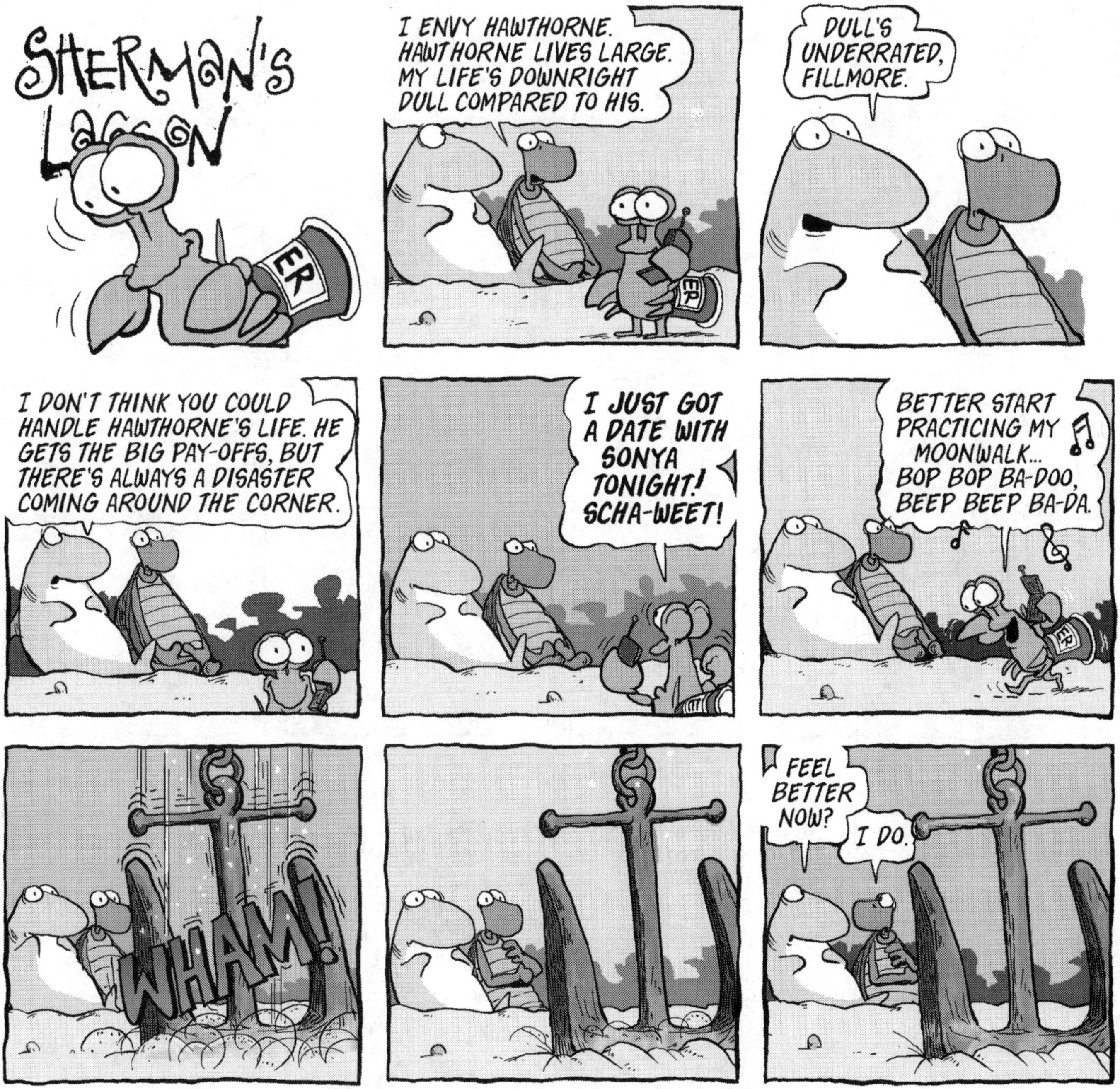
SHERMAN'S LAGOON
I ENVY HAWTHORNE. HAWTHORNE LIVES LARGE. MY LIFE'S DOWNRIGHT DULL COMPARED TO HIS.
DULL'S UNDERRATED, FILLMORE.
I DON'T THINK YOU COULD HANDLE HAWTHORNE'S LIFE. HE GETS THE BIG PAY-OFFS, BUT THERE'S ALWAYS A DISASTER COMING AROUND THE CORNER.
I JUST GOT A DATE WITH SONYA TONIGHT! SCHA-WEET!
BETTER START PRACTICING MY MOONWALK... BOP BOP BA-DOO, BEEP BEEP BA-DA.
WHAM!
FEEL BETTER NOW?
I DO.

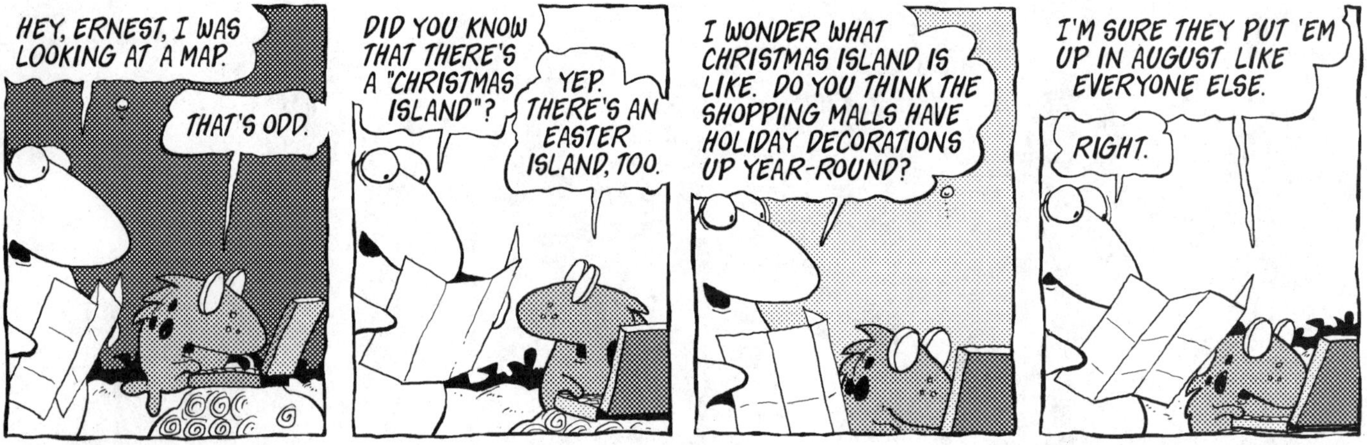
HEY, ERNEST, I WAS LOOKING AT A MAP.
THAT'S ODD.
DID YOU KNOW THAT THERE'S A "CHRISTMAS ISLAND"?
YEP. THERE'S AN EASTER ISLAND, TOO.
I WONDER WHAT CHRISTMAS ISLAND IS LIKE. DO YOU THINK THE SHOPPING MALLS HAVE HOLIDAY DECORATIONS UP YEAR-ROUND?
I'M SURE THEY PUT 'EM UP IN AUGUST LIKE EVERYONE ELSE.
RIGHT.

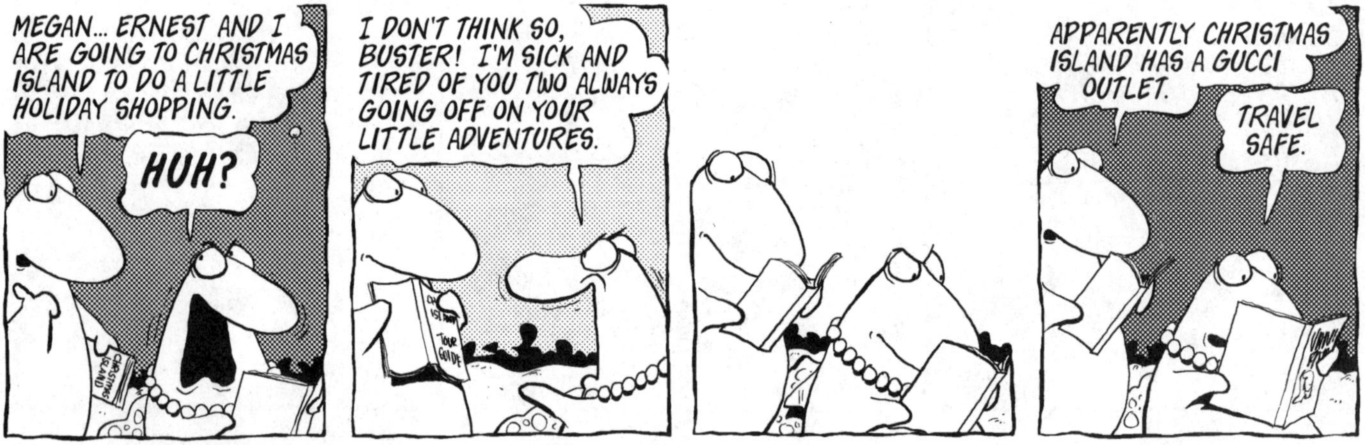
MEGAN... ERNEST AND I ARE GOING TO CHRISTMAS ISLAND TO DO A LITTLE HOLIDAY SHOPPING.
HUH?
I DON'T THINK SO, BUSTER! I'M SICK AND TIRED OF YOU TWO ALWAYS GOING OFF ON YOUR LITTLE ADVENTURES.
APPARENTLY CHRISTMAS ISLAND HAS A GUCCI OUTLET.
TRAVEL SAFE.

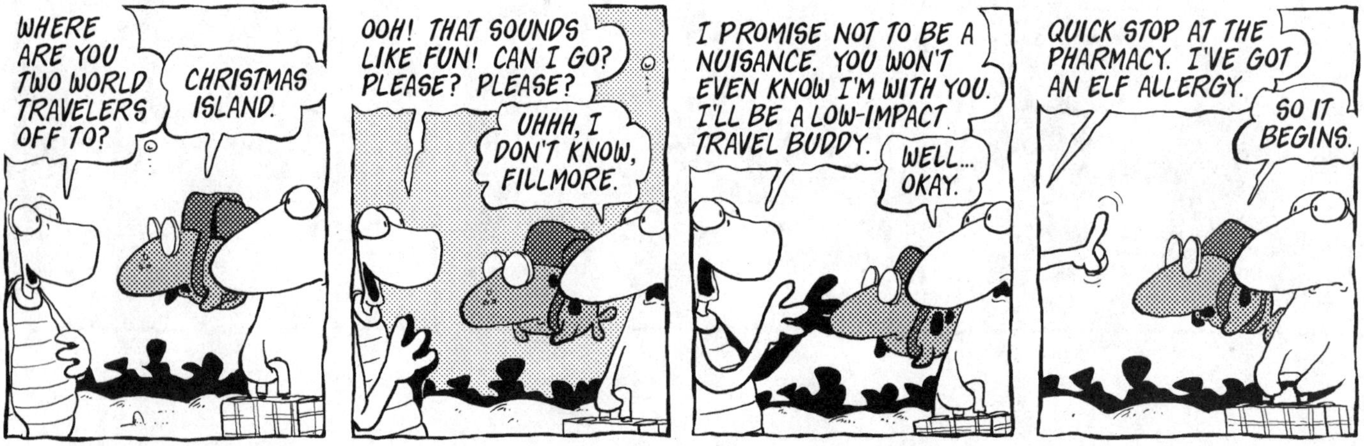
WHERE ARE YOU TWO WORLD TRAVELERS OFF TO?
CHRISTMAS ISLAND.
OOH! THAT SOUNDS LIKE FUN! CAN I GO? PLEASE? PLEASE?
UHHH, I DON'T KNOW, FILLMORE.
I PROMISE NOT TO BE A NUISANCE. YOU WON'T EVEN KNOW I'M WITH YOU. I'LL BE A LOW-IMPACT TRAVEL BUDDY.
WELL... OKAY.
QUICK STOP AT THE PHARMACY. I'VE GOT AN ELF ALLERGY.
SO IT BEGINS.

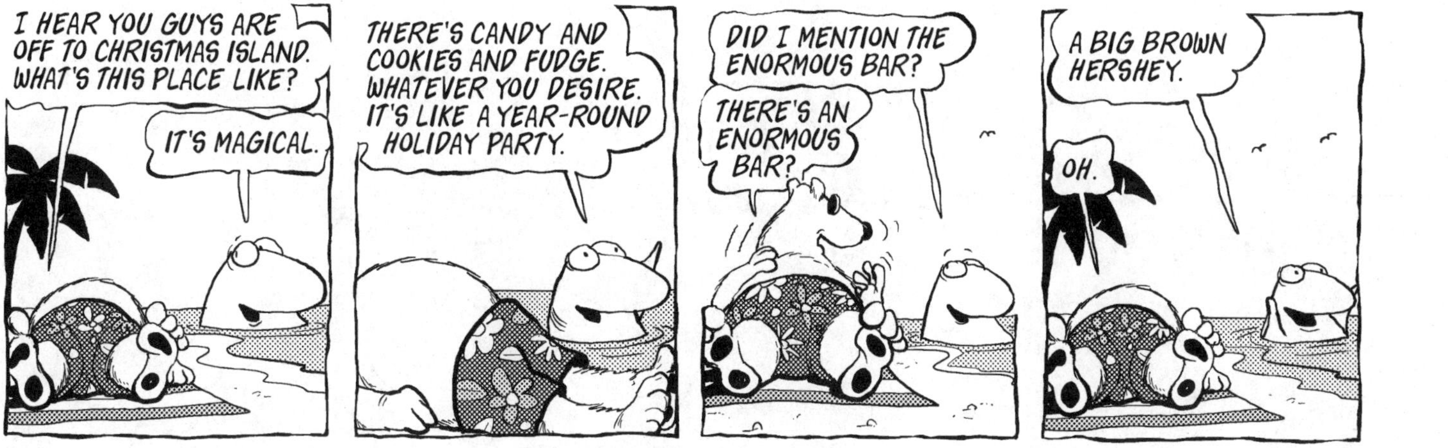
I HEAR YOU GUYS ARE OFF TO CHRISTMAS ISLAND. WHAT'S THIS PLACE LIKE?
IT'S MAGICAL.
THERE'S CANDY AND COOKIES AND FUDGE. WHATEVER YOU DESIRE. IT'S LIKE A YEAR-ROUND HOLIDAY PARTY.
DID I MENTION THE ENORMOUS BAR?
THERE'S AN ENORMOUS BAR?
A BIG BROWN HERSHEY.
OH.

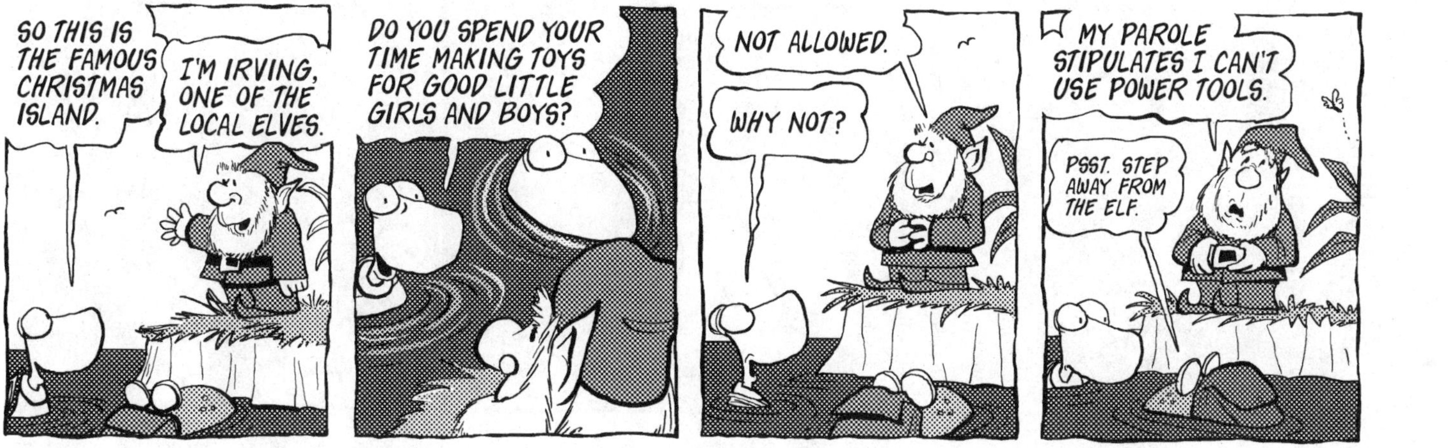
SO THIS IS THE FAMOUS CHRISTMAS ISLAND.
I'M IRVING, ONE OF THE LOCAL ELVES.
DO YOU SPEND YOUR TIME MAKING TOYS FOR GOOD LITTLE GIRLS AND BOYS?
NOT ALLOWED.
WHY NOT?
MY PAROLE STIPULATES I CAN'T USE POWER TOOLS.
PSST. STEP AWAY FROM THE ELF.

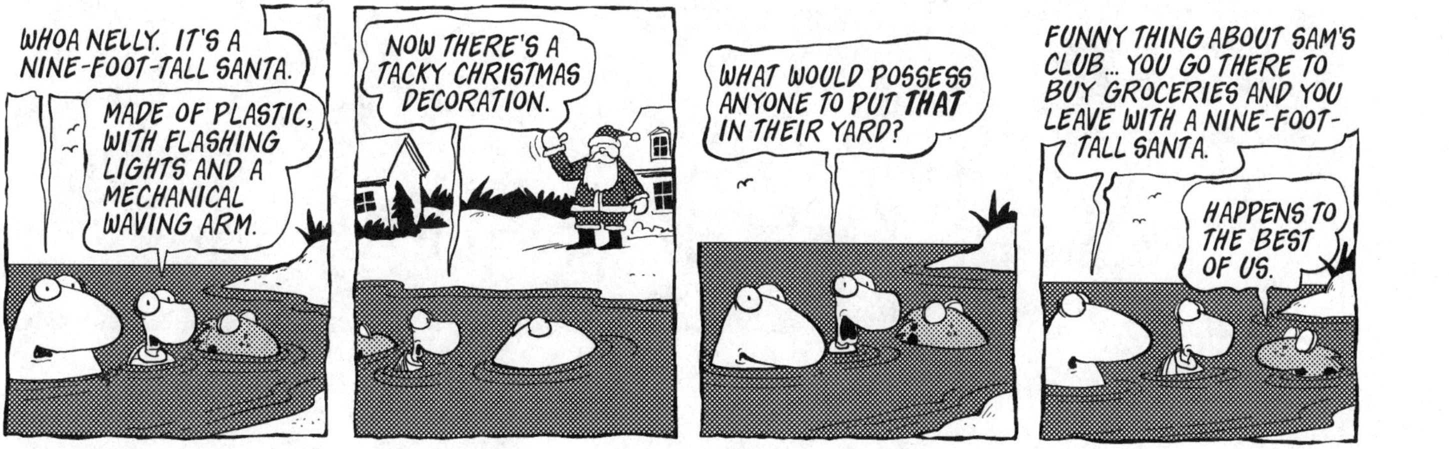
WHOA NELLY. IT'S A NINE-FOOT-TALL SANTA.
MADE OF PLASTIC, WITH FLASHING LIGHTS AND A MECHANICAL WAVING ARM.
NOW THERE'S A TACKY CHRISTMAS DECORATION.
WHAT WOULD POSSESS ANYONE TO PUT THAT IN THEIR YARD?
FUNNY THING ABOUT SAM'S CLUB... YOU GO THERE TO BUY GROCERIES AND YOU LEAVE WITH A NINE-FOOT-TALL SANTA.
HAPPENS TO THE BEST OF US.

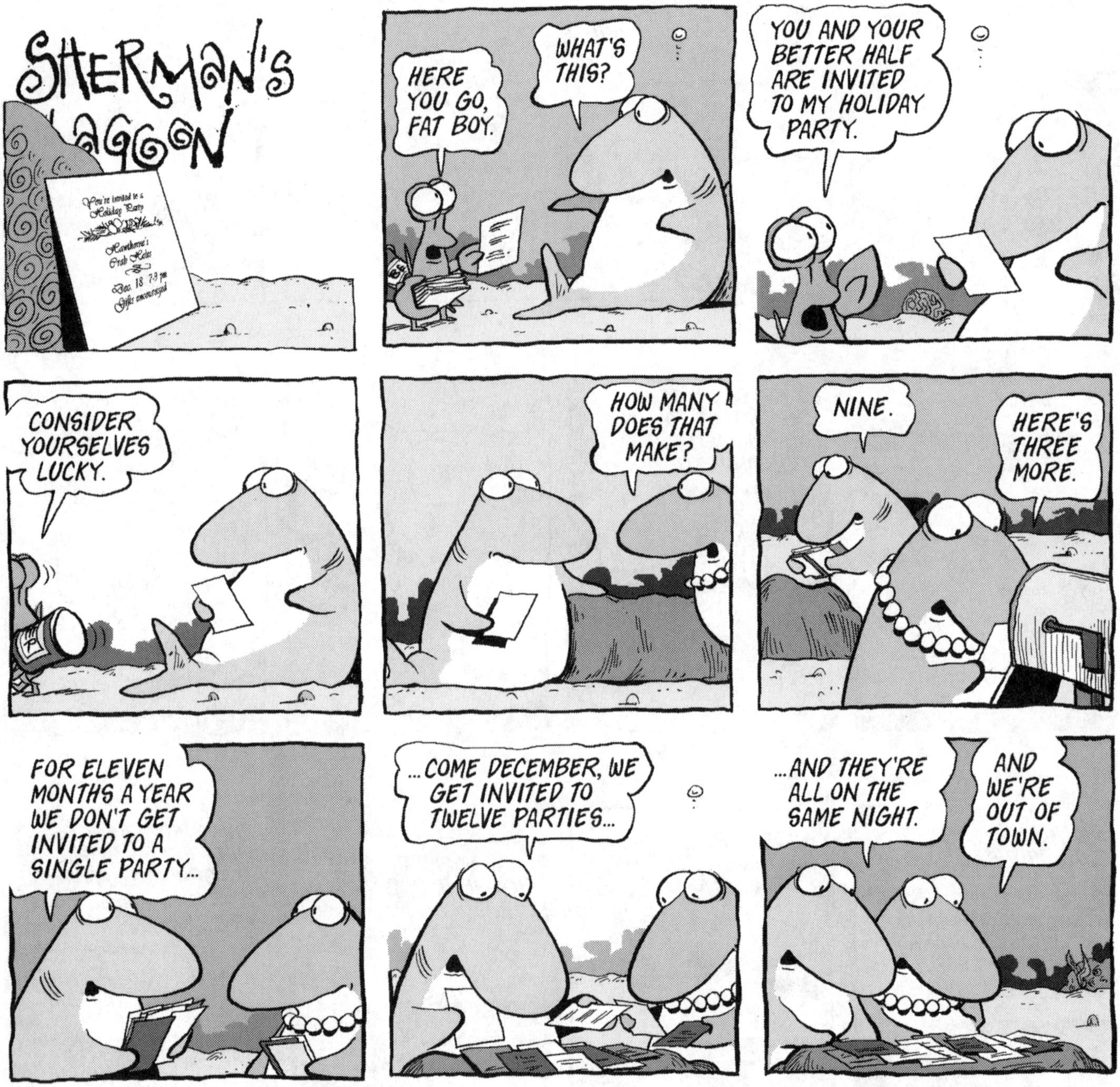
SHERMAN'S LAGOON
You're invited to a Holiday Party
Hawthorne's Crab Holes
Dec. 18 7-9 pm
Gifts encouraged
HERE YOU GO, FAT BOY.
WHAT'S THIS?
YOU AND YOUR BETTER HALF ARE INVITED TO MY HOLIDAY PARTY.
CONSIDER YOURSELVES LUCKY.
HOW MANY DOES THAT MAKE?
NINE.
HERE'S THREE MORE.
FOR ELEVEN MONTHS A YEAR WE DON'T GET INVITED TO A SINGLE PARTY...
...COME DECEMBER, WE GET INVITED TO TWELVE PARTIES...
...AND THEY'RE ALL ON THE SAME NIGHT.
AND WE'RE OUT OF TOWN.

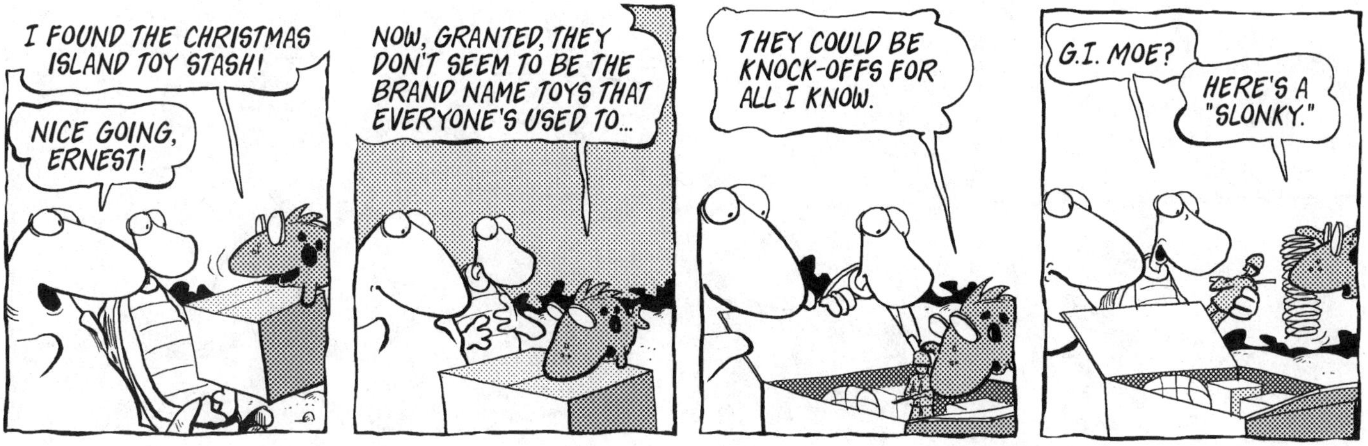
I FOUND THE CHRISTMAS ISLAND TOY STASH!
NICE GOING, ERNEST!
NOW, GRANTED, THEY DON'T SEEM TO BE THE BRAND NAME TOYS THAT EVERYONE'S USED TO...
THEY COULD BE KNOCK-OFFS FOR ALL I KNOW.
G.I. MOE?
HERE'S A "SLONKY."

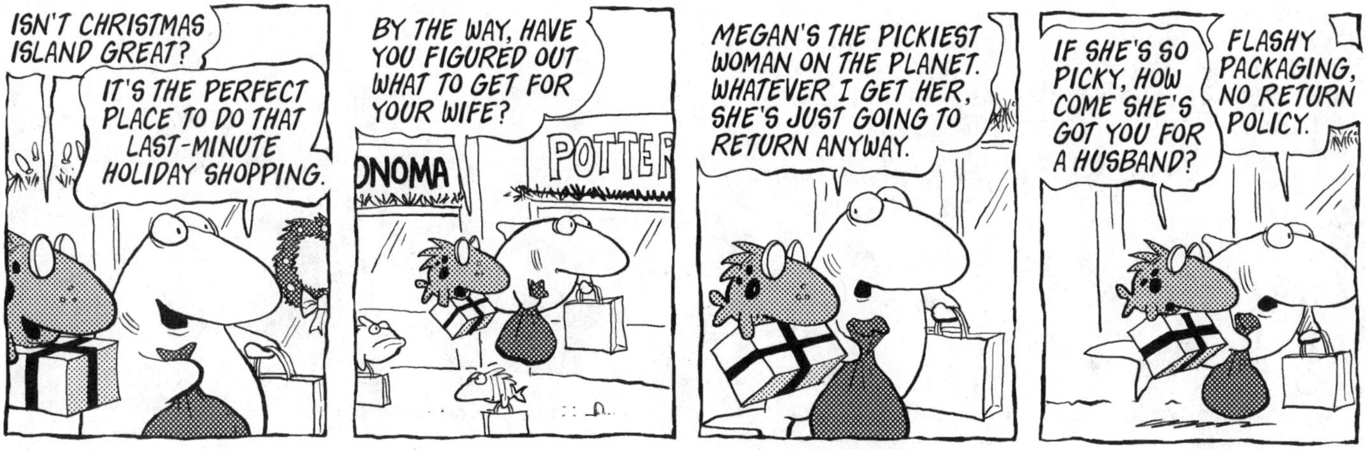
ISN'T CHRISTMAS ISLAND GREAT?
IT'S THE PERFECT PLACE TO DO THAT LAST-MINUTE HOLIDAY SHOPPING.
BY THE WAY, HAVE YOU FIGURED OUT WHAT TO GET FOR YOUR WIFE?
ONOMA
POTTER
MEGAN'S THE PICKIEST WOMAN ON THE PLANET. WHATEVER I GET HER, SHE'S JUST GOING TO RETURN ANYWAY.
IF SHE'S SO PICKY, HOW COME SHE'S GOT YOU FOR A HUSBAND?
FLASHY PACKAGING, NO RETURN POLICY.

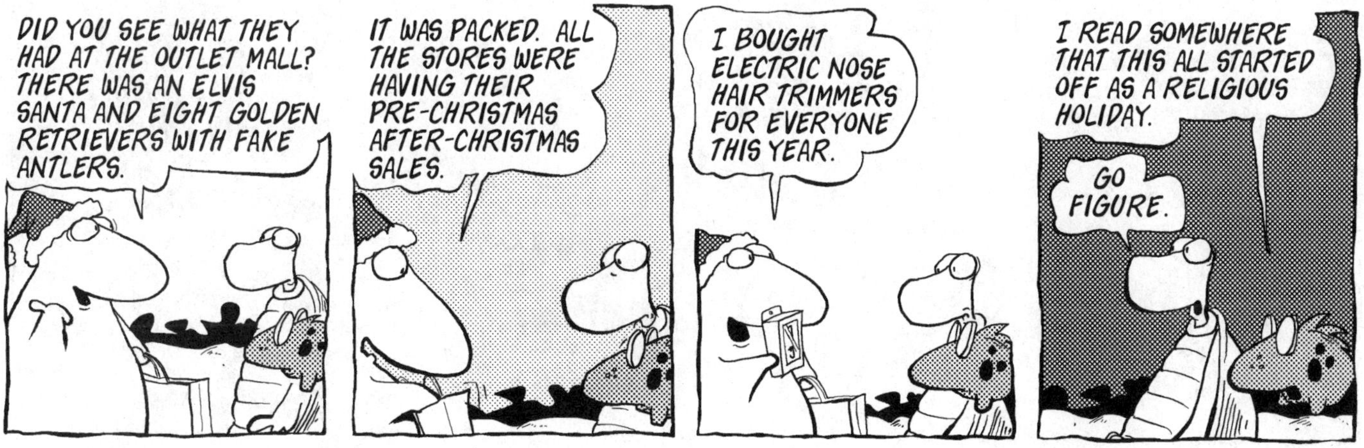
DID YOU SEE WHAT THEY HAD AT THE OUTLET MALL? THERE WAS AN ELVIS SANTA AND EIGHT GOLDEN RETRIEVERS WITH FAKE ANTLERS.
IT WAS PACKED. ALL THE STORES WERE HAVING THEIR PRE-CHRISTMAS AFTER-CHRISTMAS SALES.
I BOUGHT ELECTRIC NOSE HAIR TRIMMERS FOR EVERYONE THIS YEAR.
I READ SOMEWHERE THAT THIS ALL STARTED OFF AS A RELIGIOUS HOLIDAY.
GO FIGURE.

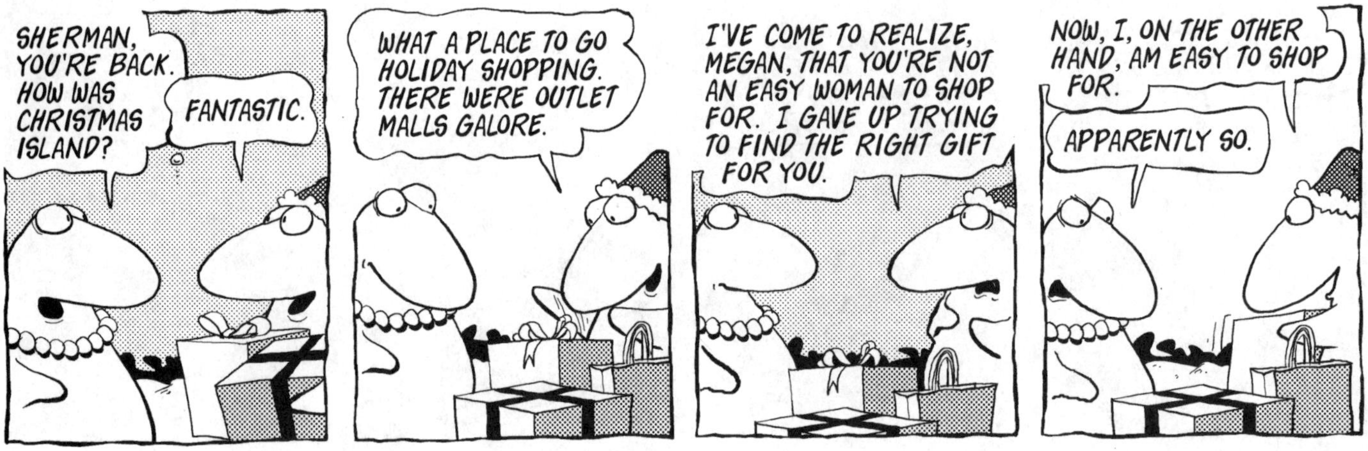
SHERMAN, YOU'RE BACK. HOW WAS CHRISTMAS ISLAND?
FANTASTIC.
WHAT A PLACE TO GO HOLIDAY SHOPPING. THERE WERE OUTLET MALLS GALORE.
I'VE COME TO REALIZE, MEGAN, THAT YOU'RE NOT AN EASY WOMAN TO SHOP FOR. I GAVE UP TRYING TO FIND THE RIGHT GIFT FOR YOU.
NOW, I, ON THE OTHER HAND, AM EASY TO SHOP FOR.
APPARENTLY SO.

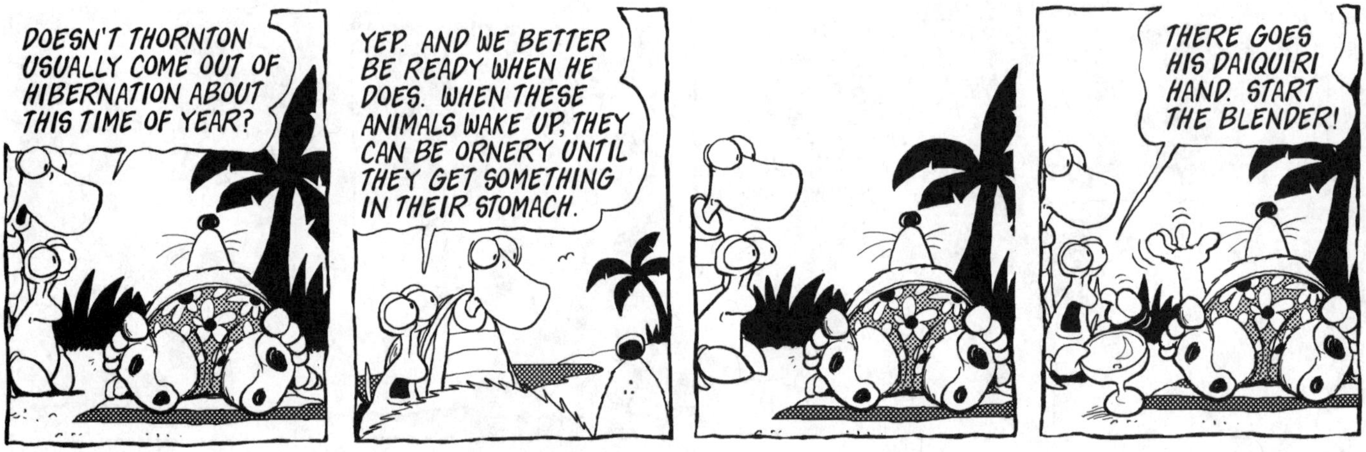
DOESN'T THORNTON USUALLY COME OUT OF HIBERNATION ABOUT THIS TIME OF YEAR?
YEP. AND WE BETTER BE READY WHEN HE DOES. WHEN THESE ANIMALS WAKE UP, THEY CAN BE ORNERY UNTIL THEY GET SOMETHING IN THEIR STOMACH.
THERE GOES HIS DAIQUIRI HAND. START THE BLENDER!

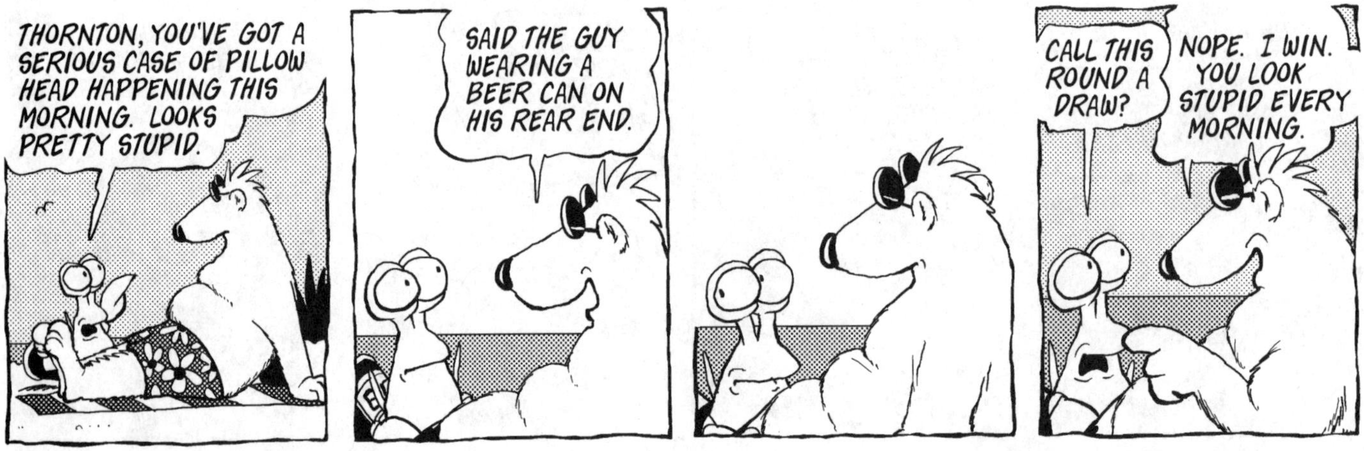
THORNTON, YOU'VE GOT A SERIOUS CASE OF PILLOW HEAD HAPPENING THIS MORNING. LOOKS PRETTY STUPID.
SAID THE GUY WEARING A BEER CAN ON HIS REAR END.
CALL THIS ROUND A DRAW?
NOPE. I WIN. YOU LOOK STUPID EVERY MORNING.

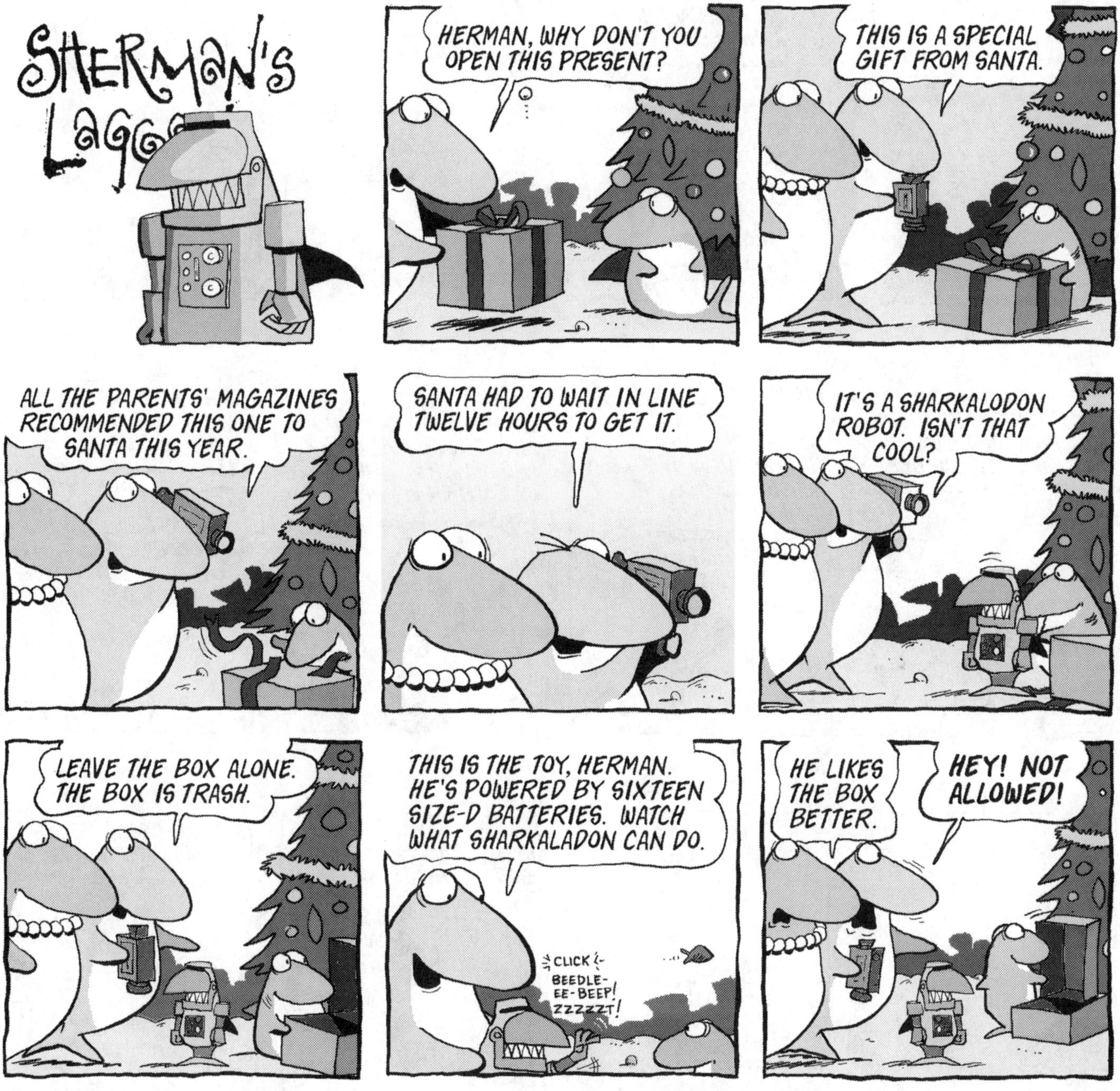
SHERMAN'S LAGOON
HERMAN, WHY DON'T YOU OPEN THIS PRESENT?
THIS IS A SPECIAL GIFT FROM SANTA.
ALL THE PARENTS' MAGAZINES RECOMMENDED THIS ONE TO SANTA THIS YEAR.
SANTA HAD TO WAIT IN LINE TWELVE HOURS TO GET IT.
IT'S A SHARKALODON ROBOT. ISN'T THAT COOL?
LEAVE THE BOX ALONE. THE BOX IS TRASH.
THIS IS THE TOY, HERMAN. HE'S POWERED BY SIXTEEN SIZE-D BATTERIES. WATCH WHAT SHARKALADON CAN DO.
CLICK
BEEDLE-EE-BEEP!
ZZZZZT!
HE LIKES THE BOX BETTER.
HEY! NOT ALLOWED!

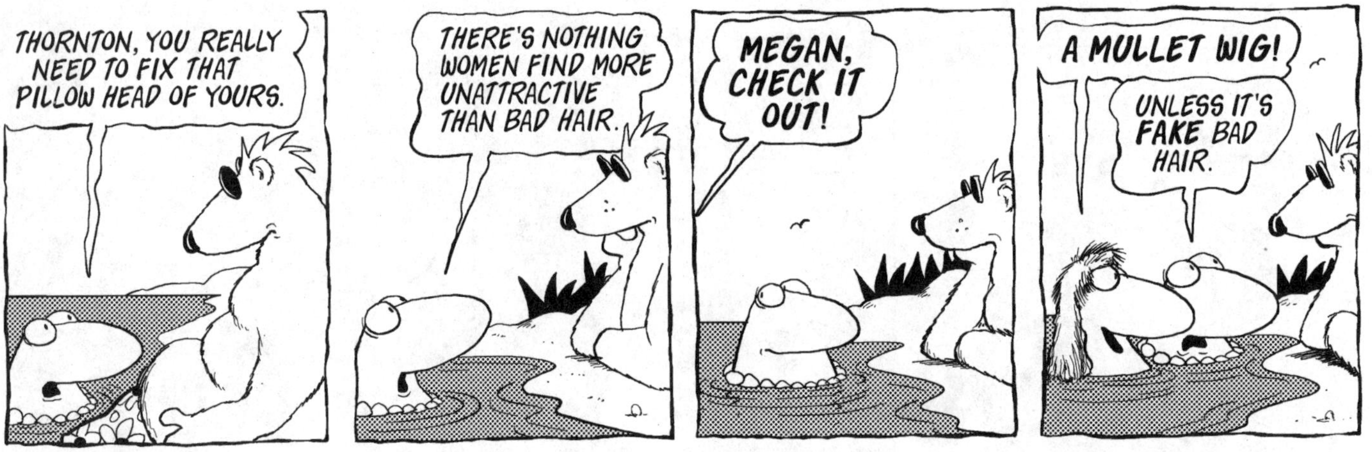
THORNTON, YOU REALLY NEED TO FIX THAT PILLOW HEAD OF YOURS.
THERE'S NOTHING WOMEN FIND MORE UNATTRACTIVE THAN BAD HAIR.
MEGAN, CHECK IT OUT!
A MULLET WIG!
UNLESS IT'S FAKE BAD HAIR.

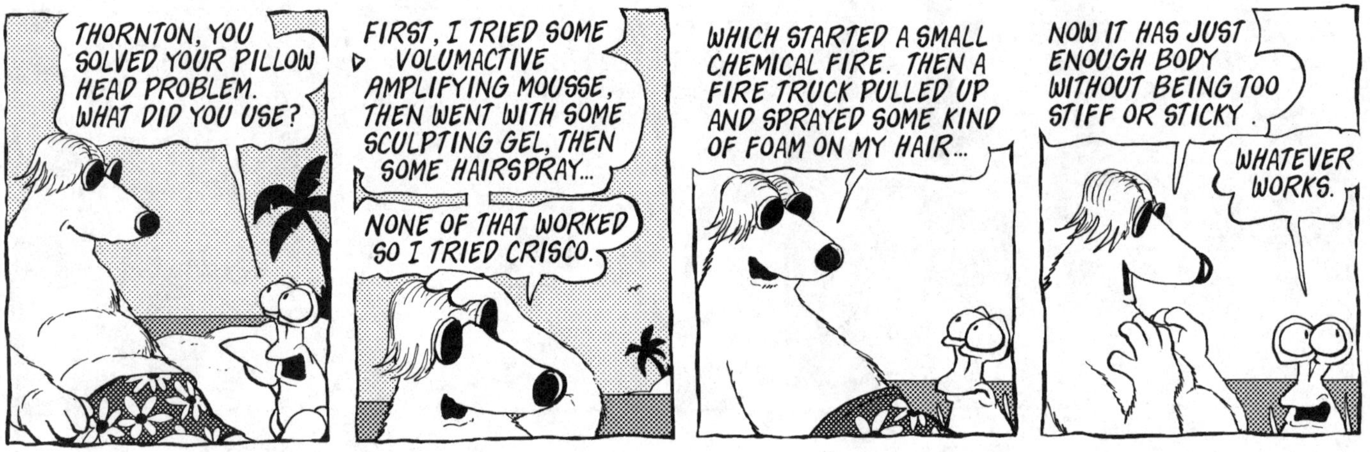
THORNTON, YOU SOLVED YOUR PILLOW HEAD PROBLEM. WHAT DID YOU USE?
FIRST, I TRIED SOME VOLUMACTIVE AMPLIFYING MOUSSE, THEN WENT WITH SOME SCULPTING GEL, THEN SOME HAIRSPRAY...
NONE OF THAT WORKED SO I TRIED CRISCO.
WHICH STARTED A SMALL CHEMICAL FIRE. THEN A FIRE TRUCK PULLED UP AND SPRAYED SOME KIND OF FOAM ON MY HAIR...
NOW IT HAS JUST ENOUGH BODY WITHOUT BEING TOO STIFF OR STICKY.
WHATEVER WORKS.

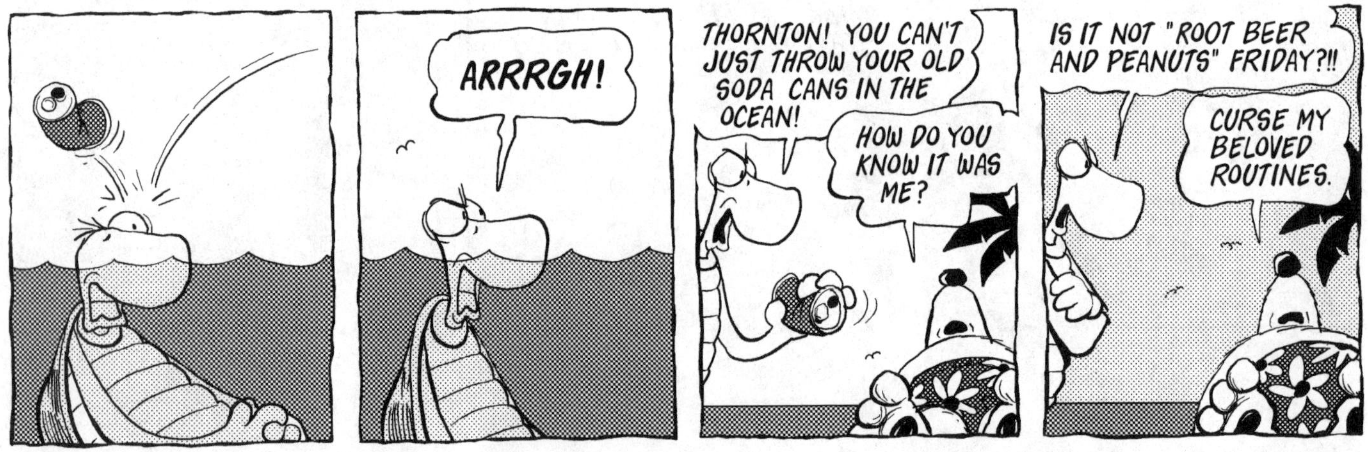
ARRRGH!
THORNTON! YOU CAN'T JUST THROW YOUR OLD SODA CANS IN THE OCEAN!
HOW DO YOU KNOW IT WAS ME?
IS IT NOT "ROOT BEER AND PEANUTS" FRIDAY?!!
CURSE MY BELOVED ROUTINES.

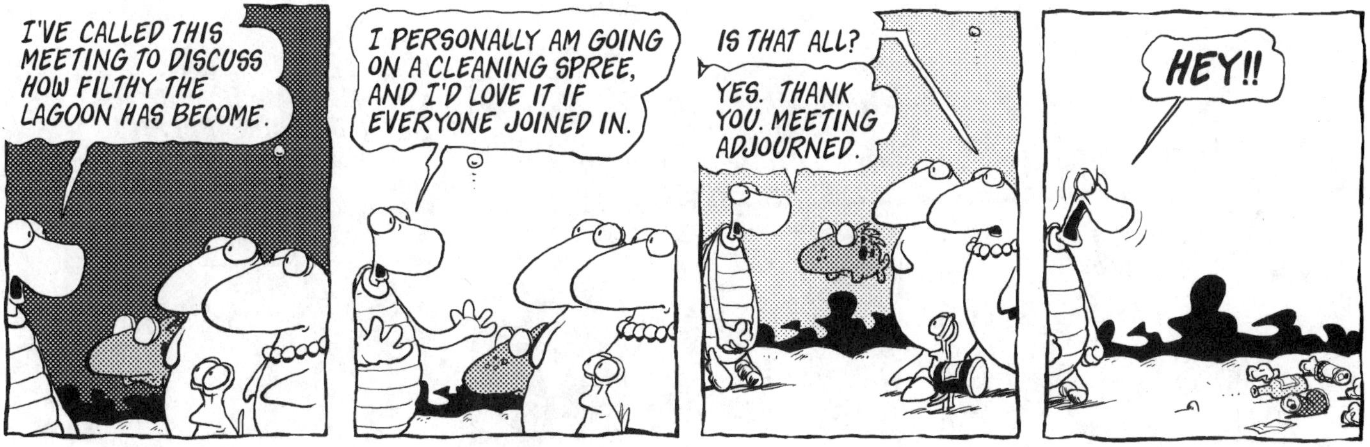
I'VE CALLED THIS MEETING TO DISCUSS HOW FILTHY THE LAGOON HAS BECOME.
I PERSONALLY AM GOING ON A CLEANING SPREE, AND I'D LOVE IT IF EVERYONE JOINED IN.
IS THAT ALL?
YES. THANK YOU. MEETING ADJOURNED.
HEY!!

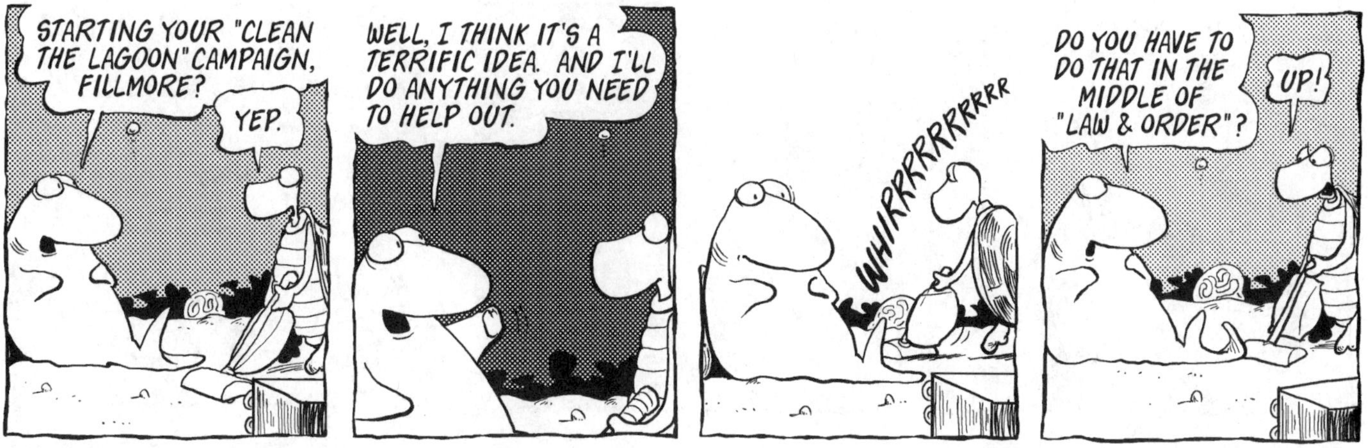
STARTING YOUR "CLEAN THE LAGOON" CAMPAIGN, FILLMORE?
YEP.
WELL, I THINK IT'S A TERRIFIC IDEA. AND I'LL DO ANYTHING YOU NEED TO HELP OUT.
WHIRRRRRRRRRRRR
DO YOU HAVE TO DO THAT IN THE MIDDLE OF "LAW & ORDER"?
UP!

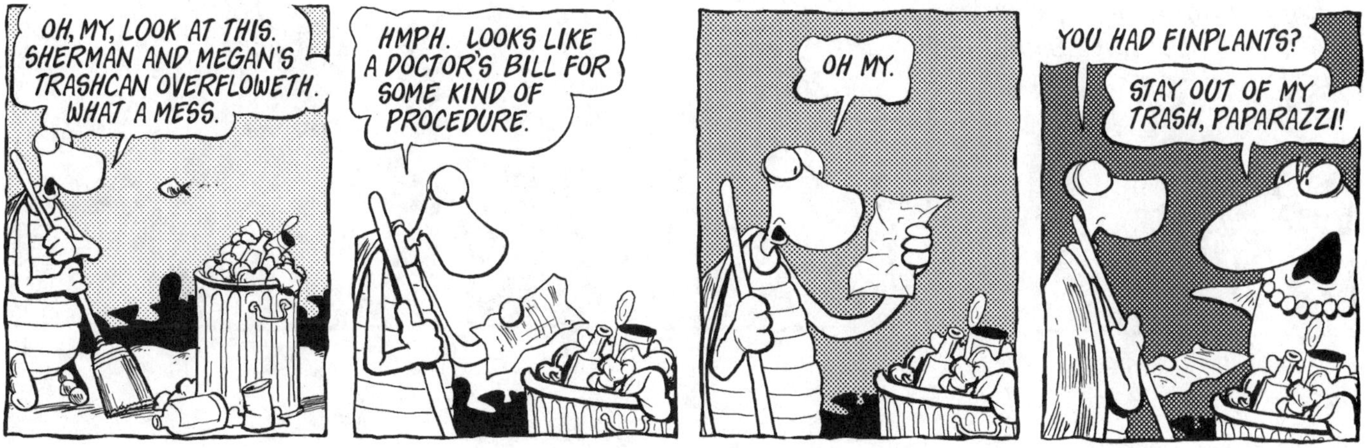
OH, MY, LOOK AT THIS. SHERMAN AND MEGAN'S TRASHCAN OVERFLOWETH. WHAT A MESS.
HMPH. LOOKS LIKE A DOCTOR'S BILL FOR SOME KIND OF PROCEDURE.
OH MY.
YOU HAD FINPLANTS?
STAY OUT OF MY TRASH, PAPARAZZI!

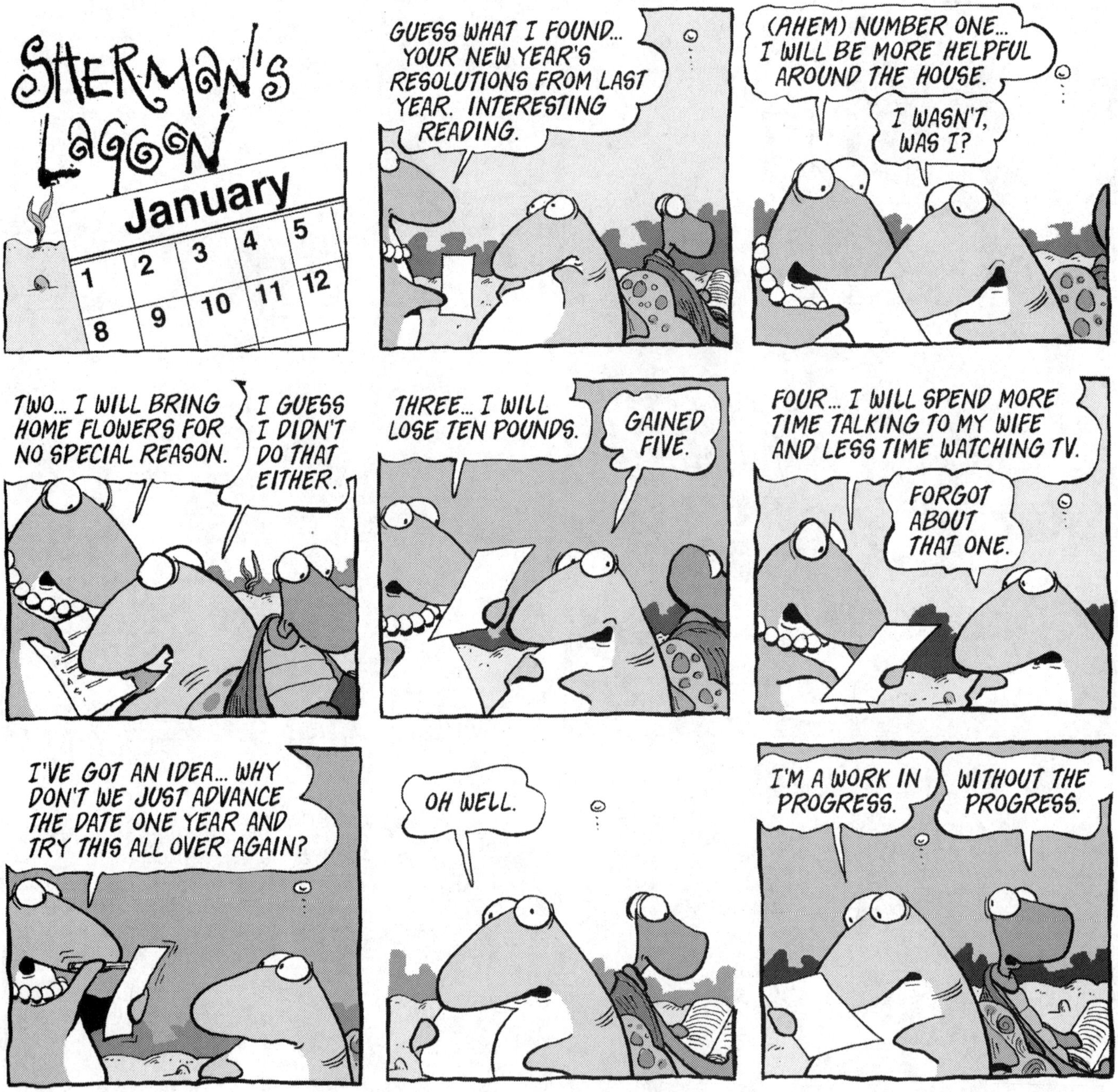
SHERMAN'S LAGOON
January
1 2 3 4 5
8 9 10 11 12
GUESS WHAT I FOUND... YOUR NEW YEAR'S RESOLUTIONS FROM LAST YEAR. INTERESTING READING.
(AHEM) NUMBER ONE... I WILL BE MORE HELPFUL AROUND THE HOUSE.
I WASN'T, WAS I?
TWO... I WILL BRING HOME FLOWERS FOR NO SPECIAL REASON.
I GUESS I DIDN'T DO THAT EITHER.
THREE... I WILL LOSE TEN POUNDS.
GAINED FIVE.
FOUR... I WILL SPEND MORE TIME TALKING TO MY WIFE AND LESS TIME WATCHING TV.
FORGOT ABOUT THAT ONE.
I'VE GOT AN IDEA... WHY DON'T WE JUST ADVANCE THE DATE ONE YEAR AND TRY THIS ALL OVER AGAIN?
OH WELL.
I'M A WORK IN PROGRESS.
WITHOUT THE PROGRESS.

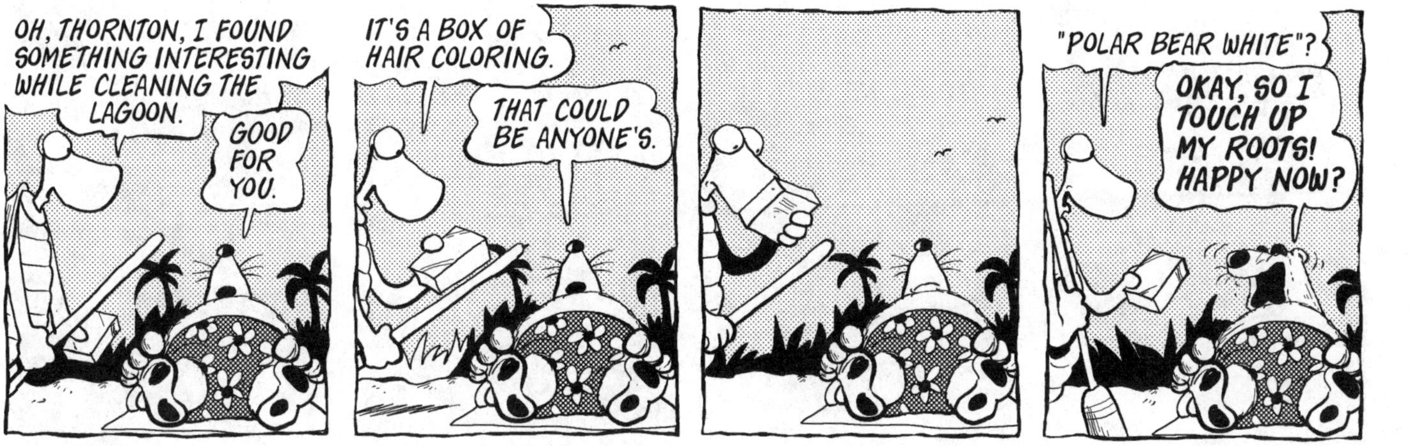
OH, THORNTON, I FOUND SOMETHING INTERESTING WHILE CLEANING THE LAGOON.
GOOD FOR YOU.
IT'S A BOX OF HAIR COLORING.
THAT COULD BE ANYONE'S.
"POLAR BEAR WHITE"?
OKAY, SO I TOUCH UP MY ROOTS! HAPPY NOW?

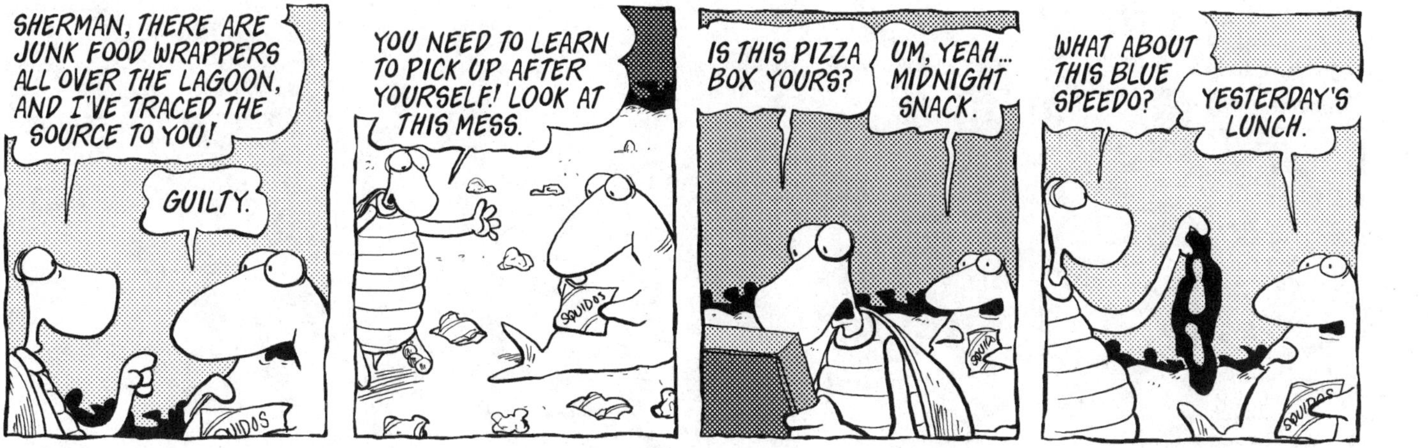
SHERMAN, THERE ARE JUNK FOOD WRAPPERS ALL OVER THE LAGOON, AND I'VE TRACED THE SOURCE TO YOU!
GUILTY.
YOU NEED TO LEARN TO PICK UP AFTER YOURSELF! LOOK AT THIS MESS.
SQUIDOS
IS THIS PIZZA BOX YOURS?
UM, YEAH... MIDNIGHT SNACK.
WHAT ABOUT THIS BLUE SPEEDO?
YESTERDAY'S LUNCH.
SQUIDOS

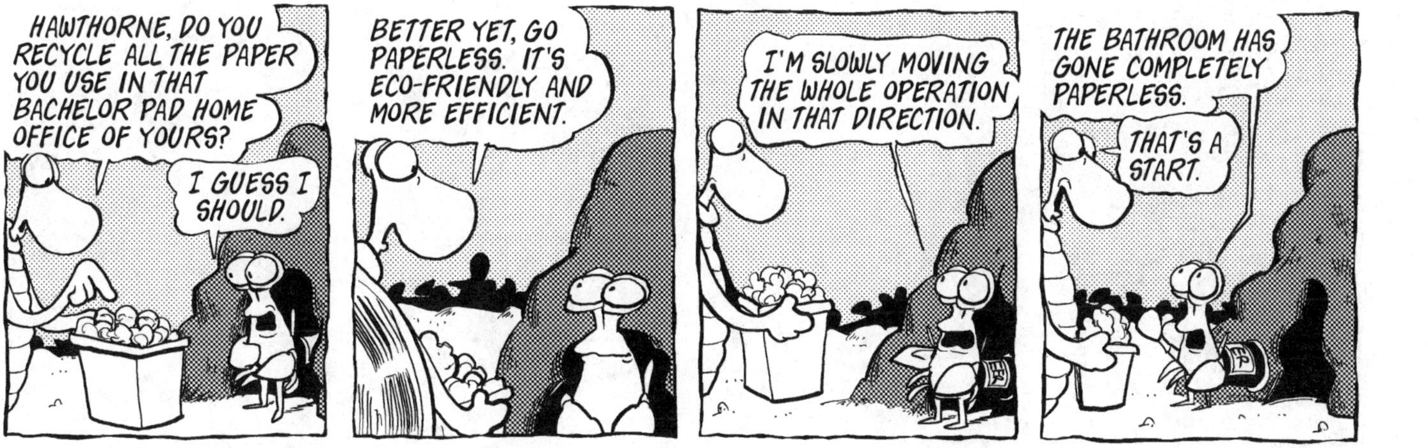
HAWTHORNE, DO YOU RECYCLE ALL THE PAPER YOU USE IN THAT BACHELOR PAD HOME OFFICE OF YOURS?
I GUESS I SHOULD.
BETTER YET, GO PAPERLESS. IT'S ECO-FRIENDLY AND MORE EFFICIENT.
I'M SLOWLY MOVING THE WHOLE OPERATION IN THAT DIRECTION.
THE BATHROOM HAS GONE COMPLETELY PAPERLESS.
THAT'S A START.

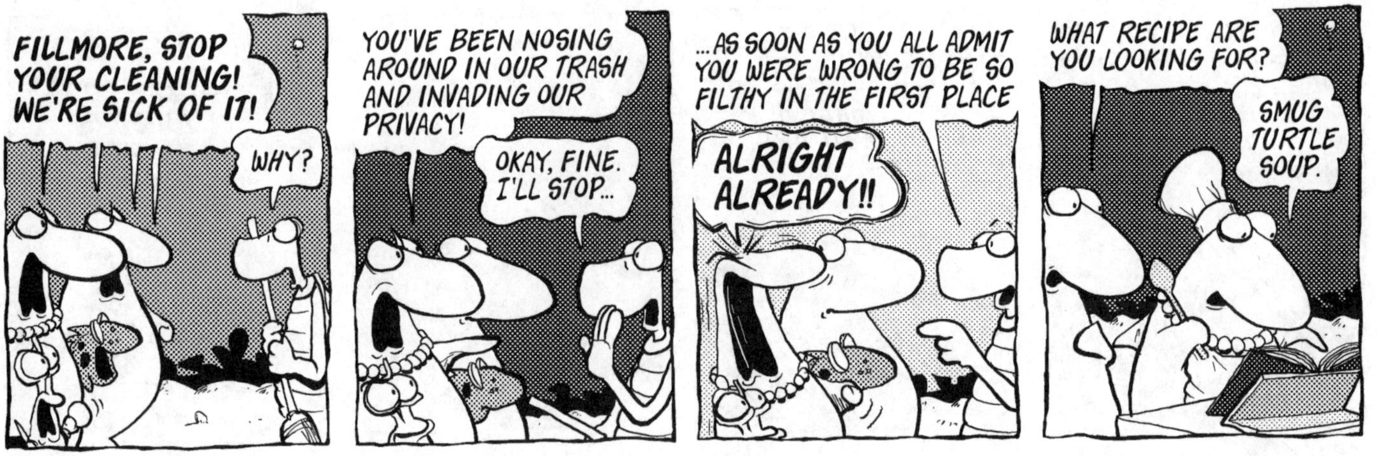
FILLMORE, STOP YOUR CLEANING! WE'RE SICK OF IT!
WHY?
YOU'VE BEEN NOSING AROUND IN OUR TRASH AND INVADING OUR PRIVACY!
OKAY, FINE. I'LL STOP...
...AS SOON AS YOU ALL ADMIT YOU WERE WRONG TO BE SO FILTHY IN THE FIRST PLACE
ALRIGHT ALREADY!!
WHAT RECIPE ARE YOU LOOKING FOR?
SMUG TURTLE SOUP.

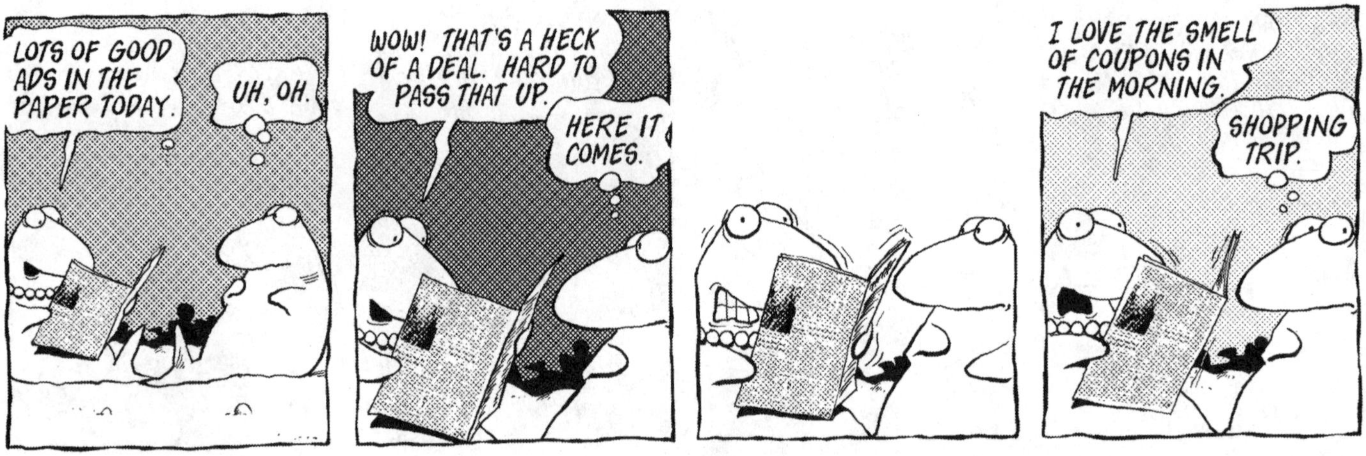
LOTS OF GOOD ADS IN THE PAPER TODAY.
UH, OH.
WOW! THAT'S A HECK OF A DEAL. HARD TO PASS THAT UP.
HERE IT COMES.
I LOVE THE SMELL OF COUPONS IN THE MORNING.
SHOPPING TRIP.

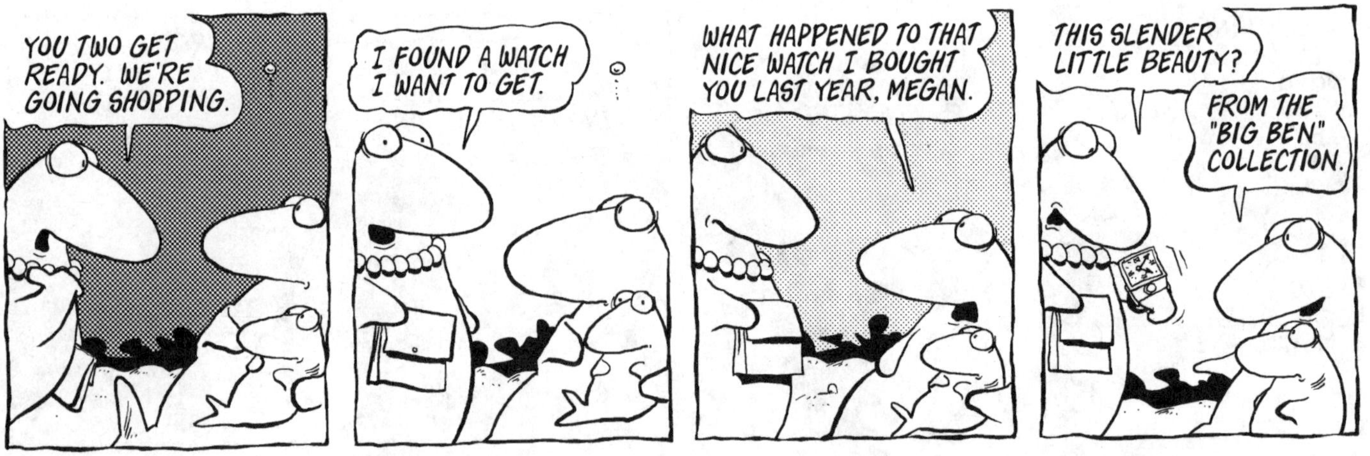
YOU TWO GET READY. WE'RE GOING SHOPPING.
I FOUND A WATCH I WANT TO GET.
WHAT HAPPENED TO THAT NICE WATCH I BOUGHT YOU LAST YEAR, MEGAN.
THIS SLENDER LITTLE BEAUTY?
FROM THE "BIG BEN" COLLECTION.

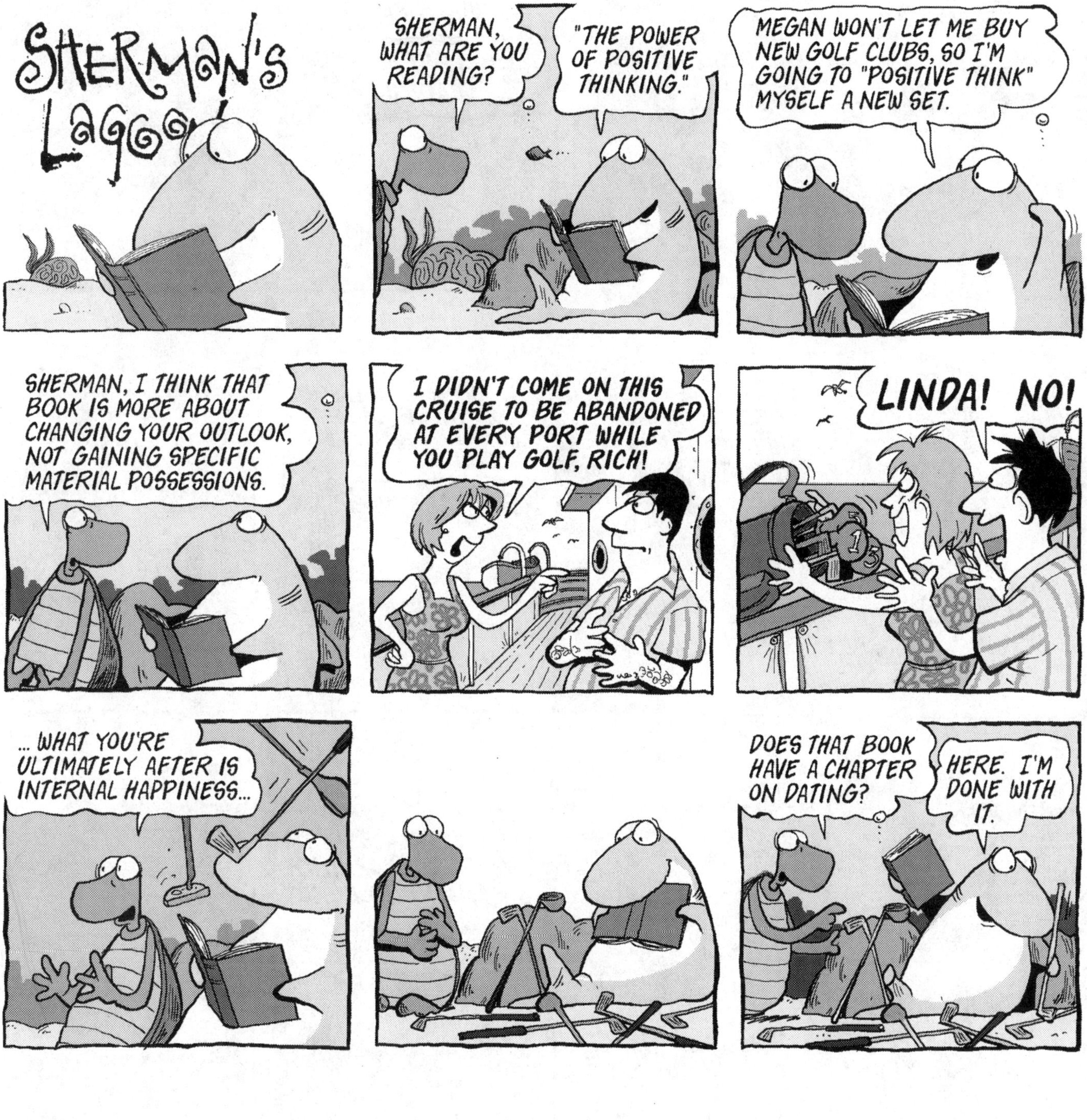
SHERMAN'S LAGOON
SHERMAN, WHAT ARE YOU READING?
"THE POWER OF POSITIVE THINKING."
MEGAN WON'T LET ME BUY NEW GOLF CLUBS, SO I'M GOING TO "POSITIVE THINK" MYSELF A NEW SET.
SHERMAN, I THINK THAT BOOK IS MORE ABOUT CHANGING YOUR OUTLOOK, NOT GAINING SPECIFIC MATERIAL POSSESSIONS.
I DIDN'T COME ON THIS CRUISE TO BE ABANDONED AT EVERY PORT WHILE YOU PLAY GOLF, RICH!
LINDA! NO!
... WHAT YOU'RE ULTIMATELY AFTER IS INTERNAL HAPPINESS...
DOES THAT BOOK HAVE A CHAPTER ON DATING?
HERE. I'M DONE WITH IT.

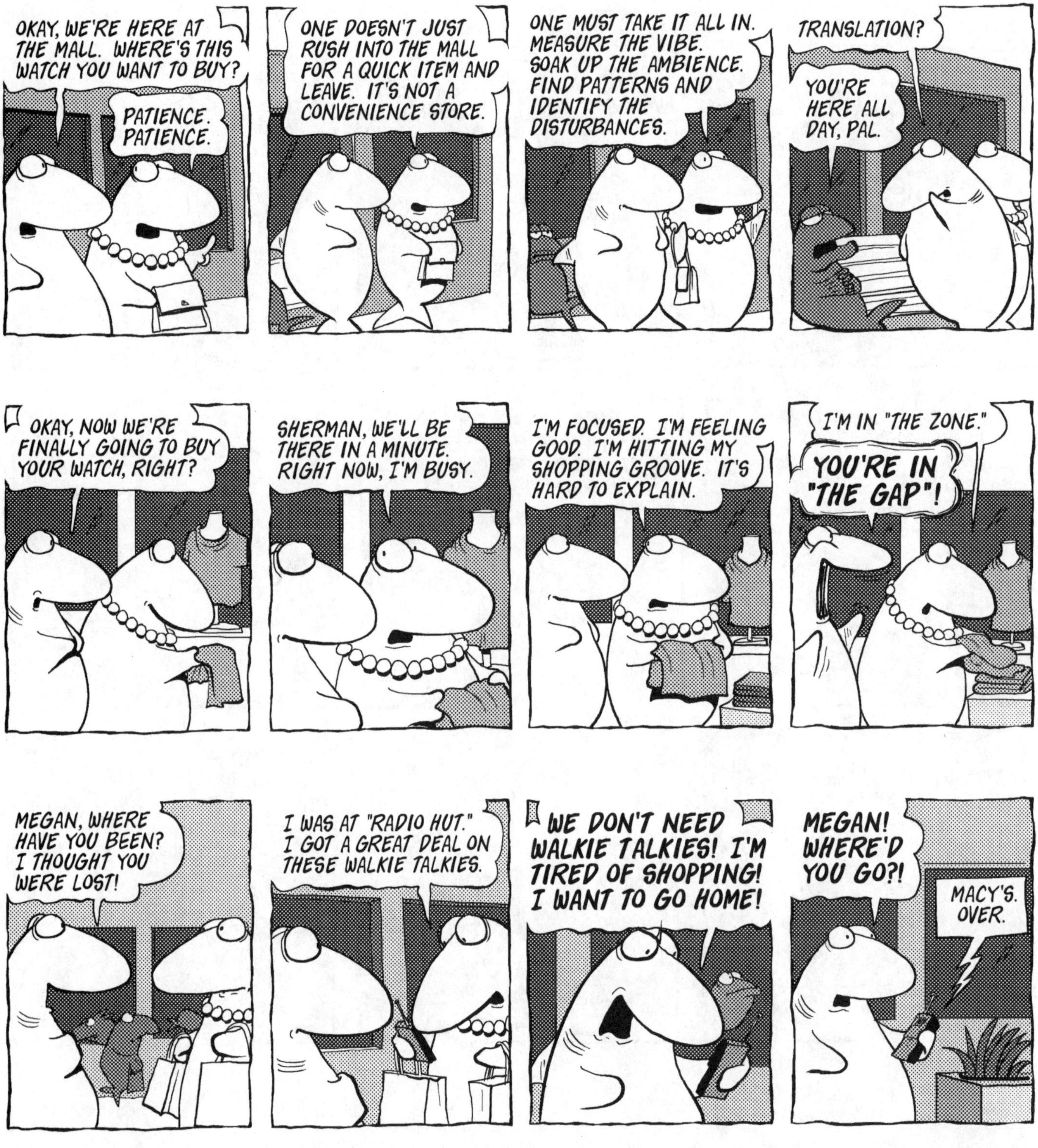

OKAY, WE'RE HERE AT THE MALL. WHERE'S THIS WATCH YOU WANT TO BUY?
PATIENCE. PATIENCE.
ONE DOESN'T JUST RUSH INTO THE MALL FOR A QUICK ITEM AND LEAVE. IT'S NOT A CONVENIENCE STORE.
ONE MUST TAKE IT ALL IN. MEASURE THE VIBE. SOAK UP THE AMBIENCE. FIND PATTERNS AND IDENTIFY THE DISTURBANCES.
TRANSLATION?
YOU'RE HERE ALL DAY, PAL.
OKAY, NOW WE'RE FINALLY GOING TO BUY YOUR WATCH, RIGHT?
SHERMAN, WE'LL BE THERE IN A MINUTE. RIGHT NOW, I'M BUSY.
I'M FOCUSED. I'M FEELING GOOD. I'M HITTING MY SHOPPING GROOVE. IT'S HARD TO EXPLAIN.
I'M IN "THE ZONE."
YOU'RE IN "THE GAP"!
MEGAN, WHERE HAVE YOU BEEN? I THOUGHT YOU WERE LOST!
I WAS AT "RADIO HUT." I GOT A GREAT DEAL ON THESE WALKIE TALKIES.
WE DON'T NEED WALKIE TALKIES! I'M TIRED OF SHOPPING! I WANT TO GO HOME!
MEGAN! WHERE'D YOU GO?!
MACY'S. OVER.

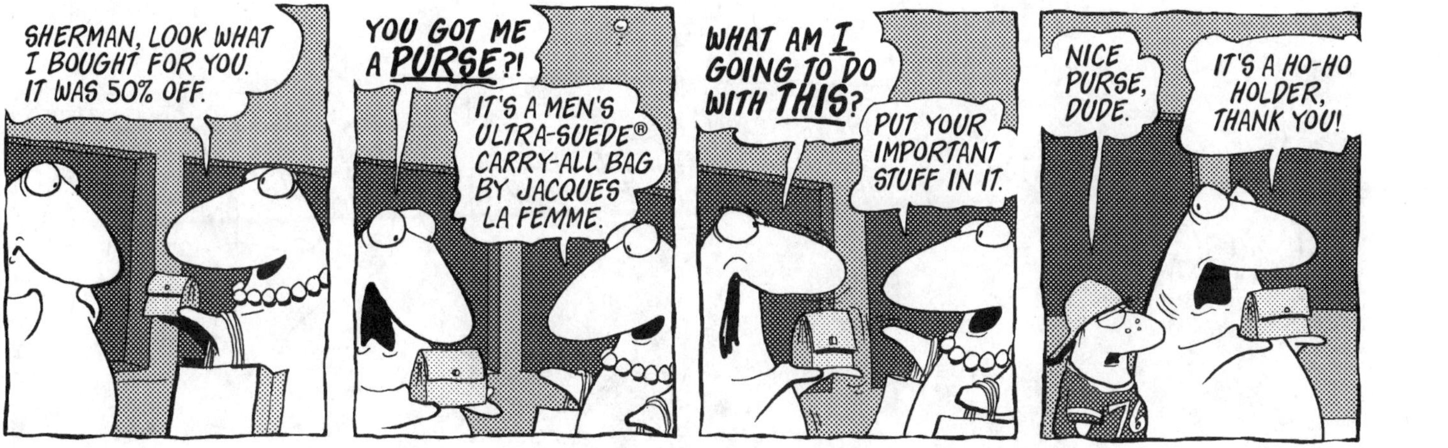
SHERMAN, LOOK WHAT I BOUGHT FOR YOU. IT WAS 50% OFF.
YOU GOT ME A PURSE?!
IT'S A MEN'S ULTRA-SUEDE® CARRY-ALL BAG BY JACQUES LA FEMME.
WHAT AM I GOING TO DO WITH THIS?
PUT YOUR IMPORTANT STUFF IN IT.
NICE PURSE, DUDE.
IT'S A HO-HO HOLDER, THANK YOU!

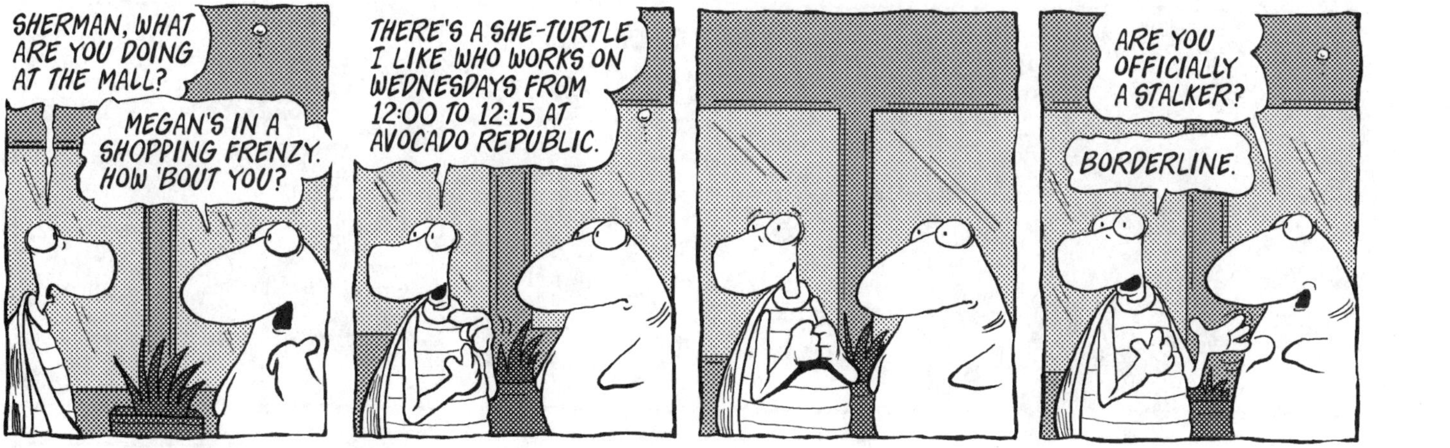
SHERMAN, WHAT ARE YOU DOING AT THE MALL?
MEGAN'S IN A SHOPPING FRENZY. HOW 'BOUT YOU?
THERE'S A SHE-TURTLE I LIKE WHO WORKS ON WEDNESDAYS FROM 12:00 TO 12:15 AT AVOCADO REPUBLIC.
ARE YOU OFFICIALLY A STALKER?
BORDERLINE.

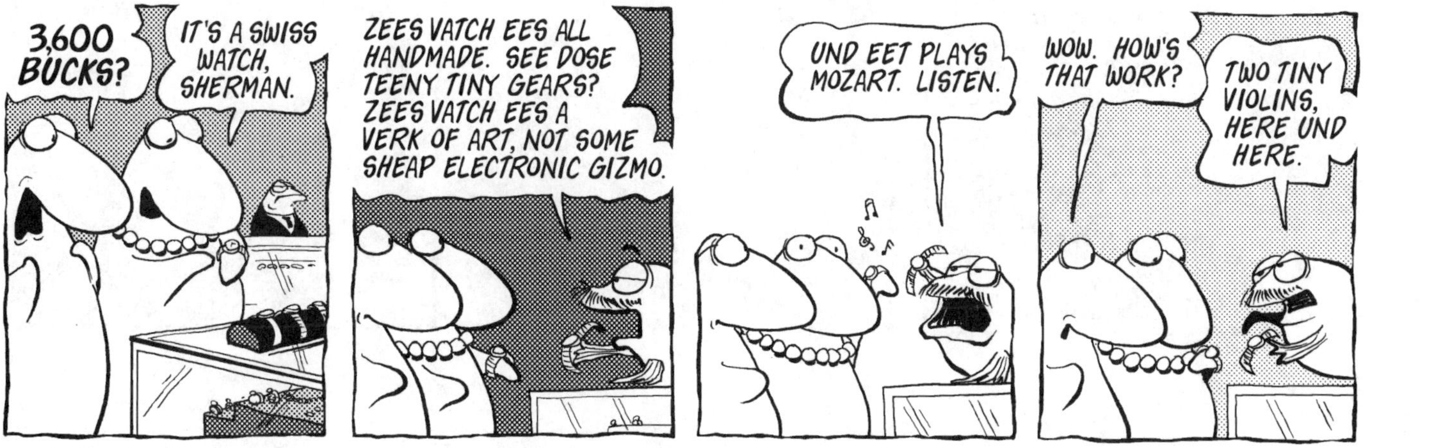
3,600 BUCKS?
IT'S A SWISS WATCH, SHERMAN.
ZEES VATCH EES ALL HANDMADE. SEE DOSE TEENY TINY GEARS? ZEES VATCH EES A VERK OF ART, NOT SOME SHEAP ELECTRONIC GIZMO.
UND EET PLAYS MOZART. LISTEN.
WOW. HOW'S THAT WORK?
TWO TINY VIOLINS, HERE UND HERE.

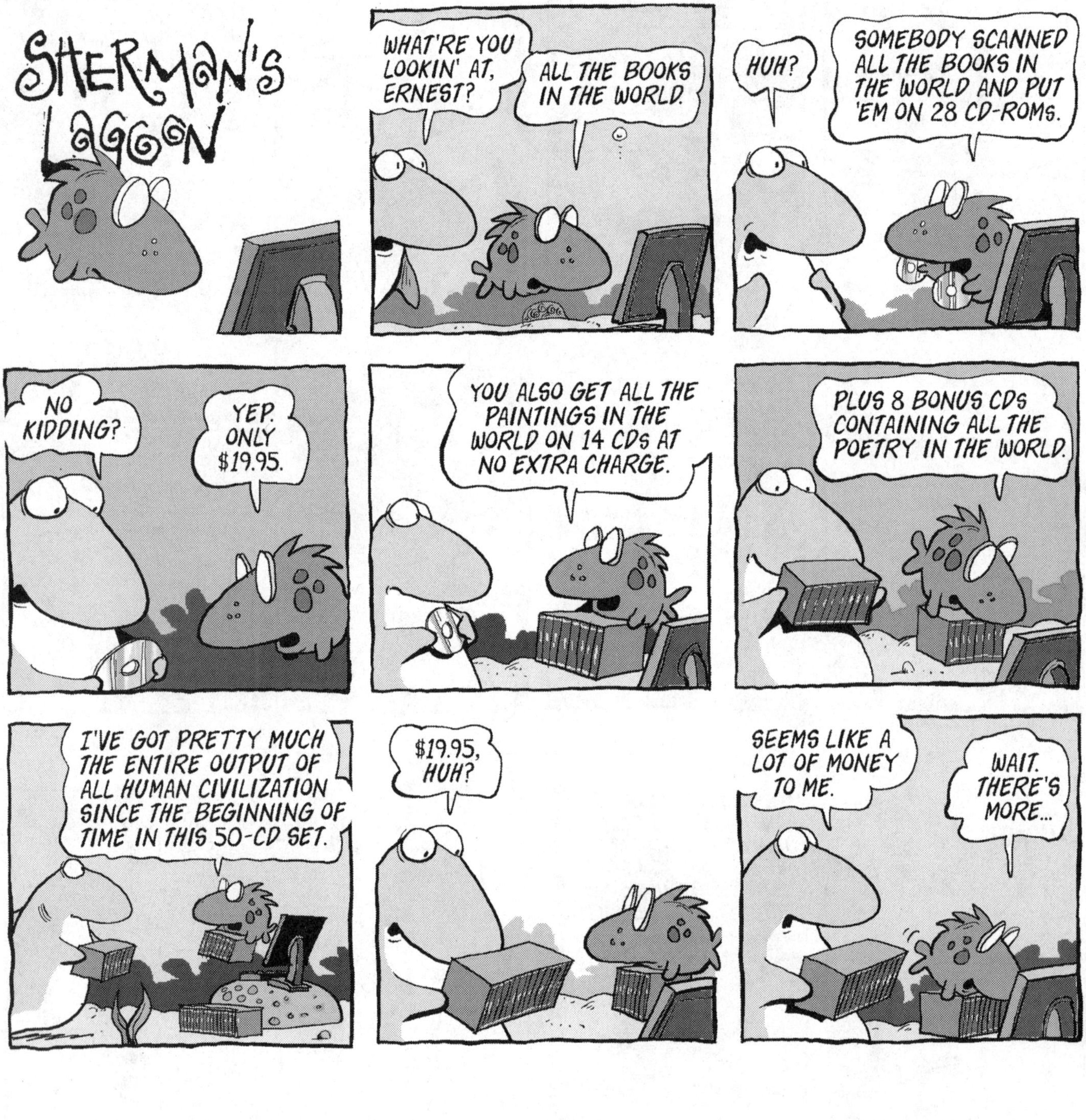
SHERMAN'S LAGOON
WHAT'RE YOU LOOKIN' AT, ERNEST?
ALL THE BOOKS IN THE WORLD.
HUH?
SOMEBODY SCANNED ALL THE BOOKS IN THE WORLD AND PUT 'EM ON 28 CD-ROMS.
NO KIDDING?
YEP. ONLY $19.95.
YOU ALSO GET ALL THE PAINTINGS IN THE WORLD ON 14 CDs AT NO EXTRA CHARGE.
PLUS 8 BONUS CDs CONTAINING ALL THE POETRY IN THE WORLD.
I'VE GOT PRETTY MUCH THE ENTIRE OUTPUT OF ALL HUMAN CIVILIZATION SINCE THE BEGINNING OF TIME IN THIS 50-CD SET.
$19.95, HUH?
SEEMS LIKE A LOT OF MONEY TO ME.
WAIT. THERE'S MORE...

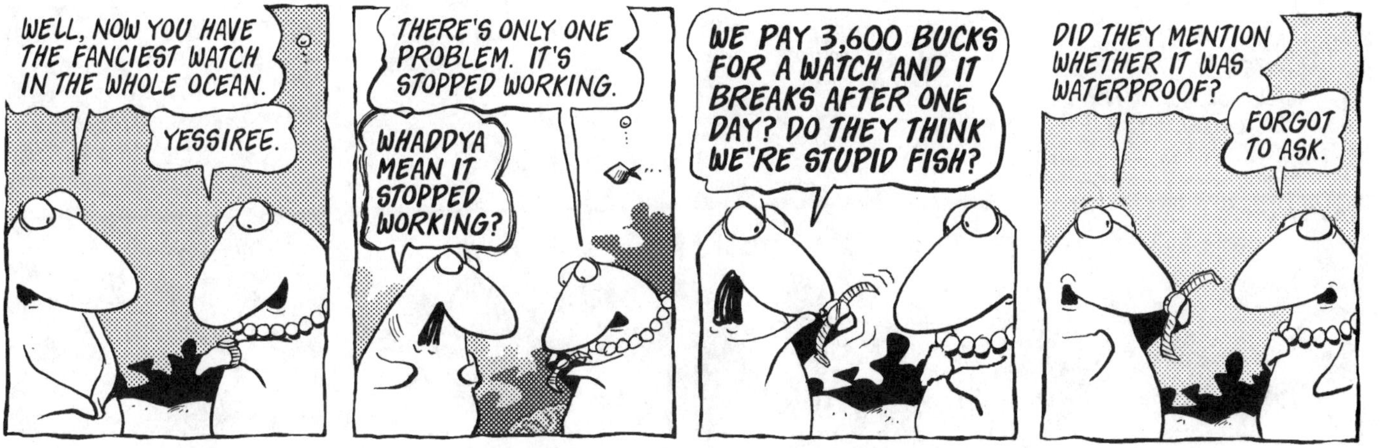
WELL, NOW YOU HAVE THE FANCIEST WATCH IN THE WHOLE OCEAN.
YESSIREE.
THERE'S ONLY ONE PROBLEM. IT'S STOPPED WORKING.
WHADDYA MEAN IT STOPPED WORKING?
WE PAY 3,600 BUCKS FOR A WATCH AND IT BREAKS AFTER ONE DAY? DO THEY THINK WE'RE STUPID FISH?
DID THEY MENTION WHETHER IT WAS WATERPROOF?
FORGOT TO ASK.

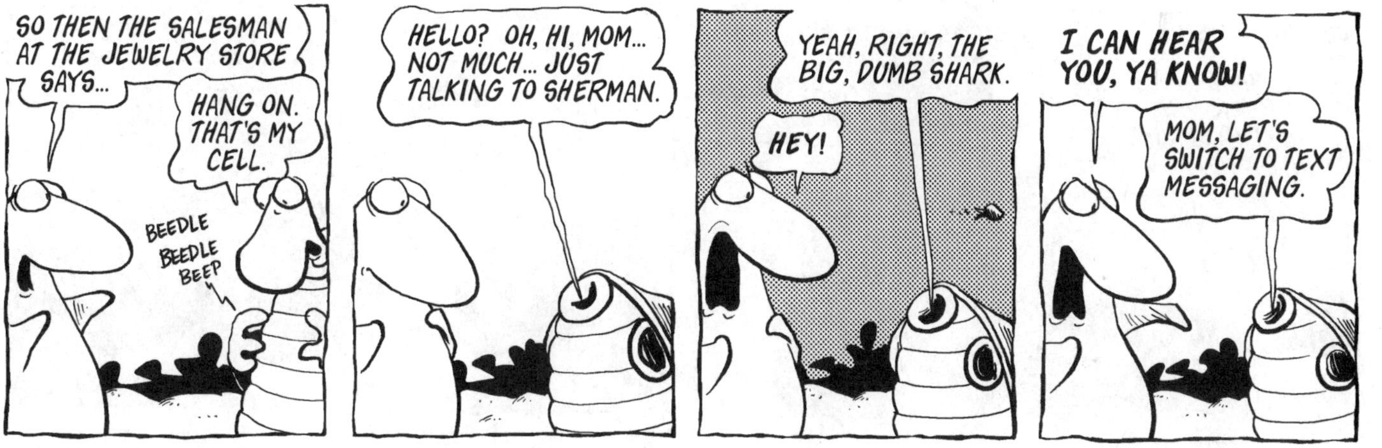
SO THEN THE SALESMAN AT THE JEWELRY STORE SAYS...
HANG ON. THAT'S MY CELL.
BEEDLE BEEDLE BEEP
HELLO? OH, HI, MOM... NOT MUCH... JUST TALKING TO SHERMAN.
YEAH, RIGHT, THE BIG, DUMB SHARK.
HEY!
I CAN HEAR YOU, YA KNOW!
MOM, LET'S SWITCH TO TEXT MESSAGING.

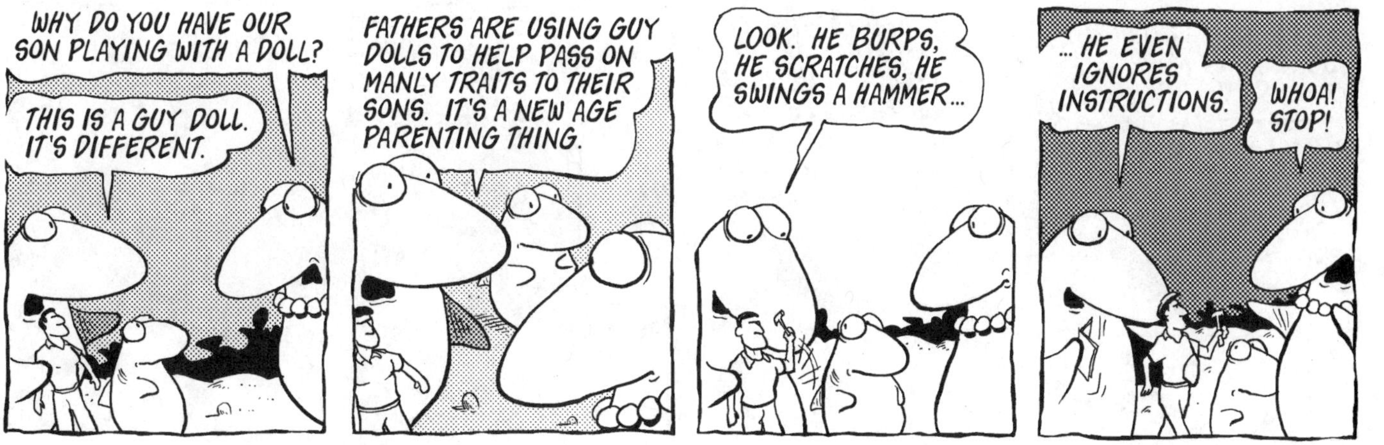
WHY DO YOU HAVE OUR SON PLAYING WITH A DOLL?
THIS IS A GUY DOLL. IT'S DIFFERENT.
FATHERS ARE USING GUY DOLLS TO HELP PASS ON MANLY TRAITS TO THEIR SONS. IT'S A NEW AGE PARENTING THING.
LOOK. HE BURPS, HE SCRATCHES, HE SWINGS A HAMMER...
... HE EVEN IGNORES INSTRUCTIONS.
WHOA! STOP!

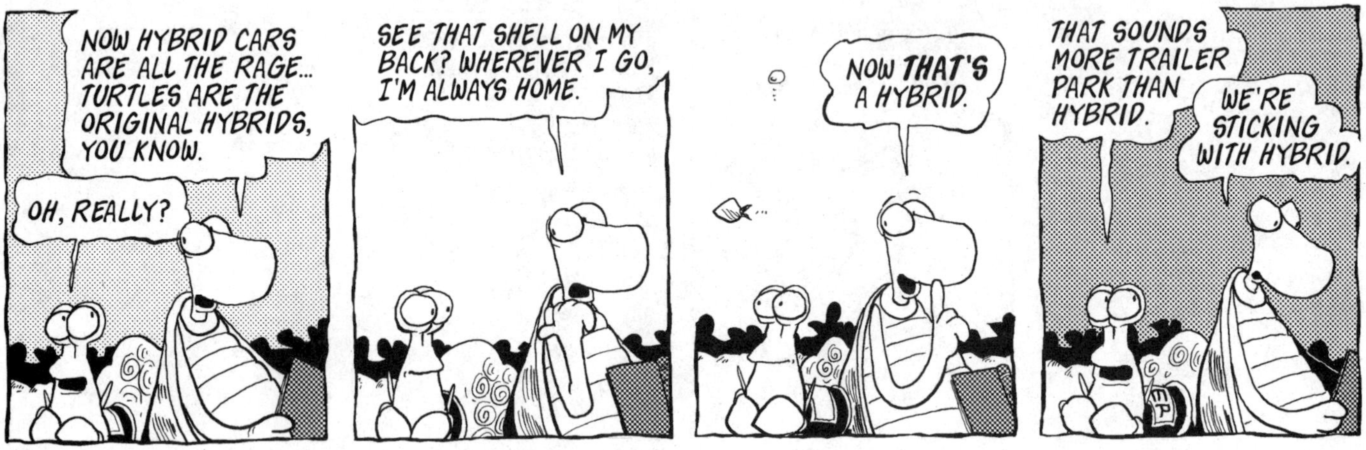
NOW HYBRID CARS ARE ALL THE RAGE... TURTLES ARE THE ORIGINAL HYBRIDS, YOU KNOW.
OH, REALLY?
SEE THAT SHELL ON MY BACK? WHEREVER I GO, I'M ALWAYS HOME.
NOW **THAT'S** A HYBRID.
THAT SOUNDS MORE TRAILER PARK THAN HYBRID.
WE'RE STICKING WITH HYBRID.

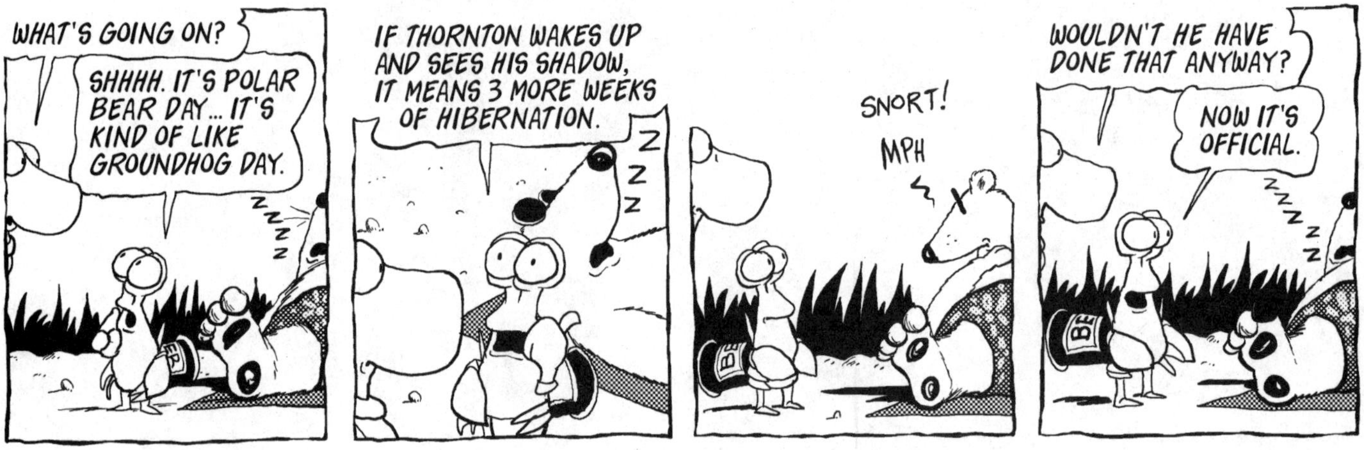
WHAT'S GOING ON?
SHHHH. IT'S POLAR BEAR DAY... IT'S KIND OF LIKE GROUNDHOG DAY.
IF THORNTON WAKES UP AND SEES HIS SHADOW, IT MEANS 3 MORE WEEKS OF HIBERNATION.
SNORT!
MPH
WOULDN'T HE HAVE DONE THAT ANYWAY?
NOW IT'S OFFICIAL.

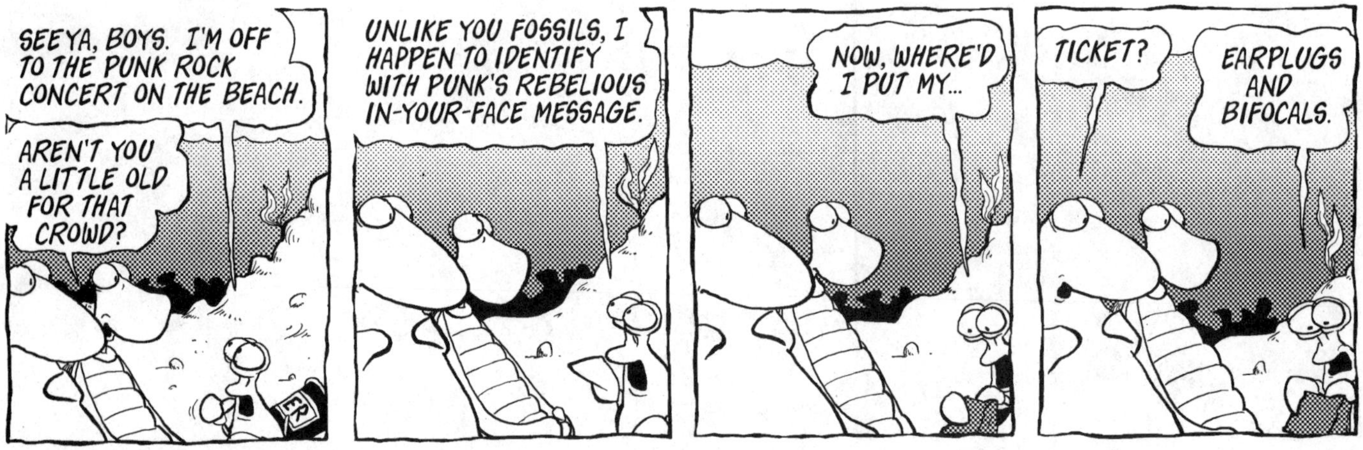
SEEYA, BOYS. I'M OFF TO THE PUNK ROCK CONCERT ON THE BEACH.
AREN'T YOU A LITTLE OLD FOR THAT CROWD?
UNLIKE YOU FOSSILS, I HAPPEN TO IDENTIFY WITH PUNK'S REBELIOUS IN-YOUR-FACE MESSAGE.
NOW, WHERE'D I PUT MY...
TICKET?
EARPLUGS AND BIFOCALS.